The Cambridge Companion to Mozart

The Cambridge Companion to Mozart paints a rounded yet focussed picture of one of the most revered artists of all time. Bringing the most recent scholarship into the public arena, this volume bridges the gap between scholarly and popular images of the composer, enhancing the readers' appreciation of Mozart and his extraordinary output, regardless of their prior knowledge of the music. Part I situates Mozart in the context of late eighteenth-century musical environments and aesthetic trends that played a pivotal role in his artistic development and examines his methods of composition. Part II surveys Mozart's works in all of the genres in which he excelled and Part III looks at the reception of the composer and his music since his death. Part IV offers insight into Mozart's career as a performer as well as theoretical and practical perspectives on historically informed performances of his music.

SIMON P. KEEFE is Lecturer in Music at Queen's University, Belfast. He is the author of *Mozart's Piano Concertos: Dramatic Dialogue in the Age of Enlightenment* (2001).

The Cambridge Companion to

MOZART

....

EDITED BY
Simon P. Keefe

CAMBRIDGE
UNIVERSITY PRESS

PUBLISHED BY THE PRESS SYNDICATE OF THE UNIVERSITY OF CAMBRIDGE
The Pitt Building, Trumpington Street, Cambridge CB2 1RP, United Kingdom

CAMBRIDGE UNIVERSITY PRESS
The Edinburgh Building, Cambridge, CB2 2RU, UK
40 West 20th Street, New York, NY 10011-4211, USA
477 Williamstown Road, Port Melbourne, VIC 3207, Australia
Ruiz de Alarcón 13, 28014 Madrid, Spain
Dock House, The Waterfront, Cape Town 8001, South Africa

http://www.cambridge.org

First published 2003

Printed in the United Kingdom at the University Press, Cambridge

Typeface Minion 10.75/14 pt   *System* LaTeX 2$_\varepsilon$ [TB]

A catalogue record for this book is available from the British Library

ISBN 0 521 80734 4 hardback
ISBN 0 521 00192 7 paperback

Contents

[v]

Contributors

David J. Buch is Professor of Music History at the University of Northern Iowa. His publications include *Dance Music from the Ballets de cour 1575–1651* (1994) and recent articles in *Acta Musicologica*, *The Musical Quarterly*, *Journal of the Royal Musical Association*, *Acta Mozartiana*, *Mozart-Jahrbuch* and *Cambridge Opera Journal*. He is currently preparing a book, *Magic Flutes and Enchanted Forests: Music and the Supernatural in the Eighteenth-Century Theatre*. He was the University of Northern Iowa Distinguished Scholar in 1998–9, and received the Donald N. McKay Research Award (1998) and the Iowa Board of Regents Award for Faculty Excellence (1999).

Paul Corneilson is managing editor of *Carl Philipp Emanuel Bach: The Collected Works*. He has published articles in *Mozart-Jahrbuch*, *Journal of Musicology*, *Early Music* and *Journal of the American Musicological Society*. His critical edition of Gian Francesco de Majo's *Ifigenia in Tauride* is available from A-R Editions as vol. 46 in the series *Recent Researches in the Music of the Classical Era* (1996).

John Daverio is Professor of Music and Chairman of the Musicology Department at Boston University, School of Music. The author of numerous articles on nineteenth-century topics, he has written two books: *Nineteenth-Century Music and the German Romantic Ideology* (1993) and *Robert Schumann: Herald of a 'New Poetic Age'* (1997). A third book – *Crossing Paths: Schubert, Schumann, and Brahms* – is forthcoming.

Cliff Eisen is Reader in Music at King's College London. His recent publications chiefly concern Mozart, performance practice and music of the late eighteenth century. He is co-author, with Stanley Sadie, of *The New Grove Mozart* (2001) and co-editor of the journal *Eighteenth-Century Music*, the first issue of which will appear in 2004.

Edmund J. Goehring is Assistant Professor in the Program of Liberal Studies at the University of Notre Dame. He is the author of recent articles on Mozart and late eighteenth-century opera in *Cambridge Opera Journal* and *Opera Buffa in Mozart's Vienna* (edited by Mary Hunter and James Webster, Cambridge University Press, 1997) and is currently completing a monograph on *Così fan tutte*.

Simon P. Keefe, Lecturer in Music at Queen's University, Belfast, is the author of *Mozart's Piano Concertos: Dramatic Dialogue in the Age of Enlightenment* (Boydell and Brewer, 2001) and recent articles on late eighteenth-century aesthetic and stylistic issues pertaining to Mozart in *Music and Letters*, *The Musical Quarterly*, *Journal of Musicology*, *Journal of Musicological Research* and *Acta Musicologica*. He is currently working on a monograph on Mozart's Viennese instrumental music.

Katalin Komlós, musicologist and fortepiano recitalist, is Professor of Music Theory at the Liszt Academy of Music, Budapest. She received her Ph.D. in musicology from Cornell University. Professor Komlós has written extensively on the history of eighteenth-century keyboard instruments and styles, her publications including *Fortepianos and Their Music* (1995).

Robert D. Levin, Dwight P. Robinson Jr Professor of the Humanities at Harvard University, divides his performance activities between the Steinway and a variety of historic keyboard instruments, appearing in recital, with leading orchestras, and as chamber musician in North America, Europe, Australia and Asia. His recordings include ten CDs in the Edition Bachakademie, a Beethoven concerto cycle with Sir John Eliot Gardiner and a Mozart concerto cycle with Christopher Hogwood. His cadenzas and completions to unfinished works by Mozart have been published by Breitkopf & Härtel, Hänssler, Henle, Peters and Universal Editions.

Dorothea Link teaches at the University of Georgia. Her publications include *The National Court Theatre in Mozart's Vienna* (1998), *Arias for Nancy Storace* (A-R Editions, in press) and recent articles in *Cambridge Opera Journal, Journal of the Royal Musical Association* and *Wolfgang Amadè Mozart: Essays on His Life and His Music* (edited by Stanley Sadie, 1996). She is the editor of *Mozart Essays* (forthcoming).

Julian Rushton, West Riding Professor of Music at the University of Leeds (1982–2002), is Chairman of *Musica Britannica*, for which he has edited a symphony by Cipriani Potter. He has also edited four volumes of the New Berlioz Edition. His books include *The Musical Language of Berlioz* (1983), *Classical Music: A Concise History* (1986), *The Music of Berlioz* (Oxford University Press, 2001) and Cambridge Handbooks on Mozart's *Don Giovanni* and *Idomeneo,* Berlioz's *Roméo et Juliette*, and Elgar's *Enigma Variations*. He was President of the Royal Musical Association from 1994 to 1999, and was elected a Corresponding Member of the American Musicological Society in 2000.

David Schroeder is Professor of Music and Associate Dean of Arts and Social Sciences at Dalhousie University in Halifax, Canada. His books include *Haydn and the Enlightenment* (1990), *Mozart in Revolt: Strategies of Resistance, Mischief and Deception* (1999), and *Cinema's Illusions, Opera's Allure: The Operatic Impulse in Film* (2002). He has also written articles on Schubert, Enlightenment issues and Alban Berg, and is a former advisory editor to *Eighteenth-Century Studies.*

Jan Smaczny, Hamilton Harty Professor of Music at Queen's University, Belfast, was educated at the University of Oxford and the Charles University, Prague. A specialist on the life and works of Dvořák and on Czech opera, he recently published a Cambridge handbook on Dvořák's Cello Concerto (1999). He has also written on other topics, including Mozart and Prague (for the *Oxford Companion to Mozart*, forthcoming), and Prague as a musical city.

William Stafford is a Professor of History in the School of Music and Humanities at the University of Huddersfield. He is a historian of ideas with wide-ranging interests in late eighteenth- and early nineteenth-century thought and culture.

His publications include *Mozart's Death: A Corrective Survey of the Legends* (1991) and articles in the revised *New Grove*.

W. Dean Sutcliffe is University Lecturer at the University of Cambridge and a Fellow of St Catharine's College. He edited the volume *Haydn Studies* (1998) and is co-editor of the journal *Eighteenth-Century Music*, the first issue of which will appear in 2004. His book *Domenico Scarlatti and Eighteenth-Century Musical Style* is forthcoming from Cambridge University Press.

Ian Woodfield is Professor of Historical Musicology at Queen's University, Belfast. Recent publications include *Music of the Raj: A Social and Economic History of Music in Late Eighteenth-Century Anglo-Indian Society* (2000) and *Opera and Drama in Eighteenth-Century London: The King's Theatre, Garrick and the Business of Performance* (2001). His current research project is a study of the autograph score of Mozart's *Così fan tutte*.

Acknowledgements

First and foremost, I would like to thank all of the contributors to this volume, not only for delivering their chapters in a timely fashion, but also for responding to my queries in a prompt, good-natured manner; it has been a genuine pleasure working with them. In particular, Cliff Eisen has offered constructive support, invaluable advice and sensible guidance at every stage of the project – not to mention lively, entertaining correspondence on a wide range of musical and non-musical topics – and receives my sincere gratitude.

Closer to home, Queen's University, Belfast, granted me sabbatical leave from teaching and administrative duties in spring 2002, facilitating completion of the volume. I would also like to thank my wife, Celia Hurwitz-Keefe, who provided a sounding board for numerous ideas relating to design and content, and combined, in customary fashion, erudite criticism and loving support. My son, Abraham, offered regular, welcome distractions from work on the book; I hope that one day he will want to read it.

The plates from the autograph of *Così fan tutte* in chapter 3 are reproduced by kind permission of the Bild-Archiv in the Staatsbibliothek, Berlin.

Simon P. Keefe
Queen's University, Belfast

Abbreviations

Books and editions

LMF Emily Anderson (ed. and trans.), *The Letters of Mozart and His Family* (3rd edn, London, 1985).

MBA Wilhelm A. Bauer, Otto Erich Deutsch and Joseph Heinz Eibl (eds.), *Mozart: Briefe und Aufzeichnungen, Gesamtausgabe* (7 vols., Kassel, 1962–75).

MDB Otto Erich Deutsch, *Mozart: A Documentary Biography*, trans. Eric Blom, Peter Branscombe and Jeremy Noble (Stanford and London, 1965).

MDL Otto Erich Deutsch, *Mozart: Die Dokumente seines Lebens* (Kassel, 1961).

NMA Wolfgang Amadeus Mozart, *Neue Ausgabe sämtlicher Werke* (Kassel, 1955–).

Journals

COJ *Cambridge Opera Journal*

EM *Early Music*

JAMS *Journal of the American Musicological Society*

JMR *Journal of Musicological Research*

JM *Journal of Musicology*

JRMA *Journal of the Royal Musical Association*

ML *Music and Letters*

MQ *The Musical Quarterly*

MT *The Musical Times*

Chronology of Mozart's life and works

SIMON P. KEEFE

The most comprehensive and systematic chronology of Mozart's life, in which late eighteenth-century documents are interspersed with biographical details, is Otto Erich Deutsch, *Mozart: A Documentary Biography*, trans. Eric Blom, Peter Branscombe and Jeremy Noble (Stanford and London, 1965; paperback edn London, 1990). A complete, up-to-date list of Mozart's works is found in Cliff Eisen and Stanley Sadie, '(Johann Chrysostom) Wolfgang Amadeus Mozart', in Stanley Sadie (ed.), *The New Grove Dictionary of Music and Musicians*, 2nd edn (29 vols., London, 2001), vol. 17, pp. 305–37.

1756: Born 27 January in Salzburg, the seventh child of Leopold (1719–87) and Maria Anna Mozart (1720–78). Baptized Joannes Chrysostomus Wolfgangus Theophilius on 28 January. Of Leopold and Maria Anna's preceding children, only Nannerl (born 30 January 1751) survives.

1761: Learns to play minuets, a march and a scherzo by Wagenseil. *Composition*: Andante for Piano, K. 1a.

1762: Performs with Nannerl in Munich for the Elector Maximilian Joseph III (January). Travels to Vienna to give numerous performances with Nannerl at court; audience members include Emperor Francis I and Empress Maria Theresia (September 1762–January 1763).
Select compositions: violin sonatas K. 6, 7 (1762–4).

1763: Leaves for a three-and-a-half-year grand tour of Europe with his father, mother and sister (9 June). Performs in Munich, Augsburg, Frankfurt-am-Main and Paris.
Select compositions: violin sonatas, K. 8, 9 (1763–4).

1764: Performs for King Louis XV in Paris before travelling on to London, where the Mozart family are received by King George III and befriended by Johann Christian Bach and Italian castrato Giovanni Manzuoli.
Select compositions: violin sonatas K. 10–15; symphony K. 16.

1765: Remains in London until 24 July, travelling via Canterbury, Lille, and Antwerp to The Hague, where he performs for Prince

William V of Orange. In Holland, both Nannerl and Mozart are seriously ill with intestinal typhoid.

Select compositions: symphonies K. 19, 22.

1766: Performs in The Hague, Amsterdam, Utrecht and Antwerp, travelling on to Paris via Brussels (January–July). Gives concerts in Dijon, Lyon, Lausanne, Zürich and Munich en route back to Salzburg (July–November). Arrives home on 29 November.

Select compositions: violin sonatas K. 26–31.

1767: Travels with his family to Vienna (September) and Bohemia (October). Contracts smallpox, as does Nannerl, but both soon recover (October–November).

Select compositions: oratorio, *Die Schuldigkeit des ersten Gebots* (Part 1), K. 35; symphony K. 43.

1768: Received in Vienna by Empress Maria Theresia and her son, Emperor Joseph II (January). *Bastien und Bastienne* is performed at Dr Anton Mesmer's house in Vienna (September/October).

Select compositions: symphonies K. 45, 48; Singspiel, *Bastien und Bastienne*, K. 50; opera buffa, *La finta semplice*, K. 51.

1769: Appointed as an unpaid Konzertmeister at the Salzburg court (November). Leaves on his first Italian trip with Leopold, travelling via Innsbruck to Verona (December).

Select compositions: cassations K. 100, 63, 99; march K. 62.

1770: Performs in Verona, Milan, Bologna, Florence, Rome and Naples and is received by noblemen and dignitaries in every city. He is awarded the Order of the Golden Spur by the Pope (8 July) and membership of the Accademia Filarmonica in Bologna (9 October). *Mitridate* is staged at the Teatro Regio Ducale in Milan (26–8 December), following a week of rehearsals.

Select compositions: string quartet K. 80; symphonies K. 81, 97, 95, 74; opera seria, *Mitridate, re di Ponto*, K. 87.

1771: Following performances in Venice (February–March), Mozart returns to Salzburg with his father (28 March) after a fifteen-month trip. Takes a second Italian trip (13 August–15 December), the highlight of which is a production of *Ascanio in Alba* at the Teatro Regio Ducale in Milan (October).

Select compositions: opera seria, *Ascanio in Alba*, K. 111; symphonies K. 110, 120, 96, 112, 114.

1772: Gives a performance of *Il sogno di Scipione* (May) in honour of Count Hieronymus Colloredo's election as Prince-Archbishop of Salzburg. Appointed Konzertmeister at the Salzburg court at a

salary of 150 gulden per annum (August). Leaves Salzburg
(24 October) on a third trip to Italy, participating in the rehearsals
and first performances of *Lucio Silla* (November–December).
Select compositions: opere serie, *Il sogno di Scipione*, K. 126, and
Lucio Silla, K. 135; symphonies K. 128–30, 132–4; divertimenti
K. 131, 136–8; string quartets K. 155–8 (1772–3).

1773: Completes the motet 'Exsultate, jubilate' for a first performance at
the Theatine Church in Milan by the celebrated castrato Venanzio
Rauzzini (17 January). Arrives back in Salzburg (13 March).
Travels to Vienna with Leopold (14 July–26 September) in an
unsuccessful attempt to procure a post.
Select compositions: motet, 'Exsultate, jubilate', K. 165; string
quartets K. 159, 160, 168–73; symphonies K. 184, 199, 162, 182,
183; piano concerto K. 175; violin concerto K. 207.

1774: Remains in Salzburg until a trip to Munich (6 December) for the
first performance of *La finta giardiniera* (13 January 1775).
Select compositions: Bassoon Concerto, K. 191; opera buffa, *La finta
giardiniera*, K. 196; symphonies K. 200–2; serenade K. 203.

1775: Returns to Salzburg from Munich (7 March). *Il re pastore* is
premiered at the Archbishop's Palace in Salzburg (23 April).
Select compositions: serenade K. 204; opera seria, *Il re pastore*,
K. 208; violin concertos K. 211, 216, 218, 219.

1776: Remains in Salzburg throughout the year and continues to
compose prolifically.
Select compositions: piano concertos K. 238, 242 (three pianos),
246; 'Haffner' Serenade, K. 250; divertimenti K. 247, 251.

1777: Requests, and is granted, leave from the Archbishop's service
(August). Begins a sixteen-month trip with his mother (and
for the first time without his father) to seek employment
(23 September). Travels to Munich, Augsburg and Mannheim,
where he falls in love with the singer Aloysia Weber.
Select compositions: piano concerto K. 271; keyboard sonatas
K. 309, 311.

1778: Leaves Mannheim for Paris (14 March), where a number of his
works, including the 'Paris' Symphony, are well received. His
mother dies (3 July). Unable to procure employment, he leaves for
Salzburg (26 September), passing through Strasbourg, Mannheim
and Munich. He stays with the Weber family in Munich, but is
rejected by Aloysia.
Select compositions: 'Paris' Symphony, K. 297; Concerto for Flute
and Harp, K. 299; violin sonatas K. 301–3, 305, 296, 304, 306;

keyboard sonata K. 310; Flute Concerto, K. 313; Flute/Oboe Concerto, K. 314.

1779: Arrives back in Salzburg (15 January). Takes a position as court organist at a salary of 450 gulden per annum. His responsibilities include teaching, playing in church and at court and composing sacred and secular music as required.
Select compositions: 'Coronation' Mass, K. 317; symphonies K. 318, 319; 'Posthorn' Serenade, K. 320; Sinfonia concertante, K. 364 (1779–80).

1780: Leaves for Munich by himself (5 November) for the rehearsals and first performances of *Idomeneo*.
Select compositions: symphony K. 338; *Vesperae solennes de confessore*, K. 339; Singspiel, *Zaide* (incomplete), K. 344; Concerto for Two Pianos, K. 365.

1781: *Idomeneo* is successfully premiered (29 January) with Leopold and Nannerl in attendance. Mozart arrives in Vienna (16 March) to begin his career as a freelance performer and composer. Archbishop Colloredo's chief steward Count Arco unceremoniously dismisses Mozart from his Salzburg post (8 June). Leopold repeatedly expresses doubts about Mozart's prospects in Vienna, but Mozart decides to stay.
Select compositions: opera seria, *Idomeneo, re di Creta*, K. 366 (1780–1); wind serenade K. 375; violin sonatas K. 376, 377, 380.

1782: *Die Entführung* is premiered at the Burgtheater (16 July) to great acclaim and is subsequently staged in honour of the Grand Duke of Russia (8 October). Mozart marries Constanze Weber, sister of Aloysia (4 August).
Select compositions: Singspiel, *Die Entführung aus dem Serail*, K. 384; 'Haffner' Symphony, K. 385; string quartet K. 387; piano concertos K. 414, 413 (1782–3), 415 (1782–3).

1783: Gives a grand concert at the Burgtheater with Emperor Joseph II in attendance (23 March). His first child, Raimund Leopold, is born (17 June) but dies two months later. Visits Salzburg with Constanze (29 July–27 October). Stopping in Linz on the return trip, he hastily writes a symphony, K. 425, for a performance at the city's theatre (4 November).
Select compositions: keyboard sonatas K. 330–2 (all 1781–3); horn concerto K. 417; string quartets K. 421, 428; 'Linz' Symphony, K. 425; C minor Mass, K. 427.

1784: Begins his thematic catalogue ('Der Verzeichnüss aller meiner Werke') (9 February). Presents a series of subscription concerts at the Trattnerhof (March) featuring newly composed piano concertos and boasts about the large number of subscribers to his father. In addition, he gives numerous private performances and a concert at the Burgtheater (March–April). His son Carl Thomas is born (21 September; d. 31 October 1858). On 14 December he is admitted to the masonic lodge 'Beneficence' ('Zur Wohltätigkeit'). *Select compositions*: piano concertos K. 449–51, 453, 456, 459; Quintet for Piano and Winds, K. 452; violin sonata K. 454; keyboard sonatas K. 333, 457; string quartet K. 458.

1785: Leopold visits Mozart in Vienna (February–April), witnessing Mozart's successful series of Friday concerts at the Mehlgrube and performances at the Burgtheater. Mozart, Leopold and Haydn play through three of Mozart's six quartets subsequently dedicated to Haydn (12 February), prompting Haydn's remark to Leopold that Mozart is 'the greatest composer known to me either in person or by name'.
Select compositions: Serenade for Winds in B flat major ('Gran partita'), K. 361 (probably 1783–4); string quartets K. 464 and 'Dissonance', K. 465; piano concertos K. 466, 467, 482; oratorio, *Davidde penitente*, K. 469; songs, K. 472–74, 476, 483, 484; piano quartet K. 478; violin sonata K. 481.

1786: *Le nozze di Figaro* is premiered at the Burgtheater (1 May), and receives eight more performances there before the end of the year. Mozart's son Johann Thomas Leopold is born (18 October), dying one month later.
Select compositions: Singspiel, *Der Schauspieldirektor*, K. 486; piano concertos K. 488, 491, 503; opera buffa, *Le nozze di Figaro*, K. 492; piano quartet K. 493; horn concerto K. 495; 'Kegelstatt' Trio, K. 498; 'Hoffmeister' String Quartet, K. 499; piano trio K. 502; 'Prague' Symphony, K. 504; concert aria, 'Ch'io mi scordi di te', K. 505.

1787: Travels twice to Prague (January–February, October–November), first for the highly successful performances of *Figaro* and the 'Prague' Symphony, and subsequently for the revival of *Figaro* and premiere of *Don Giovanni* (29 October). Meets the sixteen-year-old Beethoven in Vienna (April). Leopold dies in Salzburg (28 May). Mozart's daughter Theresia is born (27 December), but dies six months later.
Select compositions: horn concerto K. 447; string quintets K. 515, 516; songs, K. 517–20, 523, 524, 529–31; 'Eine kleine Nachtmusik', K. 525; violin sonata K. 526; opera buffa, *Don Giovanni*, K. 527.

1788: *Don Giovanni* receives its Viennese premiere (7 May 1788). Mozart composes his final three symphonies inside two months (June–August), although it is not known where and when the works were first performed. Suffering financial hardship, he starts to borrow money from his Viennese friend and fellow freemason Michael Puchberg.

Select compositions: 'Coronation' Piano Concerto, K. 537; piano trios K. 542, 548, 564; symphonies K. 543, 550 and 'Jupiter', K. 551; keyboard sonata K. 545; violin sonata K. 547; string trio K. 563.

1789: Travels alone to Dresden, Leipzig, Potsdam, Berlin – performing for King Friedrich Wilhelm II – and Prague in an attempt to obtain commissions (April–June). A new daughter, Anna Maria, dies soon after birth (16 November).

Select compositions: keyboard sonatas K. 570, 576; string quartet K. 575; Clarinet Quintet, K. 581.

1790: *Così fan tutte* is premiered at the Burgtheater (26 January). Mozart travels to Frankfurt (23 September), participating in celebrations for the coronation of the new emperor, Leopold II, following the death of Emperor Joseph II on 20 February. He gives concerts in Frankfurt, Mainz and Munich, making little financial gain, and returns to Vienna (November).

Select compositions: opera buffa, *Così fan tutte*, K. 588; string quartets K. 589, 590; string quintet K. 593.

1791: Gives his final performance at a public concert, with a programme including the Piano Concerto, K. 595 (4 March). His son Franz Xaver Wolfgang is born (26 July; d. 29 July 1844). He travels to Prague with Constanze for the premiere of *La clemenza di Tito* (6 September), possibly conducting a performance of *Don Giovanni* a few days earlier. Soon after his return to Vienna, *Die Zauberflöte* is successfully premiered at the Theater auf der Wieden (30 September) and performed more than twenty times in the next six weeks. He works on the Requiem, even when taking to his bed for his final illness (20 November). The unfinished Requiem is rehearsed at Mozart's bedside (4 December), but he dies a few hours later (12:55 am, 5 December), probably of rheumatic inflammatory fever. He is buried at St Marx's Cemetery a few miles outside Vienna (6 December).

Select compositions: horn concerto K. 412; piano concerto K. 595; string quintet K. 614; motet, 'Ave verum corpus', K. 618; Singspiel, *Die Zauberflöte*, K. 620; opera seria, *La clemenza di Tito*, K. 621; Clarinet Concerto, K. 622; Requiem, K. 626.

Introduction

SIMON P. KEEFE

Friedrich Kerst, assessing the significance of Mozart early in the twentieth century, introduces *Mozart: The Man and the Artist Revealed in His Own Words* in unashamedly hagiographical fashion:

> Mozart! What a radiance streams from his name! Bright and pure as the light of the sun, Mozart's music greets us. We pronounce his name and behold! The youthful artist is before us – the merry, light-hearted smile upon his features, which belongs only to true and naïve genius.[1]

Packing his prose with overworked generalizations about Mozart and his music – brightness and purity, eternal youthfulness, blissful ignorance aligned with genius – Kerst is one of countless late eighteenth-, nineteenth- and twentieth-century writers to worship at Mozart's shrine. In the last fifty years in particular, Mozart scholars have attempted either directly or indirectly to negate such stereotypes and the laudatory tone that accompanies them. Thanks to pioneering archival work on written and musical sources, and on late eighteenth-century aesthetic and theoretical trends manifest in his music, scholars are now in a better position than ever to evaluate both Mozart's impact on his contemporaries and successors, and his continuing relevance to an ever-changing musical world.

While unadulterated hyperbole about Mozart is a distant memory in scholarly circles, it flourishes as never before outside the academy. The bicentennial celebrations in 1991 outstripped in scope and worldwide participation all preceding and succeeding celebrations of a composer's work; the critical and commercial success of the cinematic version of *Amadeus* (1984) demonstrated the extraordinary public fascination with Mozart and his life story; and predictable millennial polls, aimed at identifying the greatest composers of all time, put Mozart close to the top, even in the company of twentieth-century pop artists who were always likely to garner the popular vote.[2]

We might dismiss Mozartian hyperbole as media-charged exaggeration, of course, but in so doing would be ignoring a significant implication of the composer's exalted public profile. For Mozart captures the popular imagination in a more pronounced fashion than any other composer of the classical tradition; relentless marketing has turned him into the principal standard-bearer for classical music. In spite of this state of affairs, could it be credibly argued that Mozart does *not* deserve his elevated status, that he is *not* a touchstone for musical greatness? Judgements of greatness, as out of fashion in post-modern scholarly discourse as they are in fashion outside academia, seem somehow superfluous where Mozart is concerned. Respected and admired in all quarters, his music defines greatness, rather than being circumscribed by it. In short, his place in the artistic pantheon is as secure as those of Shakespeare, Raphael and Goethe.

Irrespective of the critical validity of Mozart's lofty status, the huge gulf between scholarly understandings of the composer and public perceptions of him needs to be broached. Like its illustrious predecessor from an earlier era, *The Mozart Companion*,[3] *The Cambridge Companion to Mozart* brings new, up-to-date scholarship into a public arena. Intended for students, scholars and music lovers alike, it aims to bridge the gap between scholarly and popular images of the composer by enhancing a reader's appreciation of Mozart and his remarkable output regardless of musical aptitude or prior knowledge of Mozart's music.

Each of the four sections of *The Cambridge Companion to Mozart* aligns with a major area of Mozart research; moreover, the sections together paint a balanced portrait of the composer. Part I, 'Mozart in context', builds a foundation for the study of Mozart's works, focussing on the musical environments that most clearly shaped the composer's development (Salzburg and Vienna), the intersection between Mozart's aesthetic views and those prevalent in the late eighteenth century, and Mozart's compositional methods. Part II, considering the most important genres in which Mozart excelled, likewise paves the way for discussions in Part III of how his works – indeed his career as a whole – have been received in critical, cultural and compositional contexts. Part IV complements contextual discussion in Part I by offering insight into Mozart's career as a performer as well as theoretical and practical perspectives on historically informed performances of his music. Although an entirely comprehensive survey of Mozart's works is a practical impossibility in a single volume of essays, this collection will hopefully provide a simultaneously rounded and focussed picture of the composer and his output.

If a common theme runs through this *Cambridge Companion* – in fact through the Mozartian secondary literature as a whole – it is that Mozart and his music demand repeated scrutiny and interpretation. Each generation of music lovers has found something new and different to admire in the composer, identifying an element or elements in his music that speak directly to the spirit of that time; there is every reason to believe that this pattern will continue for a composer commonly regarded 'as the most universal... in the history of Western music'.[4] Just as the great twentieth-century landmarks of Mozart scholarship – the collected letters, the *Documentary*

Biography of Otto Erich Deutsch, the various editions of the Köchel catalogue and the new edition of Mozart's works (*Neue Mozart-Ausgabe*) – immeasurably enhanced (and continue to enhance) our understanding of the composer, so we trust that twenty-first-century monuments (beginning with the forthcoming *Neue Köchel Verzeichnis* under the general editorship of Neal Zaslaw) will do the same. Evaluation and re-evaluation of Mozart's music, and of sources, documents and material pertaining to it, is not only a historical obligation for musicologists and music lovers generally, but a privilege for professionals and amateurs alike; few composers repay systematic examination and re-examination in so unambiguously pleasurable and inspiring a fashion as Mozart.

PART I

Mozart in context

1 Mozart and Salzburg

CLIFF EISEN

> In the mornings we woke to the most wonderful sounds, floating through
> the air like the sound of a psalterion. Three times the sweet melody ended,
> and three times it began again. It was the glockenspiel in the tower across
> from the *Residenz* which regularly at seven and eleven in the mornings,
> and at six in the evenings, played a well-chosen melody. We tried, as often
> as we could, to listen in the square.[1]

For the eighteenth-century traveller, Salzburg could be a paradise. Off
the beaten track[2] and set at the foot of the Alps, it boasted natural beauties
and a rich history: the city owed its post-Roman origin to the founding of
the abbey of St Peter by St Rupert of Worms in 696 and of the cathedral
by St Virgil in 774. In 1278 Rudolph of Habsburg made the archbishops of
Salzburg imperial princes and during centuries of relative peace (except for
the Peasants' War of 1525–6) the power and prestige of the court increased
until it was the most important and influential archdiocese and sacred state
in German-speaking Europe. By 1700, half a century before Mozart's birth,
its boundaries stretched north and west into what is now Bavaria and east
and south as far as Wiener Neustadt and Graz.

What the anonymous visitor to Salzburg praised so highly was the mechanical clock tower facing what is now the Mozartplatz. Constructed in
the early eighteenth century, it was renovated in the 1750s to include music
by the Kapellmeister Johann Ernst Eberlin and the court violinist Leopold
Mozart. The works were published in 1759 by Lotter of Augsburg, together
with a lengthy description of the Salzburg fortress, a short history of the
city, and a charming, engraved cityscape.[3] More than a music print, it was
a souvenir for the sophisticated tourist, a memento of pleasant hours spent
near the banks of the river Salzach or roaming the numerous churches, open
squares and fountains that gave Salzburg its nickname, 'the German Rome'.

For the local citizenry, however, life in Salzburg could be less than ideal:
the state was old-fashioned, education was out of date, censorship was frequent and society highly stratified. For local musicians, work at the court
was full of vexations. This was less the case, perhaps, during the reign of
Archbishop Siegmund Christoph, Count Schrattenbach (ruled 1753–71),
Mozart's first employer. Schrattenbach was often lavish in his support of
the court music, exhibited a keen interest in instrumental works, sent his
composers and performers to Italy to study, and rewarded composition with

generous presents. And he was a strong supporter of the Mozarts: Leopold advanced rapidly in the court music establishment during Schrattenbach's reign, and during the 1760s and 1770s, when Wolfgang and his father travelled to Vienna, Paris, London and Italy, the Archbishop subsidized their travels, at least in part. Still, Schrattenbach and the archbishops before him were not always attuned to the political currents of court musical life, as an incident from 1743 shows:

> At the Archbishop's order, Eberlin's promotion to deputy Kapellmeister had already been drawn up and was considered by everyone to be a closed matter. Then his rival, Herr Lolli (Eberlin's inferior by far in musical experience), grasped a last means, threw himself at the prince's feet, and promised that, should he take over the office, he would serve without [additional] pay. And so the Archbishop, who was determined to economize in every possible way, appointed him to the post, to [Eberlin's] detriment and much grumbling by almost the entire court and others.[4]

Situations like these were exacerbated during the reign of Archbishop Hieronymus, Count Colloredo (ruled 1772–1803), who not only pinched pennies but also tended blindly to hire and promote Italian musicians at the expense of local talent. What is more, Colloredo was far less interested in the court music than many of his predecessors.

To judge by traditional Mozart biographies, Colloredo was a narrow-minded tyrant. And to judge by the Mozart family letters (one of the richest sources of information concerning music in the archdiocese) music making was more or less restricted to the court and cathedral. Seen in this way, it was Colloredo's mean-spiritedness that was largely responsible for Mozart's mistreatment and sorry life in his native city. But the situation was not so simple. Colloredo had an agenda: to modernize Salzburg, to overhaul the education system, to rescue a financially failing court, and to promote both the sciences and the arts. Although he was hampered in these attempts by an unattractive personality, by his aloofness, and by his general unpopularity,[5] his reforms nevertheless favoured some aspects of local cultural life: a new sense of toleration and freedom of the press in particular attracted prominent writers, scientists and teachers to the court.[6] At the same time, however, many of his reforms did away with traditional music-making opportunities in the archdiocese: instrumental music at local churches was restricted during some services, German hymns were made obligatory in place of more traditional liturgical compositions, and the important university theatre, home to the school drama, was permanently closed in 1778. For the court music establishment, these reforms represented a dilution of musical life and a source of dissatisfaction. Yet music in Salzburg was not entirely dominated by the court and any musician willing to negotiate the city's numerous musical opportunities was able to carve out a decent life for himself. A musician who thought only in terms of the court, however, and who failed to understand its implicit and explicit expectations and deliberately flaunted the Archbishop – whether out of excessive ego, political miscalculation or both, as seems to have been the case with the Mozarts – was bound to be disappointed. It was not Colloredo who was primarily responsible for their misery, but the Mozarts themselves.

The Salzburg court music was a sprawling institution and when Leopold joined as fourth violinist in 1743 its organization was much the same as it had been at the time of its founding in 1591. In general, it was divided into four distinct and independent groups: the court music proper, which performed in the cathedral, at the Benedictine university and at court; the court- and field-trumpeters, together with the timpanists (normally ten trumpeters and two timpanists), who played in the cathedral, at court and provided special fanfares before meals and at important civic functions; the cathedral music (*Dommusik*), which consisted of the choral deacons (*Domchorvikaren*) and choristers (*Choralisten*) and performed in the cathedral; and the choirboys of the Chapel House (*Kapellhaus*), who also performed at the cathedral and who were instructed by the court musicians.

The chief duty of the court music proper, together with the cathedral music and the choirboys, was to perform at the cathedral. For elaborate performances, the musicians numbered about forty, sometimes more; on less important occasions the performing forces were reduced. Sometimes musicians did double duty: because the woodwind players, trumpeters and timpanists played less frequently than the strings and vocalists, they were often expected to perform on the violin; when needed, they filled out the ranks of the orchestra both at the cathedral and at court, where concerts and table music were a regular if occasional part of court life. The trumpeters and timpanists were under the control of the *Oberststallmeister*; their duties are described in a court memo of 1803:

> each day, two [trumpeters] sound the morning signal at court and at the court table where another plays the pieces and fanfares; accordingly, each day three [trumpeters] are in service and they are rotated every eight days . . . For the so-called *festi palli*, all the trumpeters and two timpanists are divided into two choirs, and play various fanfares in the courtyard before the court table . . . Every three years the trumpeters receive a uniform of black cloth with velvet trim, as well as red waistcoats with wide gold borders and ornamental tassels for the trumpets and gold-rimmed hats. They receive [new] trumpets every six years, but on festive occasions the silversmith sends them silver trumpets.[7]

Additionally, they performed festive music at Christmas and New Year.

The boys of the Chapel House (founded in 1677 by Archbishop Max Gandolph) usually consisted of ten sopranos and four altos. In addition to their duties at the cathedral, where they sang on Sundays and feast days, they performed at the university, at local churches and occasionally as players of instrumental music at court as well as receiving musical training from the court musicians: Eberlin, Adlgasser, Leopold Mozart, Michael Haydn and the theorist Johann Baptist Samber all taught the choirboys. (Leopold began giving violin instruction at the Chapel House as early as 1744 and it may be that his *Violinschule* of 1756 was based at least in part on his lessons there; it is possible that other didactic music and music theory originating in Salzburg was similarly intended for the choirboys.) Teaching the choirboys meant extra income for the court musicians. It also provided compositional opportunities: the Unschuldigen Kindleintag (Feast of the Holy Innocents) on 28 December was traditionally marked by music composed especially for the choirboys: Michael Haydn's *Missa Sancti Aloysii* (for two sopranos and alto, two violins and organ) of 1777 is only one example (other works composed by Haydn for the chapel boys include the cantata *Lauft ihr Hirten allzugleich*, a *Laudate pueri*, an *Anima nostra*, a litany and several other Masses, among them his last completed work, the *St Leopolds-Messe*, dated 22 December 1805).

In addition to their service at court and at the cathedral, the court musicians also performed at the Benedictine university, where school dramas were regularly given.[8] These belonged to a long tradition of spoken pedagogical Benedictine plays that developed into an opera-like art form during the seventeenth century. Salzburg University, the most important educational institution in south Germany at the time, played a leading role in this development.[9] At first, music in the dramas was restricted to choruses that marked the beginnings and ends of acts. By the 1760s, however, the works consisted of a succession of recitatives and arias, based at least in part on the model of Italian opera. A description from 1670 of the anonymous *Corona laboriosae heroum virtuti* shows the extent to which Salzburg school dramas represented a fusion of dramatic genres:

> The poem was Latin but the stage machinery was Italian . . . The work could be described as an opera. The production costs must have been exceptionally great. It drew a huge crowd. Part of the action was declaimed, part was sung. Gentlemen of the court performed the dances, which in part were inserted in the action as entr'actes. It was a delightful muddle and a wonderful pastime for the audience.[10]

Mozart's sole contribution to the genre was *Apollo et Hyacinthus*, performed in 1767 between the acts of Rufinus Widl's Latin tragedy *Clementia Croesi*.

It was the university that also gave rise to an orchestral genre unique to Salzburg: the orchestral serenade.[11] Every year in August, in connection with the university's graduation ceremonies, the students had a substantial orchestral work performed for their professors. Typically these serenades consisted of an opening and closing march and eight or nine other movements, among them two or three concerto-like movements for various instruments. Although the origin of this tradition is not known, it was certainly established as a regular fixture of the academic year by the mid-1740s. Leopold Mozart, who had composed more than thirty such works by 1757, was the most important early exponent of the genre. Wolfgang followed in his steps: K. 203, K. 204 and the so-called 'Posthorn' Serenade, K. 320, were all apparently written for the university. Other serenades, similar in style and substance to those for the university, were composed for name days or, as in the case of the so-called 'Haffner' Serenade, K. 250, for local weddings.

Aside from the court, Salzburg was home to several important religious institutions closely tied to, but still independent from, the state church establishment. Foremost among them was the archabbey of St Peter's, where the music chapel consisted largely of students; only a few musicians at the abbey were professionals, among them the *chori figuralis inspector*, who was responsible for the music archive.[12] Nevertheless, St Peter's offered the court musicians numerous opportunities for both performance and composition. In 1753, Leopold Mozart composed an *Applausus* to celebrate the anniversary of the ordination of three fathers, and some years later, in 1769, Wolfgang wrote the Mass, K. 66, for Cajetan Hagenauer, the son of the Mozarts' landlord Johann Lorenz Hagenauer. Cajetan, who took the name Dominicus, was also the dedicatee of two of Michael Haydn's works, the *Missa Sancti Dominici* and a *Te Deum*, both composed to celebrate his election as abbot of St Peter's in 1786. Haydn had established close ties with St Peter's almost immediately after his arrival in Salzburg in 1763 and it was the source of his most important students and closest friends, for whom he composed his innovatory lieder for men's chorus.

In addition to St Peter's, Salzburg also boasted the important *Frauenstift* Nonnberg, founded by St Rupert *c.*712–14.[13] Although strict cloistering was in effect from the late 1500s – access to the church and other external areas was walled off – some court musicians were excepted: Franz Ignaz Lipp, a contemporary of Leopold Mozart, served as music teacher there and the court music copyist Maximilian Raab as cantor. The court music frequently appeared for special occasions, such as the election of a new abbess: when M. Scholastika, Countess Wicka, was elected in 1766, the Archbishop celebrated her installation with a grand feast at which the court music played instrumental works and performed a cantata by Michael Haydn (*Rebekka als Braut*). For the most part, however, the nuns performed themselves, not only at Mass, but also the fanfares traditionally given on festive occasions or to welcome guests. Of the instruments traditionally used for these purposes only the high-pitched clarino seems not to have been cultivated by the nuns, who instead played the tromba marina. A description from 1704 of a Mass celebrated by the Bishop of Chiemsee and performed by the court music is telling:

> On 10 September at ten o'clock the Bishop celebrated Holy Mass in the cloister church with the women performing the music. In the Johannes Chapel, where Baron Firmian also celebrated Mass, a song was sung, written specially for the occasion and set to music by Frau Anna Ernestina, who also accompanied.[14]

The uncommon festivity of the ceremonies described here notwithstanding, this account includes a reference to what was perhaps the chief musical distinction of Nonnberg and other local churches: the performance of German sacred songs. Such works were composed and printed in Salzburg as early as the first decade of the eighteenth century, including the anonymous *Dreyssig Geistliche Lieder* (Hallein, 1710) and Gotthard Wagner's *Cygnus Marianus, Das ist: Marianischer Schwane* (Hallein, 1710). These songs, frequently performed instead of an offertory, continued to be written throughout the century, some of them by Salzburg's most important composers, including Eberlin and Leopold Mozart. More importantly, the cultivation at Nonnberg of German sacred songs provided opportunities for women composers; aside from singing at court, women in Salzburg had little opportunity to shine musically, no matter how exceptional they may have been (as the case of Nannerl Mozart shows).

Beyond the court and other religious institutions in Salzburg, civic music making was important as well. Watchmen blew fanfares from the tower of the town hall and were sometimes leased out to play for weddings, while military bands provided marches for the city garrisons.[15] Often there was a close connection with the court: it was the watchmen, not the court music, that played trombone in the cathedral during service. By the same token, private citizens – or court musicians off duty – also played. Concerts to celebrate name days and serenades to celebrate weddings were common, as was domestic music making generally. In a letter of 12 April 1778, Leopold Mozart wrote:

> on evenings when there is no grand concert [at court], he [soprano Francesco Ceccarelli] comes over with an aria and a motet, I play the violin and Nannerl accompanies, playing the solos for viola or for wind instruments. Then we play keyboard concertos or a violin trio, with Ceccarelli taking the second violin.[16]

Nannerl Mozart's diary for 1779–80 documents other, similar occasions, and possibly as a result of Colloredo's relative lack of interest in the court music the local nobility started up a private orchestra, the first meeting of which was described by Leopold Mozart:

> Count Czernin is not content with fiddling at court and as he would like to do some conducting he has collected an amateur orchestra who are to meet in Count Lodron's hall every Sunday after three o'clock . . . A week ago today, on the 5th, we had our first music meeting . . . Nannerl accompanied all the symphonies and she also accompanied Ceccarelli who sang an aria *per l'appertura della accademia di dilettanti*. After the symphony Count Czernin played a beautifully written concerto by Sirmen alla Brunetti, and *doppo una altra sinfonia* Count Altham played a frightful trio, no one being able to say whether it was scraped or fiddled, whether it was in 3/4 or common time, or perhaps even in some newly invented and hitherto unknown tempo. Nannerl was to have played a concerto, but as the Countess wouldn't let them have her good harpsichord (which is *casus reservatus pro summo Pontifice*), and as only the Egedacher one with gilt legs was there, she didn't perform. In the end the two Lodron girls had to play. It had never been suggested beforehand that they should do so. But since I have been teaching them they are always quite well able to perform. So on this occasion too they both did me credit.[17]

Finally, there were numerous institutions within the state, or just outside its borders, that maintained close contact with the court and other musical establishments within the city. These included the Benedictine monastery at Michaelbeuern, four of whose abbots were rectors at Salzburg University and some of whose musicians, among them Andreas Brunmayer, studied in Salzburg and remained there as part of the court music; and the Benedictine monastery at Lambach, which purchased music and musical instruments from Salzburg and maintained close ties with the Salzburg court and the Salzburg court musicians. Both Michael Haydn and Leopold Mozart were welcome guests at Lambach. Other institutions allied with Salzburg stretched up the Salzach, along what is now the border with Bavaria: Landshut, Tittmoning, Frauenwörth, Wasserburg am Inn, Beuerberg and others. All of these institutions relied heavily on the city, and their surviving archives are still home to important early copies of otherwise unknown works by Salzburg composers.[18]

Mozart's Salzburg was hardly a musical backwater: it offered numerous opportunities for composition and performance, it maintained close ties with nearby cities and religious institutions, and music circulated freely there, including the most recent works of composers active throughout Europe. (The Salzburg archives preserve a wide-ranging eighteenth-century repertory including the latest orchestral music from Vienna and elsewhere, in addition to operas, vocal music and church music.) Leopold Mozart was in regular contact with Breitkopf in Leipzig, the most prominent German dealer in music manuscripts (and in instruments, several of which Leopold purchased for the court); he was himself the Salzburg sales agent for the music publisher Haffner in Nürnberg. Haffner, in turn, dealt regularly in the latest works published in Holland, Paris and London.

Nevertheless, there were local performance traditions – and beyond that, there were local compositional expectations, even if these were not always spelled out. One of these expectations concerned church music: it was the primary obligation of Salzburg composers to write works for the cathedral. And while Mozart appears to have fulfilled this obligation – his church compositions amounted to some thirty works, including Masses, litanies and offertories – he was, in fact, one of the least productive of Salzburg composers. During the same period, from 1763 to 1780, Michael Haydn composed at least eleven Masses, fifteen litanies and Vespers and more than ninety other sacred works. Several aspects of Mozart's church music fall in line with Salzburg traditions: word-painting is common – including fanfare motives at 'Gloria in excelsis' and 'Et resurrexit' and falling melodies for 'descendit', 'Crucifixus' and 'miserere' – as are multi-movement Credos with changes of tempo and fugues at 'Et vitam venturi'. In other respects, however, Mozart stands outside this tradition. His sacred works are more Italian in style than those of other Salzburg composers, no doubt a result of his contact in the early 1770s with Padre Martini in Bologna and Eugène, Marquis of Ligniville, in Florence, and his composition of Italian opera, a genre not widely cultivated in Salzburg.[19] Beyond that, the disruptive and disjunctive elements that inform his instrumental music of the Vienna period are often adumbrated in the Salzburg church music. Chromaticism is frequent and destabilizing while the Benedictus from the Mass in C major, K. 262, includes choral exclamations of 'Hosanna in excelsis' that interrupt the solo quartet. (In the Benedictus from the *Missa brevis* in C major, K. 258, the fast tempo and antiphonal exchanges between chorus and soloists are also atypical.)

It is with respect to instrumental – and in particular orchestral – music, however, that Mozart most clearly flaunted Salzburg norms. During Schrattenbach's reign, orchestral music was assiduously cultivated: in the 1750s, the court boasted three composers who were associated primarily with instrumental music – Leopold Mozart, Ferdinand Seidl and Caspar Christelli.[20] By the 1770s, however, orchestral music was little cultivated, especially at court. A letter written by Leopold to Wolfgang in September 1778 makes it clear that he was disappointed both with the frequency of the concerts and with their length:

> Yesterday I was for the first time [this season] the director of the great
> concert at court. At present the music ends at around a quarter past eight.
> Yesterday it began around seven o'clock and, as I left, a quarter past eight
> struck – thus an hour and a quarter. Generally only four pieces are
> performed: a symphony, an aria, a symphony or concerto, then an aria,
> and with this, Addio![21]

Indeed, the infrequency of the court concerts is indirectly documented by
Nannerl Mozart's diary. Of the 151 entries for the period from 26 March 1779
to 30 September 1780, a mere two describe Mozart's official duties and both
state only 'my brother had to play at court'.[22] Apparently Colloredo did not
allow much time for music, nor was he as concerned with the music establishment as he was with other aspects of court life. The historian Corbinian
Gärtner, an observer well disposed towards the Archbishop, paints a picture of court life that leaves little room for entertainment, even if he does
mention Colloredo's own occasional participation in the performances:

> Social gatherings began after six o'clock, during which [the Archbishop]
> often discussed business with his civic officials; otherwise he entertained
> foreign visitors, or played cards, or mingled with the court musicians and
> played the violin with them. Afterwards he had his evening meal, said his
> prayers, and went to bed at about ten o'clock.[23]

And Koch-Sternfeld, in his early nineteenth-century account of Salzburg,
noted that 'the Prince was less concerned with the court music than with
court society and the pleasant life in Salzburg'.[24]

On the other hand, Nannerl's diary includes numerous entries describing
private music making, including performances of quartets and quintets and
rehearsals for a concerto. One entry describes a public concert given at the
town hall while references to two presumably private academies are given
in March 1780.

Another venue for orchestral music was the university. Although it is
generally thought that the serenades and cassations performed by the court
musicians were mostly composed for the traditional August graduation
exercises, this may be only part of the story. The university diary for 1769
records a student performance of a *Platzmusik* in May and a similar event
is documented – again by Nannerl Mozart's diary – for 24 September 1779
(the work performed was Mozart's 'Haffner' Serenade).[25] The university
students, then, regularly performed (or had performed) orchestral works
throughout the year, including works of a sort traditionally thought to have
been given only at graduation. The same is true of other institutions. The
estate inventory of Martin Bischofreiter, *chori figuralis inspector* at St Peter's,
shows that orchestral music was a regular feature of musical life at St Peter's,
while the monastery at Michaelbeuern at one time had a collection of more

than 120 symphonies, primarily works by composers from Salzburg and Vienna.[26] Salzburg's citizens also required music for their entertainment, and some of Mozart's best-known works of the 1770s were demonstrably written for private performance, including not only the 'Haffner' Serenade (for the wedding of Elisabeth Haffner and Franz Xaver Späth) but also the Concerto for Three Pianos, K. 242 (for Countess Lodron and her daughters), and the Divertimento in D major, K. 334 (for Georg Sigismund Robinig on the occasion of his law examination). The diary of the court councillor Johann Baptist Schiedenhofen describes a private concert made up entirely of Mozart's compositions:

> [25 July 1777:] to Gusseti's where the music by young Mozart, which he wanted to perform for his sister in the evening, was rehearsed. It consisted of a symphony, a violin concerto, played by young Mozart, a concerto for transverse flute, played by the violone [double bass] player Herr Castel, and everything was young Mozart's work.[27]

All of this suggests that the court was probably not the principal venue in Salzburg for the performance of symphonies and other orchestral works – and it is in this context that Mozart's overwhelming interest in instrumental music seems more than a curiosity: it seems a provocation. Not only does the number of his symphonies alone almost exceed his entire output of Masses, litanies, offertories and shorter sacred works, but by comparison with his contemporaries Mozart clearly positioned himself as the city's dominant composer of orchestral music.[28]

An obvious question, then, is why Mozart composed so many symphonies and other instrumental works in Salzburg. He was not obliged to. In fact, composition was not a specific obligation of the court musicians, not even the composition of church music. Mozart's appointment as court organist states only that 'he shall . . . carry out his appointed duties with diligent assiduity and irreproachably, in the Cathedral as well as at court and in the chapel, and shall *as far as possible* serve the court and the church with new compositions made by him'.[29]

One possible answer to this question is hinted at in Leopold Mozart's letter of 28 May 1778 to his wife and son:

> The Archbishop of Olmütz was consecrated on the 17th. If you had not had so much to do for other people at Mannheim, you might have finished your mass and sent it to me. For at our practices Brunetti was chattering about who should compose the consecration mass and was hoping to arrange for Haydn to get the commission from the Archbishop. But the latter never replied; nor did Counts Czernin and Starhemberg who were approached by Brunetti and Frau Haydn. I therefore produced Wolfgang's mass with the organ solo, taking the Kyrie from the Spaur mass.[30]

Leopold's freedom of action was possible because the choice of works to be performed at court depended almost entirely on whoever was in charge that week, a practice documented by the 'Nachricht':

> The three court composers play their instruments in church as well as in the chamber, and in rotation with the Kapellmeister each has the direction of the court music for a week at a time. All the musical arrangements depend solely upon whoever is in charge each week, as he, at his pleasure, can perform his own or other persons' pieces.[31]

This may explain why so few of Wolfgang's works seem to have been heard at court. Music making in Salzburg was strictly *ad hoc*: the choice of works to be performed fell to the music director; the choice of works to be written fell to the composer. And because the Mozarts were not well liked by many of the court musicians, it is possible that Wolfgang's music was performed only when Leopold was weekly director (and even then under duress).

To Colloredo, it may have seemed that Wolfgang, given the opportunity, was slacking off. Certainly Mozart gave him plenty of ammunition, not only during the mid-1770s but also after the disastrous trip to Mannheim and Paris of 1777–8 when he was reinstated at Salzburg under favourable conditions as court and cathedral organist. For although in 1779 and 1780 he composed the 'Coronation' Mass, K. 317, and the *Missa solemnis*, K. 337, the Vespers K. 321 and 339, and the *Regina coeli*, K. 276, Colloredo was not satisfied. In an ambiguously worded document appointing Michael Haydn to replace Mozart in 1782 he wrote:

> we accordingly appoint [Johann Michael Haydn] as our court and cathedral organist, in the same fashion as young Mozart was obligated, with the additional stipulation that he show more diligence . . . and compose more often for our cathedral and chamber music, and, in such cases, himself direct in the cathedral on every occasion.[32]

Why this apparent criticism of Mozart? The answer, perhaps, is to be found in Mozart's other compositions of the time: the Concerto for Two Pianos, K. 365, the accompanied sonata K. 378, the symphonies K. 318, 319 and 338, the 'Posthorn' Serenade, K. 320, the Divertimento in D major, K. 334, the Sinfonia concertante, K. 364, incidental music for *Thamos, König in Ae-gypten*, K. 345, and *Zaide*, K. 344, and, from the end of the 1770s, *Idomeneo*. Few if any of these works would have been heard at court.

Even the few orchestral works by Mozart that came to the court's notice must have surprised the Archbishop – their complexity, colourful scoring, harmonic richness and, above all, expressive density, even among symphonies of the early 1770s, are not like other comparable works composed in Salzburg. A case in point is the Symphony in D major, K. 133, which has been compared with Michael Haydn's symphony Sherman 81 (Perger 9).[33]

Haydn's symphony, which originally consisted of three movements composed in 1766, was augmented in 1772 by the addition of a finale; the autograph of this new movement is dated 15 June 1772. K. 133 was completed a month later, in July 1772. Parallels between the works seem clear: both have quiet, lyrical main themes that are withheld at the beginning of the recapitulation and reappear only at the conclusion of the movement. And in both works, the theme returns *forte*, with augmented scoring (as early as the development in Haydn's symphony but not until the recapitulation in Mozart's). But these similarities are mostly on the surface and the two composers work out their ideas in strikingly different ways.

Like other Salzburg symphonies of the 1760s and 1770s,[34] Haydn's work consists essentially of blocks of material that are shifted about and rearranged in a different order, occasionally with varied scoring and dynamics, but only rarely with different functions. It begins with a two-part theme contrasting *piano* and *forte* which is then repeated and extended into a transition; the dominant-area material is also given a double statement before moving on to closing material. The recapitulation, as noted, begins with dominant-area material before bringing back the main tune and its continuation as well as the closing. There is little that is dramatic about the movement. The restatement of the opening theme in the central section is developmental only by virtue of its location: the material is tonally stable. Even the return at the end of the movement is unexceptional: the material is stated once, more or less exactly as at the beginning of the work, and it leads directly to the exposition's cadential material, thus preserving a sense of closure that not even the reversed order of the recapitulation can disturb.

Mozart's symphony, on the other hand, invites critical response. For although it begins straightforwardly enough, with three *forte* chords, the character of the primary material is already different from Haydn's: where Haydn's main theme is harmonically and rhythmically stable, Mozart's – beginning in the second bar – has no downbeat root-position tonic chords and only deceptive cadences. The entire gesture, from the opening of the movement to the beginning of the transition, is ambiguous. Nor does Mozart anticipate the effect of his reversed recapitulation by giving out the theme in the development. In fact, its reappearance at the end of the movement is not recapitulatory at all: by any conventional description, the movement has run its course and the closing group has already signalled its end. What is more, the weak, unstable theme in Mozart's movement is immediately juxtaposed with its opposite: the full orchestra, *forte*, 'straightens out' the material, investing it with full cadences and strong root movements. It is functionally changed and, as closing material, makes palpable a meaningful reversal between the opening and closing of the movement. For where the opening juxtaposes a stable, *forte* gesture (the three chords) with an unstable, *piano* one (the main theme), the ending not only reverses this order but at the same time draws out the 'hidden meaning', so to speak, of the three chords: the final apotheosis is, in effect, a 'realization' of the three opening chords and the one gesture that finally gives the movement tonal stability and a convincing close.

It is no wonder Colloredo may have been perplexed by his young composer. And he was not the only one who found Mozart's Salzburg music unsatisfactory. When Charles Burney's correspondent Louis de Visme visited Salzburg in 1772, shortly after the composition of K. 133, he wrote:

> Young Mozhard, too, is of the band, you remember this prodigy in England . . . If I may judge of the music which I heard of his composition, in the orchestra, he is one further instance of early fruit being more extraordinary than excellent.[35]

Possibly it was reactions such as these that led Mozart to write to his father:

> I confess that in Salzburg work was a burden to me and that I could hardly ever settle down to it. Why? Because I was never happy . . . there is no stimulus [there] for my talent! When I play or when any of my compositions is performed, it is just as if the audience were all tables and chairs.

There is no question that Colloredo was a difficult employer. And his greatest failing may have been a blind trust in foreign-born musicians, Italians in particular, whom he frequently promoted over the heads of better-qualified local talent. Long-time employees such as Leopold Mozart and Michael Haydn, both of whom established their credentials during Schrattenbach's reign, had good reason to be disgruntled: not only were they repeatedly passed over for promotion, but Colloredo's choices, even with respect to ordinary court musicians, inevitably turned out badly. Following the incapacitation in December 1785 of the violinist Wenzl Sadlo, Colloredo enlisted the two oldest choirboys from the Chapel House to play violin in the cathedral, a stop-gap action until the arrival in Salzburg of a new violinist from Italy, Giacomo Latouche. Leopold was upset. Not only had he hoped his pupil Joseph Breymann would be taken on, but Latouche made the worst possible impression:

> The new violinist arrived on Good Friday, but hasn't played a note of a solo yet, and as far as I can see, we'll hardly get to hear a concerto from him very soon either; something like a *quartet* maybe, because the Italians are saying: *the poor man – he's a good professor, you've got to give him that, and he'll be good leading the second violins*; but he *hasn't been used* to playing concertos. *At most he can play a trio or quartet cleanly, and what's more he's timid.* Now it can't be held against him that he's timid either, because after all he's only *30 years* old. So the archbishop has once again been nicely

diddled and with a salary of 500 fl. to boot, plus 40 ducats travel money here and back making 700 fl. good luck to him! – on top of that the man isn't good looking. He's of medium build, has a pale rather puffed up face, and yet has certain bony bits to it too, like a horse's head, hangs his head forward, and chews tobacco like the Zillerthal farmers; that's what the Italians say. I pity the man, all the same it's a piece of Italian audacity to undertake something you're not capable of.[36]

The upshot was that Latouche left court service in late 1786, excusing himself to Colloredo on grounds of poor health: the truth of the matter is that he left behind a pregnant girl.

At the same time, however, the Mozarts were not good employees. Leopold made no bones about his dissatisfaction. (Although he often wrote in cypher to keep his plans hidden from Colloredo and his censors, it is almost certain they were public knowledge.) And Mozart took over many of Leopold's opinions – whether musical or political – lock, stock and barrel. Most importantly, Leopold wrote from Schwetzingen on 19 July 1763: 'The orchestra is undeniably the best in Germany. It consists altogether of people who are young and of good character, not drunkards, gamblers or dissolute fellows.' And Mozart wrote, some fifteen years later: 'one of my chief reasons for detesting Salzburg [is the] coarse, slovenly, dissolute court musicians. Why, no honest man, of good breeding, could possibly live with them! Indeed, instead of wanting to associate with them, he would feel ashamed of them . . . [The Mannheim musicians] certainly behave quite differently from ours. They have good manners, are well dressed and do not go to public houses and swill.'[37]

Men of good breeding, honest men, the Mozarts withdrew from the court music – from Colloredo who at least implicitly sanctioned ill behaviour and from their drunken, dissolute colleagues. And this withdrawal, at least in Wolfgang's case, manifested itself not simply as non-participation but in the seemingly deliberate cultivation of non-institutional music making, of a type of music – instrumental and orchestral music – openly shunned by the court, and of a style foreign to local taste.[38] Clearly the Mozarts saw themselves as moderns: Leopold says as much when in 1755 he describes one of his symphonies as 'composed in the most up-to-date fashion'.[39] And they may have felt trapped in Salzburg, Colloredo's reforms notwithstanding. Certainly they felt unappreciated.[40] Nevertheless, considering their strong attachment to the court and neglect of other institutions in the archdiocese, the Mozarts' reaction – haughty withdrawal – was bound to cause friction.

If blame is to be apportioned for the breakdown of Mozart's relationship with his native city, then, it is clear that both sides were at fault. And yet history has adopted only one side of the story, namely Mozart's. It is worth asking how this came about.

Biographical accounts of Mozart published prior to the late 1820s make virtually no mention of his mistreatment in Salzburg. Not even Nannerl Mozart, in her reminiscences, has much to say about this. But with the publication in 1828 of Georg Nikolaus von Nissen's *Biographie W. A. Mozart*, the story of Mozart's early suffering became a standard biographical trope. What gave Nissen (Constanze's second husband) such authority was his publication of lengthy abstracts from the family correspondence – indeed, his is as much an epistolary biography (and as such at least indirectly related to the idea of the epistolary novel) as a scholarly one. The biographical power of these abstracts, including bitter complaints and frequent accounts of abuse, was beyond measurement: not only were they 'authentic', straight from the horse's mouth, but they reinforced the then current 'idea' of Mozart as a quintessentially Romantic artist – discarded and neglected, passed over in favour of lesser talents, sickly and impoverished, doomed to an early grave. And the music composed between 1784 and 1788: so powerful, so moving, so 'absolute', so Viennese. Could a better foil be found for the creation of this classical (in the sense of exemplary) style than his miserable life in Salzburg, where he was subjugated by his father and the Archbishop and where, as most accounts have it, he was forced to toe the line musically? Almost inevitably, Salzburg came to occupy an important and thoroughly negative place in Mozart's history, fuelled by the composer's own words. Most important of all, perhaps, he was relieved of any personal culpability: it was not Mozart's fault that his life turned out the way it did – his true spirit, and the rewards that he deserved, are manifest in the grace and beauty and purity of his works.

It is a convenient story but not a convincing one. Salzburg, like all courts large and small, had its share of problems. And it was the Mozarts' misfortune to be just as problematic as their employer. Curiously, however, recognizing the complexities and realities of the situation does not much change the final outcome: whether he was a neglected Romantic artist or a rebellious *ancien régime* hothead, Mozart's story remains exceptional. And that, above all, is what posterity wants to believe.

2 Mozart in Vienna

DOROTHEA LINK

On his own in Vienna for the first time, the twenty-five-year-old Mozart wrote to his father on 4 April 1781: 'I can assure you that this here is a Magnificent place – and for my Métier the best place in the world.'[1] He had decided to stay, although the famous kick in the arse from the agent of Archbishop Colloredo in Salzburg did not take place until 9 June. And while his father would never be persuaded that any city was the right city if one did not have a fixed appointment, Mozart was not naive about his prospects in Vienna. Had death not cut him off just as he was emerging from four financially difficult years, he would have been proven right. In the ten years since his arrival he had obtained the coveted court appointment, he had secured the reversion of the post of Kapellmeister at St Stephen's Cathedral, he had enjoyed notable, often lucrative, successes as a performer and as a composer, and he was patronized by the nobility. The present essay will examine these sources of employment and the extent to which Mozart was able to realize them.

The court

In 1781 the court was still the best employer in Vienna. Although Joseph II led an austere and conspicuously frugal court life, he did not dissolve the court's established musical institutions, the Hofkapelle (court chapel) and the theatre.[2] The Hofkapelle provided music for the court's church services. In addition to the musicians, the Hofkapelle in 1781 consisted of the Hofkapellmeister Giuseppe Bonno and the composer Christoph Willibald Gluck. It also carried on its rosters pensioned personnel drawing full salaries, including the court poet Pietro Metastasio, the soprano Maria Theresia Reutter and the altos Pietro Ragazzoni and Pietro Galli. In addition to the Hofkapelle, and sometimes considered part of it, were the Kammer Musici, personal attendants to Joseph who regularly made music with him in his private chambers. In 1781 these musicians included the composer Antonio Salieri, the violinists Franz Kreibich and Karl von Ordonez and, unofficially, the valet Kilian Strack. As court employees, all these people enjoyed employment for life, occupied positions within the court's hierarchy according to which they were automatically promoted, and were entitled to pensions. The exact make-up of the Hofkapelle and the Kammer Musik changed slightly over the years, but the important point as far as Mozart was concerned was that both bodies maintained at all times at least one composer within their ranks.

It was to one of these composer positions that Mozart aspired. In a letter to his father of 11 April 1781 Mozart assesses his chances. He describes the line of succession as consisting of Bonno, Salieri, Joseph Starzer and possibly himself: 'When Bono dies, Salieri will become Kapellmeister – then Starzer will get Salieri's position and Starzer's position? – Well, no one has been mentioned yet.'[3] Starzer, the former ballet composer, was receiving a pension from the theatre account but could be pressed back into active service if a composer position became free. Significantly, Mozart does not mention Gluck, for reasons that will become apparent below.

Mozart's ambitions were obvious to everyone, as a letter to his father of 10 April 1782 makes clear, notwithstanding his protests of having done nothing to make them known:

> What you are writing about the rumors going around that I will be taken into the service of the emperor – well, the reason that I haven't written anything to you about it is that – I myself know nothing. – One thing is certain: the whole town is full of this talk and a good number of people have already congratulated me; – and I can readily believe that there has been some talk about this matter in the emperor's presence and that he may even be giving it some thought, – but so far I haven't heard a word. – It's interesting that matters have proceeded to the point that the emperor is thinking about something of this sort when, I, in fact, – haven't taken one step to further such a move![4]

Despite repeated signs of approval, the Emperor continued not to take Mozart into his service. Then on 22 April 1787 Joseph Starzer died. As a ballet composer had long been surplus to requirements he was not replaced. On 15 November 1787 Gluck died. As his appointment was a special case, he was not replaced either. On 6 December 1787 Mozart was appointed to the Kammer Musik. This move was part of a larger plan of Joseph's, which he implemented in stages. On 12 February 1788 he pensioned off the aged Bonno and replaced him as Kapellmeister of the Hofkapelle with Salieri, who consequently gave up his position in the Kammer Musik, leaving Mozart as its sole composer. In the end, there were two composers at court: Salieri and Mozart. Salieri received 1200 gulden as Kapellmeister of the Hofkapelle and Mozart 800 gulden as composer in the Kammer Musik.

Mozart's duties were not defined in his letter of appointment, but for the time being they were practically non-existent, as Joseph went off to war at the end of February. Salieri, on the other hand, had to work for his salary as Kapellmeister. The issue of salaries is somewhat complex and superficial comparisons are misleading. When Salieri had been composer in the Kammer Musik he had been paid 426 fl. 40 x., which compares unfavourably with Mozart's 800 gulden for a more or less identical position.[5] Gluck on the other hand had received 2000 gulden as court composer in the Hofkapelle. His appointment was honorary, however, bestowed in 1774 to keep him from accepting an invitation from Marie Antoinette to go to France. He had no real duties other than to represent the court at official functions, as happened in late 1781 when the Russian Grand Duke Paul and his wife Marie von Württemberg visited Vienna. The important point to note is that within six years of arriving in Vienna Mozart had achieved his goal of obtaining a court position. Had his father lived half a year longer he would have had the satisfaction of seeing his son established at one of the greatest courts in Europe.[6]

The other court institution that supported music was the theatre. In 1781 the theatre consisted of a main company that performed German spoken theatre (established in 1776) and a smaller, experimental company that performed Singspiel (established in 1778). At Easter 1783 the German Singspiel company was upgraded to an Italian opera buffa company, for which the leading singers were imported from Italy. The Singspiel company was revived in October 1785 and played alongside the opera buffa company (and the German spoken theatre company) until it was again dissolved, at Easter 1788. These, then, were the court opera companies for which Mozart composed. The theatre's personnel, unlike those in the Hofkapelle, were not court employees but were engaged on a contract basis. Salieri alone had some security attached to his position as Kapellmeister of the opera buffa company, for which he was paid 853 fl. 20 x. (200 ducats at the time the salary was set).[7] The temporary nature of the appointments resulted, especially after 1783, in a steady stream of singers and composers passing through the capital. Composers were paid a fee of 100 ducats (450 gulden after 1786) for an opera. As the repertory consisted largely of imported operas, however, commissions for new operas were not essential and their number varied from season to season. Overall they amounted to between a quarter and a third of the entire repertory.[8] Theoretically the best Mozart could have hoped for from the court theatre was one opera commission a year, but that was wildly unrealistic as even Salieri composed only seven new operas in the eleven opera seasons from 1781–2 to 1791–2. Mozart came next with four (including *Don Giovanni*), followed by Vicente Martín y Soler with three.

Although emanating from the same institution, Mozart's commissions all came about in different ways. When Mozart arrived in Vienna on 16 March 1781, the court was producing Singspiel. One month later Mozart already reports that the actor and playwright Johann Gottlieb Stephanie was searching for a libretto for him. By the end of July it was in Mozart's hands and by August Mozart had finished the music of the first act. The premiere of *Die Entführung aus dem Serail* had to wait until 16 July 1782, however, owing to the state visit of Grand Duke Paul in the autumn of 1781, for which three Gluck operas were revived. Although July was a poor time for a premiere, as most of the nobility were out of town, the opera was enormously successful and continued to draw full houses for the remainder of the season.

In December 1782, Joseph's theatre manager Count Franz Orsini Rosenberg suggested to Mozart that he compose an Italian opera for the new opera buffa company that was due to replace the Singspiel the following Easter. Yet not until the new company's third season, 1785–6, did Mozart begin composing *Le nozze di Figaro*. To what can the delay be attributed? The uncertainty over the continued existence of the opera buffa beyond its first year may have been partly responsible for the issue of only one commission in 1783–4, to Josef Bárta for an opera that was withdrawn after three performances. That season Salieri composed an opera for Paris. The next season saw a commission for a new opera from Salieri (*Il ricco d'un giorno*), an impromptu commission to Giovanni Paisiello as he was passing through Vienna and a mysterious commission to Giacomo Rust for an opera that did not survive beyond its first performance. It is conceivable that Mozart could have obtained commissions in these two seasons had he been able to find a libretto or, more importantly, a librettist. Lorenzo Da Ponte states that he established himself as a librettist only with the success of *Il burbero di buon cuore* for Vicente Martín y Soler on 4 January 1786.[9] Except for his disastrous collaboration with Salieri on *Il ricco d'un giorno*, he had not worked with any composer on any new opera, despite being the librettist of the opera buffa company since its inception. In 1785–6, however, Da Ponte got into his stride. He furnished librettos for three of the six operas commissioned that season, from Vincenzo Righini, Stephen Storace, Vicente Martín (*Il burbero di buon cuore*), Giuseppe Gazzaniga, Salieri and Mozart, although Mozart's opera was not performed until the beginning of the next season. It is hard to gauge the success of *Le nozze di Figaro*. On the one hand, so many encores were demanded by the audiences at the first performances that Joseph issued a decree preventing the repetition of ensembles. On the other hand, the opera lasted for only nine performances.

The subsequent phenomenal success of *Le nozze di Figaro* in Prague, however, led to the commissioning of *Don Giovanni*. Although issued by the impresario Domenico Guardasoni for his own opera company, the commission was followed with a certain amount of interest in Vienna. Da Ponte, engaged as the librettist, had a draft libretto printed in Vienna, an unusual occurrence that might have been connected with the choice of *Don Giovanni* as the festive opera to be given when Joseph's niece, the Archduchess Maria Theresia, passed through Prague on her wedding procession to Dresden.[10]

As the appointed day neared and *Don Giovanni* was not ready, *Le nozze di Figaro* was performed instead, by express command of the Emperor. *Don Giovanni* was eventually performed on 29 October to great acclaim, the public being particularly appreciative of its difficulty.[11] Mozart received the proceeds of the fourth performance, which probably came to more than the fee for the opera.[12] Joseph arranged both for the opera to be given in Vienna at the beginning of the following season (7 May 1788) and for Mozart and Da Ponte to be paid again for their composition, at half the standard fee. He left for war before he could see the opera, but from the field he learned that the Viennese did not take to it, to which he remarked that Mozart's music was too difficult for singers.[13] Things were not helped by the fact that, with the exception of Leporello and Zerlina, the Viennese production had a weak cast.[14]

By the end of August 1788 Joseph had dissociated himself from the management of the opera. Da Ponte's doubled salary and his claim to have saved the opera from dissolution suggest that henceforth he assumed a greater role in its administration. To keep costs down only two operas were commissioned that season, one from Salieri and one from his pupil Joseph Weigl. The 1789–90 season proceeded with a similar eye to economy. A number of lapsed operas were revived, among them *Le nozze di Figaro*. This production, for which Mozart made a number of changes that included writing two new arias for the new singer who was to play Susanna, lasted for twenty-eight performances, extending into 1791. The season also saw two new commissions, one to Salieri for *La cifra* and one to Mozart for *Così fan tutte*. Mozart's commission must have come about hastily, as Da Ponte did not have time to write a libretto for him but offered him a libretto rejected by Salieri.[15] Perhaps Da Ponte offered him the libretto so as not to forfeit his librettist's fee of 200 gulden.[16] Despite the libretto not having been designed for him, Mozart wrote what turned out to be the most popular opera of the season.[17]

In all this we see an opera composer who, far from being marginalized by his supposedly scheming rivals and uncomprehending audiences, is in the thick of things, supported by the Emperor and taking advantage of every opportunity that came his way.

The church

The other traditional source of employment for musicians was the church, and, as Burney observed in 1772, the Viennese were exceptionally devoted to having music in church and insisted on fairly elaborate performances. Almost all of the churches and religious houses in Vienna performed musical Masses with organ, choir and strings on a daily basis.[18] All this activity provided work for many musicians, who supplemented it with jobs in the

Hofkapelle, the two court theatre orchestras and the orchestras of the commercial theatres. In 1783, however, Joseph implemented church reforms that, while not directed specifically at music, had an inadvertently negative impact on it. The primary aim of his reforms was to regularize church services across the country and to curtail costly and excessive ceremonies. The monies thus saved were redirected to a newly created capital fund that financed social-service projects.

Joseph began his overhaul of church services by categorizing all churches according to locale – cities, towns, villages, country, monasteries, convents and hospitals – and to the number of priests and other ecclesiastical personnel employed. The category determined the frequency and lavishness of the services prescribed. Details in the new regulations hint at some of the excessiveness that had crept into use. All processions except those for three feast days in the church year were banned. The three permissible processions were limited to fifteen minutes around the church. They were to begin from the church and no other place. They were to be held on the day of the feast itself and could not be postponed. Some non-liturgical devotions were banned altogether, such as blessings for good weather, pilgrimages and elaborate celebrations of Christ's resurrection. The forty-hour prayer said during the three days of carnival was limited to churches in the larger cities and only to those that already had a tradition of performing this ritual. Nowhere among these and other directives were there any aimed specifically at music. Indeed, Joseph's reforms overall were considerably more moderate than those advocated by some of his advisors, who urged, among other things, that all instrumental music should be abolished.[19]

The church reforms had unintended devastating consequences for Vienna's musicians in that many lost their jobs completely and others saw their income reduced by a third or a half. The city's church musicians wasted no time petitioning the Emperor for relief, who in response instructed his officials to draw up a list of all church musicians together with their earnings before and after the imposition of the reforms. The matter was then deliberated by the appropriate authorities, but by the time they arrived at the point of considering some action a year later the crisis had passed. The musicians had perforce solved their financial problems individually.

In 1781, even before the reforms, the church was probably at the bottom of the list of Mozart's job prospects. The best positions in Vienna's churches were those of music director, filled variously by Kapellmeister, *regens chori* and organists, but their salaries, lying somewhere between 300 and 350 gulden, were well below Mozart's expectations. There was one notable exception, however. St Stephen's Cathedral reportedly paid its Kapellmeister a salary of 2000 gulden.[20] The cathedral was administered by the city magistracy and was independent of the court and its decrees, including the one laying down the church reforms. In the spring of 1791, St Stephen's aged

Kapellmeister Leopold Hofmann became gravely ill. Although he recovered, Mozart took the opportunity to petition the city for the post of unpaid assistant to Hofmann. According to the practice of the day, he was thereby placing himself first in line for the latter's position upon his death. Mozart's petition was granted. Hofmann died in 1793.

Freelance teaching

We return to spring 1781. For the present Mozart urgently needed to find work. He wrote to his father on 19 May that he would sell sonatas by subscription, write an opera and give a concert in Advent. A few days later he also mentioned taking piano pupils: 'As far as pupils are concerned, I can have as many as I want; but I don't want that many – I want to be better paid than other musicians – so I can afford to have fewer pupils.'[21] That he took pupils reluctantly and only as a last resort, he had already emphatically expressed to his father from Mannheim in 1778:

> To be obliged to go to a house at a certain time – or to have to wait at home for a pupil – is what I cannot do, no matter how much money it may bring me in. I find it impossible, so must leave it to those who can do nothing else but play the clavier. I am a composer and was born to be a Kapellmeister. I neither can nor ought to bury the talent for composition with which God in his goodness has so richly endowed me ... and this I should be doing if I were to take many pupils.[22]

In June he obtained a first pupil in Countess Rumbeke and a second one in Josepha von Auernhammer.[23] But students were harder to come by than he had expected, and in September he was faring so badly that he was thinking of trying his luck in Paris. For a few weeks in December he entertained hopes of being appointed keyboard teacher to Princess Elisabeth von Württemberg, who, as the chosen bride of Archduke Franz, had been sent to Vienna to finish her education there. Mozart initially thought that Salieri had been given the appointment, but it eventually went to an organist known only as Summerer or Summer at a salary of 400 gulden. In reporting the news to his father, Mozart explains why he would not have wanted the position anyway:

> You write that 400 gulden a year *as an assured salary* is not to be despised. What you say would be true if in addition I could work myself into a good position and treat these 400 gulden simply as an extra. But unfortunately that is not the case. I should have to consider the 400 gulden as my chief income and everything I could earn besides as an extra, the amount of which would be very uncertain and consequently in all probability very meagre. For you can easily understand that you cannot act as independently towards a pupil who is a princess as towards other ladies.[24]

By the end of December he had found a third pupil in Frau von Trattner, after which he claimed that he needed only a fourth to have enough income to survive. He also changed his fee structure. Instead of charging by the lesson (or the traditional block of twelve lessons), he now charged his pupils a set monthly fee (6 ducats or 25 fl. 36 x.), which they paid whether or not they cancelled a lesson. The desired fourth pupil did not materialize until November 1782, in the person of Countess Zichy, and in January 1783 he obtained a fifth in Countess Palffy. That is the last we hear of countesses. Subsequent pupils seem to have been taken on for reasons other than building up a studio of well-paying pupils.

Barbara Ployer, a pupil from 1784, was an extremely fine pianist for whom Mozart wrote two concertos. Franziska von Jacquin, who studied with Mozart in 1787, was the sister of Mozart's friend Gottfried von Jacquin. The professional pianist Marianne Willmann may have had some lessons with Mozart, for she performed a piano concerto of his in the court theatre in 1787.[25] Johann Nepomuk Hummel started receiving sporadic instruction from Mozart around 1787 when he was seven or eight. Few names crop up after that, even in the financially straitened years. Ignaz von Seyfried was a fifteen-year-old keyboard student in 1791. Increasingly in later years Mozart also gave instruction in composition. Thomas Attwood, Franz Xaver Süssmayr, Franz Jacob Freystädtler and Joseph Eybler all received some form of tuition from him. As in the case of the young keyboard students, however, it is hard to know how much of this teaching, Attwood probably excepted, was undertaken as a source of income.

Freelance performing

Although he assured his father in May 1781 that he intended to give a concert in Advent, he did not appear in a public concert until the following May, and then not in his own concert but in a series of outdoor concerts organized by Philipp Jakob Martin. The following November he appeared in a concert in the Kärntnertortheater given by his pupil Josepha von Auernhammer. He was not able to organize a concert of his own until Lent 1783, in the Burgtheater. Giving public concerts in Vienna at a time when they were just beginning to be established was not easy.[26] Part of the problem was the lack of designated concert halls. The two court theatres, the Burgtheater and the Kärntnertortheater were the optimum facilities, but they were available only during Lent when operas and plays were not performed.[27] Other concert venues included all-purpose halls connected to restaurants and casinos, such as the Mehlgrube, the Trattnerhof and Jahn's Hall. In the summers, outdoor concerts were given in the Augarten and the Neumarkt as well as in other improvised settings.

A period of intense concert activity for Mozart began in 1784. He gave a Lenten concert in the court theatre. He also organized a series of three concerts in the Trattnerhof, which overlapped with three concerts given there by the Dutch pianist Georg Friedrich Richter. Mozart played in those as well as in his own. In spring 1785 Mozart gave his by now usual concert in the court theatre as well as six subscription concerts in the Mehlgrube, all of which his father attended. In Advent of that year he gave a series of concerts at an unknown location. In 1786 he gave his Lenten concert in the court theatre and a series of Advent concerts in the Trattnerhof. Thereafter concerts practically cease. We know of one more, in November 1788 in Jahn's Hall. The three subscription concerts that he planned to give at his own home in 1789 did not come about for lack of subscribers. In May 1790 Mozart again brought up the idea of giving subscription concerts at his home and in October referred to subscription quartet concerts, but we do not know whether either of these projects was realized.

Organizing a concert was a large undertaking, but the effort could be well worth it. A few surviving figures for the Lenten concert season of 1785 show how lucrative concerts could be. The Le Bruns, an oboist and a singer, cleared (or possibly took in) 1100 gulden, 900 gulden, and 500 gulden in three concerts they gave in the court theatre. Mozart's concert on 19 March yielded 559 gulden, exceeding his own and his father's expectations, since he had just given six well-attended subscription concerts at the Mehlgrube and had also performed extensively in private concerts.[28]

It should be obvious that no amount of virtuosic playing and brilliant composition could ensure success in concertizing if not accompanied by strong entrepreneurial skills. Mozart's continual casting about for new sources of income also led to his well-known collaboration with the actor, impresario, composer, director, singer (Papageno) and librettist Emanuel Schikaneder in what may have been a joint financial venture in 1791, the production of *Die Zauberflöte* at the Theater auf der Wieden.[29] This theatre, erected in 1787, was one of the three most important commercial theatres to have sprung up in Vienna since 1776 when Joseph had lifted the court's monopoly on theatre, the other two being the Leopoldstädtertheater, established in 1781, and the Josefstädtertheater, built in 1788. The immediate and resounding success of *Die Zauberflöte* should have brought Mozart some much-needed income, but we have no record of what he received or, indeed, whether he received anything at all.

Freelance publishing

Earning one's living solely from publishing was practically impossible in 1781. The biggest obstacle for composers lay in the limited rights of ownership they had to their works. They lost possession of a composition once they sold it to a publisher, which they did for a flat fee, without royalties. All too often they were denied their fee by unscrupulous publishers who pirated their music, not to mention a whole industry of arrangers who, for example, would make and sell vocal scores of popular numbers from a new opera, from which the composer would of course receive nothing. Four days after the premiere of *Die Entführung aus dem Serail* Mozart wrote to his father that if he did not complete his arrangement of the opera for wind instruments in a week, someone else would do it, which is what happened. Vienna was unusual among European musical centres at this time for carrying on much of its trade in sheet music in the form of handwritten music sold by commercial music copyists. Chief among these were Johann Traeg, Lorenz Lausch and Wenzel Sukowaty, also the court theatre copyist. The principal publisher of engraved music from 1778 was Artaria and Company, although in the following decade Franz Anton Hoffmeister, Christoph Torricella and Leopold Kozeluch also established publishing houses. Artaria was Mozart's major publisher, bringing out forty-five editions of Mozart's music during his lifetime.[30] We know of only one fee that Artaria paid Mozart: 100 ducats (then 433 fl. 20 x.) for the six 'Haydn' Quartets in 1785.

From Wolfgang and Leopold's long experience in dealing with publishers, Wolfgang was predisposed to avoid them and to try to maximize his profits by publishing his works himself. In his letter to his father of 19 May 1781 he reports that he will sell some sonatas by subscription. He never mentioned exactly how and even whether the subscription scheme was realized. The chances are that he abandoned the idea and sold the sonatas to Artaria just to get them out, for in November 1781 Artaria issued six violin sonatas, K. 296 and 376–380. The following year Mozart made another attempt to sell his works by subscription, this time in manuscript copies, but it failed as well. The failure can be clearly traced through the letters.[31] On 28 December 1782 Mozart explained to his father that he was writing three keyboard concertos (K. 413, 414, 415) which he was going to sell by subscription for 6 ducats (25 fl. 36 x.). In his letter of 4 January 1783 he had lowered the asking price to 4 ducats (17 fl. 4 x.), which is the price listed in the advertisement that appeared in the *Wiener Zeitung* on 15 January. When in April the deadline had passed without his having obtained sufficient subscribers, Mozart offered the set to the publisher Jean Georges Sieber in Paris for 30 *louis d'or* (about 330 gulden), which, as Ruth Halliwell points out, is the profit he would have realized from selling twenty-five sets by subscription. Sieber declined, and the concertos were next advertised by Traeg in Vienna in September 1783 at 10 gulden for all three. The terms of this arrangement are unknown, but Halliwell does not rule out that Traeg might have sold a pirated score. Eventually Mozart reverted to Artaria, who in March 1785 offered the concertos, now engraved, for sale at 2 fl. 30 x.

each, which made the set 7 fl. 30 x. When compared with Mozart's original figure of 25 fl. 36 x., it is clear that the price he placed on his compositions vastly exceeded their market value.[32]

In his dealings with Artaria, Mozart shows himself not to have been entirely above reproach. Rupert Ridgewell chronicles the relationship between them from 1787 to Mozart's death. In July 1787 Artaria commissioned, and perhaps paid for in advance, six piano trios, the first three of which were published in November 1788 (K. 502, 542, 548). The next trio, K. 564, was completed in October 1788, but was not published by Artaria until October 1790, and then as a single composition, suggesting that Artaria had given up waiting for the other two trios that would have made a set of three. Meanwhile, Mozart arranged to have the trio published in London in July 1789, thereby earning a second fee for it. Curiously he never repeated this stratagem. As with the trios, Mozart failed to deliver a complete set of twelve songs, forcing Artaria to publish just four. Having brought things to a standstill between Artaria and himself, Mozart sought to publish his next compositions at his own expense with Kozeluch, but again failed to finish the sets, the 'six easy clavier sonatas for Princess Friederika and six quartets for the King', and nothing came of his plan. In June 1790, Mozart sold the three 'Prussian' Quartets, K. 575, 589 and 590, to Artaria 'for a pittance'. In October 1790 Mozart negotiated with Franz Anton Hoffmeister over future publications but nothing came of that either. While Mozart soured his relationship with Artaria by defaulting on the delivery of promised compositions, the inadequate compensation received by composers for their works constituted a serious problem, and publishers, as the first in line to have to pay, appeared and often acted like villains. One has only to follow Constanze Mozart's attempts to publish her dead and by then famous husband's oeuvre with Breitkopf and Härtel to understand Beethoven's profound loathing for publishers and his many attempts to outmanoeuvre them.[33]

The nobility

From his association since childhood with a large part of Europe's nobility Mozart had acquired an ease in consorting with them. No sooner arrived in Vienna, he aggressively courted the resident nobility for their support. He looked to them for pupils, for invitations to give private concerts, for attendance of his own concerts and for the exertion of their influence with the Emperor. But that was all he could expect, for although the nobility in Vienna had a reputation for being music lovers, their patronage of musicians during the 1780s was limited to providing occasional or short-term engagements.[34] No princely household maintained a private orchestra or even a chamber ensemble, apart from a Harmoniemusik kept by Prince Johann Nepomuk Schwarzenberg and one acquired in 1789 by Prince Alois Liechtenstein. The social calendar of the aristocracy was agreeably filled with numerous musical events marking birthdays, fulfilling social obligations and rounding out dinner parties, but the number of serious patrons of music was surprisingly small. The most consistent sponsor of private concerts was undoubtedly the Russian ambassador Prince Dimitrj Galitzin, who for many years held regular concerts in his palace, for which he engaged a wide variety of musicians, including Mozart. Baron Gottfried van Swieten tried to establish a tradition of oratorio performances, which members of the nobility took turns financing. In the late 1780s he engaged Mozart to re-orchestrate and direct a number of Handel oratorios. Count Johann Baptist Esterházy took an active role in sponsoring a number of cultural activities: in 1786 he hosted a series of German plays; in 1788 he began supporting van Swieten's oratorio productions; and in 1784 he mounted a series of at least nine concerts, for which he engaged Paul Wranitzky as music director and Mozart as a performer.

The nobility also produced operas, but in small numbers and almost always as domestic comedies, in which they themselves performed the roles with the support of professional musicians. The driving force behind the opera productions seems to have been Countess Hatzfeld, who was accomplished enough as a singer to take the leading roles in most of the operas. Prince Alois Liechtenstein hosted three such productions in 1784, Prince Karl Johann Baptist Dietrichstein one in 1787 and Prince Johann Adam Auersperg three in 1786, which included *Idomeneo* under Mozart's direction.

However limited the nobility's financial commitment to music was, when at the start of the Turkish war in 1788 they cut back on their entertainments, Mozart felt the effects, for he lost not only the occasional engagement but the better part of his audience for his subscription concerts.

The Tonkünstlersozietät

It remains to mention one professional option that Mozart failed to exercise. He did not take out membership in the Tonkünstlersozietät. This organization was founded by the court under Florian Gassmann in 1772 to provide pensions both for its own musicians who did not have court-employee status (those working in the theatre, for example) and for any other Viennese musician who joined the society voluntarily. The musicians' premiums were supplemented by the fundraising concerts put on twice a year by the members of the society, two at Easter and two at Christmas. The pension scheme proved to be extremely successful. By 1781 the society had grown to 104 members and a hundred years later counted as one of the most venerable institutions in Viennese musical life.

Mozart applied on 11 February 1785 for admission to the society, but failed to complete the application – it was a matter of a birth certificate – although he was extremely active in their concerts. Already on 3 April 1781 he had contributed a symphony and piano variations to a concert that took in a record-breaking 2394 gulden. He participated in the Christmas concert of 1783 with a piano concerto and a vocal rondo. In 1785 he provided the oratorio *Davidde penitente* for the Easter concert and a piano concerto for the Christmas concert. His clarinet quintet was performed at Christmas 1789 and a symphony and an aria at Easter 1791. His failure to complete the application may reveal negligence in bureaucratic matters, but more probably betrays an unconscious wish not to associate too closely with the class of musicians who joined the society. He would lend his not inconsiderable assistance to their cause, but he had his sights on a court position with a court pension. Consequently, at his unexpectedly early death, Mozart's widow had no claim on any pension. The court pension became effective only after ten years of service, and his application to the Tonkünstlersozietät had never been approved. In her petition to the court for its mercy she admitted that her husband had been negligent in not having obtained membership in the Tonkünstlersozietät. Although the court had no legal obligation to do so, it granted her an annual pension of 266 fl. 40 x., a third of Mozart's salary.

Conclusion

In all spheres of employment open to him, it appears Mozart did exceedingly well. To inquire into the question of why Mozart's considerable income was insufficient for his needs is beyond the scope of this essay.[35] Even allowing for the fact that the freelance portion of his income was uneven and particularly low in the last four years of his life, his dire situation cannot be satisfactorily explained away by the effects of the Turkish war, his wife's costly illnesses or his financial mismanagement, although the latter is hard to gauge. Some scholars have gone so far as to propose that Mozart had a gambling problem or other psychological disorders. More revealing, if exasperatingly cryptic, is the recent discovery of a judgement won by Prince Lichnowsky in a lawsuit against Mozart in 1791 for over 1400 gulden.[36] Whatever his personal misfortune in the last years of his life, however, his decision in 1781 to make his career in Vienna was a sound one.

3 Mozart's compositional methods: writing for his singers

IAN WOODFIELD

In a famous passage concerning an aria he was composing for the singer Anton Raaff, Mozart wrote:

> I asked him to tell me candidly if he did not like his aria or if it did not suit his voice, adding that I would alter it if he wished or even compose another one. 'God forbid,' he said, 'the aria must remain just as it is, for nothing could be finer. But please shorten it a little, for I am no longer able to sustain my notes.' 'Most gladly,' I replied, 'as much as you like. I made it a little long on purpose, for it is always easy to cut down, but not so easy to lengthen' . . . When I took leave of him he thanked me most cordially, while I assured him that I would arrange the aria in such a way that it would give him pleasure to sing it. For I like an aria to fit a singer as perfectly as a well-made suit of clothes.[1]

A few years later when he was composing *Idomeneo*, Mozart again expressed his readiness to accommodate Raaff's wishes, but on this occasion the singer was so pleased with what had been written for him that he did not want a single note to be changed.[2] There was nothing out of the ordinary in the flexibility of Mozart's attitude; it was widely accepted that a singer had the right to influence the musical character of an aria.[3] When a member of an opera cast left a production, it was common for replacement arias to be commissioned to suit the voice and the dramatic persona of the new singer. In the months before the composition of *Così fan tutte*, a lean period with few major projects, Mozart was called on to provide several of these substitutes. Only a few months before this he had written some new arias for a revival of *Le nozze di Figaro*.

Mozart's correspondence during the late 1770s and early 1780s contains much valuable information about his relationship with singers, and his practice of taking work-in-progress to them is very clear. So, too, is his cautious attitude to comments on drafts of pieces. He expressed great delight at Countess Thun's approval of several arias he was composing for *Die Entführung*, but insisted that he would pay no attention whatever to anyone's 'praise or blame' until the work as a whole was completed.[4] After Leopold's death, these informative exchanges of letters about opera ceased, and from the last years of Mozart's life there is hardly any information at all. For clues

Table 3.1. *The original cast of* Così fan tutte

Adriana Ferrarese del Bene	Fiordiligi
Louise Villeneuve	Dorabella
Dorotea Bussani	Despina
Vincenzo Calvesi	Ferrando
Francesco Benucci	Guglielmo
Francesco Bussani	Don Alfonso

about the role of singers in the composition of the late operas we must have recourse to the scores themselves. In this chapter I shall examine evidence in the autograph of *Così fan tutte* which suggests that singers continued to exert a significant influence on the composition of their arias.[5] The six members of the cast are listed in table 3.1.

The first pieces drafted in *Così* were the ensembles as these were less subject to the whims of singers. A clear sign that the arias came later is their exclusion from the main folio numbering sequence, added by Mozart once the overall order of the opera was settled. Each act of *Così* thus has a long numbering sequence for the ensembles, recitatives and finale, interrupted by the arias all numbered individually. This arrangement allowed Mozart to continue to abbreviate, extend or change the position of an aria, even after the main sequence had been applied. If an aria had to change key or position at a late stage, it might well then be necessary to rewrite the end of the preceding recitative to enable it to cadence in the appropriate key. The recitative leading into Guglielmo's Act 2 aria originally ended in C minor. When 'Donne mie' in G major was inserted here, Mozart had to add an extra leaf with a revised ending.[6] To keep track of what was happening, he could rely on his system of continuity instructions. At the end of a recitative, he would usually write a 'segue' or an 'attacca' direction providing a link with the following piece, and to further clarify matters, especially if there had been changes which might confuse a copyist, he sometimes added a 'dopo' at the head of a recitative to show what was to precede it.

Before starting work on an aria, Mozart had first to make an allocation of blank sheets from his stock of horizontal twelve-stave paper. For all but the largest arias, this consisted of four double folios or sixteen sides that he numbered '1' to '4'. If more pages were needed, he would add another bifolium, sometimes forgetting to put in the '5'. The first musical element to be written down was the brace, which usually incorporated eight, ten or twelve staves. Although the detail of the orchestration might not yet have been worked out, Mozart at least knew the approximate scale of his intended aria. Light *buffa* arias such as Despina's 'In uomini' or 'Una donna' were often written on eight-stave braces. Although he usually pre-ruled the braces for a whole aria, it was easily possible to adapt part way through by making

Plate 1 The first seven bars of the quartet 'La mano a me date' from Act 2 of *Così fan tutte*. Two bar-lines were erased and five were crossed out when Mozart changed the *particella* from a 'segue' to an 'attacca'.
Reproduced by kind permission of the Staatsbibliothek zu Berlin, Preussischer Kulturbesitz, Musikabteilung mit Mendelssohn-Archiv.

use of any blank staves above or below, by doubling up two parts on a single staff, or, if a fuller orchestra were required, by having recourse to an 'extra blatt' (supplementary leaf) for the remaining wind parts.

When he started to write down the music, Mozart began with the short score, often known as the *particella* or continuity draft. In an opera aria, this would contain only the vocal line, the bass line and occasional fragments in other parts such as an opening phrase or intermediate instrumental inter-jection. The idea was to record the structure of the piece in an abbreviated form. On a few occasions, Mozart began to write a *particella* but for some reason stopped after the first melodic statement. For example, he wrote eight bars of the *particella* of an aria for Don Alfonso entitled 'La mano a me date'. If he had then decided to abandon this short draft completely, it would have become one of many 'fragments', works started but then set aside. In this case, however, he returned to the piece in order to transform it into a quar-tet, and at that stage he decided to make it an 'attacca' from the preceding recitative. The result was that all the bar-lines were in the wrong place. He scratched out a few and put wavy lines through the remainder (see plate 1).

In several arias, a break in the ink colour of the *particella* shortly before the end suggests a pause before its completion.[7] This supports the idea that the composer's usual practice was to run through an aria with its singer before committing himself to a conclusion, leaving open the possibility, as in his offer to Raaff, of lengthening or abbreviating the piece. The short score without its ending might well be termed a 'consultation *particella*', for almost certainly this is what Mozart would have taken to show his singer, who might have glanced through the draft or tried it out with the composer accompanying at the keyboard. At this point, a troublesome individual might reject an aria entirely, in which case Mozart would be left with several sheets of paper, lightly scored but unusable. (There were of course many other reasons why a *particella* might be abandoned before being scored up: a cast change; a plot change; or indeed a simple rejection of the piece by the composer himself.) Little of the perhaps large amount of waste paper generated during the composition of this opera now survives, but there are two fragments from earlier *particelle* of Guglielmo's Act 2 aria 'Donne mie'. One is completely different from the finished version, showing that Mozart, even though now a much more experienced composer than the young man who had deferred to Raaff, was still willing to countenance a replacement aria.[8]

Once an aria had been accepted, Mozart could make any final adjustments to the *particella* and then set it aside to be orchestrated. Whether the first draft taken to the singer could be used for this purpose would depend on the state of the manuscript. Beyond a certain point, changes to the structure would necessitate recopying. Paradoxically, this means that an aria such as 'Donne mie', which in the autograph has quite a large number of small alterations, might have needed less work than other arias apparently in pristine condition. Distinguishing between these two types, the scored-up *particella* and the fair copy, will provide a useful chronological framework for a discussion of late revisions made after consultation with singers.

There are four types of evidence that can be used to determine whether an aria score in the autograph is an original *particella* scored up, or whether it is a fair copy made from an earlier draft too heavily altered to be of use. These are: brace design; ink colours; structural alterations; and variants in the earliest manuscript copy of the opera.

When Mozart came to score up an aria, he quite often discovered that his original choice of brace size was insufficient to cope with all the wind and brass parts he now wanted. If this happened, the logical thing to do was to make use of any blank staves above or below the brace, which could easily be done with a small extension to the original. The instruments would not be in the conventional order, but the copyist would have no difficulty rearranging them for the official score. It is clear from its brace design that the unnumbered quintet in Act 1 'Di scrivermi' was first scored for strings only, and that the clarinets and bassoons were added later, above and below the brace. In contrast, the number of staves used to copy Fiordiligi's Act 2 rondò 'Per pietà' varies from ten to twelve. In this case, Mozart appears not to have pre-ruled the braces, but drew them in as he was copying. He could not have done this without knowing how many wind staves were needed on the next page, which suggests that he was copying from a draft containing fairly full indications of the obbligato wind instruments.

The study of ink colours is highly subjective, and a full discussion of the problems and opportunities of this kind of work cannot be given here.[9] One feature of particular use for our present purpose is the identification of copying breaks at the *particella* stage, as represented by a resumption in a differently coloured ink. There is nothing conclusive about an ink break as such; it might merely be the moment when Mozart ran out of ink. However, their location throughout the opera as a whole seems far from random. That a sharp break in ink colour usually represents a chronological pause in copying is borne out by the fact that many ensembles in Act 1 are strikingly multicoloured in appearance because the orchestration was done much later than the short score, while the ensembles in Act 2 appear increasingly uniform in colour because there was less delay before they were orchestrated.

Visible alterations in the autograph usually concern minor matters such as refinements of figuration, instrumentation or dynamics. These provide fascinating insights into Mozart as a reviser of his own music, but they do not in themselves enable us to distinguish a *particella* from a fair copy. As a perfectionist, Mozart never ceased to look for small details which could be improved even in a fair copy. Analysis of structural changes, however, can be much more revealing, because any passage cut at the *particella* stage would be left unorchestrated and is thus easily distinguished from later cuts.

Thanks to the pioneering work of Alan Tyson, the earliest Viennese copy of *Così* (Österreichische Nationalbibliothek, Musiksammlung, O.A.146) has been convincingly identified as the 'official' Hoftheater score, made for the first run of performances, but still in use decades later.[10] Mozart's own hand appears on several occasions, smoothing over the joins caused by a series of small cuts to the opera that were under consideration. There is good reason to believe that this score was produced in parallel to the writing of the autograph. A clear example is the way the copyist wrote out 'Di scrivermi' with string accompaniment only, as Mozart himself had done. When the composer decided to add clarinets and bassoons to the autograph, the copyist had to go back and add them to his score as well. Further evidence of the composer's proximity to its production lies in a small number of musical corrections that derive directly from the autograph. It is clear that Mozart was still making small changes in his own score even after the copyist thought he had finished work on his. In the copy, these changes were entered (or at least their location indicated) in very light red crayon (*rötel*) that was later smudged out, probably when the required amendments were added in ink. It appears likely that these marks were added by someone employed to check the accuracy of the copy against the original, who from time to time noticed inconsistencies. Alterations of this kind could have occurred quite late in the process of producing the opera score, and this increases the likelihood that Mozart made them during or after a rehearsal.

The four kinds of evidence discussed above produce generally consistent results. Benucci's Act 2 aria 'Donne mie' has all the characteristics of a consultation *particella* subsequently scored up: a single brace size; additional instruments above and below the brace; two copying breaks towards the end of the *particella*; some layered effects in the ink colours; and a fairly large number of corrections. On the other hand, 'Per pietà' has a variable brace size, a single ink colour, and a cut passage with completed wind parts, all of which indicate that it was probably copied from an earlier draft.

A review of the substantive changes made to arias in *Così* during the process of composition reveals one very striking fact: they are heavily concentrated (as are the *particella* ink breaks) around the climactic points, just prior to the orchestral postludes. Again this supports the idea that it was Mozart's usual practice to leave the ending of an aria until he had checked it with his singer. In a distinct (though not necessarily long-delayed) phase of composition, he would complete the piece. In this respect, the composer was making use of the end-orientated convention of aria construction in which the clear expectation was that the musical climax would come late on. Some of the changes made at climactic points concern a matter about which any singer would have had views: the upper range of the vocal line.

Four examples will illustrate the issues involved. The first comes towards the climax of what was to be Benucci's Act 1 aria 'Rivolgete a lui lo sguardo'. (The piece was in fact taken out of the opera shortly before the premiere.) Mozart had originally included an extra fifteen bars that he crossed out at the *particella* stage. The most notable feature of the excised material is that Benucci was apparently to be asked for one more high F♯ to add to the three (one immediately before the cut passage, two after it) which give this conclusion its power. As has been pointed out by Julian Rushton, the reiteration of this high F♯ results in a part with an unusually high tessitura for this singer.[11] Because the cut was made at the *particella* stage, it is not possible to say for certain what the continuation would have been, and it is far from certain that the fourth F♯ was the issue. There is no doubt, however, that the revision alters the approach to the aria's high point. Arguably, the cut passage would have resulted in some loss of momentum.

In a significant piece of rewriting, what would have been a rather understated climax to Fiordiligi's magnificent rondò 'Per pietà' was transformed into a spectacular display of vocal agility. The three cut bars (see example 3.1) contain full obbligato wind instrumentation that must have been put in

Example 3.1 Three bars cut from the climax of Fiordiligi's Act 2 rondò 'Per pietà'

Example 3.2a Original version of the end of the vocal line in Fiordiligi's 'Per pietà'

Example 3.2b Revised version of the end of the vocal line in Fiordiligi's 'Per pietà'

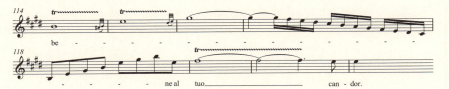

before Mozart carried on to write the seven replacement bars in the *particella*. The more measured approach greatly enhances the impact of the cadence. Other improvements include the loss of the routine chugging bassoons and the gain in clarity from separating the flute scales from the horn arpeggios. More importantly, the range required from Adriana Ferrarese del Bene was extended upwards by a minor third. Fiordiligi was now liberated to ascend to her thrilling high B♮ where in the first version she was to remain earthbound on G♯ (see examples 3.2a and 3.2b). It is quite likely that Mozart took this *particella* with its original ending to Ferrarese, and that it was she who requested the higher note, the better to show off her top register, and perhaps also a more generally showy ending with which to make a memorable exit.

Earlier in his career Mozart famously wrote of having to 'sacrifice' a little to the 'flexible throat' of the singer Cavalieri, which apparently resulted in the inclusion of a greater amount of virtuoso passagework in her aria than he would have liked.[12] Throughout 'Per pietà', mindful of the deeply personal qualities of Fiordiligi's soliloquy, Mozart kept the amount of overtly florid writing under very strict control. It would be interesting to know whether he regarded the more virtuosic replacement ending as in any sense a concession to his latest *prima donna*. In the case of Cavalieri's aria he appeared confident that he had still been able to express the character's feelings 'as far as an Italian bravura aria' would allow. If the revised ending of 'Per pietà' came about as the result of a direct request from Ferrarese, it presumably satisfied her needs, but it is also a memorable musical improvement which adds an appropriate sense of climactic power to this great rondò, without any apparent sacrifice in the characterization of Fiordiligi. With good reason, Mozart was proud of his ability to make a virtue out of necessity.

A similar extension to vocal range occurs at the end of Dorotea Bussani's Act 2 aria 'Una donna', and there is also a splendid improvement to the dramatic characterization of its climax. The additional material is copied on hand-ruled extensions to the staves at the end of the recto and the beginning of the verso of the last page (see plate 2). The first two additional bars extend the upper range of the vocal line, this time by a major third. Up to that point, Bussani (Despina) had only been required to sing a high G, but now the addition of a high B adds punch to the climax. The second pair of extra bars introduces a charming idea: the brief false start of the final phrase. The autograph shows that these four bars cannot have been inserted after the completion of the aria. If Mozart had continued on the verso in the usual way (before adding the extra bars), one would expect to see signs of an erased tonic chord. On the other hand, although the word 'ubbidir' in the vocal line seems to end on the first note of the two extra bars on the recto, the syllable '-dir' is in fact written over a typically Mozartian double-dash hyphen, which shows that it was originally to have come on the verso. There is no sign of it here in the first ordinary bar, but it does appear at the start of the first of the two extra bars. This implies that the first pair of additional bars (extending the range) was put in after the second. In reshaping the end of this charming aria, Mozart, as ever sensitive to the needs of his singers on stage, incorporated an opportunity for Bussani to flirt with the audience. Even if the singer were not on hand as Mozart worked this out, he would still have known the sorts of musical features that would please her.

One aria almost certainly revised after consultation with its singer is 'Donne mie', the main showpiece for Benucci. The autograph suggests that Mozart took great pains to get it exactly right, as there are many small-scale

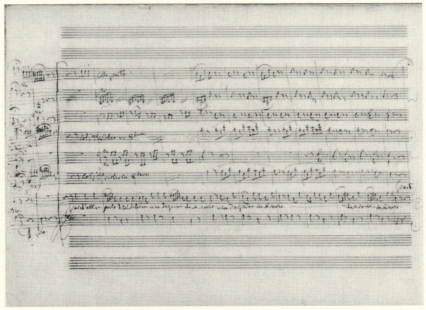

Plate 2 Two two-bar hand-ruled extensions to the end of the staves on the recto and to the beginning of the staves on the verso of the last leaf of Despina's Act 2 aria, 'Una donna'. Note the double-dash hyphen which originally ended the last ordinary bar of the recto (overwritten with the syllable '-dir') and the spacing of the vocal line on the first ordinary bar of the verso. Reproduced by kind permission of the Staatsbibliothek zu Berlin, Preussischer Kulturbesitz, Musikabteilung mit Mendelssohn-Archiv.

Table 3.2. *A section of the text of 'Donne mie', Guglielmo's*
Act 2 aria in Così fan tutte, *that is not in the libretto, showing*
the original and revised versions with the source lines

original version		*revised version*	
[Ma la fate a tanti a tanti,]		[Ma la fate a tanti a tanti,]	
Che credibile non è,		Che credibile non è,	
Siete vaghe, siete amabili	17	Io vo' bene al sesso vostro,	5
fino ai piè	20	ve lo mostro,	7
mille volte il brando presi,	11	mille volte il brando presi,	11
vi difesi,	13	vi difesi,	13
gran tesori il ciel vi diè	18	gran tesori il ciel vi diè	18
ve lo mostro	7	fino ai piè	20

alterations to instrumentation and figuration. There are other more
significant changes. At a late stage of composition, for example, the orchestration was expanded, and parts for '2 Clarini in C' and 'Timpany in
C' were written above and below the ten-stave brace. Moreover, there are
several hints that the form of 'Donne mie' could have undergone expansion.
As he had told Raaff, Mozart was quite prepared to lengthen a piece if need
be, even though this was the more difficult option. The aria is in rondo form
with episodes in the dominant, subdominant and relative minor. Mozart
returns each time to the short musical phrase that concludes the opening
tonic section, with a V^7 pedal and a catchy verbal refrain leading directly
into the new section. Curiously, this refrain line itself varies. On the first two
occasions it is 'Ma quel farla a tanti a tanti' but the third and fourth time 'Ma
la fate a tanti a tanti'. It would have been more usual to have the same line
throughout, or a new climactic line at the end, or a final return to the first
version. The third occurrence of the refrain line thus seems slightly odd.

The additional musical material might very well have been the third
episode (bars 104–27). The text of this section does not appear in the libretto at all (although there is space for it), but the lines, with one exception,
derive from earlier in the aria. This was a technique used to excellent effect in
Figaro's 'Aprite'. By telescoping and fragmenting lines already heard, a very
powerful drive to the climax is set up. When he first wrote out this section,
however, the recapitulated lines appear in something of a jumble. Later, making the corrections in a brown fuzzy ink which spreads slightly on the page,
Mozart reordered the lines into their original sequence (see table 3.2).

In adjusting the text thus, Mozart had to alter the endings of some musical
phrases to cope with a different number of syllables, such as the replacement
of 'amabili' with 'vostro'. The resulting text feels like an *ad hoc* expansion,
possibly done by the composer at the singer's behest, with the librettist later
pointing out the deficiencies. If so, then it is conceivable that the one entirely
new line ('Che credibile non è') was made up by Mozart or even Benucci

Example 3.3a Original version of the passage preceding the climax of Guglielmo's 'Donne mie'

Example 3.3b Revised version of the passage preceding the climax of Guglielmo's 'Donne mie'

himself. It is typical of the kind of punchy epithet that this singer excelled in delivering.

Because the fuzzy brown ink is rather distinctive in character, it is possible to identify other changes made with it towards the conclusion of this aria. One short passage was altered significantly when Mozart had second thoughts about the *piano* precursor to the climax (see examples 3.3a and 3.3b). The character of the revision suggests that he wanted a more *sostenuto* version. His keen eye for a harmonic improvement is also evident in the replacement of the rather fussy original with a bolder cadence, and the dull melodic ending was also enlivened.

Mozart's practice of leaving the ending in abeyance is shown with particular clarity in this *particella*. He seems to have stopped writing in bar 163. What follows is Benucci's resounding climax (bars 164–70), the bass line of which was copied in the fuzzy brown ink, probably around the time that the preceding textual and musical revisions were made. Only then was the concluding orchestral postlude put in. Its *particella* is in a third ink, rather blacker in colour.

Example 3.4a Original version of part of Dorabella's opening phrase in the Act 1 duet 'Ah guarda sorella'

Example 3.4b Revised version of part of Dorabella's opening phrase in the Act 1 duet 'Ah guarda sorella'

The nature of these changes allows us a rare glimpse of the collaboration between Mozart and one of his most admired interpreters. It is not hard to imagine a preliminary run through using the as yet incomplete *particella*. If by then Benucci's showpiece Act 1 aria had already been replaced with the lightweight 'Non siate ritrosi', he would have had good reason to argue for a bigger piece, to request the addition of trumpets and drums, or to consider carefully how the *sotto voce* statements of 'un gran perchè' would work best. Any change suggested by an artist of his stature would have been taken very seriously by Mozart, especially as he was now in danger of having nothing with which to recapture his runaway success in 'Non più andrai'.

One final example comes from an ensemble, and it represents a different area of potential concern to a singer: the start of a piece. In scene 2, Fiordiligi and Dorabella appear together in a garden to the mellifluous sound of clarinets and horns. Their A major duet 'Ah guarda sorella' in fact begins with a substantial solo for each of them in turn, before they join together in music of beguiling charm. Analysis of the ink colours suggests that Mozart worked on this piece in two halves, possibly even completing the second section before the first. The justification for so doing would have been the elaborate character of the solo writing in the first section. As this was a diplomatically sensitive moment, the first appearance of the two leading ladies, it was necessary to ensure that both women were happy with what he had written for them. In a dark-looking ink, Mozart crossed out several bars of the first phrase sung by Villeneuve as Dorabella and substituted a new version below (see examples 3.4a and 3.4b). The change in musical character is clear: the revision eliminated the octave leaps. As always, it is possible that the composer made this alteration to what seems a rather uninspired beginning for purely musical reasons, yet equally the singer could have requested it herself, wishing to avoid leaps early on, even though they are not especially daunting ones.

The reason for supposing that Villeneuve herself could have been present when this change was made lies in a paleographical feature that is hard to explain as anything other than the result of a rehearsal. Mozart did not usually write out more than once any text sung by more than one singer; especially in finales and large ensembles this saved a great deal of time. As one looks through the ensembles in the first part of Act 1 (including 'Ah guarda sorella'), it quickly becomes obvious that many sections of text sung by Dorabella (which merely duplicate Fiordiligi's words one line above) were inserted later in a black-looking ink, distinct from anything else on the page. It is hardly likely that this was done to assist a copyist as it is plainly evident that the two sisters are singing the same words. A more likely explanation is that Mozart had a preliminary rehearsal of these ensembles with Villeneuve, during which, for the ease of her reading, he added the text below her line. The ink used to make these additions looks very similar to that used to remove the early octave leaps.

The musical character of these late revisions to arias in *Così fan tutte* is certainly suggestive of a process of consultation, but in no case can study of the autograph score provide conclusive evidence that a meeting with a singer took place. From the point of view of the study of compositional process, the main point to emerge is the significance of the moment when Mozart 'rounded off' an aria. Through the careful shaping of climax, he was able to achieve an appropriate sense of closure, and in this he was very much acting in the interests of his singers. For the performer on stage, ending on the right note was something that mattered very much.

4 Mozart and late eighteenth-century aesthetics

DAVID SCHROEDER

Mozart was keenly aware of and interested in the views of his contemporaries on matters of aesthetics, but curiously it has taken almost two centuries for us to recognize this fact and to realize how critical some of this thinking may have been in influencing him as a composer. The reasons for this hiatus are not entirely straightforward, but emerge in part in the vast literature on Mozart prior to the final decades of the twentieth century. One of the simpler possibilities appears to be that writers on music in general or Mozart in particular rarely had much interest in fields other than music, and in any event often preferred to treat music as a self-contained entity, relatively free from the influence of other disciplines. The prevailing view of Mozart emerged in the late nineteenth and early twentieth centuries when the focus lay on his genius – a peculiar notion of genius shaped by early nineteenth-century Romanticism and fostered by giants of German philosophy later in the century, including Hegel, Schopenhauer and Nietzsche. For some, Mozart's genius had to be demonically inspired,[1] while for others that genius placed him as an eternal child figure, living in a childlike dream realm detached from reality and, of course, blissfully devoid of education.[2] Writing in the middle of the twentieth century, Alfred Einstein believed Mozart was 'a child and always remained one',[3] and even as late as 1971 Michael Levey continued to support a modification of the Mozart-as-child phenomenon, suggesting that 'what has often been described as the childlike quality which he retained into adulthood was in fact a retention of energy: pure, unhindered and of almost explosive force'.[4]

Leopold Mozart

In the late twentieth century a number of writers challenged various Mozart myths effectively by invoking documentation that had previously been ignored, or by interpreting evidence in the light of eighteenth-century considerations.[5] Of great importance here has been the assessment of the role of Leopold Mozart in his son's life, and the evaluation of how that role changed as the relationship between father and son changed. Before this issue could be sorted out, the full correspondence among members of the Mozart family had to be available, and this finally happened with the

[48]

publication of *Mozart: Briefe und Aufzeichnungen* commencing in 1962.[6] Earlier opinion about Leopold's role fluctuated as wildly as attitudes about Wolfgang as genius, ranging from Leopold as the wise mentor and father to Schurig's view of him as a narrow-minded philistine.[7] As long as Leopold was considered only in his capacity as a Kapellmeister, little could be understood about the breadth of education he could offer his children. While knowledge of his awareness of moral philosophy and a range of other fields has emerged gradually over a number of years, in the last decade of the twentieth century Josef Mančal gave this issue the attention it deserved, revealing Leopold's profound knowledge of the major writers of the Enlightenment.[8]

Leopold's career as a student of logic and jurisprudence at the University of Salzburg came to a shabby end after one year of study, but in no way did that diminish his love of study – especially that of moral philosophy.[9] Before leaving his native Augsburg he had developed a serious interest in the works of Johann Christoph Gottsched and Christian Fürchtegott Gellert. As the leading German writer of the Enlightenment in the mid-eighteenth century, Gellert exerted a strong influence not only at home but abroad, emphasizing the crucial role of morality in enlightened thought. Leopold took great pride in disseminating his works in Salzburg, and felt so committed to his advocacy of the Protestant Gellert that he even wrote to him, eliciting a letter of thanks in return. Not only did the young Mozart hear about Gellert from his father, but he also received a volume of Gellert's *Geistliche Oden und Lieder* from Baron von Böse as a gift, prompting Leopold to inform Lorenz Hagenauer in 1764 that the Baron had exhorted Mozart to 'read it often – and feel its god-like songs and lend them (in these spiritual hours of feeling) your irresistible harmonies: so that the callous despiser of religion may read them – and take notice – may hear them – and fall down and worship God'.[10] Just as Leopold took Gellert to be the ultimate arbiter of taste in issues of religion and morality, so he accorded Gellert's aesthetic views on issues such as tailoring works for an audience and the purpose of art in general a similarly high status.

Leopold's own education in Augsburg at the Jesuit Gymnasium of St Salvator and the Lyceum, in addition to the study of Latin, French and Italian, included instruction in astronomy, geometry, mineralogy and biology, and he passed on these interests enthusiastically to his son. In the area of music theory and criticism, Leopold knew the works of all of the major writers well, as one would expect considering his own outstanding contribution to the field. As early as 1755 he identified Glarianus, Zarlino, Bontemps, Kepler, Vogt, Neidhart, Euler, Scheibe, Prinz, Werkmeister, Fux, Mattheson, Mizler, Spiess, Marpurg and Quantz in a letter to his Augsburg friend Johann Jakob Lotter. Two decades later he wrote about these and other critics to his son:

There must be some good material in it [Vogler's *Kurpfälzische Tonschule*], since he could copy out the *Clavier Methode* from [C. P. E.] Bach's book, follow the instructions of the *Singmethode* of Tosi and Agricola, and the instructions for composition and harmony from Fux, Riepel, Marpurg, Mattheson, Spiess, Scheibe, d'Alembert, Rameau and a lot of others, and offer them as a shorter system, which I have long had in mind.[11]

Other discussions in the correspondence about specific compositional approaches or aesthetic positions, sometimes with specific writers' or composers' ideas in mind, leave us in no doubt that Mozart had been well instructed by his father on these issues, if in fact he did not learn about them from other sources.

The Mozart correspondence

While we learn much from the letters between Mozart and his father of what Mozart may have known, we must nevertheless be wary of what they tell us about Mozart's own views. Gellert turns out to be a good case in point. When he died in 1769, Leopold certainly took the news badly, lamenting the great loss. But Mozart, not yet fourteen years old, breathed a sigh of relief in complete contrast, drolly remarking to Nannerl, with a pun on Gellert and the word *gelehrt* (learned): 'I have nothing new except that Herr gelehrt, the poet from Leipzig, died, and since his death has composed no more poetry.'[12] He would not have dared to say such a thing to his father, but with his sister he could share a jest about his father's hero, undermining the authority of this celebrated moralist. When Mozart and his father discuss, in the next decade, aesthetic issues that related directly to Gellert's views, such as how to gain audience approbation or various aspects of morality, we should not necessarily assume that the two are in agreement, in spite of what Mozart may say.

The letters have proved to be fairly unreliable sources of Mozart's views, especially the letters to his father, and in this respect must be read as one would read any correspondence from the eighteenth century. Correspondents often wrote with the assumption that their letters would be widely disseminated if not actually published, especially if both parties were already famous. Leopold treated all of his early letters to Hagenhauer as raw material for the biography he intended to write about his son, and given the style of his letters to Mozart in 1777–9 we have no reason to doubt that he still had publication in mind. He uses Gellert's directives on letter writing as his model, including Gellert's persuasiveness and moral tone. Various issues on which Leopold persistently chided Mozart, especially concerning his behaviour, would have been demeaningly inappropriate for an addressee in his early twenties, but this did not deter Leopold, who apparently directed much of his chiding to a presumed larger audience.

In responding to these letters, Mozart used various strategies, counterbalancing his father's strategies with some of his own. These included adopting a tone of obsequiousness or simply being agreeable as a ruse; this tactic worked as long as Leopold could not observe (or hear about) actions to the contrary. It proved difficult for Mozart to keep this up in the face of stinging insults, and at times he could not resist lashing out, returning invective at the level he received it. This brought no success, since harsh words only prompted even more excoriating replies from Leopold. Where the bludgeon failed, the rapier proved much more successful, and Mozart discovered the effectiveness of dissimulation and outright lying, assuring his father of his industry in writing new works that in fact he had no intention of writing, or of good behaviour that actually left much to be desired.[13] An interesting deception in this respect concerns one of the great thinkers of the eighteenth century, Voltaire, whom Leopold could not respect because of his challenges to God and religion. Writing but a few hours after the death of his mother, Mozart slipped in this nasty comment about the recently deceased Voltaire: 'Now I have a piece of news for you which you may already know, namely, that the godless archrogue Voltaire, so to speak, has kicked the bucket like a dog, like a beast! That is the fruit of his labour.'[14] The chances that Mozart shared his father's view of Voltaire seem remote in the extreme. Now sharing quarters with Voltaire's dear friend Madame d'Epinay, and being on the best of terms with her, and in future years showing his subscription to Voltaire's views time and again, Mozart was indulging in the same type of epistolary deception that Voltaire himself practised, writing what he thought his addressee would want to hear.

Mozart's reading

The idea of Mozart as an active reader does not fit the psychological or genius profile that many commentators have constructed for him; even as recently as 1977 Wolfgang Hildesheimer could 'hardly imagine that Mozart was a great reader, except as a purposeful seeker of scores and libretti'.[15] According to his widow Constanze he enjoyed reading, although her remark to this effect may have been part of the mythmaking in which she immediately indulged after his death. We have the inventory of his library, included among the documents pertaining to his estate, published in Appendix II of Otto Erich Deutsch's *Mozart: A Documentary Biography*, although we should not assume that his reading was limited to these volumes or that he necessarily read them all. In fact, he personally knew a number of the authors well, figures of the German and Austrian Enlightenment, including Salomon Gessner, Christoph Martin Wieland, Joseph von Sonnenfels, and Aloys Blumauer, and it seems inconceivable that he would not have read from the works of people with whom he actually engaged in discussion. As for some of the other writers, such as Molière, Moses Mendelssohn and Johann Pezzl, evidence suggests he knew their works; the closeness of his own *Don Giovanni* to Molière's *Dom Juan* or the telltale similarity between his comments to his father in his last known letter to him and passages from Mendelssohn's *Phädon*[16] bear this out.

In all probability Mozart read at least parts of the books in his library, including authors such as Ovid, Johann Jakob Ebert, Jean Frédéric Osterwald, Ewald Christian von Kleist, Adolf von Knigge and Johann Heinrich Campe, as well as the authors noted above. One should not, of course, jump to any conclusions – positive or negative – about influence in matters of aesthetics. In most cases we lack evidence of his views about these writers, and when he expresses opinions to his father, as he does about Voltaire or Sonnenfels, we are probably hearing only what Mozart would have wished his father to have heard. Something closer to Mozart's own views, gleaned from his operas or other possible evidence, may often contradict his remarks to his father. It seems fairly safe to assume that through reading or direct contact with noted writers Mozart encountered a wide range of philosophical and aesthetic opinions.

Friends and acquaintances

From a very early age Mozart came into contact with significant figures of the Enlightenment, among them monarchs and other leaders and ministers of state, composers, poets, critics, freemasons, shapers of public opinion, *philosophes*, ambassadors and *salonnières*. Some were already friends or acquaintances of his father, and he could therefore often approach them with a letter of introduction if not the warm embrace of Leopold's friendship. In some cases the contact may have been fleeting, but in others it extended for long periods of time, sufficient for establishing thorough familiarity.

Mozart's first exposure to the Enlightenment occurred at home in Salzburg, although since the source of it was, aside from his father, the much detested Archbishop Hieronymus Colloredo, Mozart should not be blamed for not recognizing anything of an enlightened or reforming nature. In spite of his treatment of the Mozarts, Colloredo brought reforms to both church and state, promoting education, populating the Benedictine University of Salzburg with more German professors, reforming the system of privileges and agrarian economy, restructuring the military and financial

systems, and supporting the arts – especially music and the theatre.[17] If
Mozart had been able to suspend his distaste for Colloredo long enough
to notice ('the Mufti H. C. is a prick,' he wrote to his father, who did not
disagree but protested at the language Mozart used), he would have seen a
society and a role for music in society much improved from the previous
generation.

At the tender age of twelve, Mozart, with his father, encountered Gluck
in Vienna. Far from adulating the great composer, and incredulous that
someone would doubt the abilities of his precocious son, Leopold imagined
a conspiracy against them led by Gluck. As the finest composer of opera
living in the 1760s, and one with a strong position on the relative roles of
music and text, Gluck had much to offer a young composer such as Mozart,
but Mozart's view of Gluck does not accurately emerge in his comments to
his father in the early 1780s when he again met up with Gluck in Vienna.
The apparently contradictory positions will be discussed below in relation
to Mozart's famous remarks about *Die Entführung aus dem Serail*. A figure
much more congenial to the Mozarts, who met them in 1770 in Bologna,
was Padre Giovanni Battista Martini, a renowned music scholar and teacher
of composition. They discussed not only composition but also matters of
music history. Mozart surely discovered much from Martini in both practical
and aesthetic domains, and the mutual respect did not flag over the years.

While travelling with his mother in 1777 and 1778 in search of a suitable
position, Mozart met a number of leading figures, including Wieland in
Mannheim. Two individuals stand out, one of whom Leopold knew well:
the German Baron Melchior Grimm, now living in Paris, and his French
mistress Madame Louise d'Epinay. As the Russian ambassador of Catherine
the Great in Paris and the driving force behind the *Correspondance littéraire*,
Grimm was a force to be reckoned with, and he advised Mozart on numerous
matters during the half year Mozart spent in Paris in 1778, most notably on
how to win the approval of French audiences. Mozart may have followed
Grimm's advice in writing his 'Paris' Symphony, but after a falling out with
Grimm because of his alleged stinginess and apparent refusal to introduce
Mozart to important members of Parisian society Mozart had little good to
say about him.

In contrast to his relationship with Grimm, Mozart remained on the
best of terms with Madame d'Epinay, moving into her apartment shortly
after his mother's death, and regularly taking meals with her. As one of
the great intellectual forces in France, she wrote prolifically and contributed
regularly to the *Correspondance littéraire* with essays on politics, philosophy,
economics and the theatre. A close friend of all the leading *philosophes*, she
in all probability discussed with Mozart in their many hours together such
matters as Voltaire's scepticism, Denis Diderot's questions about world order

and uses of literary disguise, and Baron d'Holbach's challenges to Christian principles. She may also have talked about Rousseau, with whom she had fallen out, and the vilification she experienced from him, in part in his *Confessions*.

After moving to Vienna in 1781, Mozart quickly met leading representatives of the Enlightenment, some through his association with freemasons and others through his involvement in the world of opera and theatre. These people included Aloys Blumauer, Johann Baptist von Alxinger, Michel Denis, Lorenz Leopold Haschka, Ignaz von Born, Franz Sales von Greiner, Tobias Philipp Gebler, Joseph von Sonnenfels, Gottfried van Swieten and Gottlieb Leon. Some of these were members of the lodge 'Zur wahren Eintracht', under the leadership of Born and Sonnenfels, and Mozart regularly attended this lodge although he did not join since he already belonged to 'Zur Wohlthätigkeit'. He could also meet many of the same people at non-masonic gatherings such as the literary or music salons of Greiner and van Swieten. Also in Vienna, Mozart could not help but pay close attention to Joseph II, whose efforts to reform the Habsburg Empire during the early 1780s left a lasting impression on a grateful Viennese population, if not necessarily on people in the farther flung reaches of the Empire.

Aesthetic approaches

As Mozart matured as a composer, he approached his art and his listening public not as one possessed by some detached quality of genius living in his own ethereal world, but as an artist who fully understood the nature of his audience and how that audience should be engaged. The audience could vary from country to country or even from city to city, and Leopold, himself thoroughly familiar with the principles of gaining approbation, made certain his son understood these principles. Especially during Mozart's Paris sojourn, Leopold hammered away at this necessity, stressing that 'should you be engaged to write a contrapuntal work or something of that sort for the *concert spirituel*, work it out with the greatest care, and listen in advance to what is being composed and what people like best'. Leopold kept up this theme in other letters:

> *your whole reputation depends on your first work*. Before you write it, listen and think about the taste of the nation; hear and observe their operas. I know you well; you can imitate anything... Discuss the text in advance with *Baron Grimm* and with *Noverre* and make sketches and let them hear them. Everybody does that. Voltaire reads his poems aloud to his friends, listens to their judgement and makes revisions.[18]

Grimm himself had complained to Leopold about the poor taste of the French, and one can only imagine that Leopold had in mind that his son should appeal to the lowest common denominator among the audience.

Leopold's understanding of the connection that should exist between an artist and his audience as well as the goals of works of art came directly from principles espoused by Gellert, whose mid-century values emphasized that if a writer's works were to achieve moral value they must be made accessible to all, featuring a predominantly natural tone.[19] Gellert's own model was one of the most influential writers of the early eighteenth century, the third Earl of Shaftesbury, who noted in his *Characteristics of Men, Manners, Opinions, Times* that 'an author's art and labour are for his reader's sake alone'.[20] Eventually Leopold took this principle to the extreme, and in accounting for Grimm's advice advised his son 'to think about not only the musical, but also *the unmusical public*. You know that for every *ten real connoisseurs* there are a *hundred illiterates*. Therefore do not forget the so-called *popular* style, which tickles *long ears*.'[21] Mozart's reply, that 'concerning the so-called popular taste, do not worry about it, since there is music in my opera for all kinds of people – with the exception of long ears',[22] may have indulged a joke about *Langohren*, but it also suggests, as does his music, that he had rejected this notion.

Leopold very much admired Sonnenfels, who had become the most important authority on matters of taste and the purpose of art in the Habsburg realm during the 1760s and 1770s, and when Mozart met him in 1781 his remarks to his father about Sonnenfels' reforms appeared to take Sonnenfels' position. In a protracted and bitter fight with actors, playwrights and theatre managers, Sonnenfels had succeeded in ramming through legislation to get rid of the popular theatrical figure Hanswurst, leaving the mission of the theatre 'to defend the good, to fight evil, to uphold authority, to obviate subversion'.[23] Shortly before the famous discourse on the role of opera emerging from correspondence on *Die Entführung aus dem Serail*, Mozart discussed with his father the issue of mixing comic and serious features in opera, making unmistakable references to Sonnenfels in the process:

> do you really believe that I would write an *opéra comique* the same way as an opera seria? In an opera seria there should be less frivolity and more erudition and sensibility, as in an opera buffa there should be less of the learned and all the more frivolity and merriment. That people also want to have comic music in an opera seria, I cannot prevent. But here [in Vienna] they correctly differentiate on this point. I definitely find in music that Hanswurst has not yet been eradicated, and in this case the French are right.[24]

If Mozart suggested here, invoking the taste of the French, that the continued appearance of Hanswurst was in some way unfortunate, he contradicted this entirely in his next work, *Die Entführung aus dem Serail*, in which Hanswurst plays a large role – in a Turkish disguise as Osmin. Later in *Die Zauberflöte* Hanswurst would resurface again in the form of Papageno, whose musical role far outstrips that of the character some might imagine to be the hero, Tamino.

The letters Mozart wrote to his father in September and October 1781 while he was composing *Die Entführung* are generally taken as the clearest indicators of his aesthetic views as they apply to opera, explaining, it would seem, compositional processes and even giving what amounts to a dictum on the balancing of text and music. As with all of Mozart's letters to his father, especially after the bitter exchanges in late 1778 and the beginning of 1779, the context must be understood. Mozart had now defied his father's wish that he should stay in Salzburg and receive a meagre but steady salary to pay back the debt he owed him. On the one hand, Mozart hoped to relieve some of the tension by returning to what Leopold had always thrived on in the past – discussion of his latest composition. On the other, he needed to convince Leopold that he had made the right decision in leaving the Archbishop's service, and that he could make much more money in Vienna than in Salzburg. To succeed he would need to present the work in the best possible light, in fact in a way that would sound very much as if it were framed by Leopold's own views and biases, and in a number of instances these descriptions do not correspond to the work that finally emerged. Mozart's strategy appeared to work up to a point, provided that Leopold did not try to interfere by attempting to advise and influence, as he had in his mediation between Mozart in Munich and the librettist Giambattista Varesco in Salzburg during the composition of *Idomeneo*. Once again Leopold overstepped the bounds and as punishment Mozart excluded him from discussions of Acts 2 and 3, writing nothing more on the subject after 13 October 1780.

Of the various comments made about *Die Entführung*, including the remark that although Osmin oversteps all sense of order the music must never offend the ear and must still give pleasure, the point which receives the greatest attention, because of its apparent status as an aesthetic pronounce-ment, is his statement that 'in an opera the poetry must absolutely be the obedient daughter of the music'.[25] This seems directly to contradict Gluck's famous dictum, given in the preface to *Alceste*, that music should play a sub-ordinate role to poetry. Gluck no doubt had good reason to state his position so baldly, responding to the flimsy or distorted texts of opera seria, and the profusion of music designed for the aggrandizement of singers; taking the remark out of context as a general statement of Gluck's own aesthetic view seems to miss the point. Doing the same with the opinion Mozart expressed to his father falls even wider of the mark. Leopold, even at this late date, probably still nursed the old wound of an imagined conspiracy led by Gluck against him in 1768, and reading a view contrary to Gluck's from his son no doubt gave him the satisfaction for which Mozart would have wished. The relationship of text and music proves far too complex to be reduced to this type of epigram, and Mozart surely knew this better than anyone.

Enlightenment issues

Strictly speaking, the study of aesthetics concerns matters of taste and the principles of art, but in the eighteenth century it necessarily went further since taste and morality were inexorably linked. Aesthetics therefore represented a central issue of philosophical discourse and the unfolding of the Enlightenment. As morality was increasingly defined in secular ways, its focus shifted from a religious notion of rules of behaviour to a cultivation of the best human qualities or refinement of taste. The Enlightenment saw works of art as one of the best means for achieving this refinement, and it did not have to be accomplished through overt fostering of virtue. The more indirect cultivation of the sensibilities proved just as effective, and novels or instrumental music could reach a higher level than *geistliche Lieder* or moral weeklies. Since Gellert had been instrumental in developing these ideas in Germany, Mozart knew them well through his father and other Gellert enthusiasts in his father's circle. Among the finest writers and composers a shift occurred from the older notion of art as moral persuasion to a new conception of art as being independent of this function, existing rather for its own sake or for the satisfaction of the individual artist.

The Enlightenment also fostered lively debate on a wide range of social issues, and during much of the reign of Joseph II discussion could occur with relative freedom, at least until the crisis in the provinces in 1787 that caused the Habsburg Empire to revert back to its more traditional role as a police state. Various social reforms were not only debated actively but put into practice by Joseph and his ministers, including the abolition of serfdom, restricting the use of torture in the judicial system, and the notion of universal accessibility to education. Along with reform came a broader debate that proved troublesome to those in authority, and probably triggered some of the backlash in 1787. In the heady early days of Joseph's reign authority itself became susceptible to challenge, both religious and state, and possibilities arose for the improved lot of those previously marginalized by society, especially women. These matters could find their way into literature and music; much of this thought emanated from the *philosophes* or others in France, and as vigorously as censors tried to keep their writing out of the Habsburg territories it always managed to find its way in.

Since travel outside the realm was not restricted, as it was later in the century and early in the nineteenth century, one could visit France, as Mozart did, and gain exposure to a world of thought that had touched Austria in only a peripheral fashion. Even before reaching Paris in 1778, Mozart encountered people and ideas travelling through Protestant Germany that would later fire his imagination, such as the volume of Molière's plays he received from Fridolin Weber in Mannheim just before departing for Paris. A great new world of thought surely opened up to him in the presence of his Paris hosts – if not from the somewhat stuffy Baron Grimm, then certainly from the more liberated Madame d'Epinay. As a leading intellectual she would have had little sympathy for prevailing views about women, such as the misogynist notions of her nemesis Rousseau, and it does not seem impossible that Mozart's treatment of women in the operas written after his Paris sojourn, including Susanna in *Le nozze di Figaro*, Pamina in *Die Zauberflöte* and even Elettra in *Idomeneo*, was somehow connected to his awareness of what Madame d'Epinay represented. Even *Così fan tutte*, which on the surface appears to support an older misogynistic view of women, surreptitiously does the opposite as it dismantles the symmetry that represents the status quo.

The 1780s, a limited window on change and transformation during which Joseph tried to pull his realm into the modern world, brimmed with contradictions as some sought to gain unheard of freedoms while Joseph fully intended to keep firm control. The oxymoron 'enlightened despotism' characterized this era, and Mozart felt the pull of the reform side more than most, being acquainted with thought emanating from France, where defiance to the authority of the state would erupt into violence before the end of the 1780s and where challenges to the benevolence and even existence of God were mounted by Voltaire and d'Holbach. Some of these attitudes surface in Mozart's letters, although often obliquely so as not to offend his correspondent, especially if it happened to be his father. The challenges to state and religious authority emerge much more succinctly in the late operas, in fact in each opera from *Idomeneo* onwards, sometimes in very subtle ways that require hearing such challenges covertly in the music instead of more overtly in the texts. In these operas Mozart appeared to be pushing beyond the boundaries of the Enlightenment itself, and in order to do this he had to be acutely aware of current events, the aesthetic, political and philosophical views of the past, and the most current thought emerging from France and elsewhere. It appears that he was more than up to the task.

PART II

The works

5 The keyboard music

W. DEAN SUTCLIFFE

If the name of Mozart is a touchstone for innate, absolute musicality, probably no genre has done more to accomplish this than the composer's keyboard sonatas. Collectively associated with such attributes as simplicity and
naturalness of material, modesty of tone and facility of technique, they encapsulate the reception not only of Mozart but of a whole 'Classical style'.
This state of affairs has been encouraged by the tendency to view the keyboard as a 'neutral' medium, one useful for theoretical demonstrations in
the classroom, in which Mozart is, as it were, a model pupil. It has certainly
also been encouraged by the works' very wide exposure as piano teaching material. Both cases help to determine, and continually reinforce, the
centrality of this repertory to the canon of Western music.

Yet there is another strand of reception that suggests anxiety about this
very image of the sonatas, one that tends to imply that better Mozart can
be found in other instrumental genres, including those in which the piano
features either as soloist or in an ensemble.[1] Within the output for solo
piano alone, there is undoubtedly much that is more colourful, dramatic
and elaborate than the governing image would suggest, including some
of the sonatas themselves. In this context the pedagogical explanation has
often been invoked. Thus the discourse of the sonatas precisely reflects
the original teaching purposes the works were meant to serve, and more
broadly the amateur market for such works at the time, considerations that
have retained their relevance up to the present. These associations, which
include not only a carefully tailored simplicity but also the childlike, have
caused unease. Now that our intellectual climate no longer favours 'absolute
music', we should be more relaxed in contemplating such functionality, yet
negative connotations remain.[2]

Indeed, the image of the sonatas seems stuck in a time warp. They arguably remain more indebted to the traditional nineteenth-century imagery
than any other part of the oeuvre.[3] We might compare what has been made of
Mozartian genres such as opera, concerto or even string quartet in the recent
past. These genres, however, can be shown to embody conflict or duality, and
this has been one of the main critical levers for redefining the composer, for
getting beyond what has been perceived as an insipid Classicism. But how
can we locate a similar dynamic in the sonatas, a solo medium? There have
been two principal means of trying to ruffle their smooth surface. Readings

of individual sonata movements that play up their topical or rhetorical plurality have helped to create some of the necessary friction.[4] Secondly, historical performance practice has emphasized the extent to which the dominant imagery is conditioned by the approach of players on modern instruments. This, by typically smoothing out articulative and dynamic indications, has generated a consistent flavour of 'lyrical sweetness' that Malcolm Bilson has called 'excessively mild'.[5]

To this point, my approach is itself traditional in implying that the sonata is either the predominant or at least the most significant mode of Mozart's solo keyboard production. To clarify what is at issue, consider the thoughts of Mark Everist on Mozart's Quintet for Piano and Winds, K. 452:

> The reception of the Quintet for Piano and Wind since 1945 is dominated by questions of genre. This [is] clearly related to performance; when we compare it with a piano concerto, we are comparing a work that survives today with no easy professional performance context (the quintet) with one whose generic status is being enlarged all the time by audiences, performers, and concert-giving institutions . . . Considerations of genre also affect the critical literature: the generic organization of many scholarly texts means that such works are sidelined.[6]

Similarly, the Mozart piano sonatas have a well-established generic identity, and thus far I have continued to privilege them at the expense of other solo works. But, as a known quantity, they will inevitably remain a basic point of reference for any remarks on the keyboard output as a whole, and, to a lesser extent, for what Mozart does in other chamber forms featuring the instrument. My main focus will be on texture, including its expressive role and its social implications.

Ensemble music with piano

The Quintet for Piano and Winds, piano quartets and piano trios

Let us begin with the work Mozart claimed in 1784 as his best to date, the Quintet for Piano and Winds, K. 452. Given the novel forces assembled, four single wind instruments (oboe, clarinet, bassoon and horn) and piano, it shows particularly clearly one of his fundamental textural predilections, namely the permutation of material. Mozart is never happier than when working in what might be termed an antiphonal field, in which various strands of a total texture can be rearranged or reallocated in numerous ways. This will often take on a concertante character, involving relatively formal alternations of material at the level of the phrase or period. In K. 452, though, the breathing requirements of winds as well as their inherent differences of timbre promote a more intricate interaction. Rather than a whole (melodic) unit being carried by one player, it is more characteristic for it to be completed by another instrument or group. Mozart is here exploiting the conversational properties of contemporary musical syntax to enact a particular kind of social exchange. What arises is less the sort of 'hard' conversational style we might associate with Haydn than a sense of complementarity, in which personal fulfilment arises from the corporate participation in pattern making.

This consensual textural mode meshes with two of Mozart's most favoured syntactical devices, imitation and sequence. Fundamental constituents of the permutation technique, they promote a sense of punctiliousness within the dialogue, of an agreed larger purpose. In K. 452 this is juxtaposed with the more detailed manoeuvres that arise from Mozart's conception of the medium. An example may be found in the Largo introduction. We might expect to hear from bar 5 a textural block dominated by the winds in reply to the piano's leadership in the first four bars. However, the main melodic cell quickly changes hands before horn and bassoon offer more individual contributions. The other instruments then line up to take their turn in a rising sequence based on the bassoon's idea, leading to a cadence. In this way the medium determines the syntax: closure cannot arrive until every player has participated in the larger pattern.

The textural versatility of K. 452 does eventually extend to the creation of blocks of sound. The most striking of these occur in the Larghetto and involve harmonic exploration. The middle section contains a real purple patch in which the piano has a sort of soliloquy while the winds sustain a mysterious sequence of harmonies. In an earlier chromatic passage the keyboard provides constant figuration while the winds mark out the chord changes on each quaver. Such material would be hard to shape satisfactorily in a solo piano context, nor would it occur readily in a work for winds alone. The piano can hold the harmony together and aid intonation, while the winds can provide a leading edge and textural definition to the piano's full harmonic outline. In line with its closing function, the finale tends to adopt a broader textural manner, but this is compensated for by a lengthy 'Cadenza in tempo' for all of the players. In the subsequent coda the ensemble turns into a tutti, humorously abandoning this differentiation between the parts.

Another unusual, indeed novel, grouping for the time is represented by the two piano quartets written in 1785 and 1786. The thematic concentration of the first movement of K. 478 in G minor determines a fairly intimate level of textural interplay, albeit less detailed than in the Quintet, K. 452. The first real solo episode does not occur until the piano's cantilena at the start of the central section, which lyrically transforms the initial motto material. This is then sequentially imitated in several stages by the strings. Such devices can, in serving as agents of textural exchange, promote social flexibility within a chamber ensemble. The effect of the whole apparatus here, though, is more like a severe rejoinder to the piano's moment of introspection.

In the coda the strings expand the motto into a larger declamatory statement. In the final bars the piano joins the strings in unison for another extended form, the dotted rhythms lending it a *recitativo accompagnato* flavour. Notice how all this comes about through rather looser piano writing than one might find in a solo environment and with the strings able to band together as a realistic group against the piano.

Aided by passages where each line conveys a strong sense of agency – so that, for instance, an apparently subordinate part can suddenly take the lead – Mozart's reallocation and reweaving of lines in the Andante tends to have a meditative effect. This includes pedal points, such as those in the cello from bar 43 or the viola from bar 52, with its high c" that penetrates the texture.[7] Although not melodically 'active' – the normal terms for assessing a place in a textural hierarchy – such elements can form the most eloquent part of the discourse. Once more the piano readily covers a wide range, with frequent gaps between the hands and considerable use of lower registers.

The finale invests much more heavily in the concertante principle – most material is given a dual presentation, once by piano and once by string trio – as do the outer movements of K. 493 in E flat major. The first movement of K. 493 also centres on sequences of canonic string writing, while in the finale the two lower strings are only melodically independent in imitative passages. This tends to suggest that Mozart is not easily able to create detailed interaction without some form of contrapuntal or antiphonal underpinning.[8] That said, at a given speed even quite formal alternations of material can provide a vivid sense of interchange.

Slow movements, though, require different means. This is apparent in the Larghetto of K. 493. The composer in fact retains the outlines of a basic alternating pattern between strings and piano but achieves surprising and even dramatic effects. The alternating phrases rarely just echo or balance each other. For instance, the *pianissimo* passage for strings alone from bar 32 mysteriously takes the music in a new direction. The only sustained exception to this competitive interchange comes in the development. Here the technique of imitation is transformed by context: group identity is briefly put to one side while the three string players compete with each other.

Such manoeuvres are barely possible in the piano trio. For Mozart in particular the form allowed fewer opportunities for antiphonal thinking, something he must have felt keenly since all but one of his trios were written after the piano quartets. On the other hand, this was an inherited genre, one whose amateur ethos tended to demand an active keyboard part and strings that played a mainly supporting role. Much is made of the traditional doubling role of the cello in the early Trio in B flat major, K. 254 (1776), but within this frame Mozart actually writes carefully for the instrument. It is just that, in common with all the later works, this may mean sitting out much of the action. Charles Rosen has noted how the 'relative independence' of the cello in the trios 'is bought at the price of a great many patches of silence'.[9]

In fact there is some nice social comedy to be found in K. 254. In the outer movements this tends to occur at transition points. In the opening Allegro assai the last part of the development features a laboured effort to secure the necessary dominant, with the violin and piano topping and tailing every few bars but unable to progress forward. Even the cello, as if impatient, contributes independently to the imbroglio. The finale features two separate gags based on the imitative interchange of a one-bar unit. Near the end these are brought side by side so that we can appreciate their common textural root.

Towards the end of each part of the Adagio the violin and piano sound like two competing singers, as they find different ways of bringing eloquence to the closing melodic formulae. There is also a nice sense of competition to their respective versions of the opening theme, especially in the different harmonic twists that undermine the expected cadential closure. In the reprise the piano goes first and surprises us by proceeding straight to the tonic cadence, without the expressive detour. The fact that the order of appearance is swapped here shows how the principle of alternation can operate on a larger scale. Although this often exemplifies the courteous reciprocal spirit animating so much of Mozart's chamber music, in this case it seems to have a harder edge.

The first movement of the Trio in G major, K. 496 (1786), begins with an extremely leisurely paragraph for piano alone. The repetition, with violin leading, turns into a transition. That this leisurely opening is marked for attention, rather than simply manifesting a relaxed chamber style, is made clear by the development, which concentrates quite exclusively on the material of the very first two bars. The block dialogue apparent when violin answers piano in the exposition is already telescoped through the fact that the piano shares the melodic material during this passage, but this is now taken much further. The development opens with a tutti presentation of the initial melodic incise, but within a few bars the cello and piano left hand have embarked upon an imitative dialogue involving this unit. This is exactly the opposite of the treble-centred texture that animated the opening exchanges.

This plot is clearly taken further in the Andante, which resembles the development of the first movement in its dialogue involving a short figure.[10]

Now, however, it is contracted so that the imitative distance is very quickly just half a bar. Again in the finale, a set of variations on an Allegretto theme, the cello is slowest to make its voice felt, but, dramatically, it then initiates the *minore* variation by itself. In this section the strands are unusually lacking in melodic clarity and thus the textural focus is uncertain; our composer is normally much neater in this respect.[11] It is not surprising that this unusual conception returns, in the major, as part of the coda after Variation 6, which reprises the opening and alternates it with the simplest figurative variation technique. Such contrasts encapsulate a certain technical anxiety in K. 496, as if Mozart is not quite sure how to dispose his trio textures. Yet it makes for an absorbing work, not 'characteristic' nor especially winning. The very choice of variations is surely part of the plot of textural investigation.

In the following three trios, K. 502, 542 and 548, each first movement is a variant on the plan devised for K. 496. Each starts with the piano in the ascendant and the cello reluctant to speak independently, and the development uses fragmentation of part of the first theme to generate a more egalitarian texture. It is noteworthy that imitative counterpoint is associated in these movements, as in the equivalent points in the piano quartets, with harmonic tension, with the centre of a structure. It is not a natural 'presentational' texture[12] in the context of these chamber genres – the coalition of piano with strings as well as their more amateur provenance made such writing far less likely than in all-string chamber music.

The slow movement of K. 548 contains yet another central section involving imitation of a fragment from a first theme, but here the material extracted is rather unlikely (it seems to be a filler between the melodic gestures of the first two bars and the cadence point) and the imitation is more flexibly treated. First it is heard in four versions one bar apart, in a logical trio syntax, played by the two strings and the two hands of the keyboard. But then it is heard in dialogue between the strings, every two bars, while the piano has a cantilena that takes wing from the exposition's second subject. This provides a nice layering, as the figure that was the centre of attention moves out of immediate focus. The very elevated Larghetto of K. 502 matches this movement in impact, and the finales of both works are much preoccupied with the exchange of short figures, as if taking wing from the dialogue textures arrived at during their respective first-movement developments. Once more the sheer pace with which the figures are rotated creates a vivid sense of interchange.

Piano duos and duets

Music for piano four hands is not always immediately thought of as 'chamber music', but it does share comparable social dimensions. Part of its image, especially the piano duet, arises from a long history of arrangements, particularly of orchestral works. This has clearly been thought to interfere with the legitimacy of the medium in its own right, but even music conceived for four hands often shows strong traces of an orchestral typology. This should hardly be seen as problematic, though, given the free way in which genres borrow from each other in the later eighteenth century; our medium is hardly exceptional in this regard. While one would also expect some more intimate aspects to the texture, there are social considerations that reach beyond the specific nature of the material. This is apparent in the outer movements of the duet sonatas K. 358 (1774) and K. 381 (1772). These set the tone of untrammelled exuberance and sheer joy in movement that marks nearly all Mozart's four-hand music. Although predominantly 'orchestral', their meaning is not exhausted by noting such derivations. First there is the thrill for the performers in evoking a public arena; then there is the peculiar energy produced through duet playing. It is unnatural for pianists to share an instrument and to have to co-ordinate with another of their kind. Two of the four elbows do not have much freedom of movement, leading to the feeling of a feat of management on the part of performers as well as those who watch. Also unusual is the sonority produced, so much bigger, wider-ranging and, simply, louder than what we would expect from a keyboard at the time. This is especially apparent in the case of Mozart, given the modest textures found in many of the solo sonatas.

Indeed, there is often a sense of relish for such sonorities. This is apparent from bar 21 of the Andante of K. 381, with a magical doubling of the melody two octaves apart in the right hands of primo and secondo parts.[13] Mozart in fact achieves many of his most striking textures through octave scoring.[14] It can be especially effective as a closing device, fitting socially because of its unanimity and sonorously because it clears out the texture. Another instance is found in the slow movement of K. 358, in the doubling of a semiquaver accompanimental figure between the right hand of the secondo and left hand of the primo at bars 5–7. Its accompanimental status is no longer self-evident due to its doubling between the two players; for a start, it will require careful consultation and matching in preparing a performance. The same is true on a larger scale for whole accompanimental passages. This of course partakes of the nature of all ensemble music, and especially chamber music, but is I believe more pointed when two players at the same instrument are involved.

The Sonata for Two Pianos in D major, K. 448 (1781), enables the composer to generate even fuller textures. It has a stronger than usual predilection for binary symmetries, and this suits the medium very well, given its natural disposition towards stereo effects. Indeed, particular emphasis on the spatial dimension is part of the delight of the genre. For example, the brilliant passage that ends the first section of the finale, from bar 34, consists of a two-bar unit in octaves for Piano I which it then repeats twice, an octave lower each time. In itself this is a typical section-concluding gesture. But Piano II joins in on the first repetition, an octave higher than Piano I, an apparently simple case of octave doubling used here to increase the textural mass and momentum towards the cadence. Curiously, it is the left hand of Piano II that does this, a seemingly unnatural placement of the hand. Two bars later, though, its right hand joins in, again starting with the original Piano I right-hand register. Thus we have a threefold imitation that greatly enriches the basic gesture. It is used as a sort of conceit, absorbed into a 'natural' texture. Thus the initial flourish of Piano I is twice echoed through time and space, coexisting with the more direct downward plunge we can follow through in the Piano I part. Also impressive is that by the end we hear the basic semiquaver figuration in four separate octaves – an unusual combination of mass and speed.

In the Fugue for Two Pianos in C minor, K. 426, of 1783, imitative exchange naturally takes on a rather different form. This was one of a number of pieces Mozart attempted around this time that reflect his introduction to the music of Handel and Bach. The result here is a rather grotesque, not to say Gothic, counterpoint. There is the same sense of strain, of striving after something no longer readily accessible to the contemporary composer, that we sometimes find in Clementi's polyphony (and later, indeed, in Beethoven's). Yet the inflated rhetoric is part of the historical moment and part of the fascination of this music.[15]

The Variations for Piano Duet in G major, K. 501, form an amusing contrast in manner. Here compositional technique is laid out in an accessible way for pleasure, a hallmark of Mozart's creativity, and especially notable once more is the way in which strands are fitted in or together. Further, there is a constant probing of the grey area between imitation and complementary motion, producing an intrinsic type of texture that does not rely as heavily as usual on the exchange of clearly defined units of invention.

The sense of a deliciously packaged musical art, a real 'Mozart effect', is particularly well embodied by Variation 3. There is a finicky elegance to the figuration and high spirits in the rich supply of grace notes; Robert Levin writes of 'music-box enchantment',[16] a quality we will consider further with the solo keyboard works. Variation 4 introduces the first antiphony, meshing beautifully with the change to minor to produce an affect of lonely melancholy. In its first half the players largely perform separately, quite unlike the sociable cohesion of earlier sections.

The Sonata in F major, K. 497, demonstrates a comparable sensitivity to sound. In the first bar of the slow introduction a figure is presented in four separate octaves; the second bar is louder, with an extra low octave added (which obviously has something to do with the lower compass of the instrument of the time); bar 3 features high octaves for primo only, and *piano*; bar 4 returns to four lines, as in the first bar, but now in close four-part harmony, and *pianissimo*. In the following few bars the performers are physically even closer in the notes that they play, matching the warmth of this typical lyrical riposte to an imposing opening gesture. A much more aerated and stratified texture follows, in a series of grand gestures in a high style. This includes eleven consecutive repetitions of a rising arpeggio figure, hardly a natural modern syntax.

The elevated feeling to the whole introduction makes the initial lively Allegro di molto material a characteristic puncturing of the balloon. The whole development is built around reworkings of this material, generating a single-mindedness that is not so different from the rhythmic monomania of the introduction after all, while in the coda the music dissolves into a fit of grace-note giggles, based on the latter part of our material.[17] The subsequent movements play with learned material and high style in a similarly ambivalent manner.

Solo keyboard music

While we have been able to consider all genres so far in terms of interaction within an 'antiphonal field', no such social exchange is built into a solo keyboard texture. Our primary context for this medium is a cluster of associations with that stylistic quantity known as the galant. This of course represents another model of sociability. Notions of pleasure and entertainment are often invoked and just as often qualified, reflecting a larger problem of reception of Mozart's art and indeed of the 'Classical style' altogether.[18] For instance, we can read of the Piano Quartet in G minor, K. 478, that 'it is no longer in any sense music of mere sociability, which can be listened to superficially and with a smile', or of the composer's 'mature masterpieces that transcend the *galant* aesthetic of delightful entertainment and colourful juxtaposition'.[19] With the more transparent textures of a solo work, though, the sociable simplicity stares us in the face. The great critical ambivalence about the galant reflects long-held assumptions about artistic value, about the sort of techniques and tone with which we are most comfortable. One continued symptom of ambivalence, especially in Mozart criticism, is the notion that the pathetic and chromatic, as well as the use of the minor mode in general, is more 'authentic' than the affirmative major-mode typology that is statistically dominant.[20] Why assume that such darker colours represent a truth hidden by convention rather than, for instance, a means of increasing pleasure once they are dispersed?

Variations

It is not just the sonatas that fall conspicuously into this category, but also the variations, by virtue of their form. Traditionally they have not been highly regarded. Again this is ultimately an issue that affects all the variations of the Classical era.[21] The form has been seen as too simple, too mechanical. So either a composer such as Mozart simply achieved less in this area than all other forms and movement types he undertook – part of a general failure to do anything interesting with the genre in the eighteenth century – or we are wrong and need to readjust our perceptions and expectations. A set such as K. 265, the well-known variations on 'Ah, vous dirai-je, Maman', can be very helpful in this regard. Most independent variation sets of the day (which generally meant for keyboard solo) were based on popular tunes, most commonly from operatic arias. The trouble is that almost none of these tunes are known today, or, if so, they are not familiar favourites. But the tune used in K. 265 has particular resonance as a nursery rhyme ('Twinkle, twinkle little star'). It would be difficult to maintain that Mozart's variation set is particularly well known and frequently played because of any intrinsic superiority in the handling of the variations. We love it and want to hear it simply because of the familiarity of the tune, and this brings alive the *raison d'être* of the form, the pleasure of recognition. It is fun to recognize it in different guises, and because it is well ingrained, the tune (more properly, the entire material, which includes harmonic progression, texture, register and so forth) will bear many (altered) repetitions. This must approximate to the pleasure contemporary listeners derived from other tunes more familiar to them.

Another relevant issue is that, simply, some tunes seem to be more shapely than others. It is helpful if they feature particular high points that can form the focus of attention for each variation. Mozart often shapes his sets around just such a criterion. In the Variations on 'Mio caro Adone' by Salieri, K. 180, the high point comes after the double bar, in the treble progression by step from f♯'' up to b''. There is a natural crescendo effect to this rising progression, built over a dominant pedal, which is reinforced by the markings *p – cresc. – f*, but then there is a *piano* at the completion of the line. Mozart's technique is to leave the basic line largely unaltered so that it forms a foil to the more extensive alterations elsewhere. Nevertheless, each variation provides some registral or dynamic deformation that complicates the picture. It is only with the final Variation 6, an Allegretto in 2/4, that we hear an absolutely direct presentation of the line; it is *forte* throughout and there is no registral elaboration. This is less a simple variant than the climax to the operations surrounding this focal part of the theme's material.

The Variations on 'Je suis Lindor', K. 354, written in Paris in 1778, also work towards a climactic articulation of the most 'characteristic' passage, in a very elaborate Adagio (see bars 301–2). The Adagio of the other Paris set, K. 264 ('Lison dormait'), is also exceptionally expansive, even extravagant, in its gestures. Katalin Komlós notes that the 'infinitely elaborate notation and rich rhythmic vocabulary' of these two Adagios, found to a lesser extent in several later sets, 'have no parallel in Mozart's keyboard music'. As she notes, the very tempo designation is quite rarely found in Mozart, Andante being much more common.[22] The conjunction of these attributes forms quite a contrast to the assumed character of Mozart's solo keyboard output. K. 264 also shows a relish for the big gesture in the cadenza that concludes the fast Variation 9. Yet the following da capo merges into a coda with a modest ending that takes us back to the character of the theme – an ironic restoration after what has been largely an expansive, big-boned set.

Some other sets, such as K. 353 ('La belle Françoise'), work more within the modest character of their themes throughout. On the other hand we have K. 398 (based on a theme by Paisiello) and K. 455 (based on a theme by Gluck), both of which seem to have originated in a concert given at the Burgtheater in 1783, during which Mozart improvised variations on these two themes. These are not only more exuberant and technically difficult, they remind us of the especially strong performative element in the genre of variations. Of the two sets, K. 398 is remarkable for its blurring of the edges of the later variations to approach the more truly through-composed state of an improvisation.[23] Like K. 264, it dissolves its virtuosic exuberance in a humorously low-key manner at the end. In K. 455 (on Gluck's aria 'Unser dummer Pöbel meint') the humorous glance at variation technique is found throughout. The focal point of the theme as treated by Mozart lies in its unison opening, descending a fourth from G to D. This contrasts with the clear three- or four-part harmonies found elsewhere.[24] The game played throughout the set concerns whether or not to harmonize this opening.

Mozart seems to have retained a fascination with the unpromising opening, since his next set, K. 500, on an original theme, starts with two and a half bars of tonic harmony in gavotte time. The whole theme in fact is just eight bars long, and so has a rather epigrammatic flavour. In similar spirit, his final set of 1791 ('Ein Weib ist das herrlichste Ding', K. 613) reflects the popular origins of the tune through a fairly transparent variation technique.[25]

The impression arising from the literature is that Mozart is too fluent for his own good in his piano variations, even though this very fluency is so much admired elsewhere. Coupled with the more general reservations concerning the whole genre, this means that few of these works are known or played. We are used to emphasizing the negative, what they do not apparently contain, yet variations bring delights not offered by most other formal-expressive types. In the case of the current series of works these include an inventiveness with sound and texture that the genre itself naturally tends to spotlight.

Miscellaneous pieces

Mozart's numerous youthful piano pieces, including the London Notebook of 1764, have, like the sonatas, had a considerable influence in shaping the image of the composer. They are not only encountered frequently by learner-pianists, but also – by their very existence – substantiate the story of the child prodigy. The more mature pieces consist of one-off works, individual sonata movements, arrangements and exercises in stylistic imitation; a number of these are unfinished. They can suffer, of course, for being miscellaneous, hard to classify; however, some rank among Mozart's most memorable solo keyboard compositions.

Indeed, Mozart can be defined as a supreme occasional composer – in that a sense of occasion tends to bring the best out of him and that he likes to be challenged by unusual circumstances. Some genres have an in-built sense of occasion, such as opera and concerto; and his achievements in less established genres are often thought to outshine those in more established ones. Thus there has been a critical preference for piano quartet rather than piano trio, string quintet rather than string quartet. (Nor should we forget the novel instrumental forces assembled by the Quintet, K. 452.) And the same might apply to the keyboard output: the greatest riches are dispersed untidily according to particular circumstances rather than being concentrated in the fundamental genre of the sonata. Such a claim, though, seems historically problematic. Nearly all music produced at the time was occasional, in the sense of being written for specific performers and circumstances. Furthermore, what we now regard as mainstream genres may not originally have had quite the same secure identity; consider the fact that a higher proportion of Mozart's duets and variation sets than sonatas was published in his lifetime. Nevertheless, the feeling persists that non-routine productions did inspire the composer.

The A minor Rondo, K. 511, of 1787, evokes a *larmoyante* tradition of sensibility, saturated with chromaticism and with appoggiaturas that represent sighs or tears. (This is also found in the Adagio sections of the popular D minor Fantasia, K. 397.) This engenders a degree of pathos that is rather uncomfortable, for all the celebration of the composer's 'dark side'. Arthur Hutchings commented that the piece has 'a unique mood, lovely in musical expression like this, but morbid beyond pathos in a man's behaviour'.[26] We may smile at the anxiety behind this statement – the fear of the feminine – but it gets to the heart of such critical discomfort. The work in fact ends up contradicting its title, since the episodes ultimately provide little contrast. They are overrun by chromaticism when both set out to be plainer, countering the theme with a show of diatonic scales. Indeed, the very relentlessness of the chromatic movement altogether almost suggests the technical spirit of a chromatic ricercare. The writing ranges freely over the whole keyboard, something one finds less often in the sonatas. While much of the rondo theme itself occupies a high tessitura, the episodes are much more expansive. The coda shares this greater width, but also presents the thinnest textures of the work and leaves a gap between the hands. This eloquent gap in the sound is filled, inevitably, by the final, soft, close-position chords.

The enigmatic Minuet in D major, K. 355, also features heavy chromatic writing, but in a more unlikely generic context. This tends to go with the contrapuntal; as in K. 511, the chromatic or 'difficult' and the learned are closely associated. In K. 574, 'Eine kleine Gigue', the two features combine to produce a skittish atmosphere: repeated chords on strong beats near the end of each half are needed to curb the runaway counterpoint. Mozart seems confident enough to have a dig at the sort of material he so earnestly tried to imitate at the beginning of the decade.

In the Adagio in B minor, K. 540 (1788), the composer does without much chromaticism until the coda, when it is even more in *larmoyante* style than in the D minor Fantasia. A linking chromatic scale, the formula so strangely overplayed in the retransitions of K. 511, is repeated twice with rhythmically accelerating decoration. The effect is melodramatic, an appropriate contrast near the end of a piece that uses different methods to generate a highly emotional atmosphere. K. 540 has harder outlines: the first chord we hear in the piece is a diminished seventh, played *sforzando*. Even more surprising, though, is that the resolving 6/4 chord at the start of bar 2 is also *sforzando*. The severity is also found in the economical thematic conduct of the piece – the opening melodic unit is heard many times throughout and its outlines can often be glimpsed in apparently contrasting material. Indeed, the development section is dominated by reiterations of the opening in various remote keys, creating a series of frozen gestures. This gives the recapitulation a disorientating effect, since it both continues the pattern and represents a fresh start. The dominant expressive device is the appoggiatura, but it is most frequently heard in isolation rather than as part of a more fluent melodic line; this also aids the frozen, chiselled quality of the discourse. Again K. 540 is notable for the assurance with which Mozart exploits register and texture, for its great variety of colour and mass.

Sonatas

As we have seen, defensiveness about the pedagogical and infantile associations of the sonatas has been a constant factor in their reception. William

S. Newman sought to shift the perception of the works by reminding us that, far from existing 'merely for teaching purposes', most of the sonatas were in fact vehicles for Mozart's own playing.[27] Even granted this, what remains rare is any attempt to characterize their expressive climate in a positive way, not surprising given the reception of the galant outlined earlier. Wye J. Allanbrook and Robert Levin are among the few who have squared up to this challenge. In her topical readings of the first movements of K. 332 and K. 333 Allanbrook offers a number of attractive formulations that might constitute the basis of a reorientation. She uses 'the sensitive style' as an umbrella term for the manner we associate with this music; and within this, we find characterizations of a 'private reflectivity', and of passages that are 'intense yet demure' or in 'music-box' style, the term applied by Levin to the duet variations, K. 501.[28] Levin himself evokes such attributes as 'stagey coyness', 'conversational ease' and 'teasing flirtatiousness', within a basic discourse that is dominated by 'dapper banter'.[29]

Another attempt at renewal has come from the historical performance movement. Malcolm Bilson, for example, has questioned the whole edifice of 'good Mozart playing' in a consideration of the opening slow movement of K. 282; he suggests the 'extraordinary expressive power' that can emerge when the notation is taken seriously rather than being ironed out in the familiar way.[30] (This is what Alfred Brendel, a performer on modern instruments, of course, terms 'touch-me-not' or 'pampered Mozart'.)[31] Nevertheless, these two strains pull in different directions – one tends to reconceptualize the existing image, the other to deny it. Both in fact are needed, since we must acknowledge both the centrality of a 'sensitive style' as well as the more diverse character of the total output. On the latter count, we might note that the abrupt dynamics of which Bilson writes so persuasively are commonly found in the sonatas, especially the earlier ones. Juxtapositions of loud and soft generally occur in contexts in which the changes can only be sudden, not 'subtle', as they are so often rendered.

In regard to the 'sensitive style', we need to remember that this idiom is a shared one. It not only exemplifies a fundamental galant orientation but is particularly widespread in solo keyboard writing. Indeed, such a musical style achieved specific theoretical recognition. The theorist Friedrich Rochlitz, for instance, dubbed it 'niedlich', meaning, in the words of Annette Richards, a manner that was 'playful and naïve, childlike and dainty'.[32] To call such an idiom 'Mozartian' is largely a convenient historical fiction – although there are of course particular nuances in the way Mozart handles it. A central part of this orientation is the focus on pure and 'natural' melody, with accompaniments contrived so as not to compromise this, and speeds that tend to be moderate, and hence easy on the ear as well as the player.

Sonatas such as K. 330, 545 and 570 are among the best examples of the Arcadian manner this tends to promote; in memory at least, they seem to consist of an unbroken stream of idyllic lyricism. This impression does not disappear even with the more varied and dynamic declamation demanded by Bilson. Further, it can mute contrasts of material and figuration, something insufficiently emphasized in topical readings of the sonatas, which have in any case tended to tackle only the more promising cases. This is often allied with a concentration on high and bright register, one of the elements that has done most to determine the image of children's music. Within its world this music seems not to know lower sounds. It is this self-sufficiency, this lack of an internal foil, that tends to make the tone of the music hard to assess. It is at once self-evidently innocent and mock-innocent (hence the references to coyness, flirtatiousness and the like).

Some works do of course contain foils, sometimes between movements. K. 332, after a first movement that is indubitably fragmented from a topical perspective, presents an Adagio whose totally concentrated, continuous cantabile is in pointed contrast; in K. 283 the lusty final Presto, with its strong physical presence and abundant rhythmic wit, hints at a lower style than that found in the refined first two movements. And then there are entire works that belie the notion that Mozart adhered to one basic, indispensable idiom for his solo sonatas. K. 310 in A minor has a first movement that rushes by in a torrent of figuration, making full and dramatic use of the bass registers of which the more galant sonatas are simply not conscious. Textures are much less nuanced, and there are no tunes. The slow movement compensates for this with a stream of melody, but the writing remains on a grand scale and there is a strong internal foil in the middle section. This is a sustained outburst of the same mood we heard in the Allegro's development, with even more obvious Baroque echoes – sequence, suspensions and dotted rhythms. The Presto is a virtual *perpetuum mobile*. Texture and sonority are often rather rough, especially with all the prominent fourths and the passages of low parallel thirds in the left hand. Another innovative and surprising feature is that the movement is predominantly quiet: there are of course louder passages, and the ending is forceful, but there are no explosions. There is in fact little variety in the type of material, another contrast with the 'sensitive' manner. The nearest we get to its more self-contained nature is the major-mode 'trio' at bars 143–74. Here the narrow register and melodic style have real expressive point. In fact, they sound uncomfortable, especially in the rather rushed, square, unexpansive four-bar units of the melody.

The Fantasia in C minor, K. 475, published together with the Sonata in C minor, K. 457, almost functions as a negative image of the prevailing style of writing in the sonatas. Within its wider range there is a striking preponderance of low and thick scoring. Note, for instance, the treatment of the Andantino theme, where each version is one octave lower than the last. This subject of register is elaborated with the reprise of the material from bar 119, when the three registers are mixed within each phrase unit.[33] The very consciousness of this parameter is of course much more muted in most of the sonatas. The frequent low tessituras have clear connotations of mystery and uncertainty in this piece – and this suggests, again as a negative image, that the usual high tessitura is cognate with the clear, bright, innocent and idealized (yet 'natural').

In a sense this comparison is unfair. The keyboard writing may be more inventive and varied in K. 475, but then one would expect this of a fantasia. All it may show us is Mozart respecting generic boundaries. Nevertheless, it does offer a perspective on the practices of the Arcadian manner. The sonata that does this most radically is K. 533 in F major. It breaks with the house style not only through much contrapuntal exuberance but through an eccentricity rarely found in other sonatas. The very opening is unclear in shaping, almost diffident, and the Alberti bass – that most common means of supporting the lyrical stream – is here deconstructed. It enters in bar 4, which makes it seem strange, since it is normally the underpinning for a complete unit. Adding to the strangeness, it is not a particularly suitable companion for the rising then falling scale of bars 5–6. In fact, this is the only real appearance that this all-but-indispensable textural feature makes in the entire movement (along with its return in the recapitulation). It is, in other words, no longer self-evident. The Andante does without Alberti-type figuration altogether. It is written more in parts, in the Haydn or Clementi manner. Many of its expressive high points derive not, as has usually been the case, from melodic shaping, but from other types of line. (See, for example, the right-hand figuration in the passage from bar 23 or the immediately fol-lowing cadential progression, expressed simply in terms of rising arpeggios shared between the hands.) The contrapuntal impulse resurfaces in a very unexpected manner in the development. Tortured invertible counterpoint between the hands, doubled in thirds, produces something startling.

The point of this discussion is not to disparage the 'sensitive' manner and its seemingly limited range of textural and registral options, but to raise awareness of its situatedness, its specificity. There is a general difficulty ap-parent in the apprehension of much of Mozart's solo keyboard writing when it is compared with what we find in the ensemble forms. Eric Blom got at this when he claimed to miss the 'interplay' found when the keyboard is used in combination (which for our purposes includes the duos and duets).[34] Mozart, it has been stressed, cannot readily trade in his favoured tech-niques, alternation and antiphony, and so these works can feel unfocussed from registral and textural perspectives. Similarly elusive is the question of expressive tone, at once immediate and idealized. Our continuing challenge is to construe this 'sensitive' solo manner – one that has done so much to shape the image of the composer – not in a negative but rather in a positive fashion, so that it can offer us the depth of pleasure it clearly gave to players and listeners of the late eighteenth century.

6 The concertos in aesthetic and stylistic context

SIMON P. KEEFE

Writing in haste to his father, Leopold, shortly before a musical *soirée* on 28 December 1782, Mozart described three new piano concertos he was composing, K. 413 in F major, K. 414 in A major and K. 415 in C major:

> These concertos are a happy medium between what is too easy and too difficult; they are very brilliant, pleasing to the ear, and natural, without being vapid. There are passages here and there from which the connoisseurs alone can derive satisfaction; but these passages are written in such a way that the less learned cannot fail to be pleased, though without knowing why.[1]

One of the most frequently quoted passages in Mozart's entire body of correspondence, these words have been taken to signify many different things: that Mozart was capable of thinking through 'the problem of the interaction between composer and listener' in an extremely lucid and erudite fashion, believing 'an audience could be simultaneously charmed and challenged'; that Mozart's compositional philosophy is 'fragmentary... [enshrining] a duality, some might say a dialectic, between whole and part'; and that each of the three works exhibits 'events of an unusual nature such as... sallies into invertible counterpoint', while also demonstrating 'a string of connections and progressions... that serve to coalesce the three concertos into one splendidly integrated larger work'.[2]

Since the risk of overinterpreting Mozart's passage is considerable given the simultaneously broad and incisive nature of his prose, it is as well to remember what the passage is *not*. Above all, it is certainly not an original assessment and articulation of widespread appeal. The idea that a musical piece or set of pieces would be attractive to connoisseurs and amateurs (*Kenner und Liebhaber*) alike was voiced with great regularity in eighteenth-century critical and commercial circles, often with a view to a composer or publisher enhancing the marketing potential of the work (or works) in question.[3] In addition, Mozart's belief that both the musical cognoscenti and the 'less learned' should comprehend his concertos ultimately has its roots in formulations of venerable writers on rhetoric such as Quintilian and Cicero.[4] Moreover, the context in which Mozart expresses his ideas – a letter to his father only eighteen months or so after his move to Vienna – and the nature of an additional comment he makes on K. 413–15 make us wary of interpreting his remarks simply as an idealistic statement of aesthetic intent. Leopold was sceptical about Mozart's chances of professional success in Vienna, and Mozart no doubt wanted to reassure his father that his compositional strategies were orientated in practical fashion towards cultivated and popular tastes and towards broad, commercial appeal. In any case, Mozart was clearly mindful of pragmatic matters in regard to K. 413–15, proposing in an announcement in the *Wiener Zeitung* that these works offered on subscription to the Viennese musical public 'may be performed either with a large orchestra with wind instruments or merely *a quattro*, viz. with 2 violins, 1 viola and violoncello'.[5]

Even with due recognition of the commonplace nature of Mozart's *Kenner/Liebhaber* formulation, of the implications of his remarks for his relationship with Leopold and of his pragmatic orientation at the time, Mozart's comments offer considerable insight into his aesthetic and stylistic priorities *vis-à-vis* the concerto genre. His reference to K. 413–15 as 'very brilliant, pleasing to the ear, and natural, without being vapid', for example, engages with prevailing trends in late eighteenth-century concerto criticism. While concertos were expected to feature 'brilliant' writing for the solo instrument – passage work, figuration and other types of virtuosic display – they were usually perceived as possessing an overabundance of 'brilliance', and thus regarded with deep suspicion by aestheticians, theorists and music critics alike. Invariably, writers and musicians in the second half of the century explain that excessive display in concertos detracts from their aesthetic import and their articulation of musical content: Johann Georg Sulzer and Johann Philipp Kirnberger note in the influential *Allgemeine Theorie der schönen Künste* (*General Theory of the Fine Arts*) that 'the concerto has no fixed character ... At the most basic level, it is nothing but a practice session for composers and players, and a totally indeterminate aural amusement, aimed at nothing more'; Johann Karl Friedrich Triest condescendingly excuses the concerto composer from exhibiting an 'aesthetic sense and inventiveness' in instrumental writing on the grounds that 'concertos are the special proving ground of virtuosity, and hardly one in a hundred can claim to possess any inner artistic value'; and Carl Dittersdorf, on being told that he should imitate the work of Antonio Lolli, a composer and performer of violin concertos renowned for virtuosic exhibitionism, exclaims 'God forbid! ... I must do exactly the opposite, and try to cut a better figure ... through good solid playing and expression.'[6] In his own estimation, Mozart avoids the kind of 'vapidity' often wrought by brilliance and lack of substantive content, striking a balance – or 'happy medium' – between excessive displays of virtuosity and plain, straightforward writing.

The most eloquent contemporary advocate of Mozart's concertos was the celebrated German aesthetician and theorist Heinrich Christoph Koch

(1749–1816). In a similar vein to Mozart, Koch believed that the late eighteenth-century concerto need not constitute empty display and could be more than 'mere pleasure for the ear'. Citing Mozart's concertos as exemplary models in his *Musikalisches Lexikon* of 1802, Koch described a 'well worked-out concerto' as a

> passionate dialogue between the concerto player and the accompanying orchestra. He expresses his feelings to the orchestra, and its signals him through short interspersed phrases sometimes approval, sometimes acceptance of his expression, as it were . . . In short, by a concerto I imagine something similar to the tragedy of the ancients, where the actor expressed his feelings not towards the pit, but to the chorus. The chorus was involved most closely with the action and was at the same time justified in participating in the expression of feelings.[7]

Ever since Koch's *exposé* of the dramatic characteristics of the late eighteenth-century concerto, analogies between Mozart's concertos and drama have been central to our understanding of these works, especially analogies between his concertos and his operas. Thematic and gestural similarities between Mozart's five violin concertos from 1775 (K. 207, 211, 216, 218, 219) and arias from *Il re pastore*, K. 208, first performed in Salzburg on 23 April 1775, testify to the cross-fertilization of his concerto and operatic material;[8] and formal and procedural parallels between Giunia's aria 'Ah, se il crudel periglio' from his opera seria *Lucio Silla* of 1772 and the first movements of the Violin Concerto in A major, K. 219, and the Piano Concerto in B flat major, K. 238 (1776), bear further witness to the confluence of operatic and concerto techniques in the music of Mozart's Salzburg period.[9] This convergence is no less productive in his Viennese concertos and operas, especially in cadential and ending gestures, although formal parallels – particularly in regard to important distinctions between orchestral ritornellos and aria introductions – are more problematic than is generally acknowledged.[10]

Koch's analogy between the interaction of the soloist and the accompanying orchestra in the late eighteenth-century concerto and dialogue in spoken drama also provides the catalyst for a fresh perspective on drama in Mozart's concertos, one rooted in late eighteenth-century dramatic criticism. Above all, seminal writers on drama such as Gotthold Ephraim Lessing, Johann Wolfgang von Goethe and Denis Diderot believed that dramatic processes – the plan, structure, plot and character interaction in a play, for example – should be conveyed to the audience in a clear, consistent and systematic fashion, without recourse to much-derided *coups de théâtre*, gratuitous on-stage surprises or 'miraculous' events. In short, plays had to engage audiences through carefully crafted dramatic processes rather than ingeniously designed suspense, a fact acknowledged succinctly by Lessing:

> I rather think it would not exceed my powers to rouse the very strongest interest in the spectators even if I resolved to make a work where the *dénouement* was revealed in the first scene. Everything must be clear for the spectator . . . and there are hundreds of instances when we cannot do better than to tell him straight out what is going to occur.[11]

Given that the self-evident centrality of dialogue in late eighteenth-century drama finds an analogy in Koch's description of the ebb and flow of dramatic dialogue over the course of a late eighteenth-century concerto ('[the orchestra] signals him [the soloist] through short interspersed phrases sometimes approval, sometimes acceptance of his expression, as it were. Now in the allegro it tries to stimulate his noble feelings still more; now it commiserates, now it comforts him in the adagio'),[12] it seems that a historically informed analysis of dialogue between the concerto soloist and accompanying orchestra will probe the dramatic significance of Mozart's concertos in an effective fashion. As a result, dialogue will also show how Mozart imbues these works with an aesthetic significance that decisively transcends the vapidity associated with the concerto genre by late eighteenth-century writers.

The second movement of Mozart's Piano Concerto in C major, K. 467, offers a poignant illustration of his systematic approach to dialogue in the concerto genre. Adopting Antoine Reicha's comprehensive four-fold definition of musical dialogue from the *Traité de mélodie* of 1814 – culled in large part from relatively unsystematic eighteenth-century writings on the topic – as alternating full periods, antecedent and consequent phrases split between voices, imitations of motivic material, and individual phrases split between voices, we recognize that dialogue in K. 467/ii mainly constitutes a sophisticated version of Reicha's third type, imitation.[13] Above all, dialogic procedures witnessed in the opening ritornello (bars 1–22) – namely the F–A–C and C–C♯–D accompanimental figures in the lower strings in bars 1 and 18–19 taken up immediately in the first violin's and winds' melodic material respectively and the perpetual quaver-triplet accompaniment passed from strings to winds in bars 21–2 – form the basis of dialogic interaction between piano and orchestra in the remainder of the movement, thus demonstrating procedural consistency commensurate with the prescriptions of dramatists such as Lessing, Diderot and Goethe for late eighteenth-century plays.[14] The piano's entry in bar 23, for example (see example 6.1), integrates both types of dialogue: the left hand takes up the quaver-triplet accompaniment where the winds leave off (bars 22–3), while the arpeggiated right-hand melody grows from the preceding

Example 6.1 Mozart, Piano Concerto in C major, K. 467/ii, bars 22–6

F–A–C figure in the strings (see bars 23–4). We could hardly envisage a subtler, more mellifluous introduction of a concerto soloist. The three-way dialogue of the quaver triplets segueing into the main theme (strings–wind–piano, bars 21–3) reappears in reverse at the end of the piano's presentation of the theme leading into the transition (piano–wind–strings, bars 34–7) and then again at the beginning of the middle section (bars 55–61); the dialoguing of accompanimental material to the principal voice subsequently resurfaces in the arpeggiated writing passed from the cello/double bass to the piano in the four-bar sequence (bars 66–9) shortly before the reprise. Finally, in the coda, a 'new' fragment of piano material (bars 99–103, example 6.2) again grows out of an F major arpeggio in the strings, set against the backdrop of quaver-triplet figures passed from piano (bars 94–8) to wind (99–103). The technique of overlapping dialogue in these concluding bars evokes the piano's original entry, as does the concluding bar in the wind (103–4), a near exact replica of the winds' concluding bar

Example 6.2 Mozart, Piano Concerto in C major, K. 467/ii, bars 99–104

from the ritornello (bar 22–3). The formal function of the coda – bringing back ritornello material (bars 8ff., returning in 94ff.) postponed from earlier in the reprise – coincides with an exquisite summary of dialogic procedures from the movement as a whole.[15]

While general vocal and operatic qualities of the second movement of K. 467 have long been acknowledged by eminent Mozartians – Cuthbert Girdlestone likens it to a 'cantilena' and Alfred Einstein to an 'aria freed of all the limitations of the human voice', Arthur Hutchings compares its spirit to 'an operatic character with a human soul' and Charles Rosen labels it 'an aria with muted strings and a pizzicato bass'[16] – manifestations of piano–orchestra dialogue cast the movement's drama in a sharper critical perspective. Mozart's careful exploitation of specific dialogue techniques and processes lends his exchange a 'formality' characteristic of drama rather than an 'informality' characteristic of conversation. In addition, his dialogue can be said to be *about* the relationship between the piano and the orchestra – as Koch stipulates for dramatic dialogue in the concerto – since the collaboration between piano and orchestra subtly realized at the soloist's entry is meticulously reinforced in the remainder of the movement. Moreover, the *sine qua non* of both eighteenth-century drama and the ever-popular formal dialogue – that they should ultimately edify and instruct their spectators and readers – does not appear to have been lost on Mozart, at least judging by a passage later in the letter to Leopold of 28 December 1782 already quoted. Reflecting that the 'golden mean of truth in all things is no longer either known or appreciated', Mozart suggests his own instructional remedy: 'I should like to write a book, a short introduction to music, illustrated by examples, but, I need hardly add, not under my own name.'[17] Given that Mozart had just identified K. 413–15 as a 'happy medium' in stylistic and aesthetic terms, it is not far-fetched to suggest that, in a general way, he would have envisaged his concertos fulfilling a similar instructional function to that fulfilled by contemporary drama.

Stylistic issues

Mozart's Piano Concertos, K. 413–91

As well as illuminating aesthetic concerns, Mozart's references to the easiness and difficulty and to the brilliance, naturalness and lack of vapidity of K. 413–15 pertain specifically to the *style* of these works. Crucially, Mozart's 'happy medium' necessitates an integration of two different stylistic dimensions in his concertos, especially in the fast-paced first and last movements: display on the part of the soloist (without which a late eighteenth-century work's generic status as a concerto would be called into question) manifest in the 'spirited, lively' and 'glittering' nature of the 'brilliant' style;[18] and engagement between the soloist and the accompanying orchestra (primarily through dialogue) ensuring a level of musical 'content' distributed among participants that counteracts criticisms of vapidity. While each of Mozart's concertos negotiates this balance in a slightly different way, the nature of the balance is best exemplified, perhaps, by the first movements of those works written contemporaneously with and in the years immediately following Mozart's 'happy medium' proclamation, namely the Viennese piano concertos K. 413–91 (1782–6).[19]

A comparison of types of piano–orchestra involvement and engagement at several key formal junctures of the first movements of Mozart's piano concertos K. 413–91 – the entry of the soloist at the beginning of the solo exposition, the transition, the second theme, the passage between the end of the second theme and concluding cadential trill, and the end of the development section running into the recapitulation – reveals a consistent approach on Mozart's part to the integration of virtuosic passagework and piano–orchestra dialogue.[20] The soloist's initial entry in the 1782–6 concertos, for example, almost always features dialogue with the accompanying orchestra – following Reicha's historical definition – irrespective of whether the piano begins by stating the main theme or ostensibly 'new' thematic material; only four of the fourteen concertos (K. 415, 450, 482, 491) do not work in this way.[21] In contrast, the transition (which usually coincides with the end of the orchestra's first interjection in the solo exposition) highlights pianistic display through quaver-triplet and semiquaver figurations, often to the exclusion of dialogue with the accompanying orchestra (see, in particular, K. 413, bars 82–120; K. 414, bars 86–114; K. 450, bars 87–103; K. 453, bars 97–109; K. 456, bars 87–128; K. 488, bars 87–98; K. 491, bars 124–46).

The alternation of dialogue and piano passagework in the first theme and transition sections at the beginning of the solo exposition is complemented by a similar alternation of the secondary theme and close-of-secondary-theme-to-cadential-trill sections at the end. With the exception of three movements (K. 415, 450, 482), the secondary theme always features dialogue between the piano and the orchestra, incorporating, for example, full themes and phrases passed between interlocutors, antecedent–consequent dialogue and split phrases.[22] In contrast, the passage between the end of the presentation of the secondary theme and the cadential trill concluding the solo exposition brings solo virtuosity to the fore. Most movements showcase the piano immediately after the secondary theme with an unaccompanied solo passage of between three and eleven bars that incorporates either passagework (K. 413, bars 138–44; K. 414, bars 127–36; K. 415, bars 108–18; K. 449, bars 154–61; K. 450, bars 119–25; K. 482, bars 171–8) or a solo extension to the preceding thematic material (K. 451, bars 138–40; K. 456, bars 136–41; K. 459, bars 144–8). (K. 467 works differently, since the end of the secondary theme coincides with the piano's solo statement of the head motif of the main theme, a motif that subsequently prevails in imitation in the orchestra while the piano's figuration takes hold.) Moreover, figurative writing for the piano either coincides with the final cadence of the secondary theme and does not relent until the cadential trill (K. 413–15, 449–51, 466, 482), or, in related fashion, begins directly after ritornello material restated following the secondary theme (K. 453, 488). Of the remaining four movements, three contain only brief digressions from the piano passagework stretching from the end of the secondary theme to the cadential trill (K. 456, 467, 459).[23]

The consistent approach to piano–orchestra dialogue and solo display in the solo exposition of the first movements of Mozart's piano concertos K. 413–91 gives way to a more heterogeneous approach in the development sections. While every development section – beginning with the piano's re-entry after the middle ritornello and ending at the moment of recapitulation – features piano passagework, the amount of it varies from movement to movement (from sixteen bars in K. 456 (202–10; 222–28) to forty-two bars in K. 467 (231–73) and fifty-two bars in K. 491 (309–61)) as does its placement in the section. In addition, retransitional passages leading into the recapitulation divide into two different categories: those in which dialogue or straightforward piano–orchestra alternation prevails (K. 413, bars 225ff.; K. 450, bars 189ff.; K. 453, bars 219ff.; K. 459, bars 241ff.) and those in which solo figuration and/or a lack of dialogue are conspicuous (K. 414, bars 180ff.; K. 415, bars 192ff.; K. 449, bars 219ff.; K. 451, bars 211ff.; K. 456, bars 222ff.; K. 466, bars 242ff.; K. 467, bars 266ff.; K. 482, bars 253ff.; K. 488, bars 189ff.; K. 491, bars 354ff.).

There is a point of connection among Mozart's first movements K. 413–91, however, at the beginning of the recapitulation. At this moment in almost every movement Mozart brings together musical procedures from the onset of the orchestral ritornello and solo exposition sections – often incorporating new dialogue between the piano and the orchestra in the process – as if to acknowledge at the outset of this section that it will necessarily involve the integration of thematic material from *two* expository sections. In K. 414, 449, 453, 459 and 482, for example, Mozart more or less cuts and pastes segments of material from the orchestral ritornello and solo exposition: K. 414 repeats the first eight bars of the orchestral ritornello followed by the first eight of the solo exposition (bars 196–211)[24] and K. 449 the first eight of the orchestral ritornello and the second eight of the solo exposition (bars 234–49), creating full-theme and split-theme dialogues respectively; K. 453 restates the first ten bars of the orchestral ritornello followed by the eleventh and twelfth from the solo exposition (bars 227–38); K. 459 brings back the initial eight bars of the solo exposition then the second eight from the orchestral ritornello (bars 247–62); and K. 482 restates the first eight bars of the orchestral ritornello followed by four bars from the solo exposition with a slightly modified piano part (bars 264–75). Other movements integrate the beginnings of the orchestral ritornello and solo exposition sections in related fashions, albeit without *exact* repetitions of earlier material: the first eight bars of K. 450's recapitulation is a slightly modified version of the beginning of the orchestral ritornello, rescored to incorporate a new split-theme dialogue between the wind and the piano, and the next four bars an exact repetition of the corresponding bars in the solo exposition (see bars 197–208); the first ten bars of K. 451's recapitulation feature a version of the main theme in the orchestra (as heard in the orchestral ritornello) juxtaposed with ascending semiquaver writing in the piano that occurs in the piano left hand every other bar at the beginning of the solo exposition (bars 219–28); the opening twelve bars of K. 456's recapitulation combine rescored versions of bars 9–12 from the orchestral ritornello and bars 78–81 from the solo exposition and a repetition of bars 5–8 from the orchestral ritornello (see bars 232–43), maintaining the dialogue from the earlier sections; the first thirteen bars of K. 466's recapitulation restate the first eight bars from the orchestral ritornello followed by a modified version of bars 99–103 from the solo exposition (bars 254–66); and the first sixteen bars of K. 488's recapitulation bring together rescored versions of the first eight bars of the orchestral ritornello and the second eight bars of the solo exposition – the latter including slight modifications to the piano's elaboration of the theme – presenting the entire main theme in dialogue between the piano and the orchestra for the first time (bars 198–213). The presence of a 'recapitulatory tutti' in most of Mozart's piano concerto first movements partially explains how Mozart is able to fuse orchestral ritornello and solo exposition sections so succinctly in the opening bars of the recapitulation, although the less fashionable practice of including a 'modulatory ritornello' immediately before the recapitulation also surfaces in one movement from the 1782–6 piano concertos, K. 459.[25]

The balance struck by Mozart in the first movements of his piano concertos K. 413–91 between 'brilliant' writing for the soloist and intricate, substantive piano–orchestra engagement gets to the heart of the stylistic significance and aesthetic import of these works. Requirements of first-movement concerto form – integrating the soloist into the orchestral fabric at its initial entry in the solo exposition, demarcating the end of the solo exposition and bringing together orchestral ritornello and solo exposition sections in the recapitulation – operate within this balance, contributing to an impression that musical and aesthetic concerns are meticulously aligned. While Mozart's method of integrating passagework and piano–orchestra dialogue is comparable from work to work in the 1782–6 piano concertos, procedural similarities do not obscure the subtleties and intricacies of individual movements. Ultimately, Mozart's 'happy medium' extends beyond aesthetic and stylistic realms to the manner in which unique and common characteristics of individual works in the K. 413–91 sequence seem effortlessly to coexist.

Mozart's final concertos

Mozart's concerto writing reaches a climax in the Piano Concerto in C minor, K. 491 (1786). The first movement, for example, is longer and more formally complex than earlier concerto first movements and projects an unrivalled level of intensity in the interaction between the piano and the orchestra, including an extraordinary confrontation between the two forces in the development section (bars 330–45). What is more, the recapitulation not only unveils a *tour de force* of dialogic activity, again without precedent in Mozart's earlier concertos, but also combines thematic material and dialogic procedures from the orchestral ritornello and solo exposition sections in so forceful and systematic a fashion as to integrate symmetrical arrangements from both earlier sections.[26]

Given the climactic nature of K. 491, it was perhaps inevitable that Mozart should adjust certain aspects of his style in his final concertos. While his next piano concerto, K. 503 in C major (completed in December 1786), is, in its way, just as imposing as the great K. 491, it shows signs of stylistic experimentation. The entry of the piano leading into the statement of the main theme in the first movement, for example, combines intimacy and grandeur in a manner unprecedented at this juncture of Mozart's piano concertos. Mozart himself coined the term 'grand' concerto to denote works from the Piano Concerto in B flat major, K. 450, onwards that feature a large wind section indispensable in performance terms; the corollary of a large orchestra for Mozart in his piano concertos – greater subtlety in scoring and texture – is recognized by a writer for the *Allgemeine Musikalische Zeitung* in 1800 who points out that Mozart's concertos are 'greatest from the point of view of intimacy'.[27] The assimilation of these two dimensions at the piano's entry in K. 503 is particularly remarkable. While the piano creeps into the action imitating the outlined tonic triad and oscillation of the trill presented in the strings (bars 91–6), the subsequent six-bar semiquaver approach to the main theme (bars 106–11) – integrating scalic, arpeggiated and chromatic passagework – and the main theme itself (bars 112–17) are more emphatic. The *pièce de résistance* in blending intimacy and grandeur, however, occurs at the piano's re-entry in bar 118. The f''' starting point not only revisits the registral high point of the piano's preceding semiquaver build up, but also grows exquisitely from the flute's f''' in the two preceding bars. Transforming its semiquavers from bold, virtuosic flourishes to ethereal reflection in one fell swoop, the piano's delicacy precipitates a radical alteration in the character of the theme's continuation; in place of the brash *forte* of bars 9ff. from the orchestral ritornello, the piano and the orchestra offer refined, *piano* alternations of the blocked dominant chords (bars 120–2). It is not unusual, of course, for Mozart to bring in his soloist in the first movement with ostensibly 'new' material prior to the restatement of the main theme – K. 413, 415, 450, 466, 482, 491 and 503 among the Viennese concertos all work in this way; similarly, it is standard practice for Mozart to reorchestrate the main theme in the solo exposition to accommodate the soloist. K. 503's originality resides in the existence of expressive contrasts and transformations that are unique at this juncture of Mozart's first movements.

Just as Mozart experiments with his stylistic *modus operandi* at the beginning of the solo exposition of K. 503/i, so he does the same at the end of the solo exposition and the beginning of the development. In the final bars of the solo exposition, the piano introduces a seven-quaver rhythmic pattern (bars 208–10) stated three times, against the prevailing 4/4 time signature; at the exact point at which we expect a rhythmically decisive drive to the cadential trill in order to reinforce sectional closure, Mozart introduces momentary metric ambiguity. He departs again from his standard practice at the beginning of the development section. Whereas the piano and the orchestra in this section of the first movements of Mozart's preceding Viennese piano concertos invariably move away from the intimate dialogue characterizing their exchange in the solo exposition, they engage in a panoply of dialogic combinations at the beginning of the K. 503 development (bars 228–53), in the process strengthening their bond considerably.[28]

Mozart's remaining piano concertos – K. 537 in D major (1788), nicknamed the 'Coronation', and K. 595 in B flat major (completed 1791) – take stylistic experimentation further than K. 503, particularly in their first movements. Unfairly dismissed by many scholars and critics as second rate, K. 537 can be understood more positively as Mozart's reappraisal of certain features of his piano concerto style pertaining to the presentation of thematic material and solo passagework. Viewed in relation to Mozart's earlier practice, K. 537's fourteen-bar passage for the solo piano (bars 180–93) after the presentation of the secondary theme, for example, is highly original. Short passages for unaccompanied soloist incorporating figurative writing are not uncommon at this point in his preceding Viennese concertos as we have seen, but K. 537 contains a unique combination of sophisticated contrapuntal and sequential writing, an *absence* of piano passagework, and a lush harmonic excursion (initiated by the Neapolitan harmony in bar 182) standing in stark contrast to the preceding thematic presentation. Similarly, in the recapitulation of K. 537 the reappearance of thematic material from the orchestral ritornello omitted in the solo exposition precipitates a severe juxtaposition of contrasting harmonic styles: the diatonic presentation of the theme (bars 383–94) is followed immediately by a terse minor subdominant – diminished (A–C–E♭–F♯) – diminished (B–D–F–G♯) progression (bars 395–400). The onset of solo figuration in a number of Mozart's earlier Viennese piano concertos coincides with the conclusion of a recapitulated theme heard for the first time since the orchestral ritornello (K. 414, bars 264ff.; K. 459, bars 348ff.; K. 467, bars 359ff.; K. 491, bars 463ff.; K. 503, bars 372ff.) as in K. 537. But K. 537's passage significantly surpasses these earlier ones in the intensity of harmonic contrast that it engenders. Viewed through the lens of Mozart's earlier concertos, moreover, the material from bars 295–300 and its placement in the recapitulation marks a moment of stylistic experimentation. The alternation between the piano and the orchestra of arpeggiated and conjunct units, equal in length and sharply contrasting in style, occurs in several of Mozart's first movement development sections, most notably K. 449 (bars 188–204) and K. 491 (bars 330–45), with units distributed in such a way as to stress conflict between the two parties. K. 537's passage is exceptional, however, in displacing this type of abrasive alternation from the development to the recapitulation section, in eradicating the confrontational dimension by conflating the rising scalar and falling arpeggiated writing into the piano part, and in directly following on from a diatonic thematic presentation. In fact, K. 537's striking passages in the solo exposition and recapitulation could be considered part of the trend towards disjunctive continuations in the movement as a whole. In the orchestral ritornello, for example, an emphasis on 'melodic succession' brought about by 'long athematic passages, setting off one section from another' supersedes subtle melodic flow.[29]

The stylistic experimentation evident in K. 537 is complemented by experimentation in K. 595. Whereas the first movement of K. 537 is at its most radical in the solo exposition and recapitulation sections, the corresponding movement of K. 595 departs from Mozart's standard practice in the development section. The harmonically disjunctive opening to the section – beginning in the remote key of B minor (bar 191) and moving abruptly to C major via an outlined diminished harmony in the strings that does not prepare for the modulation (see bars 194–7) – is unprecedented in Mozart's piano concerto first movements, even though the corresponding junctures of the first and last movements of the approximately contemporary G minor Symphony, No. 40 (1788), strike a similar note.[30] In contrast to the taut opening to the section, the end features an elegant and expansive transition into the recapitulation, as if to 'correct' the earlier disjunction. Whereas the corresponding juncture of Mozart's earlier piano concertos invariably highlights *either* dialogue between the piano and the orchestra (K. 413, 450, 459) *or* passagework leading into the recapitulation, K. 595 combines both, absorbing the piano's quaver triplets into an orchestral fabric that includes main theme material passed from the piano to the wind to the strings (bars 231ff.).

Although Mozart re-evaluates certain aspects of his piano concerto style in K. 503, 537 and 595, his aesthetic views on the concerto genre as a whole do not appear to change markedly from 1782 to the end of his life, at least if the review of a roughly contemporary critic in the *Allgemeine Musikalische Zeitung* is accorded significance as historical testimony. The development section of the first movement of Mozart's last work in the genre, the Clarinet Concerto, K. 622, for example, contains as striking a combination of terse, contracted modulation and harmonic expansiveness as the corresponding section in K. 595. Following an extended passage at the beginning of the section in the dominant, E major (bars 172–86), a fully prepared modulation to F sharp minor (bars 188–91), and a four-bar articulation of V of F♯ minor (bars 192–5), the clarinet and orchestra move abruptly from V of F♯ minor to a confirmation of D major (bars 196–200) – via consecutive diminished harmonies (bars 196–7) – subsequently assigning these three tonalities central roles in the spacious 'modulating ritornello' that concludes the section (F♯ minor, bar 227; E minor, bar 233; D major, bar 239).[31] The writer for the 1802 *Allgemeine Musikalische Zeitung*, however, emphasizes very similar aesthetic qualities in the Clarinet Concerto to those articulated by Mozart himself in K. 413–15. Just as the 'happy medium' and brilliance of K. 413–15 steer clear of the 'vapidity' commonly associated with the genre, thus implicitly acknowledging important musical content, so the Clarinet Concerto is 'difficult, and even *very* difficult', but will 'secure the finest reward for an artist as artist, namely, to delight and enrapture... [the performer] and all around him by the omnipotence of true art'. In addition, the appeal of K. 413–15 to both *Kenner* and *Liebhaber* is matched by the Clarinet Concerto's equally broad appeal across a range of musical aptitudes: the 'emotional man' will have his 'deepest feeling' awoken by the Adagio of K. 622, while the less knowledgeable listener will at least 'be sufficiently *amused* by the wit and humour... of the third movement, a very pleasing rondo'.[32] Thus, Mozart's first and last Viennese concertos – the beginning and end of one of the most remarkable sequences of works in the history of instrumental music – are on a similar aesthetic plane, it would seem, demonstrating comparable objectives and similar predilections for a type and quantity of solo virtuosity that does not detract from the articulation of substantive musical content.

7 The orchestral music

SIMON P. KEEFE

Mozart was a prolific composer of orchestral music, writing numerous symphonies, divertimenti, serenades and cassations in the 1760s and 1770s, and six remarkable symphonies while based in Vienna in the 1780s. Although his contribution to the orchestral literature is predictably diverse, the genres in which he works are not as musically distinct in practical terms as nomenclature would seem to suggest. Divertimento, serenade and cassation each carried slightly different connotations in eighteenth-century Europe – according to the theorist Heinrich Christoph Koch the cassation was specifically designed for performance 'in the evenings, outdoors, or on public streets', for example – but Mozart uses the terms more or less interchangeably.[1] Many of Mozart's Salzburg symphonies, too, are closely linked to his serenade and operatic overture repertories, the symphonies K. 45, 87, 120, 135, 161/163, 121 and 102 either deriving from or being transformed into the overtures to Mozart's operas *La finta semplice*, *Mitridate re di Ponto*, *Ascanio in Alba*, *Lucio Silla*, *Il sogno di Scipione*, *La finta giardiniera* and *Il re pastore* respectively, and the cassation K. 100 and the serenades K. 204, 250 and 320 all reappearing in symphonic versions by Mozart or his father Leopold.[2]

Irrespective of generic context, Mozart was acutely sensitive to matters of instrumentation and instrumental effect where orchestral writing was concerned. His meticulous attitude towards the spacing of chords in the wind section is evident not only in adjustments he makes to his own manuscripts, but also in amendments to the work of his pupil Thomas Attwood.[3] Even in his very earliest compositions, Mozart is attuned to issues of orchestration, asking Nannerl to 'remind me to give the horn something worthwhile to do' in a symphony written in London in 1764.[4] Throughout his life, in fact, Mozart reacts to orchestral colours and effects he witnesses at home and abroad. After experiencing the famed Mannheim orchestra first-hand in 1778, Mozart laments to his father: 'Ah, if only we had clarinets too [in Salzburg]! You cannot imagine the glorious effect of a symphony with flutes, oboes and clarinets.'[5] Several months earlier in Paris, Mozart responds directly to a popular, much-used contemporary orchestral effect – the *premier coup d'archet*, comprising tutti chords or unisons heard at the outset of a work – in spite of apparent disinterest in the effect itself. Writing to his father about the 'Paris' Symphony, K. 297, he remarks:

I still hope ... that even asses will find something in it to admire – and, moreover, I have been careful not to neglect *le premier coup d'archet* – and that is quite sufficient. What a fuss the oxen made of this trick! The devil take me if I can see any difference! They all begin together, just as they do in other places.[6]

Alongside his willingness to write a second Andante for K. 297 at the request of the influential Parisian impresario Joseph Le Gros – in spite of the original movement being a 'great favourite' of Mozart – and to incorporate 'a passage that I felt sure must please' in the middle of the first movement, subsequently bringing it back at the end in order to please the audience still further, Mozart's inclusion of the *premier coup d'archet* underscores a pragmatic approach to integrating orchestral effects into his works and, indeed, to the composition of orchestral music in general.[7]

Mozart's preoccupation with orchestration and orchestral effects is part of a prevailing concern for these issues among late eighteenth-century and early nineteenth-century theorists and critics. Above all, the Classical symphony, on account of its large complement of instruments, is required to convey a 'grand' tone, whether grandeur analogous to that of a Pindaric ode and 'similar to the great plan and character of an epic poem', or grandeur that is 'powerful [and] convulsive' with 'more of the earthly about it than the sense of the sublime'.[8] Equally, symphonic composers are repeatedly urged to strive for textural equality among instrumental participants.[9] As François de Chastellux explains in 1765, drawing an analogy between the symphony and conversation, such an approach guarantees apposite instrumental effects:

> The German symphonists ... are less interested in finding simple motives then in producing beautiful effects by the harmony that they draw from the great number of instruments that they use, and from the manner in which they work them successively. Their symphonies are a kind of concerto in which the instruments shine, each in its turn, provoking and responding, arguing and making up. It is a lively and sustained conversation.[10]

Mozart's skills as an orchestrator were often remarked upon during his lifetime and in the decades immediately after his death. Leopold praises Mozart in 1780 for composing 'with so much discernment for the various instruments' and for requiring 'unusually close attention from the players of every type of instrument'.[11] In addition, Franz Xaver Niemetschek claims in 1798 that Mozart 'judged with extreme accuracy the nature and range of all instruments' and 'the exact time and place to make his effect' thus '[evoking] the admiration of all experts'. He continues: 'Never is an instrument wasted or misused, and, therefore, redundant. But he also knew how to achieve his most magical effects with true economy, entailing the least effort, often through a single note on an instrument, by means of a chord or a trumpet blast.'[12]

While Mozart's father and early biographer are hardly the most impartial witnesses to the composer's proficiency as an orchestrator, the comments of Niemetschek are certainly supported by Georg Wilhelm Friedrich Hegel's eloquent testimony to Mozart's excellence in the symphonic medium. In an extended lecture on music from the 1820s, Hegel comments:

> To blend the various kinds of string and woodwind, to learn how to introduce the thunder of the trumpet-blast, how to emphasize first one and then another class of distinctive sounds most effectively, has required long experience with the instruments themselves . . . Mozart is the great master of instrumentation in this respect. In his symphonies . . . the controlled passing from one class of instruments to another has often struck me as a dramatic interplay of dialogue of the most varied kind.[13]

Such praise for Mozart's orchestration is not universal among classical critics and isolated criticisms are voiced: one writer discovers moments in *Don Giovanni* that are 'overloaded with instrumental detail'; another identifies wind instruments that are 'too loquacious' in *Die Entführung aus dem Serail*; and a third criticizes the overly intricate orchestration of the second theme of the first movement of the G minor Symphony, K. 550.[14] However, the writer on K. 550 at least (Jérôme-Joseph de Momigny) implicitly acknowledges that the 'interruption' of the wind in bar 45–6 – one of his main bones of contention – is not up to the composer's usual standards of orchestration; according to Momigny the 'master's hand' quickly re-emerges in the subsequent 'little imitation' of the head motif of the main theme from wind to strings (bars 72–88). In any case, Mozart's extraordinary expertise as an orchestrator has never been systematically called into question either in historical sources or in the secondary literature. In fact, a consideration of matters of instrumentation and orchestration, including Mozart's instrumental effects, his prominent use of the wind and – following writers such as Chastellux and Hegel – the interaction among his orchestral instruments (especially in dialogue), will provide significant insight into Mozart's compositional priorities in his orchestral repertory as a whole.[15]

The orchestral music: 1769–1779

Mozart's interest in assigning an important role to the wind participants in his orchestra, rendering them the equal (or almost the equal) of their string counterparts, is evident in many of his early orchestral works. Although string instruments are more commonly allocated solo roles than wind instruments in Mozart's early cassations, divertimenti and serenades, the oboe and horn assume this function in three movements of the Cassation in D major, K. 100, from 1769. The Divertimento in E flat major, K. 113 (1771), features exposed wind writing throughout, including rudimentary dialogue among the wind and between the wind and the strings. The reorchestrated second version of K. 113, probably dating from spring 1773, expands the wind contingent from two clarinets and two horns to two oboes, two clarinets, two cors anglais, two bassoons and two horns, thus accentuating the musical presence of the wind still further.[16] Mozart's next divertimento, K. 131 in D major (1772), illustrates the wind's role as a potential equal of the strings in an even more direct fashion. The instruments performing each of the principal sections of the first minuet and trio movement, for example, change systematically; while the strings are heard alone in the minuet, the three trios are performed by the four horns, the flute, oboe and bassoon and the four horns respectively, with all instruments coming together – fittingly – in the twenty-four-bar coda. In the second minuet and trio, too, Mozart takes care to balance instrumental participation: the horns perform the A and A' section of the minuet and the strings and woodwind the B section; the flute and strings and the oboe and strings feature in the first and second trios; and the whole ensemble rounds off the movement with a tutti coda.

The prominent role assigned to the wind in Mozart's early orchestral works is especially striking in the G minor Symphony from 1773, K. 183, since Mozart combines succinct instrumental interaction with striking instrumental effects. The repeat of the twelve-bar main theme of the first movement, for example, is totally transformed in mood and affect by the solo oboe restatement of the first four bars plus a continuation (bars 17–25) taking over from the combined syncopated–semibreve statement in the oboe, horns and strings (bars 13–17). In place of the rhythmically driven *Sturm und Drang* tutti of bars 5–12 a pure and tranquil *piano* oboe melody in semibreves soars above accompanimental writing in the strings. Moreover, the registral highpoint of the oboe line (b♭'', bar 23), heard concurrently with the registral low point in the strings (cello E♭), coincides with the harmonic climax of the restatement (German augmented sixth). Thus, Mozart integrates an affective transformation of the theme, a new solo role for the oboe and a moment of gentle melodic and harmonic intensification in one fell swoop.

Following the first part of a development section in which the solo oboe version of the main theme is a notable feature (see bars 97–101, 103–7), Mozart introduces conspicuous interaction of strings and wind to rival the effect witnessed at the restatement of the main theme of K. 183 from the beginning of the movement. The retransition (bars 109–16) comprises the only strict alternation of strings (109–14) and wind (115–16) in the movement as a whole and contains the only segment scored *exclusively* for the full wind contingent of two oboes and two horns. The imitated, sequentially falling string lines – foreshadowing the corresponding retransitional passage in the first movement of the G minor Symphony, K. 550 (bars 160–6), in motivic and procedural terms – give way to the oboes and horns. Building on the earlier solo role of the oboe by continuing to include a semibreve rhythm and by featuring solo wind performance, the horns and oboes now assume the important structural responsibility of leading the orchestra directly into the recapitulation, a move accentuated by the *piano* to *forte* crescendo. As in bars 13–25, Mozart succinctly combines a careful distribution of instruments, a prominent role for the wind and a striking instrumental effect.

K. 183 has traditionally been identified as a landmark in Mozart's orchestral oeuvre, with critics often attributing the overall increase in musical intensity to the work's status as Mozart's first minor-key symphony.[17] Such stylistic distinction for K. 183 was not recognized in the late eighteenth century, however, at least judging by an article from the *Allgemeine Musikalische Zeitung* (1799) presumably by the then editor Friedrich Rochlitz. Failing to distinguish K. 183 from three major-key symphonies from 1773–4 and heavily prejudiced in favour of Mozart's late instrumental works, the author brands all four 'entirely ordinary symphonies … without conspicuous characteristics of originality and novelty'.[18] While it is difficult to deny K. 183 the quality of concentrated passion (*pace* Rochlitz, perhaps), as a whole K. 183 is better understood in continuity with Mozart's earlier 1773 symphonies (K. 184, 199, 162, 181, 182) – albeit as a climactic point in this particular sequence – than as a stylistic break from his earlier works resulting from a demonstrative venture into the minor mode. The dialogic engagement between strings and wind in K. 183/ii (echoes and answers in the bassoons in bars 1–9 and 40–8 and responses in the oboes and bassoons in bars 49–57) and the prominence of the wind elsewhere in the movement as well (sustained wind chords in bars 16–19 and 64–8 and unaccompanied chords in bar 36) is much in evidence in the preceding slow movements K. 184/ii, 199/ii, 162/ii and 182/ii. The *Sturm und Drang* style witnessed initially in K. 183/i in bars 5–10 is foreshadowed in bars 12–21 and 54–63 of K. 184/i and bars 71–8 of K. 199/i; similarly, the distinctive combination of a *forte* unison opening and half-step ascents incorporated into a falling line at the beginning of K. 183/i is foreshadowed in K. 162/i (bars 22–6). In addition, the strings–wind interaction preceding the recapitulation of K. 183/i is prefigured at the corresponding juncture of K. 182/i: just as the clear separation of strings and wind and the solo performance of oboes and horns in bars 109–16 of K. 183/i is reserved for this one passage in the movement, so the antecedent–consequent dialogue between the strings and horns and the oboes in bars 69–73 of K. 182/i is exceptional in providing the only strings–wind dialogue and the only moments of exclusive wind participation in its movement. If K. 183 appears more formidable and compelling than its immediate predecessors (particularly in the first movement), this is not because Mozart altered his compositional priorities wholesale in moving to the minor mode, but rather because he combined pre-existent stylistic practices in an especially taut and concise fashion.

Following three symphonies in 1774, K. 201 – often considered one of Mozart's ground-breaking early works alongside K. 183 – K. 202 and K. 200, Mozart took leave of the genre until 1778.[19] Instead, these years witnessed several splendid orchestral serenades, especially K. 203, K. 204 and K. 250 ('Haffner') from 1774, 1775 and 1776, respectively, in which Mozart continues to demonstrate keen attention to prominent wind scoring and sonorities and to the wind's interaction with the strings, in spite of also writing inner concerto movements for the solo violin.[20] The G major Andantes of both K. 203 and K. 204, for example, combine melodic distinction for selected wind instruments with dialogic interaction between wind and strings. The oboe's solo theme in bars 14–25 of K. 203 includes second violin and viola segues between phrases (bars 15, 17) taking up the oboe's demisemiquavers, and ends with a trill figure (bars 24–5) that provides the foundation for the immediately ensuing string line (bars 25–9). An even more forthright sequence of solo prominence for the oboe and dialogue with the strings is evident in the coda; a new oboe solo (bars 76–83) leads directly to semiquaver imitation (oboe and second violin, bars 83–6) that concludes the movement. The K. 204 G major Andante also combines these two traits. The flute theme in bars 9–16, partially dialogued by the bassoon (bars 17–20), highlights intricate give and take between the wind and the violins, especially when the violins' trill-like segue in the middle of the flute and bassoon phrases (bars 14, 18; see example 7.1) inspire the flute and bassoon to adopt the same figure for concluding their thematic presentations (bars 15, 19). The flute and bassoon solos lead, in turn, to an oboe solo featuring accompanimental dialogue between strings and wind (bars 21–4), an exchange of arpeggiated semiquavers between flute and violins (25–6) and a strict alternation of complete string and wind sections in a kind of antecedent–consequent dialogue (bars 30–4), thereby unveiling a rich tapestry of dialogue across the section as a whole.

In contrast to the wind in the G major Andantes from K. 203 and K. 204, the wind in the 'Haffner' Serenade, K. 250, participate in relatively few solos or dialogues with the strings. Their distinctive function emerges instead in Mozart's exploration of different sonorities, in the effects he can achieve with striking combinations of wind instruments. The minuet and

Example 7.1 Mozart, Serenade in D major, K. 204/v, bars 13–16

trio movements are especially revealing in this respect. In the trio of the first, the solo violin is accompanied only by the wind, featuring a euphonious combination of two flutes, two bassoons and two horns. In contrast, Trio II of the last minuet and trio brings together flute lines independent of the strings and a military-style trumpet part. Elsewhere, Mozart ensures a prominent presence for wind sonorities, even when they do not dominate the texture – the repeated accompanimental *piano* chords scored for the Rondeau's entire wind contingent of two flutes, two bassoons and two horns in bars 227–44 provide a case in point.

Mozart's return to the symphony in 1778 heralded a work with as large a number of orchestral parts as any of his earlier or later symphonies. The 'Paris' Symphony, K. 297, scored for two flutes, two oboes, two clarinets, two bassoons, two horns, two trumpets, timpani and strings, has recently been criticized for featuring 'grandiose gestures...strangely empty compared with his symphonic best' and for being stylistically unadventurous.[21] In one important respect, however, K. 297 illustrates how succinctly, coherently and thoughtfully conceived Mozart's orchestral works are at this stage of his career. As explained above, Mozart included the *premier coup d'archet* at the beginning of the first movement in order to please his Parisian audience. But in contrast to two of the 1773 symphonies, K. 162 and 181, in which similarly grand opening gestures are simply calls to attention failing to reappear at the corresponding point of the recapitulation, for example, the *coup d'archet* of the 'Paris' Symphony (with the ascending semiquaver scales that immediately follow) is thoroughly integrated into the musical argument of the first movement and its dramatic potential fully explored. Playing the three tutti chords *piano* in bars 7–8, the wind simultaneously echo the first statement (bars 1–4) and foreshadow the second (bars 9–12), thus creating a smooth segue between thematic presentations. Later, a tutti statement of the motto in bars 48–51 leads to the secondary theme, but via a portentous half-close on the dominant (German augmented sixth to

Example 7.2 Mozart, 'Paris' Symphony, K. 297/i, bars 174–9

V) rather than an affirmation of the new key area. As if to compensate for the temporary harmonic shadow cast over the beginning of the secondary theme by the strong orientation of this augmented-sixth harmony back to the tonic not towards the dominant, the motto next appears at the reconfirmation of the secondary key area in bar 74 following a brief excursion to the dominant minor (70–1), now heard in diminution and in imitation (see bars 74–80, then 93–9).

The development and recapitulation of K. 297/i exploit the potential of the opening motto still further. A B♭ intrudes at the end of the second statement at the beginning of the development, jolting the music away from the dominant and again emphasizing the motto's harmonic force (bar 132). While the C natural added to the presentation a few bars into the recapitulation (bar 176) 'conjures up memories of the surprising introduction of B♭ at the start of the development',[22] the motto statements at this juncture have a wider significance as well. For the opening of the recapitulation, especially the restatement of the motto (bars 174ff., see example 7.2), brings together musical workings of the motto witnessed thus far. Just as the C natural represents its force in a harmonic capacity, so the imitation in bars 174–86 – the first time the original version of the motto has been treated in this way – evokes its function in the secondary theme section of the exposition. In addition, the original echoing and foreshadowing of the motto in the wind at the beginning of the exposition is retained (bars 170–3). In short, bars 164–86 constitute both a climactic moment in the 'life' of the motto and a microcosmic representation of the uses to which it is put in the movement as a whole.

If K. 297/i marks a high point among Mozart's pre-Viennese orchestral works in its taut assimilation of an orchestral effect, the famous 'Posthorn' Serenade, K. 320 (1779) – Mozart's last serenade for full orchestra – marks

Example 7.3 Mozart, 'Posthorn' Serenade, K. 320/i, bars 46–54

a similar high point in its writing for the orchestral wind section. The high quality of Salzburg's wind instrumentalists was recognized at this time, Christian Friedrich Daniel Schubart remarking on the 'especially distinguished' performers and Friedrich Siegmund von Böcklin identifying 'several fine wind players',[23] and their talents would have been particularly well exploited in the concertante Andante grazioso and Rondeau middle movements that feature elaborate solo wind parts. Here, the wind engage in numerous imitative, split-theme and full-theme dialogues, 'forming an ensemble of exquisite conversationalists' according to one recent writer.[24] Mozart reveals elsewhere in this serenade, too, that his dialogic technique has reached a new level of sophistication, one we shall witness frequently in the Viennese concertos and symphonies; in the first violin's presentation of the secondary theme of the first movement (bars 46–65), for example, the first oboe provides not only the final bar of each phrase (bars 49, 53, 57, 61) but also the smoothest of segues between phrases, on each occasion entering and exiting on the same pitches as those on which the violin exits and enters (see example 7.3).

Mozart's Viennese symphonies, 1782–1788

Although Mozart devoted considerably less energy to the composition of symphonies in Vienna than he had devoted to symphonies, divertimenti and serenades in Salzburg (and on his travels) in the late 1760s and 1770s, it is still difficult to regard his six Viennese symphonies, K. 385 in D major, 'Haffner' (1782), K. 425 in C major, 'Linz' (1783), K. 504 in D major, 'Prague' (1786), K. 543 in E flat major (1788), K. 550 in G minor (1788) and K. 551 in C major, 'Jupiter' (1788), as anything other than climactic works in his orchestral oeuvre. This is the case for interaction among instruments, for the consistently prominent use of the wind, and for the realization of the late eighteenth-century theoretical goal of textural equality in the symphony, just as it is also the case for aspects of Mozart's style more often discussed in the secondary literature, such as the manipulation of motivic and thematic material.

Many movements from Mozart's Viennese symphonies demonstrate a systematic attitude towards the organization and development of dialogue. In the first movement of the 'Linz', for example, material close to the end of each major section is characterized by imitative dialogue in one- and two-bar units among and between wind and strings (see bars 8–18 (slow introduction), 105–11 (exposition), 158–61 (development), 251–7 (recapitulation)). While imitation is the primary type of dialogue, Mozart introduces another kind – the splitting of thematic material – in the secondary theme section (see bars 75–9 and 221–5). The coda brings together these two traits (imitation in bars 265–75 and 278–81 and split-theme dialogue in 274–8), thus encapsulating the movement's overall approach to dialogue and, fittingly, extending the process of rounding off a section with concise dialogue to the movement as a whole.

The finale of the 'Prague' Symphony reveals not only a teleological dimension to dialogue, as in K. 425/i, but also a symmetrical arrangement of dialogue in the exposition and recapitulation. The most balanced dialogue of the exposition in terms of wind and string involvement – the repeated secondary theme split between the two instrumental groups (bars 66–81 and 82–98) – occurs right in the middle of the 151-bar section and is framed by statements of the movement's primary thematic material alternating between strings and wind (bars 1–30, 31–46, 47–63 and 110–20 (including bassoon), 120–38, 138–51). This design is retained in the recapitulation, but rendered more taut through a compression of the violin's initial statement of the primary material from thirty bars into eight (216–23) and through an interpolation of *forte* tremolo-minim writing into the wind's initial statement (bars 224–43) closely resembling the procedure at the beginning of the development (bars 156–75). Thus, the newly compact wind–strings exchange and the addition of ostensibly 'dramatic' interventions in the wind's presentation of the primary material conspire to intensify dialogue at the beginning of the recapitulation.

Two further movements, K. 543/iv and K. 550/i, progressively increase the involvement of their wind participants and, as a result, strive for the kind of textural equality recognized by late eighteenth-century writers on the symphony such as Chastellux. In the first part of the exposition of K. 543/iv the strings not only dominate the statement of the main theme but also cut short the wind's attempt to engage in split-theme dialogue in the secondary theme (see bars 43–4 and 49–50). Subsequently, however, the flute and bassoon (bars 55–61) followed by the flute, clarinet and bassoon (bars 80–5) dialogue the head motif; the strings enter into dialogue with the wind in the later passage, too (bars 86–9), as if finally acknowledging the important role of the wind instruments as independent interlocutors. Emphasizing that they have found their autonomous voice, the wind add their own split-theme dialogue to the presentation of the main theme at the beginning of the recapitulation (flute and bassoon, bars 154–60).

The wind become increasingly active interlocutors over the course of K. 550/i – at least as far as presentation of the principal thematic material is concerned – just as they assert themselves with increasing confidence during K. 543/iv. The fastidiously equal dialogic distribution between strings and wind of the secondary theme and its repeat (bars 44–57) sparks greater dialogic equality in the presentation of the main theme in the rest of the movement than observed hitherto. The wind and strings twice exchange statements of the head motif towards the end of the exposition (bars 73–80 and 81–8), engage in extended imitation of the same figure in the development (bars 139–52) as well as using it to segue elegantly into the recapitulation (bars 160–6), and introduce a succession of imitative entries in the coda (bars 286–93).

While dialogic sophistication abounds in movements such as K. 425/i, K. 504/iv, K. 543/iv and K. 550/i, no individual movement surpasses Mozart's final symphonic endeavour in this respect, the finale of the 'Jupiter', K. 551. To be sure, the fugal writing integrated into the sonata-form structure ensures a large amount of imitative dialogue, but the significance of imitative dialogue in the movement as a whole goes well beyond its quantity. As in K. 504/iv but in a more intricate and pronounced fashion, Mozart combines rudimentarily symmetrical distribution of dialogue with teleological thrust. In the exposition, for example, the exchange of themes 4, 5, 3 and 2 among the first violin, oboe, bassoon and flute in the secondary theme (bars 74–86) is framed in bars 56–73 and 86–110 by a combination of sequential imitations on 3 and a stretto (on theme 2 in the earlier passage and theme 4

Example 7.4 Principal themes from Mozart's 'Jupiter' Symphony, K. 551/iv

in the later). (See example 7.4 for the five principal themes of the movement.) At the same time, dialogue increases in intensity as the exposition
progresses: the stretto in bars 98–110 features four entries and is sequentially
repeated twice in contrast to the stretto in bars 64–73 which includes three
entries and is repeated only once; and the stretto in bars 135–45, repeated
twice, takes in both theme 2 and its inversion, again going beyond the earlier stretto on theme 2 (bars 64–73) in procedural terms. The development
section is also end-orientated where instrumental interaction is concerned.
The alternation of themes 1 and 2 in bars 158–72 and the stretto on 2 in bars
172–86 are combined in bars 186–207, while the subsequent imitation of
the beginning of theme 2 leading directly to theme 1 at the beginning of the
recapitulation (bars 219ff.) negates the earlier sense of opposition between
these themes.

The recapitulation and coda of K. 551/iv take the symmetrical and teleological organization of dialogue in the exposition and development sections
to a new level. The framing of the secondary theme (imitative and stretto
passages) now extends to the framing of the section as a whole, with the
new stretto on theme 1 in the secondary development (violins, bars 241–52)
being complemented by a stretto on 1 in original and inverted forms at the
beginning of the coda (bars 360–71). Two new procedures in the recapitulation intensify the interaction witnessed in the exposition: the repeated
statement of the secondary theme (bars 278–84), unlike the corresponding
segment of the exposition, rescores the wind presentations of themes 5, 3

and 2 from the initial statement, emphasizing the invertibility of the themes and foreshadowing the invertible counterpoint in the coda; and the climactic arrival of e''' (bar 332), after an ascending sequence extended from the exposition, coincides with a dotted-crotchet–quaver cadential gesture (bars 332–4) that pre-empts the use of the same figure in the ensuing stretto, thus creating a link between material not previously linked in the exposition. Above all, the double fugue on themes 1 and 4, and the canonic combination of themes 1, 2, 3, 4 and 5 in five-part invertible counterpoint in bars 372–402 of the coda provide a fitting climax to the dialogic intensification of the recapitulation and, more generally, the profusion of dialogue in the movement as a whole; a rich tapestry of dialogue arises out of the presentation of a different theme every four bars in each of the wind and string parts. There can be few passages in Mozart's oeuvre that more powerfully exemplify his 'true economy' of instrumental effect (Niemetschek) and 'dramatic interplay of dialogue' (Hegel). Indeed, little in the entire literature better illustrates the 'lively . . . conversation' (Chastellux) and textural equality required of the symphony by late eighteenth-century writers. Even the horns and trumpets contribute to a sense of instrumental equality in bars 388–402, in spite of not participating in the intricate thematic exchange. With their direct, straightforward march, the horns and trumpets set a foundation for observing the dialogic workings of wind and strings and establish their own important presence through an assertive musical topic.[25]

While the 'Jupiter' finale marks a particularly emphatic climax to Mozart's orchestral music in interactional terms, his six Viennese symphonies also underscore stylistic high points of a more general nature. The 'Prague' Symphony, for example, is more topically and gesturally heterogeneous and complex than any of his preceding works in the genre.[26] In addition, the G minor Symphony, typically considered one of Mozart's most progressive, proto-Romantic works, contains some of his most audacious harmonic writing, particularly at the beginning of the development sections of the first and last movements (bars 101–105 and 125–35 respectively).[27] In any case, it is quite remarkable testimony to the fluidity of Mozart's compositional technique that all six symphonic masterworks (with the possible exception of the 'Prague') were composed in extraordinary haste – Mozart wrote the 'Haffner' 'as fast as possible', the 'Linz' at 'breakneck speed' and his last symphonic trilogy inside two months in 1788.[28] Surely no major works in the history of Western music as hurriedly composed as Mozart's Viennese symphonies have had such a profound, far-reaching impact on our collective musical consciousness.

8 Mozart's chamber music

CLIFF EISEN

SALIERI: ... the concert began. I heard it through the door – some serenade – at first only vaguely ... but presently the sound insisted – a solemn Adagio in E flat. It started simply enough: just a pulse in the lowest registers – bassoons and basset horns – like a rusty squeezebox. It would have been comic except for the slowness, which gave it instead a sort of serenity. And then suddenly, high above it, sounded a single note on the oboe. It hung there unwavering, piercing me through, till breath could hold it no longer, and a clarinet withdrew it out of me, and sweetened it into a phrase of such delight it had me trembling. The light flickered in the room. My eyes clouded! The squeezebox groaned louder, and over it the higher instruments wailed and warbled, throwing lines of sound around me – long lines of pain around and through me. Ah, the pain! Pain as I had never known it. I called up my sharp old God, '*What is this? ... What?!*' But the squeezebox went on and on, and the pain cut deeper into my shaking head, until suddenly I was running, dashing through the side door, stumbling downstairs into the street, into the cold night, gasping for life.[1]

Salieri's description of Mozart's Serenade for Winds in B flat major, K. 361 (example 8.1), does the work – as well as some commonly held beliefs concerning both Mozart and chamber music – surprising justice on a number of counts: it describes a sophisticated interplay of instruments (oboe and clarinet), an enveloping intimacy of expression ('around and through me') and a self-conscious manipulation of artifice and affect ('it would have been comic except for the slowness, which gave it instead a sort of serenity'). But is the serenade, composed for thirteen wind instruments with double bass and performed publicly at the Burgtheater on 23 March 1784, a piece of chamber music?

Today, 'chamber music' is understood to mean intimate, carefully crafted music for a small instrumental ensemble played one to a part and intended either for private performance or for performance in a small hall. The serenade therefore appears to be a different kind of work. For Mozart and Salieri, however, it was unquestionably chamber music. During the eighteenth century, the term – found in theoretical writings by Brossard, Mattheson, Rousseau and Koch[2] – was used to distinguish both a broad stylistic category and a normal venue, one among three: church, theatre and chamber. It included not only instrumental music for small, one-to-a-part ensembles, such as trios with or without keyboard, quartets or quintets, but also

Example 8.1 Mozart, Serenade for Winds in B flat major, K. 361/iii, bars 1–7

symphonies, concertos, works for one instrument, cantatas and songs.[3] This definition applied well into the nineteenth century and while it did not imply purity of style – eighteenth-century church music was frequently described as operatic (sometimes even borrowing traditional opera seria forms such as the da capo aria), theatrical music regularly took over gestures from church music (for example the trombones in the graveyard scene in *Don Giovanni*) and chamber music, especially symphonies, frequently approximated the theatrical style – the general boundaries were nevertheless clear enough.

It was not until the mid- and late nineteenth century that 'chamber music' took on its modern meaning, and even then the definitions proposed were retrospective, based largely on the prestige of Haydn's, Mozart's and Beethoven's quartets (as well as other similar works by these canonic composers, including string quintets and piano trios) rather than eighteenth-century practice. This meaning dictated an understanding not only of substance and style – intimate, complex and highbrow – but also of scoring, the number and order of movements, and superficial generic characteristics. Works not fitting the 'historical' description were dismissed as precursors, as light music lacking depth and compositional sophistication, intended solely for entertainment and diversion, not for serious contemplation,[4] or, in the case of non-standard scorings, as experimental, reactionary or outside the 'main stream'.

This profoundly evolutionary view of chamber music has little to do with the realities of the eighteenth century and the immense variety of chamber music traditions practised across Europe. For Mozart, these traditions were overwhelmingly the predominant context for his music. What is more, his compositional choices reflect not only time and place but also a personal aesthetic that grew and changed over the course of his life.

Early chamber music to 1780

Documentary evidence for the performance of chamber music in Salzburg notwithstanding – Mozart himself occasionally mentions performances at court – it appears that one-to-a-part ensemble music was not widely cultivated in the archdiocese during the 1760s or 1770s. And local taste, at least insofar as scoring is concerned, was less up to date than elsewhere in Europe. There is no evidence for the composition of string quartets in Salzburg before the mid-1770s[5] and virtually no chamber music with keyboard. Instead, it was trios for two violins and basso or divertimenti for string quartet and two horns that were common. Mozart's divertimenti K. 247 (1776), K. 287 (1777) and K. 334 (1779–80), belong to this tradition. They are leisurely works in six movements, often with introductory marches, and probably intended for specific occasions: K. 247, for example, was composed to celebrate the name day of Countess Antonia Lodron.[6] And he composed only one string trio in Salzburg, K. 266 (1777). On the whole, chamber music in the archdiocese was a conservative affair, although more exotic scorings can sometimes be found: during the 1750s, Leopold Mozart composed divertimenti for violin, cello and double bass and for two cellos and double bass, while Wolfgang, in the mid-1770s, composed divertimenti for two horns, bassoon and strings (K. 205) and oboe, two horns and strings (K. 251).[7]

Mozart's works for strings only, as well as his accompanied sonatas, accordingly derive from his travels. These include two sets of string quartets (K. 155–60, Milan 1772–3, and K. 168–73, Vienna 1773),[8] two flute quartets (K. 285 and 285a, Mannheim 1777–8), an oboe quartet (K. 370, Munich 1781) and a set of piano and violin sonatas (K. 301–6, Mannheim and Paris 1777–8).[9] The early Milanese quartets largely conform to Italian traditions: each is in three movements, several have expressive minor-key middle movements (K. 157–9) and there are extended contrapuntal passages (possibly Mozart was showing off for his Italian mentors, Padre Martini and Eugène Ligniville), although on the whole the works are characterized by transparent textures with the bulk of the melodic and harmonic interest situated in the first violin and cello parts. That K. 155–60 are 'Italian' quartets – or, better, that Mozart tailored his chamber music to local audiences – is clear from the Viennese set, K. 168–73, composed barely six months later. These are more serious works, featuring four movements (the prevailing Viennese style) and fully developed fugues (in the finales of K. 168 and K. 173). Until recently, Mozart scholarship pinned Mozart's inspiration on Joseph Haydn's newly composed quartets, Op. 17 and Op. 20, but it is just as likely that he adopted a generalized local style of which Haydn's are perhaps the finest examples.[10] And it is frequently suggested that K. 168–73 were composed to impress the Imperial Court, where Leopold hoped to obtain an appointment for his son.

The accompanied sonatas, on the other hand, probably owe their origin as much to Mozart's performing as to his self-representation as a composer: on the road, they gave him a chance to show off both his compositional and his performing skills in places where works of this sort were highly regarded. It is easy to forget that Mozart was a talented string player, that his first appointment in Salzburg was as a violinist and that he continued to play regularly, at least until his move to Vienna in 1781. A report from Salzburg, dated 16 October 1769, describes a private concert at which 'the daughter [Nannerl] first played the keyboard, then Wolfgangus, a youth aged thirteen, sang and played the violin and the keyboard to everyone's astonishment',[11] and his earliest independent concerto was not for keyboard but for violin (K. 207, 1773).[12] In late 1777 Mozart wrote to his father:

> The day before yesterday . . . we had a little concert here . . . I played my [keyboard] concertos in C, B-flat and E-flat, and after that my trio [K. 254] . . . As a finale I played my last *Cassation* in B-flat [K. 287]. They all opened their eyes! I played as though I were the finest fiddler in all Europe.[13]

Leopold wrote back:

I am not surprised that when you played your last *Cassation* they all opened their eyes. You yourself do not know how well you play the violin, if you will only do yourself credit and play with energy, with your whole heart and mind, yes, just as if you were the first violinist in Europe.[14]

The sonatas that Mozart wrote at Mannheim are traditionally thought to have been influenced by Joseph Schuster,[15] although at least one sonata, K. 301, began life as a work for flute. Throughout the set, Schuster's influence is not too distant: the first movement of K. 303, for example, in which an Adagio introduction represents the 'first' subject and appears again at the recapitulation, seems to be modelled on the Dresden composer's sonatas. And five of the sonatas are in two movements. Nevertheless, it is the expressive Mannheim style that dominates: frequent turns to the minor, jarring dissonances and harmonic and rhythmic disjunctions betray a sensibility close to that of north German music, a sensibility best represented in C. P. E. Bach's works. This is particularly true of the E minor Sonata, K. 304, with its stark unison opening in the first movement, abrupt shift to G major that never fully dispels the darkness of the minor, canonic, bitingly dissonant development and surprisingly reharmonized recapitulation. At the same time, it is worth noting that K. 304 was not composed at Mannheim but at Paris; consequently it has to reckon with works such as the A minor Piano Sonata, K. 310, as well. So does K. 305, also composed in the French capital, even if it is an entirely different kind of composition. One of the most genial of the sonatas composed about this time, it includes two movements: an introductory Allegro di molto and a theme and variations Andante grazioso. The 6/8 metre and triadic motives of the Allegro conjure up a bucolic pastoral-hunting atmosphere even if the chase seems to go on longer than expected: fully half of the first part of the movement is given to cadential gestures and pedal points of increasing agitation (perhaps the prey is more elusive than we are at first led to believe). The variations, on the other hand, are typically Mannheim, not least in the ornamental opening to the second variation and the *ad libitum* adagio of the fourth. Still, the hunt is never far away and the triple-time allegro variation that concludes the set re-inscribes the pastoral mood of the sonata's first movement.

Vienna 1781–1788

In Vienna, where he took up permanent residence in the spring of 1781, Mozart discovered a different chamber music culture: both his professional circumstances and the ways in which chamber music was cultivated locally gave rise to new and different opportunities for the composer. Mozart was not associated with the court, where chamber music was frequently performed, nor did it figure in public concerts. But it was widely pursued at the homes of the nobility (among them Baron van Swieten, who had Mozart arrange for string quartet several of J. S. Bach's fugues, for which Mozart also composed new preludes) and by the public at large: the bulk of music printed and sold in Vienna during the 1780s was solo keyboard and chamber music. A composer's first calling card was usually a set of accompanied sonatas and Mozart was no exception: K. 296 and K. 376–80 were published by Artaria in December 1781. The sonatas were an immediate success. According to a review from April 1783 published in Carl Friedrich Cramer's widely read and influential *Magazin der Musik*:

> These sonatas are unique of their kind. Rich in new ideas and traces of their author's great musical genius. Very brilliant and suited to the instrument. At the same time, the violin accompaniment is so ingeniously combined with the keyboard part that both instruments are constantly kept in equal prominence; so that these sonatas call for as skilled a violinist as a keyboard player.[16]

In some respects the sonatas recall the music composed just before Mozart's move to Vienna – there are traces here of *Idomeneo* and the earlier accompanied sonatas, K. 301–6. But on the whole they look ahead to the leaner textural style of the period up to 1784 and in particular the piano concertos K. 413–15. (It is worth remarking here that the 'chamber style' as we think of it was still not a fixed idea: when Mozart advertised the three piano concertos, he stated that they could be performed '*a quattro*... with 2 violins, 1 viola and violoncello', that is, as piano quintets.)[17] The works are full of surprises: K. 378 includes a sonata movement with three themes and a rondeau finale with a surprising second episode, in the main key but a different metre; the elaborate G major Adagio of K. 379 begins like a sonata (including a first half repeat) but then proceeds to a half-cadence that does not lead to a recapitulation but, rather, a stormy Allegro in G minor; and K. 380, perhaps the most brilliant of the set, exploits distant key relations (an E flat major sonata with a G minor middle movement) and includes a development section in the first movement that begins and ends with a new theme.

What is equally striking about the sonatas is their exploitation of texture as a primary engine of affect and the equality of the parts: although nominally keyboard sonatas with violin accompaniment, they require, as Cramer's critic pointed out, 'as skilled a violinist as a keyboard player'. This is even more true of the later sonatas, including K. 454, written for the Mantuan violinist Regina Strinasacchi (and performed at the Kärntnerthortheater on 29 April 1784), K. 481 (December 1785) and K. 526 (August 1787 and arguably the finest of Mozart's accompanied sonatas). Indeed, texture as a

Example 8.2 Mozart, String Quintet in G minor, K. 516/iii, bars 1–15

motivating principle is key not only among the sonatas but in Mozart's chamber music generally. The two string quintets of 1787, K. 515 and K. 516, offer numerous instances where textural interest threatens to over-power both harmony and form, none more telling than the Adagio ma non troppo of the G minor quintet. The variety of textures in the first dozen bars alone is almost overwhelming (see example 8.2): block chords in bars 1–2, melody and accompaniment in bars 3–4 and then, in bars 5–8, a sudden dis-solution of the ensemble, mere snatches of material increasingly separated from each other (the first violin's figure rises, the cello's descends), followed by a reconstitution of the middle as the second violin and the violas enter in succession (bar 6) and a fully voiced but deceptive cadence at bar 9 (which is then repeated but leading to a perfect cadence). As if the textural variety, rests, awkward intervals, disjunctions and isolation of single voices were not enough, bars 13 and 14 dissolve the ensemble into little more than sound itself: the succession of *sforzandi* (followed by *piani*) is completely static, a moment of stillness punctuated only by a succession of exploding mini-supernovas outlining the prevailing harmony. It is a unique moment, even among Mozart's works, profoundly captivating for its sheer beauty and its preoccupation not with harmony or melody or rhythm but merely with sound. Other instances of overwhelming textural interest can be found throughout the chamber music: in works such as the Quintet for Piano and Winds, K. 452, or the Trio for Clarinet, Viola and Piano, K. 498, it is the unique scoring that first commands attention. Even the two piano quartets, K. 478 and 493, are novel in this regard. Texture also serves to articulate form. In the Piano Trio in B flat major, K. 502, exposition, development and recapitulation each represent an increasingly complex dialogue between piano and violin, with the cello fully participatory only after the second theme; this recurrent textural shape is as important to the affect of the work as any formal device.

In a sense, the violin sonatas represent not only a beginning – Mozart's concerted attempt to make a good impression in his new home and a departure from the style of his earlier works – but also an ending, for they are among the last of Mozart's chamber works to be gathered and published as a traditional opus of six. All of the succeeding sonatas, as well as the two piano quartets, the 'Hoffmeister' Quartet, K. 499, the Trio for Clarinet, Viola and Piano, K. 498, the Quintet for Piano and Winds, K. 452, the string quintets and piano trios are one-off compositions, mostly intended for publication by themselves.[18] The one exception is the six quartets composed and revised by Mozart between 1782 and 1785 and published by Artaria that year with a dedication to Haydn. Mozart described the works as 'the fruits of a long and laborious endeavour', a claim apparently borne out by the relatively large number of quartet fragments from this time and by numerous corrections and changes in the autographs.[19] That Mozart sought to emulate Haydn's recent Op. 33 quartets (but not slavishly to imitate them) can hardly be doubted. Like Haydn's, Mozart's quartets are characterized by textures conceived not merely in four-part harmony, but as four-part discourse, with the actual musical ideas linked to a freshly integrated treatment of the medium. Counterpoint in particular takes on a new importance in the quartets. In the first movements of K. 421 and K. 464, each of the principal themes is subjected to imitative treatment. The Andante of K. 428

follows similar procedures, supported by increased chromaticism (characteristic of the quartet as a whole). The coda of the first movement of the 'Hunt' Quartet, K. 458, draws on the latent imitative potential of the movement's main thematic material while the famous introduction to the 'Dissonance' Quartet, K. 465, represents an extreme of both free counterpoint and chromaticism.[20] The finale of K. 387 represents a different use of counterpoint, not so much as a texture in and of itself, but as a structural topic. Here the main, stable thematic material is represented primarily by fugatos, while transitional and cadential material is generally composed in a melody-and-accompaniment *buffa* style. (Elsewhere – most notably in the finale of the piano concerto K. 459 – this procedure is reversed: in K. 459/iii fugato represents transition and instability and is explosively elaborated in the double fugue of the central episode.) The multi-functionality of Mozart's thematic material in general, as suitable for both contrapuntal and melody-and-accompaniment treatment, is already adumbrated in the C minor Fugue for Two Pianos, K. 426, and its later version for strings, K. 546, where a seemingly commonplace Baroque subject erupts at the end of the movement in the previously unimaginable guise of a melody supported by aggressive sawing away in the upper parts.[21] Beyond this, the quartets exhibit a kaleidoscopic array of gestures and topics,[22] of formal types and affects: they are the essence of 'chamber music' as it came to be defined in the nineteenth century. Early critics described them as prime examples, together with those of Haydn and Beethoven, of the 'Classical' quartet, as opposed to the *quatuor concertant* (where the different instruments take the melody in turn) or *quatuor brillant* (dominated by the first violin, with the rest of the ensemble accompanying). According to Koch, they are the finest works of their kind.[23]

Vienna 1789–1791

The major chamber works composed by Mozart during the second half of 1788, the Divertimento in E flat major, K. 563, and the Piano Trio in G major, K. 564, have curious histories. It is surprising, in a way, that Mozart composed them at all: they are the only substantial works of any sort written by him between the 'Jupiter' Symphony of August 1788 and the early summer of 1789 (when he began a set of sonatas and the three 'Prussian' Quartets, a legacy of his trip to Berlin that spring).[24] Nor do they appear to have been composed with a general Viennese audience in mind. The divertimento was written privately for Michael Puchberg (and never published during Mozart's lifetime) while the trio was first published in London by Stephen Storace, one of Mozart's English acquaintances resident in Vienna during the mid-1780s. (Stephen's sister, Nancy, was the first Susanna in *Figaro*.)

The Clarinet Quintet, K. 581, of September 1789 was written for Anton Stadler and performed by him at the Burgtheater on 22 December. It marks a rare appearance of a chamber work at a Viennese theatre (although Mozart had set a precedent with his performance of the Quintet for Piano and Winds, K. 452, also at the Burgtheater, on 1 April 1784) and is in many ways a late manifestation of the public 'Classical' style of the mid-1780s, a welding together of diverse gestures over the course of entire paragraphs and entire movements. At the arrival on the dominant in the first movement, for example, a rest in all the parts – more a signal to stop the action after a tutti arrival than an indication of any particular length of silence – is followed by a pizzicato cello line outlining the tonic and fifth of the harmony, long-held notes in the second violin and viola that seem almost to emerge from the preceding silence, and a new lyrical melody in the first violin. The re-entry of the clarinet with the same melody signals further changes: a shift to the minor mode, quieter dynamics and syncopations in the strings. All of these lead to a confrontation between the clarinet and the rest of the ensemble, an outbreak of semiquavers and a conclusive trill, on three instruments, resulting in the firmest cadence in the movement to that point. The effect is to drag the listener along on a wave of increasingly agitated activity.

Yet the Clarinet Quintet is not generally representative of Mozart's prevailing style at the time, which is often characterized as ironic, restrained or serenely detached. Some writers trace the origin of this style to the last three symphonies, others to *Don Giovanni* – whatever its origin, it is pervasive only among the so-called 'late' works. And frequently it provides grounds for dismissal, especially by comparison with the chamber music of the mid-1780s. Hans Keller described the last string quintet, K. 614, as 'a bad arrangement of a wind piece in mock-Haydn style', and adding insult to injury he comments: 'Mozart entered it in his diary on 12 April [1791], and the writing looks somewhat shaky to me; perhaps he was ill.'[25] This may be facetious but in fact Keller appeals to a long tradition of excusing Mozart's late works on grounds of ill-health, depression, financial anxiety or the necessity to compose on demand, whether string quartets for the King of Prussia or on a subject suggested to him by Emperor Joseph II for *Così fan tutte* (a theory now long discredited). Eric Blom, for instance, describes the 'Prussian' Quartets in this way: 'the wonder is that they come so near to Mozart's high-water mark in quartet writing, for all that they were written under the constraint of poverty as well as that of a royal mandate'.[26] And it is not only the twentieth century that condemns these works – the nineteenth century did as well. Blom's precursor is Jahn, writing in 1856: 'These quartets completely maintain Mozart's reputation for inventive powers, sense of proportion and mastery of form, but they lack that absolute devotion to the highest ideal of art characteristic of the earlier ones.'[27]

If the late quartets and quintets are condemned in particular, it is chiefly because they do not correspond to the 'Classical' ideal promoted about 1850 on the basis of the six quartets dedicated to Haydn and the quintets K. 515 and 516 of 1787 – in this sense, they are rejected on broad, bio-graphical grounds and because of the unfulfilled expectation (or perhaps the unfulfilled desire) that they correspond to what was then (and still is) accepted as 'the' Classical style. But there was no such expectation at the time the works were written, nor were the works received as such. An obit-uary notice published in Frankfurt less than two weeks after Mozart's death noted: 'A few weeks before his death he composed another 4 [*sic*] *Quadros* in which he nearly surpassed even himself in art, modulation and inten-sity of expression.'[28] And when Artaria published the 'Prussian' Quartets in December 1791, they advertised them as 'Classical' chamber music, fully worthy of Mozart:

> These quartets are one of the most estimable works of the composer
> *Mozart* ... they flowed from the pen of this so great musical genius not
> long before his death, and they display all that musical interest in respect
> of art, beauty and taste which must awaken pleasure and admiration not
> only in the amateur, but in the true connoisseur also.[29]

What later critics perceived as a new and often unsuccessful 'late' style, then, was not an issue for Mozart's audiences, even though the style of the works is clearly 'different'. The String Quintet in D major, K. 593, for example, has a first movement in a style more spare in texture than that of the pre-ceding quintets but polyphonically richer, especially in the recapitulation where the exposition material is extended and elaborated. The same can be said of K. 614, the minuet of which is canonic while in the finale the devel-opment section includes a double fugue. At the same time, both quintets self-consciously exploit similar topics – each first-movement Allegro begins with a passage imitating horns – while making use of textures in novel ways. The Adagio of K. 593 is a study in sonorities: each of its five large paragraphs is similarly structured around a recurring pattern, beginning with the full ensemble, reducing to three parts (the violins and first viola alternating with the violas and cello) and then returning to five. K. 614 is novel in a different way. Here the first movement can be read as a contest between the first violin and the rest of the ensemble, each vying with the other not only to assert superiority but also to control and direct the musical discourse, achieving rapprochement only in the final bars.

The notion of a contest in the first movement of K. 614 suggests that play on genre, consisting in this case of tension between the 'brilliant' and

Example 8.3 Mozart, String Quintet in E flat major, K. 614/ii, bars 79–90

'Classical' styles identified by early writers on string chamber music, is self-consciously present in Mozart's works of the late 1780s. Generic play is hardly foreign to Mozart's earlier style: the Quintet for Piano and Winds is a concerto in all but name, the slow movement of the Horn Quintet, K. 407, of 1782, is also based on the model of the concerto, and the Piano Sonata in B flat major, K. 333, includes a cadenza. But in the case of K. 614 there is a twist: Mozart manipulates not merely markers of genre but markers of form and procedure as well. The slow movement of K. 614, ostensibly a theme and variations (and among the most popular of Mozart's late variation sets as several contemporaneous arrangements for keyboard show), takes over characteristic gestures not only of the rondo, including tonic restatements of the main theme, but of sonata as well. The passages linking the variations are typical sonata transitions while the climax of the movement, which includes some of the sharpest dissonances in all Mozart, corresponds to the increase in harmonic tension characteristic of a sonata development (see, for instance, example 8.3). A clear return to both tonic and main theme characterizes the final variation (bars 88ff.), which is followed by a sonata-like coda, drawing together the main procedural gestures of the movement.

The same pervasive exploitation of underlying topics characterizes the 'Prussian' Quartets as well. K. 575 gives a hint right off the bat: three of its four movements are titled Allegretto and two of them begin *sotto voce*. In both the first and final movements, a characteristic motive is elaborated, expanded, exploited and fractured but eventually given a majestic statement towards the end. K. 590, on the other hand, is a study in asymmetries, often of an unusual sort: the first movement development is made up almost exclusively of accompanimental gestures, with hardly a tune in sight.[30] The slow movement is not unlike that of K. 614: an almost obsessive set of variations, it masks a sonata structure that eventually gives rise to a coda of stunning beauty.

The essence of the 'late' style, then, is a return to an earlier aesthetic, one of unity of affect. It is not a return to an earlier style, a style characterized by uniformity of surface: for Mozart, the surface remains as varied as ever, sometimes more varied, more disjunctive. But underneath there is a uniformity of idea or topic that motivates and is expressed by the music. In this respect, the later chamber music is strikingly different from the chamber music of the mid-1780s, where variation, change, disruption and disjunction, even at the level of the whole, is paramount. This newly conceived and executed unity of affect is not just a feature of the chamber music, however: it informs the Requiem, *Die Zauberflöte, La clemenza di Tito* and the last concertos as well. It is, in fact, a new style, and, absenting biographical tropes as well as the unrealistic wish that the composer's style remain constant, the later chamber music shares with other works of 1789–91 in a regenerated exploration of music's affective power.

9 Mozart as a vocal composer

PAUL CORNEILSON

In a memorable scene from Peter Shaffer's *Amadeus*, Salieri is introduced to Mozart's music through a performance of the Adagio from the Serenade for Winds in B flat major, K. 361. It causes him to swoon: 'It seemed to me that I had heard a voice of God,' Salieri exclaims in a mixture of admiration and bitterness, 'and that it issued from a creature whose own voice I had also heard – and it was the voice of an obscene child!' (Act 1, scene 5). Although Shaffer's play takes many poetic liberties with historical facts, this remark reflects much of the nineteenth- and twentieth-century reception of Mozart: a child prodigy (or idiot savant) who never grew up, yet wrote inspired, virtually perfect music. This comment put in the fictional Salieri's mouth also makes clear that Mozart's melodic gift is not limited to vocal music; indeed, for Shaffer you are as likely to hear the 'voice of God' in one of his secular instrumental works as in Mozart's sacred vocal music.[1]

In fact, vocal music was of great importance to Mozart, and he was a gifted composer for the human voice. In the hierarchy of music before 1800, vocal genres – opera, oratorio and cantatas – reigned supreme, while even the loftier forms of orchestral music – symphonies and concertos – took a subordinate place. The main problem was summed up in Fontanelle's oft-repeated question: how could a sonata express an *Affekt* or emotion without words to guide the performer and listener? Vocal music and professional singers enjoyed a prestige that simply was not yet available to instrumental music. Even Haydn and Mozart, who did so much to elevate the status of instrumental music towards the end of the eighteenth century, would have taken it for granted that their most important works were operas, oratorios and Masses. Today, we appreciate the entire corpus of their orchestral, chamber and keyboard music, but their early reputations were built largely on major vocal works such as *The Creation*, *Don Giovanni* and the Requiem.

By the early nineteenth century and the rise of absolute music, the tide began to turn. While Mozart's later operas, from *Figaro* to *Die Zauberflöte*, have never been out of the repertory for long, most of his other vocal works, with the exception of the Requiem, were largely forgotten. Even E. T. A. Hoffmann, an early advocate of Mozart's music, had little good to say about his sacred music (as we shall see). Nevertheless, if we want to understand Mozart and his music, we need to re-emphasize the central vocal genres of his time.

Mozart's early childhood training included not only keyboard and violin lessons with his father, but also singing studies with the castrato Giovanni Manzuoli while his family stayed in London between April 1764 and July 1765. When examined by Daines Barrington of the Royal Society, Mozart had already absorbed the basic gestures of *affetto* and *perfido*, as he demonstrated by improvising a 'Love song' and 'Song of rage' at the keyboard.[2] He also wrote his first and only setting of an English text, 'God is our refuge and strength', K. 20, which he proudly presented to the British Museum. Although the piece itself is little more than twenty bars long, it is a competent example of an English antiphon in G minor.[3]

As a young composer Mozart was able to repay his voice teacher by writing for Manzuoli the title role of *Ascanio in Alba* (Milan, 1771). In Milan he also had the opportunity to write for other outstanding singers, including Venanzio Rauzzini and Anna de Amicis. We may be shocked to read that these veteran Italian stars did not always treat the upstart Mozart with respect, as Leopold reports in his letters home to Salzburg. But throughout the eighteenth century leading singers ranked well above composers in the eye of the public, and expected them to defer to their prestige and talent. Nevertheless, Mozart's lifelong association with singers began in Italy, and singers were among his most constant companions throughout his career.

While Handel seems to have been despotic towards his singers, Mozart tried to please them, not because he had to, but rather because he wanted to. His well-known letter to his father of 28 February 1778 – in which he mentions writing two arias, K. 294 and 295, for Aloysia Weber and Anton Raaff respectively – hides no resentment whatsoever. On the contrary, the letter reveals a composer genuinely trying to suit the talents and tastes of his friends.[4] Mozart loved his singers, and he even married one.[5]

In a letter of 7 February 1778, Mozart fully discloses his ambitions to his father: 'I am a composer and was born to be a Kapellmeister.'[6] What did such a statement mean to Mozart? Until the mid-seventeenth century the *cappella* had definite associations with church music, but by the mid-eighteenth century a maestro di cappella (or Kapellmeister) typically wrote both sacred and secular music, whether employed at a cathedral or at court. Alessandro Scarlatti, Vivaldi, Hasse and Jommelli all had success writing sacred and secular music.[7] Years later in a petition to Archduke Francis, Mozart applied for the post of second Kapellmeister, a job for which he felt especially qualified because he had devoted himself to the church style since his youth.[8]

It is important for our purposes to note that the Kapellmeister was also responsible for training and coaching singers. In the letter cited above, Mozart was motivated in large part by his desire to take Aloysia Weber to Italy where she would become a *prima donna*. In other words, Mozart would teach this sixteen-year-old soprano to sing his music specially written for her to make her a star. Leopold strongly opposed this course of action, not because his son was incapable, but rather because such a move would put undue strain on the Mozart family's financial security. Although Mozart never wrote a treatise or method for training singers, his letter to Aloysia Weber of 30 July 1778 gives specific instructions about studying and interpreting his concert aria K. 272.[9] Only in the last months of his life did Mozart come close to realizing his goal of becoming a Kapellmeister.

Mozart as a provincial church musician

Alfred Einstein was not the first person to raise questions about Mozart's church music: 'Is it really Catholic? Is it sincere? Is it appropriate to the church?' One page later he asserts: 'If ever a great musician was a Catholic composer it was Mozart.'[10] Einstein goes on to argue that the composer's exposure to the enlightened ideals of freemasonry in Vienna distracted him from Catholicism. More recently, Alan Tyson has shown that Mozart began a significant number of church pieces only during his last years in Vienna, rather than in the 1770s in Salzburg.[11]

What if Mozart had stayed in Salzburg in the 1780s? On the surface this might seem a ludicrous question, but we should not forget that Mozart took a big risk in leaving the Archbishop's service in May 1781. We do not have any of Leopold's letters to his son from this period, but it is safe to assume he was very upset and hurt by Wolfgang's sudden discharge. Following the successful premiere of *Idomeneo* in January 1781, we can imagine that Mozart was very impatient with the disrespectful treatment he received while accompanying his patron to Vienna. Opportunities for further advancement were rather limited in Salzburg, especially for writing operas. Probably the best Mozart could have hoped for was the early retirement or death of Michael Haydn, the local Kapellmeister, in conjunction with an Archbishop more sympathetic towards the Mozarts than Hieronymus Colloredo had been. One thing is very clear: if Mozart had stayed in Salzburg in the 1780s, he would have continued writing liturgical music for Salzburg cathedral.

The sacred music from Mozart's years in Salzburg divides roughly into three periods. The early works include four Masses (K. 139, 49, 65, 66) written before his first visit to Italy. As an eleven year old, Mozart was commissioned to write the first part of an oratorio, *Die Schuldigkeit des ersten Gebots*, performed in Salzburg on 12 March 1767; Michael Haydn set Part 2 and A. C. Adlgasser Part 3. But it was the striking success of his 'Dominicus' Mass, K. 66, performed at St Peter's for Dominicus Hagenauer, the son of the Mozarts' landlord, on 15 October 1769 that promptly led to Mozart's first Italian trip. The work is scored for two clarini, two trombe and timpani, which create a striking effect in the closing section of the Gloria, 'Cum Sancto Spiritu'. Mozart designed the subject in C major so that in stretto (bars 386ff.) the successive entries by bass, tenor, alto and soprano cover two octaves (subject: C–D–E–F–F–E; answer: G–A–B–C–C–B) in a grand climactic sweep. In Italy he could not only refine his compositional skills but also display his talent to the church fathers in Rome.

Mozart's sojourns in Italy with his father served as a second apprenticeship. Of crucial importance was his encounter with Padre Martini, Europe's leading pedagogue in music history, theory and sacred music. Mozart had some counterpoint lessons with him, probably to test his extraordinary ability, and with Martini's recommendation Mozart received the papal Order of the Golden Spur and became a member of the Accademia Filarmonica in Verona.[12] Mozart's first major commissions also date from this period, an opera seria, *Mitridate, re di Ponto*, and an oratorio, *La Betulia liberata*. The latter, a setting of Metastasio's two-act libretto, was apparently written for Padua in the second quarter of 1771 but was not performed there. By far the most famous work from Mozart's time in Italy is his solo motet 'Exsultate, jubilate', K. 165. This was originally composed in January 1773 for the soprano castrato Rauzzini, who less than a month earlier had created the *primo uomo* role in *Lucio Silla*. This vocal concerto conforms perfectly to contemporaneous definitions of motet, opening with an allegro, followed by an andante, and closing with a presto 'Alleluia' with ample virtuoso passagework.[13]

After his extended visits to Italy, Mozart wrote nine Masses (K. 167, 192, 194, 262, 220, 258, 259, 257, 275), several Vespers or litanies (including K. 125, 195, 193, 243) and other sacred works for Salzburg between 1772 and 1777.[14] During this second period of activity, he wrote only two operas, *La finta giardiniera* and *Il re pastore*, the former written for Munich. And while there are other important instrumental works from the mid-1770s, such as the symphonies in G minor and A major and the violin concertos, the sacred works represent the most sustained and substantial works in the composer's development.[15] To cite only the most famous example of how these earlier works contribute to his later ones, the 'Little Credo' Mass, K. 192, has the same four-note motto on the words 'Credo, Credo' that Mozart used in the finale of the 'Jupiter' Symphony.

For better or worse Mozart and his Salzburg compatriots were constrained by a decree that specified that the musical settings of the Mass should not last more than forty-five minutes. In September 1776 Leopold (using Wolfgang's name) wrote a letter to Padre Martini, in which he enclosed an Offertory and described the situation:

> Our church music is very different from that of Italy, since a Mass with the
> whole Kyrie, Gloria, Credo, the Epistle Sonata, the Offertory or motet,
> Sanctus, and Agnus Dei must not last longer than three quarters of an
> hour, and this applies even to the most solemn Mass celebrated by the
> archbishop himself. You see a particular study is required for this kind of
> composition. At the same time, a Mass must use all the instruments –
> trumpets, timpani, etc.[16]

Although most commentators assume the whole service could last only
forty-five minutes, it is more likely that it was only the musical portion (not
the lessons, prayers and sermon) that had to fit within this timeframe. Even
the shortest settings of the Ordinary by Mozart last twenty minutes, which
would hardly allow for the rest of the service to be completed in forty-five
minutes. The 'particular study' mainly consisted of limiting the amount
of counterpoint and compressing the Mass by having different texts sung
simultaneously by two or more voices, creating what Konrad Küster calls
'polytextualism'.[17] Generally, the longer Gloria and Credo are not subdivided
into smaller sections, even when soloists alternate with chorus. Thus, the
overall effect is of a remarkable efficiency.

Mozart's ties to Salzburg were so deep that a number of works by
other composers, including Johann Ernst Eberlin, Anton Cajetan Adlgasser,
Michael Haydn and his father Leopold, have at one time or another been
attributed to Salzburg's most famous son. While most of the church music
he wrote in the 1770s conforms to Salzburg traditions, the arias exhibit Ital-
ianate features, especially in the litanies K. 125, 195 and 243. The castrato
Francesco Ceccarelli, who arrived in Salzburg shortly after Mozart departed
in September 1777, sang the soprano solos in the *Missa brevis* in B flat major,
K. 275, on 21 December of that year, and in April 1778 he sang the solos in
the litany, probably K. 243.[18]

Following his second continental journey in January 1779 Mozart petitioned the Archbishop and was granted the post of court organist, and
his contract specified that as far as possible he was to write new compositions for the church.[19] He fulfilled these obligations in part by writing
two complete Masses (K. 317 and 337, first performed on Easter Sunday in
1779 and 1780 respectively), two Vespers (K. 321 and 339) and probably
the *Regina coeli*, K. 276. K. 317 is called the 'Coronation' Mass because it
was probably sung at the coronation of Leopold II in Prague in 1791, and it
was certainly heard a year later for the coronation of Leopold's son Francis
as King of Bohemia. Although it is called simply a *Missa* (rather than a
Missa solemnis), it is one of Mozart's most brilliant works. As befitting a
festive occasion, it features a full complement of independent wind parts
(oboes, horns, trumpets, timpani), with three trombones doubling the lower
voices.

Example 9.1 Mozart 'Coronation' Mass, K. 317, Agnus Dei, bars 9–56

Throughout the movements of the 'Coronation' Mass, Mozart makes carefully calculated alternations between tutti and soloists. For the most part the chorus declaims the text in a homophonic texture while the violins swirl around them, giving the Gloria and Credo in particular a symphonic intensity. Each of the movements has a rounded, sonata-like thematic and tonal closure. Particularly effective is the *subito* change of tempo and the texture of the soloists' entrance on the words 'Et incarnatus est' in the Credo. Mozart obviously liked the contrast between the 'Benedictus' (Allegretto, 2/4, solo SATB) and 'Osanna' (Allegro assai, 3/4, tutti SATB) as he repeated it not once as required but twice. In the closing section of the 'Dona nobis pacem' (Andante con moto, solo SATB) Mozart recapitulates material from the middle section of the opening Kyrie (marked 'più andante', solo SATB). The concluding Allegro con spirito for tutti SATB develops the theme and serves as a coda to the work.

Many have noticed that the melodic contour of the Agnus Dei for soprano solo is very close to the opening of the Countess's aria 'Dove sono' in *Figaro*. In the former Mozart provides a modest written-out embellishment, subtly varying the vocal line on the three-fold repetition of the words 'Agnus Dei qui tollis peccata mundi miserere nobis' (see example 9.1, marked (a), (b) and (c)). Did the singer (probably Mozart's friend the castrato Ceccarelli) go further in adding embellishment? We assume not, but here the boundaries between operatic and church styles begin to blur.

In his final complete Mass, K. 337, Mozart began the first three movements, Kyrie, Gloria and Credo, in the typical condensed, Salzburg fashion. But then he plays a trick on the Archbishop and congregation: after

the Sanctus begins in a grand, homophonic style, a solo soprano introduces an unexpectedly playful 'Osanna'. This is followed immediately by a
'Benedictus' in A minor in severe counterpoint interrupted by the repeat of
the 'Osanna' in C major. The Agnus Dei for soprano solo (presumably sung
by Ceccarelli) features an obbligato organ part (played by Mozart), as well
as solo oboe and bassoon, anticipating concertante arias in his late operas.
One has the feeling that at this point in his career Mozart was determined to
write opera even if the works could only be 'staged' in Salzburg cathedral.

Mozart and operatic church music

E. T. A. Hoffmann's essay on 'Old and New Church Music' (1814) heralds the
advent of the revival of Renaissance masters, above all Palestrina. Hoffmann
singles out the church music of Alessandro Scarlatti and C. F. Fasch (the
founder of the Berlin Sing-Akademie) as worthy successors to the 'old'
church style. But the 'modern' Viennese composers of the second half of the
eighteenth century are chastised:

> increasing enfeeblement and sickly sweetness finally overcame art; keeping
> step with so-called enlightened attitudes, which killed every deeper
> religious impulse, it eventually drove all gravity and dignity from church
> music. Even music for worship in Catholic churches, the masses, vespers,
> passiontide hymns etc., acquired a character that previously would have
> been too insipid and undignified even for opera seria. Let it be frankly
> admitted that even a composer as great as the immortal Joseph Haydn,
> even the mighty Mozart, could not remain untouched by the contagion of
> mundane, ostentatious levity. Mozart's masses, which he is known to have
> composed to a prescribed pattern on paid commission, are almost his
> weakest works.[20]

On 12 April 1783 Mozart asked his father to send him some of his own
church music for Baron van Swieten's private concerts. He then makes an
enigmatic statement, which appears to be in agreement with Hoffmann's
views:

> tastes are always changing – and *unfortunately* – such changes of taste
> affect even church music; it should not be this way, but for this reason true
> church music is found in boxes and almost eaten up by worms. – If I come
> to Salzburg, hopefully in July with my wife, then we can speak more on
> this subject.[21]

We wish Mozart had said more on this subject either in this letter or in a
later one. Is he giving his father a back-handed compliment? In any event, it
seems to condemn the most recent piece of church music Mozart had been
working on.

The 'Great' Mass in C minor, K. 427, is exceptional in every sense of the word. Mozart first mentions the work (already a 'half-finished score') in a letter of 4 January 1783, in which he refers to a promise he made to his father to write a Mass in honour of his marriage to Constanze Weber.[22] For some reason, however, his vow was never fully realized, since only four of the six movements were completed. Mozart brought his bride to Salzburg in July 1783, and Constanze told Vincent Novello some forty years later that he had planned to offer a votive Mass for her recovery following the safe delivery of their first child.[23] He continued working on it after coming to Salzburg, since most of the extra wind parts are on Salzburg paper with ten staves.[24]

Most scholars believe the work was performed for the first and only time during Mozart's lifetime at St Peter's Abbey on Sunday 26 October 1783, a day before he and Constanze went back to Vienna.[25] According to Mozart's sister, Constanze sang the soprano solos.[26] But the evidence is sketchy and quite problematic, since Nannerl does not specify which of her brother's Masses was performed, nor does she mention his 'new Mass' at all.[27] In any event, only the first half of the Credo survives in a continuity draft, and the Agnus Dei is entirely lacking, and it is unlikely that an incomplete Mass would have been performed with the entire 'Hofmusik' taking part. Nevertheless, it appears that at least the completed sections of the Mass in C minor were given that October in Salzburg.[28]

Mozart salvaged the Kyrie and Gloria of the Mass in C minor by incorporating them into an oratorio, *Davidde penitente*, K. 469, for a Lenten concert in 1785 (see table 9.1). Lorenzo Da Ponte supplied the new Italian text.[29] He wrote new arias for Valentin Adamberger (the first Belmonte in *Die Entführung*) and Catarina Cavalieri (the first Constanze in *Die Entführung* and Madame Silberklang in *Der Schauspieldirektor*). According to his thematic catalogue ('Der Verzeichnüss aller meiner Werke'), Mozart finished 'Eine Arie für Adamberger zu Societäts Musique' on 6 March 1785, and 'Eine Arie für die Cavaglieri [sic] zur Societäts Musique' was entered a few days later on 11 March. Mozart did not bother to write out the score again, but rather made marginal notes in the score of the C minor Mass to indicate which singer should take the solos.

While in Vienna, Mozart served informally as Baron van Swieten's personal Kapellmeister, conducting and making arrangements of oratorios by Handel and C. P. E. Bach and of works by J. S. Bach for private concerts.[30] These various encounters with Handel's and Bach's music, beginning in the spring of 1782, had considerable influence on Mozart's own works. The chorale melody used in *Die Zauberflöte* ('Ach Gott, vom Himmel sieh' darein') is only the most obvious example of his homage to the Baroque masters. The C minor Mass is on a scale comparable to Bach's monumental B minor Mass, and Mozart probably knew this work first-hand since Baron

Table 9.1. *A comparative outline of the Mass in C minor, K. 427, and Davidde penitente, K. 469*

Mass in C minor, K. 427	Davidde penitente, K. 469[a]
Kyrie (Andante moderato, common time, C minor): soprano solo and SATB chorus	No. 1 Coro: 'Alzai le flebili voci al Signor'
Gloria in excelsis Deo (Allegro vivace, common time, C major): SATB chorus	No. 2 Coro: 'Cantiam le glorie'
Laudamus te (Allegro aperto, common time, F major): soprano solo	No. 3 Aria: 'Lungi le cure ingrate'
Gratias (Adagio, common time, A minor): SSATB chorus	No. 4 Coro: 'Sii pur sempre benigno, oh Dio'
Domine (Allegro moderato, 3/4, D minor): duet for two sopranos	No. 5 Duetto: 'Sorgi, o Signore, e spargi'
	No. 6 Aria: 'A te, fra tanti affanni' (Andante, 3/4, B flat major): tenor solo
Qui tollis (Largo, common time, G minor): double chorus (SATB/SATB)	No. 7 Coro: 'Se vuoi, puniscimi'
	No. 8 Aria: 'Tra l'oscure ombre funeste' (Andante, 3/8, C minor): soprano solo
Quoniam (Allegro, alla breve, E minor): trio for two sopranos and tenor	No. 9 Terzetto: 'Tutte le mie speranze'
Jesu Christe (Adagio, common time, C major): SATB chorus	No. 10 Coro: 'Chi in Dio sol spera'
Cum Sancto Spiritu (alla breve, C major): SATB chorus	'Di tai pericoli non ha timor' (bars 186–232 = new cadenza for soprano I, II and tenor)
Credo in unum Deum (Allegro maestoso, 3/4, C major): SSATB chorus	
Et incarnatus est (6/8, F major): soprano with obbligato flute, oboe, and bassoon	
Sanctus (Largo, common time, C major): double chorus (SATB/SATB)	
Benedictus (Allegro comodo, common time, A minor): quartet for two sopranos, tenor, bass	

[a]Nos. in the oratorio are in the same tempo and key and for the same forces as the corresponding sections of the Mass.

van Swieten owned a copy.[31] No doubt Wolfgang and Leopold spent many hours in the summer of 1783 discussing and enjoying the counterpoint of the Kyrie and the 'Qui tollis' and 'Cum Sancto Spiritu' of the Gloria.

Above all, the Mass in C minor shows the influence of operatic style in church music, and in particular of Mozart's recent works of 1781 and 1782. The most impressive aria in the work is the 'Et incarnatus est', a concertante aria for solo soprano, flute, oboe, bassoon and organ obbligato. Basically, it is a rewriting of Ilia's 'Se il padre perdei', from Act 2 of *Idomeneo*, although the cadenza (bars 92ff.) has a clear reference to Konstanze's 'Martern aller Arten' from *Die Entführung*. Mozart almost never wrote vocal music in the abstract, but rather had a particular voice in mind, and here the most likely candidate is his beloved wife, Constanze. Although never a professional singer, she received training, and the range of the aria (up to high C) would have been comfortably within the range of her two sisters (Aloysia and Josefa) who could sing the F above high C. It is even more tempting to speculate that Mozart wrote this aria (which includes the words 'and was made man') for the mother carrying his first child at the time. The intimate sensuality of the music would seem to encourage such speculation. Perhaps Mozart had to put the work aside through grief at the sudden, unexpected death of their infant son on 19 August.[32]

Mozart as a Viennese Kapellmeister

What if Mozart had become kapellmeister in Vienna? Conventional wisdom states that once in Vienna, Mozart lost interest in sacred music, and the two unfinished masterworks (the C minor Mass and the Requiem) were his only efforts. But Otta Biba has made a strong case that Mozart never lost interest in sacred music and the church style.[33] In late April and early May 1791, Mozart petitioned for and was appointed to the post of Kapellmeister designate at St Stephen's in Vienna.[34] The motet 'Ave verum corpus', K. 618, was written in June 1791 for the feast of Corpus Christi and can be seen as a test for his pending appointment at St Stephen's. According to his first biographer, Franz Xaver Niemetschek, who is generally an accurate witness:

> Church music . . . was Mozart's favourite form of composition. But he was able to dedicate himself least of all to it. The Masses which he has left were composed for various occasions, and were specially commissioned. All those we have heard in Prague bear the stamp of his genius. In the catalogue no single Mass is mentioned, a proof that all those we have must be placed in the early years of his life. He, however, composed a gradual on the text 'Ave verum corpus' in June 1791. Here in Prague some motets have been made, based on his compositions, which are sung by various church choirs with dignity and solemnity.[35]

Mozart could have shown his full powers in this branch of music only if he had, in fact, obtained the post at St Stephen's; he looked forward to it. How well his gifts could have been used for this type of serious church music is proved by his last work, the Requiem, K. 626, which certainly surpasses anything that had previously been achieved in this sphere.

The commission for a Requiem Mass arrived while Mozart was working on *La clemenza di Tito* and *Die Zauberflöte*, and these two major projects limited the time he could spend on the work. Considering all his activities in the summer and autumn of 1791, it is impressive how much of the text he was able to set before his final illness forced him to his deathbed.[36] (One of the best scenes in the Miloš Forman film adaptation of *Amadeus* has the dying Mozart dictating line by line the 'Confutatis' to a befuddled Salieri. The scene, although entirely fictional, gives insight into how Mozart composed music.) The mysterious circumstances surrounding the work and its completion emerged only gradually, years after Mozart's death.[37]

The Requiem was a favourite of the Romantics, not only because its unfinished state mirrored the life of a heavenly composer cut short, but also because of its sublime expression. As E. T. A. Hoffmann writes: 'In one church work, however, [Mozart] has revealed his innermost feelings; and who can remain unmoved by the fervent devotion and spiritual ecstasy radiating from it? His Requiem is the sublimest achievement that the modern period has contributed to the church.'[38] He continues:

> [Mozart's Requiem] is a masterpiece that combines the power and solemn dignity of the old music with the rich ornament of the new, and that can serve as a model in this respect, as also in its wisely handled orchestration, to church composers today . . . The Tuba mirum may perhaps be the one movement that lapses into oratorio style, but otherwise the music remains genuinely devotional throughout; pure devotion resonates through these awe-inspiring chords which speak of another world, and which in their singular dignity and power are themselves another world. The Requiem performed in a concert-hall is not the same music; it is like a saint appearing at a ball![39]

It seems entirely plausible that (at least near the end) Mozart believed he was writing the Requiem for himself, and he bares his soul for all posterity. The key of D minor – the tonal centre of *Idomeneo, Don Giovanni* and the Piano Concerto, K. 466 – expresses the anguished cries for the dead in the Introit, 'Requiem aeternam dona eis' – 'Kyrie eleison' ('Eternal rest give unto them' – 'Lord have mercy'). Mozart repeated much of this music for the 'Lux aeterna', from the soprano solo (bars 19–48) of the first movement to the end of the Kyrie fugue but with new words, 'Cum sanctis tuis in aeternum' ('With thy saints in eternity'). D minor also anchors the outer movements of the Sequence, 'Dies irae' and 'Lacrymosa'. The latter section breaks off after only eight measures, and a surviving sketch shows Mozart planned to set the 'Amen' to a fugue. (Süssmayr did not use it, but Robert Levin among others has produced a convincing realization.) Despite some of Süssmayr's occasional awkward completions, the Requiem stands with the Clarinet Concerto and *Die Zauberflöte* as a brilliant record of the new direction Mozart's music was taking in the last months of his life towards a nobler, more popular style.

Deutsche Arien or lieder?

At the end of his chapter on aria and song, Alfred Einstein asks a slippery question: 'Did Mozart write any German songs?'[40] He coyly answers, 'yes and no', straddling the fence on semantics. After Schubert, Schumann, Brahms and Hugo Wolf we can pretend that there is a clear difference between aria and song, but in Mozart's lifetime there was not such a clear-cut distinction. As Einstein points out, two pairs of Mozart's German songs published during his lifetime were labelled 'deutsche Arien zum Singen beim Clavier'. Indeed, there is quite a close relationship between Mozart's songs and arias, and it is worth taking up Einstein's thesis and discussing a few examples.

There seems to have been no pattern to Mozart's song writing. There are songs for public and private consumption, and most were written for specific commissions. Most were first published in Breitkopf and Härtel's anthology *Gesänge mit Begleitung des Pianoforte von W. A. Mozart* (Leipzig, 1799).[41] Two French ariettes, K. 307 and 308, were written for Elisabeth Augusta Wendling in Mannheim and were probably done as preparatory work for his trip to Paris, as Mozart implies in his letter of 7 February 1778. A set of three songs, K. 472–4, all on texts by the Singspiel librettist C. F. Weise, are dated 7 May 1785. A pair of sacred songs, 'O Gottes Lamm' and 'Als aus Aegypten', K. 343, were evidently written and published in Prague in 1787; although these were not entered in his thematic catalogue, Mozart did record six lieder (K. 517–20 and 523–4) between 18 May and 24 June 1787. Another pair (K. 529–30) is dated 6 November and one other (K. 531) 11 December that year.

Mozart was not the only composer to incorporate 'songs' in his operas. Cherubino's canzona for the Countess, 'Voi che sapete', comes directly from a scene in Beaumarchais's *Le Mariage de Figaro*, Osmin's opening *Volkslied*, 'Wer ein Leibchen hat gefunden', immediately portrays a melancholic, and Pedrillo's romance, 'In Mohrenland gefangen war ein Mädchen', imparts colour to the abduction scene in *Die Entführung*. Such incidental 'songs' create a new dimension of expression and often feature a guitar-like accompaniment. Don Giovanni's canzonetta, 'Deh vieni alla finestra', has its roots in the two lieder with mandolin accompaniment, especially 'Komm liebe Zither', K. 351. By the time we get to Papageno's strophic songs in *Die Zauberflöte*, Mozart creates a real tension between 'song' and aria, in which case we are never quite sure whether the birdcatcher is 'speaking' or 'singing' his music.

Some of the lieder are quite operatic, through-composed settings. How shall we classify 'Ridente la calma' (an Italian aria with keyboard accompaniment) and 'Un moto di gioia' (a song used as a substitute aria in *Figaro*)? Are 'Die Liebe himmlisches Gefühl' and 'Männer suchen stets zu naschen' unorchestrated arias or songs? (The latter would fit comfortably in *Die Entführung*, most likely sung by Osmin.) 'An die Einsamkeit', K. 391, has the same basic shape and character as Constanze's 'Traurigkeit' in *Die Entführung*.

Mozart's most famous song, 'Das Veilchen', K. 476, sets a ballad from Goethe's first Singspiel, *Erwin und Elmire*, although the composer probably

Example 9.2a Mozart, 'Das Veilchen', K. 476, bars 8–14

Example 9.2b Mozart, *Die Entführung aus dem Serail*, K. 384, 'Durch Zärtlichkeit', bars 9–18

did not know the original context of the poem. Compare 'Das Veilchen' with Blonde's 'Durch Zärtlichkeit und Schmeicheln' (examples 9.2a and 9.2b): the shapes of the opening melodies are similar (both are in 2/4 time, the former in G major, the latter in A major), but 'Das Veilchen' is more modest in scope and less artificial than the aria. The poetic text for Blonde's aria is not far removed from Goethe's theatre, but Mozart wrote his Singspiel for the Viennese National Theatre and the court opera company. The differences between the two pieces reflect the differences between the two genres (lied and aria) as well as the ability of the original Blonde, Therese Teyber. Unfortunately, we do not know for whom (if anyone in particular) Mozart intended 'Das Veilchen'.

Mozart's role in the development of German art song has been largely ignored. Earlier commentators such as Einstein have been uncomfortable dealing with Mozart's lieder, perhaps because there is not a clear distinction between his songs and his arias.[42] Other nineteenth- and twentieth-century critics have had difficulty with the overlapping styles of his sacred and secular vocal music, even though Mozart himself did not hesitate to write sacred music in a secular style and vice versa. Only a handful of composers beside Mozart have produced a body of music that embraces the entire gamut of human and divine.

10 The opere buffe

EDMUND J. GOEHRING

In the history and criticism of Mozart's opere buffe, all roads lead back to Carlo Goldoni. The comic works of the Venetian lawyer-turned-playwright influence every Mozart opera buffa in one way or another. Mozart's first, *La finta semplice*, comes from a Goldoni libretto (by way of Marco Coltellini); his last, *Don Giovanni* and *Così fan tutte*, use topics and language that Goldoni had treated earlier; and all of them divide the characters into the Goldonian *parti buffe, parti di mezzo carattere* and *parti serie*.[1] The pressing question about Mozart's opera buffa repertory, then, is not whether Goldoni influenced Mozart, but how he did so.

The difficulty in striking a consensus about Goldoni's influence on Mozart comes largely from tensions inherent in the Goldonian repertory itself. In the eighteenth century, as today, Goldoni's reform of comedy was generally understood in one of two contrasting ways: as a technical achievement, or as an ethical one. According to the former view, Goldoni did not reject the commedia dell'arte – the often ribald improvisations of professional actors which had been the basis of Italian popular comedy for some two centuries – but rather improved on it. Replacing improvised scenarios with fully scripted comedies gave him control over pacing and clarified the action. The finest representative of this kind of comedy was also the most famous in the eighteenth century: *Il servitore di due padroni* (1745), a work that Mozart had hoped to turn into a Singspiel.[2] It reaches its comic apex when the servant, Truffaldino, waits simultaneously at the tables of his two masters without letting either one know about the other (Act 2, scene 2). This episode is a masterpiece of comic choreography and a brilliant realization of the commedia dell'arte *lazzo*, or stock gag.

The other view of Goldoni holds that an early work such as *Il servitore* only partially represents his reform of comedy. The true reform works, which began to appear during the 1748 season at the Teatro Sant'Angelo, do far more than tinker with the machinery of comedy. They alter its very character by investing comedy with a moral dignity not found in the commedia dell'arte. The theoretical impulse behind this change was a disaffection with the long-standing Aristotelian formulation of comedy, which held that comedy promoted virtue through negative example, by making vice appear ridiculous. This apology, Goldoni worried, was a sophistry used to provide intellectual cover for admitting all kinds of vice on to the stage. Goldoni

abandoned the ethically suspect (because unregulatable) practice of improvisation for a fully scripted, hybrid form that steered a middle course
between tragedy and comedy. It took the ethos of the former – tragedy's
nobility of feeling and action – and the devices of the latter – comedy's
more probable actions and less remote characters (servants, merchants and
other common folk, rather than nobles or mythological types). Only this
kind of comedy could instruct by positive and recognizable example or, in
Goldoni's words, could fish comedies out of nature's *mare magnum*.[3]

Goldoni the moralist also attracted a large eighteenth-century following,
although generally from a different crowd – critics rather than practitioners
or the audiences themselves.[4] Especially valuable testimony to his influence
on opera comes from the composer Francesco Bianchi. His preface to *Il
disertore francese*, a *dramma serio per musica* (Venice, 1784), shows various reforms in eighteenth-century theatre converging in the creation of a
new kind of opera. Basically, Bianchi wanted an operatic equivalent for the
French *drame*, a kind of theatre espoused by Diderot and, as the following
declaration shows, one that looks very much like a Goldonian reformed
comedy:

> Why can't one similarly venture an opera that falls between a grand heroic
> one and a comic one? . . . [Its action] would be serious and important; its
> language would not be more lyrical (except in moments of passion, which
> is always lyrical), but noble, full of sentiment and truth and would come
> closer to the ideas and objects of daily life. Let these characters be cloaked
> with the propriety of real clothes not overly altered by theatrical
> decoration.[5]

Bianchi's claim that such a theatre would be more natural might strain credibility, except that nature did not mean the indiscriminate representation
of the world. It referred rather to human nature in its virtuous aspects.[6]
Nature was that which ought to be, not that which is. Such a conception
brings reforms such as Goldoni's into line with eighteenth-century sentimental theatre and literature. Both wanted to make virtue appear attractive.

The two readings of Goldonian comedy, the technical and the moral-
izing, have each been advanced as an influence on Mozart's opere buffe,
sometimes as direct ones, sometimes as mediated through contemporary
comic theory and practice. The more conventional interpretation is that
Goldoni's comedies and librettos gave Mozart the characters and, above
all, situations for translating into music the rhythms of spoken comedy.[7]
The case has also been made that Mozart took from Goldoni his ethical
vision of comedy, and thus that Mozart belongs in the company of the
great reformers of eighteenth-century spoken theatre, namely Lessing in
Germany, Diderot and his *drame* in France, and especially Goldoni. In their

works, and decidedly not in the existing opera buffa repertory, Mozart found a comedy that could render 'the moral, sentimental, and psychological complexity of life by means of a rigorous coherence of behavior, characters, and plot', in what would ultimately be 'a new and more faithful representation of reality'.[8] This interpretation makes Mozart into a progressive composer, one who shattered the conventional practices and stereotypical characters of the commedia dell'arte.

Of the two images of Goldoni, that of the craftsman is the more germane to Mozart's opere buffe, but only up to a point: well-drawn characters and varied situations meant little until there was a musical style that could convey action. The other image of Goldoni is still further removed from Mozart's opere buffe. As Mozart acquired greater facility in musical comedy, the operas render ambiguous the relation of moral virtue to technical excellence and to the creative process itself. In thus putting asunder what Goldoni had tried to unite, the Da Ponte operas challenge the ideal of a rational, virtuous theatre.

The early opere buffe

Mozart's earliest essays in opera buffa, *La finta semplice* (K. 51, 1768) and *La finta giardiniera* (K. 196, 1775), rest uneasily between buffa and seria. Their characters, situations and language are recognizably comic, but their organization comes out of opera seria. Imposing the structures of opera seria on musical comedy creates an awkward and inefficient division of labour: it gives the most interesting music to the most static part of the drama, the aria, and the least interesting music to the most active part of the drama, the recitative. A crude but useful measure of this organization can be found in the proportion of arias in each of these works. Of the twenty-five numbers in *La finta semplice*, only four are not arias; meanwhile, only six of *La finta giardiniera*'s twenty-eight numbers are not solos. Concentrating on the expression of feeling presents obvious obstacles for depicting situations. Less obvious, but no less significant, is that such a focus also restricts what one can do with character. This limitation is especially apparent in *La finta semplice*. Many of its arias approach the text too literally by giving the words of the text a status independent from the speaker. Such is the case with Polidoro's first-act aria, 'Cosa ha mai la donna indosso' (No. 7). Rosina is the eponymous feigned simpleton of the opera, but Polidoro is the real thing: socially inept, physically unappealing and, at the end of the opera, the only one who cannot find a spouse. One would know nothing of these traits from listening to this aria, however, which is a perfectly competent and *simpatico* expression of the torments of love. If there is buffoonery here, it comes from extramusical, visual sources, such as acting or design. This is not the only aria to speak of love in *La finta semplice*. Nearly every one dwells on it, frequently in ways that do not distinguish one speaker from another. The shortcoming is not of insufficiently realistic or overly stereotypical characters but of characters who are not sufficiently delineated as types.

La finta giardiniera is much more successful in its musical characterization. This is Mozart's first opera to exploit the full range of characters envisioned in a Goldonian opera. Musical depictions run from the *buffa* arias of the servant Nardo (No. 5, 'A forza di martelli'), through the enchanting middle style of Sandrina, the noblewoman disguised as a gardener (No. 11, 'Geme la tortorella'), all the way up to the high passion of the seria figure Arminda (No. 13, 'Vorrei punirti'). Mozart lavished brilliant orchestral effects and elaborate melodies on these characters. Even the avaricious Mayor gets a full complement of obbligato writing in his first-act aria, 'Dentro il mio petto io sento' (No. 3). Similarly, Nardo's aria 'Con un vezzo all'italiana' (No. 14) contains passages in three different languages and national styles: Italian, French and (in Mozart's only operatic foray there) English. *La finta giardiniera* has a fecundity, a creative exuberance, that was not common in the genre. Or, as Leopold Mozart put it: 'All who attended the rehearsal say that they never heard a finer piece, in which all the arias are beautiful.'[9]

Leopold's comment stumbles on to a problem with *La finta giardiniera* as a comedy. If the aria is conceived primarily as a soliloquy, then, no matter how beautiful, it can do little to advance dramatic action. It seems that this static approach also troubled Mozart, because some of the set pieces in these early works attempt to convey action. Both operas, for example, occasionally call for pantomime. In *La finta semplice* this happens in a recitative that has a measured, orchestrated accompaniment ('Me ne vo' prender spasso', Act 2, scene 7). *La finta giardiniera*, in turn, occasionally calls for pantomime from its arias, as in 'Care pupille belle' (No. 15), which tries to choreograph the stock comic gag of mistaken identity. Here, Count Belfiore thinks he is addressing Sandrina (his back is turned to her), when it is actually the Mayor. The anticipated surprise comes when Belfiore, turning to take Sandrina's hand, takes the Mayor's instead. This event fails to provide convincing musical comedy not because the action is predictable but because the humour resides only in the staging and acting, not in the musical language itself.

One might argue in response that the proper place to find dramatic action is not in the aria but in the lengthy finales of these early operas. The chain finale had indeed been a fixture of opera buffa since 1760, and Goldoni was its most visible practitioner.[10] Built around a series of individual

Example 10.1 Mozart, *La finta semplice*, K. 51, Act 1 finale, bars 38–42

scenes arranged in a trajectory of increasing activity, the chain finale was an ideal setting for injecting comic action into music. Mozart's first opere buffe, however, lacked a musical style that could do much with it. The main impediment was writing that was dominated by continuo homophony, a procedure that generates motion by laying down a regular pulse (usually quavers) beneath frequently changing harmonies.[11] The resulting steadiness brings stability over long movements such as a multi-sectional finale, but at the considerable cost of variety and long-range tension. An example of both the character and liabilities of continuo homophony comes in an early passage from the first-act finale of *La finta semplice* (see example 10.1). The text calls for two postures: first, fear from the pusillanimous Polidoro; second, sternness from Ninetta, who orders him on his knees to beg forgiveness (for an offensive note he has written). The musical setting is as appropriately deprecatory in the first instance as it is strict in the second: not only does the minor mode yield to the major, but Ninetta even appropriates Polidoro's melody for her command. Supplying the background to this activity, however, is the steady gait of the continuo. Its undifferentiated pulse weakens the melodic and harmonic contrasts between the two, and its rapid motion gives insufficient time for the audience to absorb the two contrasting affects. The long-range presentation and resolution of tension is beyond the capabilities of this style. At this point, the music is an ornament to action rather than a source of it. So, even with important Goldonian elements in place – a varied cast of characters, a model of spoken comedy that emphasized situation over character, and the chain finale – a genuinely *musical* comedy could not be established until there was a change in musical language.

Table 10.1. *Organization of the finale of* L'oca del Cairo, *K. 422*

Bar	Key	Tempo	Metre	Vocal texture	Remarks
1–93	B♭	Allegro	4/4	Solo, then ensemble at 72–93	Harmonically closed, *ottonari*
94–126	B♭	Allegro	6/8	Ensemble	*Quinari*
127–9	F:V	–	C	Recitative	Transitional passage
130–42	F	Adagio	3/4	Ensemble	New key area established, harmonically closed
143–88	d, a, C	[Allegro]	C	Dialogue	*Sturm und Drang*, *ottonari*, two-bar transition bars 187–8
189–214	C, A♭, c		C	Ensemble, reflective	Brief canon bars 196–204
215–26	E♭		C	Dialogue	*Quinari*
227–51	C		C	Solo vs ensemble	Entrance of Don Pippo, *settenari*
252–7	C		C	Solo	Pippo summons guards, *quinari*
258–300	c, E♭, C		C	Varied textures	Peak of tension: triplet motion, chromaticism
301–9	F	Andante maestoso	C	Solo	French overture style for Don Pippo
310–28	B♭:V	Allegro	C	Solo	Retransition to tonic
329–72	B♭		C	Solo and ensemble	*Buffo* patter, *ottonari*, tonic re-established
373–461	B♭	Presto	C	Stretto	Harmonic and rhythmic acceleration

New stylistic paths in opera buffa

In 1783, Mozart began composing an opera that he eventually abandoned, *L'oca del Cairo* (K. 422). Enough of this fragmentary work exists to show that it puts music on a new footing in opera. For perhaps the first time in an opera buffa, the music itself presents a comic style of rapid changes of mood and long-range control over them. Such musical comedy was possible largely because continuo homophony gave way to writing based on the musical period. Periodic writing had two great virtues for musical comedy: rhythmic pliancy and harmonic control. The more plastic sense of rhythm was possible because the emphasis moved up from the beat to the bar, or even to the phrase. The greater harmonic control, meanwhile, came from a deceleration of harmonic rhythm. When harmonies change less frequently, a move to a new key can become a dramatic event. This new formal control is best seen in the most ambitious number of the opera, the 461-bar finale (see table 10.1). For example, its scene of greatest dramatic tension – Don Pippo's entrance, which momentarily thwarts the lovers' escape – is also the most tense from a musical perspective. Bars 143–300 have the most frequent and dramatic changes of harmony, the most complex textures (including a brief canon) and the greatest rhythmic activity of the finale. And despite the preponderance of common-time metres, this finale has a rhythmic flexibility that, with the assistance of harmony, generates a momentum unavailable in the earlier works. The obvious place to look for this dynamism is in

Example 10.2 Mozart, *L'oca del Cairo*, K. 422, finale, bars 375–7

Example 10.3 Mozart, *L'oca del Cairo*, K. 422, finale, bars 398–9

Example 10.4 Mozart, *L'oca del Cairo*, K. 422, finale, bars 406–7

Example 10.5 Mozart, *L'oca del Cairo*, K. 422, finale, bars 428–32

the stretto, whose customary duty was to generate turmoil before the end of the act. It begins with a line from Don Pippo which stretches a B-flat sonority out over three bars (see example 10.2) and is followed by one that adds to it syncopation and a doubled rate of harmonic change (see example 10.3). A subtle, efficient increase in momentum occurs at bar 405, where the syncopation now starts on a dissonance (the texture also becomes thicker here) (see example 10.4). But the most impressive stroke comes after the repeat of this section. Up to this point, the g″ that had first appeared in bar 405 was the highest pitch in the stretto. Now it is extended over five bars to form a melodic cadence at bar 432 (see example 10.5). Harmonically, of course, this melodic arrival comes on a deceptive cadence, and Mozart needs ten more bars to bring everything back to the tonic and twenty more in the tonic to close off the act. None of Mozart's earlier opere buffe create this kind of large-scale dramatic tension.

Where might Mozart have acquired the resources for this conception of musical drama? It is true that the Classical style as a whole, including instrumental genres, owed a heavy debt to comic opera. Johann Adam Hiller had already noted the contamination of instrumental music by comic opera as early as 1768:

> Everyone knows that comic opera is the reigning taste these days, at least in Italy. As wretched as their plots often are, the characters are caricatured and the plots exaggerated to such a degree that it is impossible to suppress a laugh ... Comic opera has become the best school for today's composers. Symphonies, concertos, trios, sonatas – all, nowadays, borrow something of its style, which would not be objectionable were it only possible to avoid the low and tasteless elements.[12]

But it is important to note that the influence also went in the other direction: developments in instrumental music gave Mozart musical control over long-range dramatic action. The beginning of the finale to *L'oca del Cairo*, for example, sounds like a ritornello to a concerto and even treats some of the later vocal themes as elaborations on this orchestral exposition. Years prior to the composition of this work, Mozart already had at his disposal all of the textual and most of the musical resources for musical comedy: the conventional plots, the finales and contrasting character types from Goldoni, and a syllabic vocal style and short phrases from contemporary musical language. But these devices, without the additional support of periodicity and long-range control over harmony, left music as an accompaniment to comedy. Instrumental music had the burden, absent in vocal music, of creating drama without recourse to words, and so it necessarily had to turn to harmony, rhythm, form and melody for drama and coherence. This shows one limitation of Goldoni's influence on Mozart in the technical development of his comedies. It is not primarily a failure of the Goldonian libretto to be sufficiently operatic. The limitation stems, rather, from the translation of one medium, in this case, spoken drama, to another.

The power of the new style extended not only to situation but also to character. As we have seen, the text-centred approach of opera seria left characterization mostly to word and feeling rather than to action. The steady beat of continuo homophony supported this stable, reflective posture. The development of periodic writing changed all this because it introduced a flexibility that also brought action into the definition of personality. This more animated approach to character is exemplified in a figure such as Leporello in *Don Giovanni*, and the opening of 'O statua gentilissima' (No. 22) provides one of numerous examples of the effectiveness of

Example 10.6 Mozart, *Don Giovanni*, K. 527, 'O statua gentilissima', bars 1–10

periodicity in portraying character. Its first quatrain compresses several actions and emotions into a short space. First, Leporello starts to invite the Statue to dinner, but, overcome with fear, breaks off the invitation and turns to his master for mercy; the quatrain ends with his observation that he cannot stop shaking. Mozart's musical setting attends to these actions and sentiments with an array of images: the invitation with a deferential march; the fear with the disintegration of the march into minims spanning a minor seventh (bars 6–8); and the trembling with a move to quavers at the end of the period and into the next section (see example 10.6). This description may make Mozart's dramaturgy seem as text-centred as that of the opera seria he abandoned, but the quatrain's organization of events fits periodic structure like a glove. A usual feature of a coherent period is an acceleration at the end to articulate closure, which is precisely what happens here: the peak of tension (the C♯s at bars 7–8) also has the slowest note values and the slowest harmonic rhythm. From this point of relative suspense there follows a stepwise melodic descent to the tonic (this makes the two halves of the period melodically symmetrical), an acceleration of harmony – from one to four changes per bar – and also one of rhythm – from minims to quavers with a subdivision of semiquavers. (The increased rhythmic activity in the melody leads Mozart to repeat most of the last line of text.) The formal economy of such periodic writing has its own elegance, but it is also indispensable to this new style of musical comedy. Its compressed presentation of a range of musical gestures allows action as well as emotion to depict character, something unattainable in the earlier style.

What we begin to see in Mozart's mature opere buffe is a conception of comedy tied less to a specific subject matter than to a way of treating material. A later passage in 'O statua gentilissima' is an especially useful instantiation of this principle, because it is analogous to a passage from a

Example 10.7 Mozart, *Idomeneo*, K. 366, No. 28a

serious opera, *Idomeneo*. The episode in question involves the subterranean
voice of Poseidon (Act 3, scene 10). This scene gave Mozart a lot of trouble,
because he thought the original text was too long to allow the scene to inspire
awe. Frustration with the episode prompted him to register a rather notori-
ous complaint about the speech of the ghost in *Hamlet*, which he says would
have been far more effective had it been shorter.[13] (Lest Mozart be accused
of literary rusticity, the speech he attacks is almost certainly from Friedrich
Ludwig Schröder's translation of 1777, not Shakespeare's original.) In the
end Mozart produced four settings of this scene, which move from a total
of seventy bars to one of only nine (see example 10.7). The principle – that
one awakens the imagination most powerfully by not belabouring a point –
finds an extreme of compression in an analogous passage that comes towards the end of 'O statua gentilissima'. This time, the sepulchral voice is
compressed into one bar and one note (see example 10.8). Of course, it is
not brevity alone that makes this moment so compelling. The Commendatore's 'Sì', which restores the tonic, follows upon a passage of accompanied
recitative (bars 78–83) that brings all motion to a halt. (The setting of this
entire trio in seven-syllable lines allows Mozart to switch to recitative without a change of poetic metre.) Leporello's subsequent interjection is also
important to the pacing and pathos. His extension of the syllable 'Mo-' to
an entire bar is marvellously comic, but the harmonic plunge to the minor
mode has a violence that the category of the mock tragic cannot adequately
explain.

If it is difficult to take a proper measure of the proportions of humour
and sublimity in this number, the trio can still clarify what the word 'natural' might have meant for Mozart. For Goldoni and others, it is largely
synonymous with decorum, propriety and fidelity to the morally appealing

Example 10.8 Mozart, *Don Giovanni*, K. 527, 'O statua gentilissima', bars 81–5

sides of the real world: hence the call for recognizable rather than mythological or remote characters. The term also turns up frequently in Mozart's
own correspondence, most commonly as a demand to make a scene more
natural. Given the obvious improbabilities of scenes with subterranean or
sepulchral voices, 'natural' must mean something different in Mozartian
poetics, something like 'convincing within the laws of theatrical representation'. Mozart is too opportunistic a composer and unsystematic a thinker
for one to find a consistent poetic theory in his activity or writings. Nor
does one want to give in to the tyranny of teleology by trying to conscript
the operas into an inexorable march towards a preordained end. Nonetheless, the evidence of the correspondence as well as that of the early opere
buffe suggests that the conventions of opera seria could not meet Mozart's
desire for a quick-paced, convincing musical drama. Mozart eventually discovered (or invented) an outlet in opera buffa instead. Far from sacrificing
pathos, the turn to buffa actually expanded the range of sentiments and
situations.[14]

Moral ambiguity in the Da Ponte operas

Libertines inviting statues to dinner do not populate daily life, and only a
degenerate or a Romantic would commend Don Giovanni's behaviour here,
which is, basically, blasphemous. A scene like this, in other words, implicitly
challenges the Goldonian model of well-behaved comedy. It is not the only
one in the opera to do so. The opera's brilliance as a comedy stands in a
more tenuous relationship to virtue than the ideals of reformed comedy
would like. One of the least satisfying interpretations of *Don Giovanni* is
to take seriously as a moral statement rather than a simple observation the
other part of the opera's title, 'the libertine punished' (*Il dissoluto punito*).
Virtue's weak hold on technique is largely implicit during most of the opera,

Example 10.9 Mozart, *Don Giovanni*, K. 527, 'Ah taci, ingiusto core', bars 14–16

Leporello: Zit - to! di Don - na El - vi - ra si - gnor,__ la vo - ce io sen - to!

but one number, 'Ah taci, ingiusto core' (No. 15), draws explicit attention to it by raising questions about the creative process itself.

Although lacking otherworldly characters, this episode is not proba-ble by any reasonable standard. Its artificiality resides primarily in self-conscious references to theatre. Leporello and Don Giovanni stumble once again upon Elvira, and the ever-impulsive Don Giovanni decides to seize the moment ('Cogliere io vo' il momento') by playing the seducer-as-theatre-director. Swapping outfits with his servant, Don Giovanni directs a little comic episode by serenading Elvira and having the disguised Leporello pro-vide pantomime. Although composed out, this scene has popular theatre written all over it. Like the *lazzi* of the commedia dell'arte, this number is contrived, artificial and accidental.

Understood only as a text, the scene appears too inconsequential to reg-ister on anyone's moral radar screen. Its musical craftsmanship, however, invests this trivial situation with a perplexing moral significance. This ambi-guity is possible because Elvira now cuts a much more sympathetic musical figure than in the analogous first-act trio, 'Ah chi mi dice mai' (No. 3). In this earlier ensemble, her excessive passion (she wants to carve out Don Giovanni's heart) and a truly Baroque melody render her rage comic.[15] In 'Ah taci, ingiusto core', by contrast, a graceful melody quiets this comic fury, its pulsing quavers and semiquavers delicately registering the beating of her renegade heart. It is not her tune but the larger musico-dramatic situation that turns Elvira into an object of ridicule. Intruding upon her touching self-recrimination are scraps of *buffa* patter from Leporello and Don Giovanni (of whom she is not yet aware) (see example 10.9). This is a very low musical style, a mechanical, vamp-until-ready diatonic line that repeats itself a full eight times.

These opening bars put into play the components of the overall conflict, and it is their collective musical and affective range that generates irony: on the one side, Donna Elvira's dignity, on the other, Don Giovanni's bot-tomless callousness, and, somewhere in between, Leporello, caught between laughter and sympathy. Musically, this tension climaxes at bars 49–51 (see example 10.10). It is a patently artificial moment. Don Giovanni's declara-tion that he will kill himself burlesques the heroic lover, as does his melody, with its exaggerated downward leap of a minor seventh; the mock pathos of this marionette show brings Leporello to the brink of laughter. None

Example 10.10 Mozart, *Don Giovanni*, K. 527, 'Ah taci, ingiusto core', bars 49–54

of this mischief appears staged to Elvira, of course, whose gullibility seems alternately desperate, comic and moving. With the high pathos of its musical style, an episode such as this defies a Goldonian canon regarding the regulation of elevated language. Goldoni tried to exclude or at least restrain the *stile antico*, with its metaphors and other rhetorical devices, because of its potential for making noble actions and sentiments into grist for the comic mill.[16] One will recall a similar exhortation from Bianchi, who did not want his operatic equivalent of the *drame* overly altered by theatrical decoration. Yet sabotage of the high style is exactly what goes on in this trio and elsewhere in *Don Giovanni*. The inclusion of the seria mode may give some parts of the opera a dignity that they would not otherwise have, but, as in this case, they can also expand the possibilities for farce.[17]

This is not the only ambiguity in this remarkable trio. Another one comes in the resolution of this episode. From the standpoint of harmony, the re-establishment of the tonic is one of the more unusual in the repertory: normally, the bass holds out a dominant, with the upper parts moving. Here, the bass moves instead, and by a chromatic rather than diatonic descent to the tonic (bars 52–4, example 10.10). The result is a resolution that seems unanticipated yet deeply satisfying. But it is hard to find a commensurate

Example 10.11 Mozart, *Don Giovanni*, K. 527, 'Ah taci, ingiusto core', bars 67–71

sentiment in the text: the musical line that ushers in this return is Leporello's inane patter on 'rido'. The formal control and elegance of the trio are more out of step with the contrivance and frivolity of the situation.

The mismatch between the music and the situation is neither a sign of compositional incompetence nor an invitation to critical indeterminacy. Rather, the incongruity has a purpose, which is to separate creativity from virtue. The second half of the trio makes this point explicit in the way it relates the text to the music. The posture of the second half is all reflective, which means that the dialogue of the first half yields to ensemble writing. Moving from action to commentary is standard operating procedure in opera, but nothing in the trio quite prepares one for the musical transformation. Mozart weaves the earlier strands of *buffa* patter into a tapestry of beauty unmatched in the trio (and, arguably, in the opera as a whole) (see example 10.11). The point of such beauty is not to make the characters appear true to life. They are never anything more (or less) than deftly drawn stereotypes: the ingénue, the guileful libertine, the servant who rebukes his master's mendacious lips. And true to the setting, the characters and the overall moral ambiguity of the opera, the polyphonic layers of this closing ensemble offer not a single perspective on the scene but three discrete ones. This is another manifestation of the economy of Mozart's comic muse, the same one that wanted fewer words from the voice in *Idomeneo*. Mozart does not overreach by reducing ambiguity to moral platitudes. Rather than systematize, he merely observes. The most disturbing observation, from Don Giovanni, distils the danger of this trio into a few words. After noting what an impressive improvisation ('bel colpetto') he has given, he then exalts himself for his unrivalled fecundity of invention: 'A more fertile talent than mine? No, there is none.' This is not a flattering, or at least tidy, view of the creative process. The Goldonian reformed theatre, it will be recalled, wanted to harness creative exuberance to virtue. Mozart's inventiveness, spurred on by low comedy, bridles at such restrictions. A scene such as this one in 'Ah taci, ingiusto core', where beauty and virtue part company, reveals the ethical distance separating *Don Giovanni* from some of the great reform movements in eighteenth-century theatre.

The coarseness with which *Don Giovanni* handles high passion distinguishes it from the other Da Ponte operas only in degree, not in kind. Even *Figaro*, the work that comes closest to a Goldonian ideal, is sparing in its use of sentimentality. Such reserve is the rule in Mozart's favourite number in the opera, the third-act sextet (No. 19). This is the episode in which Figaro and Susanna learn that Marcellina is Figaro's mother, a (mostly) joyous discovery for all but the Count and Bartolo. Exalting familial ties is a cornerstone of sentimental, realistic theatre, where even the mere invocation of a familial name – 'mia madre!' – can be a sign of piety. Not quite in this sextet, however: its piled-on repetitions of 'madre' and 'padre' (more than fifty of them) smother whatever reverence these epithets might have had.[18] What is more, real life, the raw material of reformed comedy, never enters into this scene. The discovered birthmark or its equivalent (this is how Marcellina recognizes Figaro) is as old as literature itself (in the tales of Odysseus and Oedipus, for example); the foundling tale, too, is an enduring convenience of theatre. At the same time, not all is parody in this sextet. Its ending (bars 102–36) projects a radiant solemnity that casts a new light on to this parody of sentimental reunions. The music – a hymn, really – is not just a representation of social harmony, it is that harmony itself, an ideal that persists despite the obvious shortcomings of the *dramatis personae*. But, again, this splendour is the contrivance of musical theatre, with all of its attendant symmetries, its artificialities, its sporting with convention.

The anti-Goldonian conflation of sympathy with ridicule reaches an extreme in *Così fan tutte*. Mozart's last opera buffa can be usefully read as a refutation of sentimental theatre. The very first number, 'La mia Dorabella', sets forth the central tenet of sentimental psychology: that external beauty is a reflection of inner virtue. This thought betrays an exceptionally transparent, deeply sentimental but also rigid view of human nature. It is on this basis, for example, that Fiordiligi, the opera's archetype of the sentimental heroine, can equate her fidelity to a rock that withstands the tempests. It cannot withstand twenty-four hours of scrutiny, however. The opera erodes such confidence by creating scenarios that make it impossible – for players and audience alike – to sort out sympathy from ridicule. By the second act, Fiordiligi is left pondering how the heart can change in a single day (Act 2, scene 10) and, two scenes later, how unlike herself she seems (Act 2, scene 12). Now deprived of such certainty, she and the lovers are invited to replace their heroic, sentimental *Weltanschauung* with one that founds sympathy not on perfection but on contingency and irony. The ultimate rejoinder to Fiordiligi's heroism is the benediction of Da Ponte's subtle and richly allusive libretto, which insists that only a comic outlook will give one the flexibility to weather life's storms. Replacing the standard of *homo sentimentalis* – which is, basically, the Goldonian ideal of heroism made attractive – is one of *homo comicus*.

The theatrical reforms sometimes associated with Mozart's opere buffe in many ways betray an anti-theatrical impulse. Demanding restrained language, admirable protagonists and probable situations amounts to a belief that comedy, if left unsupervised, would misbehave. By way of contrast, Mozart's finest opere buffe seem unruly in their resistance to such discipline. This is not to say that the operas are immoral (a claim that is made from time to time about *Don Giovanni* and *Così fan tutte*). It is just that much of their activity takes place beyond the purview of virtue and vice, categories which regulate sentimental, realist theatre. It might seem contradictory to make such claims about a composer whose works have been celebrated for a classical feeling for balance and symmetry, which all sounds very virtuous. But these technical properties only aided the creation of an irrepressible musical comedy. The balanced phrase, the exquisitely prepared return, invested Mozart's opere buffe with a comic energy that the structures of opera seria had dissipated. In the end, Mozart took an old form of comedy, wedded it to a new musical style, and to this union brought a technical mastery that gives his opere buffe a range – from the irreverent to the sensuous to the transcendent – that grants them a place of their own in eighteenth-century theatre.

11 Mozart and opera seria

JULIAN RUSHTON

Mozart is treasured today for his opera buffa and Singspiel, the foundation of the modern repertory. His serious Italian operas belong to the most abundant operatic genre of the eighteenth century, and share its modern neglect. Yet there is no reason to suppose that Mozart despised the rhetorical grandeur of opera seria, with its cast of tyrants, suffering princesses, courtiers and soldiers, and its plots of treachery overcome and magnanimity in suffering. It played a larger role in his pre-Vienna works than any other type of opera, and was by no means neglected thereafter. Mozart was brought up on opera seria, and an opera seria was his last stage work.[1]

The majority of Mozart's serious operas were composed for specific occasions connected to the Austrian ruling house of Habsburg, yet none was written for its capital, Vienna. What today we loosely call 'opera seria' comprised a number of sub-genres, selected according to the circumstances of a commission. For Milan, Mozart composed two traditional opere serie, *Mitridate, re di Ponto*, and *Lucio Silla*.[2] Such operas acted as a mirror to the upper echelon of society, and an enlightened monarchy is directly reflected, or indirectly admonished, when the tyrant sees the light and forgives his enemies. Although concerned almost entirely with aristocratic characters, this kind of opera seria, whose form was established by the librettist and Imperial poet Pietro Metastasio, was designed for public theatres; yet in a city such as Milan, governed by the Austrian Archduke Ferdinand, the court certainly attended the premiere. Mozart wrote only one further opera along these lines, *La clemenza di Tito*, for the 1791 coronation of Leopold II in Prague. Two operas fall into an exclusively courtly genre, the *festa teatrale*, which relieves the succession of recitative and aria with an occasional chorus and dance. *Ascanio in Alba* was written for Ferdinand's marriage, again for Milan, and *Il sogno di Scipione* for the Salzburg Prince-Archbishop's Golden Jubilee in January 1772.[3] Also for Salzburg, in 1775, he composed a cut-down version of Metastasio's *Il re pastore* for the visit of the Archduke Maximilian. In form, this is a traditional opera seria, but as in the *festa* the intrigue is comparatively slender. These three works can be associated with the category of serenata, which implies less than full staging. Mozart's very first opera, *Apollo et Hyacinthus*, was a Latin-text serenata, written for Salzburg University when he was eleven (1767).[4] It conforms to the expected pattern of recitative, sometimes harmonically daring, and arias which, with performers scarcely older than the composer, were naturally more pleasing, or brilliant, than individually expressive. At the other extreme, *Idomeneo*, commissioned for the court theatre in Munich for the Carnival of 1781, is the masterpiece of an operatic type cultivated mainly in German court theatres, based on Greek myth rather than Roman or medieval history, with heavy involvement of chorus, and partly modelled on French lyric tragedy. Gluck's 'reform operas' composed for Vienna were the principal but by no means only forerunners.[5] In *La clemenza di Tito*, Mozart tried to retain the advances made in *Idomeneo* and, indeed, in opera buffa; his collaborator Caterino Mazzolà simplified the intrigue and compressed some dramatic situations into ensembles rather than letting them unfold in a sequence of arias: in short, he boiled down Metastasio 'into a proper opera'.[6]

The aria

Opera seria is represented in our theatres today mainly by Handel. Its basis was great solo singing, and therefore the aria; it thus requires a special kind of attention, focussed on the discharge of single, intense emotions into long pieces of music of almost abstract symmetry that, in their role as vocal concertos, balance direct emotional expression with virtuosity. The conventions of opera seria required most of the dramatic motivation to be channelled into arias, assisted by only a handful of elaborately orchestrated recitatives. This concentration on aria is the feature of opera seria that most disconcerts audiences accustomed to Mozart's comedies, charged with dramatic electricity in their ensembles and finales. Yet even the comedies depend on arias for full presentation of the characters' internal dilemmas. Parts of *Così fan tutte*, in particular, resemble opera seria viewed through a looking glass; when he wrote it, Mozart was probably already on the look-out for the chance to write a tragedy.

Mozart's musical education included singing lessons, and he is recorded as singing in public, with a thin voice but much expression, up to his thirteenth year.[7] In a report written for the Royal Society of London, Daines Barrington testified that the nine-year-old boy, who was having lessons with the castrato Giovanni Manzuoli, could extemporize music proper to arias of love and rage, complete with preceding recitatives.[8] Mozart's understanding at such a young age of the conventional passions of opera seria may testify to his genius, but also, to the sceptical, may seem to mark the musical language as over-conventional. At the height of his powers, Mozart overcomes any such reservations, and his dramatic objectives were fully compatible with his sensible policy of getting to know the singers before composing. This policy brought practical problems in preparing his first opera seria, *Mitridate, re di Ponto*: as his father wrote, 'he has only written one aria for the *primo uomo* because he hasn't arrived, and he doesn't want double the work; he prefers to await his arrival so he can measure the suit to fit the body'.[9] In the event Mozart had to rewrite several numbers, but the *prima donna*, Antonia Bernasconi, refused an insidious suggestion that she might substitute arias from an earlier setting of the same libretto by Quirino Gasparini.[10] One of Gasparini's arias ('Vado incontro') seems to have been included by the recalcitrant tenor Guglielmo d'Ettore, who had sung the same role (Mitridate) in Gasparini's opera.

The typical aria text had two stanzas, complementary or contrasting, returning to the first stanza after the second. This design, established as the Baroque da capo aria, is found in *Apollo et Hyacinthus*. But by 1770 most composers preferred a modified form of this design, in which the first stanza ends in a related key, so that when it returns after the second stanza the music is recomposed like a sonata recapitulation, ending in the main key, often with a cadenza. It is tempting to look with a favourable eye on departures from these conventional patterns, but this would do scant justice to Mozart's ability to make conventional designs work dramatically. A number of arias make their effect by using varied tempi, and a favourite design of the 1780s formalised this into the rondò, a slower then a faster movement, in each of which a main theme receives two statements; a dramatic advantage of this form is that the character and hence the drama appear to have moved on during the aria.

It needs to be remembered that aria-based opera was designed for a more formal society than ours, and is used to characterize people whose relationships were governed by class and rank, so that even relatives and lovers (married couples seldom appear) must observe decorum when addressing each other. The coupling of orchestrated recitative and aria, usually marking a dramatic climax within an opera, could be detached as a freestanding scena, precisely the form Mozart used in many of his so-called 'concert arias', written for particular singers he wished to oblige, or for whom he acted as teacher.[11] In Mannheim (1777–8), he fell in love with Aloysia Weber (later Lange), and determined to establish her career; over nearly ten years, during which time he married her sister Constanze, he composed for her some of his most intense and brilliant arias. The intensity results as much from exploration of her extraordinary high tessitura as from other forms of compositional inventiveness; one aria extends higher than those of the Queen of Night in *Die Zauberflöte*, a role created by her sister Josefa.[12] Mozart set Metastasio's text 'Alcandro, lo confesso... Non sò d'onde viene' for Aloysia (K. 294) in 1778, and then again in 1787 (K. 512) for the magnificent bass, Ludwig Fischer, who had created Osmin in *Die Entführung*. The settings have little in common beyond the broadest aspect of form, a modified da capo with the middle section in a faster tempo. Both exploit the singers' enormous range and flexibility in singing large intervals. The Fischer version is musically more sophisticated; but, like several of the Aloysia arias, it suffers from its own cleverness. The same could be said of one of Mozart's most celebrated scenas, 'Bella mia fiamma…Resta, o cara', K. 528 (1787). This was written for Josepha Duschek, who allegedly locked Mozart in her summerhouse until he had completed it; in revenge he filled it with awkward intervals. Insertion arias for comedies are usually shorter and warmer; and excess intellectualism is entirely absent from the beautiful 'Ch'io mi scordi di te?…Non temer, amato bene', another text Mozart composed twice, first as an additional aria with obbligato violin in the 1786 *Idomeneo* revival, and a few months later for the farewell performance of the first Susanna, Nancy Storace, with obbligato piano for himself. For this popular mistress of opera buffa overwhelming difficulties were not required, and her raptly beautiful dialogue with the piano led to unsubstantiated rumours that Mozart was in love with her; for him, however, the chance to combine two of his favourite forms, the rondò and the piano concerto, was sufficient motivation.

Dramatic themes

A new opera seria was a major cultural event requiring co-ordination of poetic, musical, histrionic and scenic arts. The visual dimension is irretrievably lost, although surviving illustrations suggest considerable lavishness. Acting skill was expected, or at least desired; Leopold Mozart recounts an incident at the premiere of *Lucio Silla*, when the inexperienced tenor's tyrannical fury was so exaggerated that the audience laughed, seriously discomposing the *prima donna*. In reviving its emotional poetry and elaborate music, we should remember that its favourite topics – arbitrary imprisonment, exile and tyranny – were rife during the Enlightenment, of which opera seria is a characteristic product. Mozart's German operas are famed for the magnanimity of Pasha Selim and Sarastro, but in this they imitate the older Italian form. Mitridate yields to his better instincts on his deathbed, renouncing his intended queen Aspasia in favour of his faithful son, Sifare. Less convincingly, Lucio Silla arbitrarily forgives his enemies and retires into private life. Curiously, his action has some historical basis, yet in the opera nothing is done to make it plausible; Silla is the least interesting and least musically rewarding role. The clemency of Tito, however, follows from a clear, if bland, analysis of his personality by means of arias. In this last opera seria commission, Mozart accepted this method of characterization, which sets into higher relief the rages of his antagonist, Vitellia. Her final recitative and aria ('Non più di fiori') are the musical embodiment of resignation, as ambition is abandoned and she resolves to confess her role in the attempted assassination of Tito. Significantly, Mozart used the modern rondò form, in which a thought represented by theme or tonality continually returns to haunt the mind. Only aria can achieve such introspection; in a committed performance the very floridity of the instrumental obbligato (basset-horn) contributes positively, through musical beauty, to the sentiment, and to the conviction of the musical rhetoric.

The complexities of plot preclude detailed dramatic discussion here, and in what follows a few features are isolated which show Mozart's remarkable grip on the potentialities of the genre. In the early serenatas, the slenderness of plot, divinely controlled and allegorical, is barely sufficient scaffolding for the musical elaboration, although *Ascanio*, according to Leopold Mozart, eclipsed the opera seria of the season, Hasse's *Ruggiero*. But *Mitridate* and *Lucio Silla* have shown themselves well worthy of revival, and although it takes a leap of faith from producers, singers and audience to mount or attend a production, the effort is rewarded by the satisfactory symmetry of *Mitridate*, in which the old King breathes his last while his sons are reconciled to their brides, as it is by the finest scenes of *Lucio Silla*.

Despite its success, *Lucio Silla* was Mozart's last commission for Italy, a fact that profoundly affected his future. Mozart respected the Milanese taste for long arias, without relinquishing characterization. Where a secondary character, Cinna, has a loquacious and open-hearted first aria, the *primo uomo* Cecilio immediately reveals a more introspective personality: Cinna picks up the tune of the orchestral introduction, while Cecilio's entry floats above the instrumental bustle, asserting the expressive independence of the voice. As Giunia defies the tyrant, her aria tempo twice changes to allegro. Behind such multi-tempo arias we may sense the influence of Gluck's *Alceste* (1767), stronger still in the magnificent scene in which Cecilio awaits Giunia by the tomb of her ancestor Marius; the atmosphere conveyed by instrumental texture and harmony would have done credit to any composer, never mind one of sixteen, and the solo and choral music for the processional entry of Giunia, and her mistaking Cecilio for a ghost, form the strongest passage of Mozartian opera seria before *Idomeneo*. There follows a rapturous duet; the rest of the opera never quite matches this superb and complex scene.

In *Il re pastore*, with Metastasio's libretto cut to fourteen numbers, the dénouement is convincing because each character is fully developed in the arias (there is one duet, and a finale for all the voices). At the heart of this pastoral opera seria lies an aria for the eponymous hero, Aminta: 'L'amerò, sarò costante' (the resources of Salzburg were enriched by the castrato Tommaso Consoli in this role). Muted violins, pairs of flutes and cors anglais, support a solo violin melody that curls back on itself, then develops an impassioned

continuation. The voice completes one of Mozart's most gorgeous paragraphs, the violin gliding above the orchestra like a benediction. This aria is
a literal show-stopper: for over seven minutes nothing happens – or should
happen – on stage. The young shepherd has discovered that he is the rightful
king, and believing himself alone pours out his love for Elisa. Instrumentation and the rondo form assist in conveying romance, tenderness, constancy.
That, at least, is what *we* hear. Those who witness Aminta's declaration assume that it is not meant for Elisa, but for Tamiri, daughter of the deposed
usurper; Alessandro (Alexander the Great), with the best of intentions, has
arranged this dynastic marriage. Agenore, who loves Tamiri, believes that
ambition has led Aminta to throw over Elisa. Such misunderstandings are
the stuff of serious and comic opera alike, but we may well ask why music
of such transparent sincerity fails to register with Agenore. There are no
unsympathetic characters in *Il re pastore*, but all are victims of Alessandro's
well-meaning statesmanship. The beauty of this aria contributes to the irony
of its misinterpretation within the dramatic context, and allows Agenore to
be no mere confidant but a dramatically interesting person, whose own
passions motivate the only minor-mode aria of the opera, a fine piece of
Sturm und Drang. With unintended cruelty, Alessandro sings an aria of
self-satisfied triumph; but when the women boldly confront him with their
preferences in love, and Aminta determines to renounce glory for Elisa,
the King duly displays enlightened magnanimity, and love and duty are
reconciled.

This thoroughly moral opera is uncharacteristic of Metastasio only in
the absence of any opposition other than well-intentioned ignorance. The
orchestral sound is richer and more varied than in the earlier serious operas.
Near the end of the overture, a horn melody precedes the first flute entry;
flutes take the lead in the short aria that follows without a break.[13] Elisa
interrupts it before its cadence (but such continuity between numbers does
not recur). Trumpets in Alexander's first and final arias contrast with the
flute solo in the second, inspired by Johann Baptist Becke who accompanied
Consoli from Munich. Form and style are sufficiently varied to be considered
symbolic. Elisa, suffering noble anguish in her aria 'Barbaro! oh Dio', twice
explodes into a fast tempo because she cannot contain her anger; then, with
'L'amerò', rondo form embodies the loving nature and nobility of Aminta,
and the essence of this surprising early masterpiece.

Idomeneo is the only serious opera generally recognized to be among
Mozart's finest achievements. The adaptation of a French original by the
Salzburg cleric Gianbattista Varesco is no mere translation, but a reinterpre-
tation of the myth previously treated in a French opera.[14] Perhaps *Idomeneo*
never reached formal perfection; after three performances in Munich, in
which much music was cut and some restored, it was performed only once

more, by aristocratic amateurs in Vienna (1786). Although Mozart was writing with all the singers present in Munich, he struggled to express the drama through the medium of (so he claimed) an inexperienced castrato, Dal Prato (Idamante), and the all-too-experienced and elderly Anton Raaff as Idomeneo. Neither could act; 'Raaff is like a statue', Mozart wailed, in one of the letters home that provide unique insight into the compositional thinking behind this opera. In the event, that the King sings in a dignified, if old-fashioned, style is dramatically to the purpose. That his heroic son is overshadowed by the women in the cast is less so, given that Idamante slays the monster ravaging Crete, and then voluntarily offers himself for sacrifice to placate the god Neptune. Two members of the Wendling family sang Ilia, the captive Trojan princess, and Elettra, daughter of Agamemnon, both of them in love with the young Prince; and for them Mozart wrote superbly dramatic arias, contrasting the saint-like forbearance of Ilia with the alternate fury and exacerbated tenderness of Elettra. In the last act, Ilia's aria evokes a tender garden of love, while Elettra's, following the god's oracular pronouncement that her rival Ilia must marry Idamante, is neurotic venom personified.[15] Between these personal epiphanies, the dramatic climax is the quartet, a piece of harrowing beauty which Mozart was never to surpass and which he could not hear again without weeping.

Not the least remarkable aspect of *Idomeneo* is the richness of its orchestral invention. The fury and charm of natural phenomena are unforgettably limned: the storm in Act 1, fantastically merged with the rage of Elettra, and the calm sea in Act 2. The orchestra conveys heroism, tenderness and resignation, through instrumentation as much as tempo and style, and supports splendid choral writing and fine dances. (Mozart was delighted to compose his own ballet music, instead of, as was usual, leaving it to a local hack.) No doubt Mozart never surpassed this work only because he never had the opportunity to do so; aspects of *Idomeneo*, matched by such works as the C minor Mass, K. 427, and the Requiem, K. 626, bridge the world of Gluck and that of Beethoven and Berlioz, even Wagner, for *Idomeneo* is a treasure-trove of motivic allusion, anticipating leitmotiv technique in its continual thematic cross-references.[16]

Idomeneo immediately preceded Mozart's move to Vienna, and his first efforts to revive it there, probably with a redistribution of voice-types (a tenor Idamante, a bass Idomeneo), were abortive. The version given a single performance by aristocratic *dilettanti* in 1786 makes Idamante a tenor, while Idomeneo's role was essentially unaltered (except for simplification of passagework in his central aria, 'Fuor del mar'). At least in adapting *La clemenza di Tito*, Mozart could include one low male voice, the Imperial confidant Publio, in addition to the experienced tenor Antonio Baglioni, who sang Tito. He may have wanted to cast his young hero, Sesto, as a tenor, but the impresario supplied the castrato Domenico Bedini; his music, however, confirms that he was experienced and reliable, and his two arias are high points of the score. The first, 'Parto, parto', allows the young man, cowed by the beautiful and imperious Vitellia, to articulate his subservience to her will so that it almost becomes a strength of character; this feat is achieved with the support of a glittering clarinet solo.[17] The second is a substantial rondò ('Deh, per questo istante solo'), which Sesto addresses to Tito. This expresses his tangled thoughts while saying nothing to implicate Vitellia in the (fortunately unsuccessful) plot to assassinate his friend and protector, the Emperor. Sesto fully expects to be put to death; his eloquence is the musical equivalent of silence in the face of an accusation that can neither be refuted nor explained. Vitellia was sung by Maria Marchetti Fantozzi, a competent actress as well as a singer of power and wide range. The rondò form of 'Non più di fiori' (see above), with the obbligato on the hollow-sounding basset-horn, forms an unacknowledged bond between these characters. Vitellia recognizes that her fate is intertwined with Sesto's, and although she does not love him as he loves her she cannot be responsible for his death. The clemency of the Emperor is thus richly justified, not only by his own character, but by the empathy the audience must feel, thanks to the musical powers of aria, with its beneficiaries. The happy ending foreshadowed in the opera's title is no less persuasive than that of the opera's contemporary, *Die Zauberflöte*.[18]

This concentration does not detract from the force and beauty of the opera's ensembles. The duet for Annio and Servilia is an enchanting evocation of young love resigned to frustration; the trio when Vitellia hears too late that the Emperor is willing to marry her, and tries to stop the conspiracy without revealing its existence, is blood-curdling in a good performance, and not only because she is required to sail up to d''' (this in a role which descends, in the last aria, to g). Shorter than Mozart's opera buffa finales, the first-act finale is a conception of concentrated grandeur. It opens with Sesto evidently about to sing an aria; confronted by the other characters, he rushes off to try to save Tito, his confusion represented by a disturbing modulation. When he returns he seems about to confess everything; a solo oboe again makes silence eloquent.[19] The characters and chorus unite in lamenting the death of a beloved monarch.

Denounced as 'very bad' by the Empress at the premiere, *La clemenza di Tito* has had the most disputed reception of all Mozart's mature operas. It is too readily assumed, however, that its immediate popularity in the fifteen years or so following Mozart's death was a response to a perceived simplification of style.[20] It remains essentially unfinished; the recitatives were not composed by Mozart, and he would surely have revised it before any second production. But we cannot assume that the speed with which it was composed equates to perfunctory invention or execution, or that he was already dying and his powers failing. There is reason to suppose that he was eager once more to try his hand at this genre, as he was with church music, and to measure his mature style against its rigorous demands on the musician.

Conclusion

In the modern fashion for musical revival, serious opera remains relatively neglected. Mozart's remain among the finest products of the genre. In Milan, Mozart acted under instruction from his father, from the singers and from the requirements of the court; these operas succeeded, and the absence of any revivals merely reflects a culture in which few operas outlived their first season. We might wonder whether, young as he was, Mozart could have grasped the political and human implications of the stories. Undoubtedly he worked from a stylistic template that enabled him to select a manner appropriate to each dramatic situation, as the remarks of Daines Barrington testify (see above). But in working with the signifying conventions, and thus of audience expectations, Mozart was no different from his peers, and in actual inventiveness within these constraints he can match any master of the previous generation. In *Lucio Silla* he added a powerful dose of post-Gluckian drama in the tomb scene, anticipating the glories of *Idomeneo*. In *Il re pastore* he captured the pastel shades of the libretto to perfection, and working on vulnerable characters on an intimate stage prepared him not only for the richer humanity of *Idomeneo* but also for his comedies. Although not without flaws, and uncertainty as to his final intentions, *Idomeneo* is quite simply one of his greatest works; modern performances of *La clemenza di Tito* have restored it to a significant place in the repertory; and if we add the opera seria arias which belong to no opera – the 'concert arias' – we have a Mozartian repertory so richly various that it must be considered unequivocally to be among the glories of his magnificent oeuvre.

12 Mozart's German operas

DAVID J. BUCH

Mozart wrote German opera throughout his compositional career – from the age of twelve until three months before he died. His career comprised the first flowering of German opera, from its origins as an adaptation of *opéra comique* (which was in the process of integrating elements of Italian comic opera), with its characteristic alternation of spoken dialogue and music,[1] to its emergence in a distinctly Viennese dialect.

Mozart's two greatest theatrical successes in his lifetime were in fact German operas, *Die Entführung aus dem Serail* and *Die Zauberflöte*. Without these two operas the transformation of that provincial adaptation (just one of many at the time) into an exportable commodity might not have occurred. They were essential for the development of an international German repertory, one that became translated rather than one that was the result of translation. While Mozart's German operas were not the only ones that contributed to this development, operas such as Peter Winter's *Das unterbrochene Opferfest* and Franz Xaver Süssmayr's *Der Spiegel von Arkadien* (both 1794) would not have enjoyed their international and long-lived success without the precedent established by Mozart. In fact, these operas would probably not have been written in the first place.

Mozart's German operas exemplify the historical development of the genre: both his early and his later works are stylistically consistent in a general way with those of his contemporaries. But Mozart was not a typical late eighteenth-century opera composer. *Die Entführung* and *Die Zauberflöte* form only a miniscule part of the contemporary repertory, yet they were works of the highest compositional virtuosity and were performed in virtually every German opera house. The scope of his output in other vocal and instrumental genres, the consistently high quality of his music and the virtuosity of his compositional mastery were unmatched.

This chapter has contrasting objectives. On the one hand, I demonstrate how these operas underscore the blossoming of German musical theatre in the last two decades of the eighteenth century. On the other, I explore the individuality of Mozart's art, and show that this individuality ensured his enshrined status as one of the first 'classic' composers. By the early nineteenth century Mozart had become a mythical figure in that it was deemed unnecessary for him to be viewed in any other context than that of singular genius. As a result, knowledge of the immediate context of his

German operas – the blossoming of German musical theatre – was all but forgotten.

First, a word on terminology. The modern definition of 'Singspiel' denotes a German opera with dialogue and no 'semplice' recitatives. But in the eighteenth century 'Singspiel' stood for any kind of musical theatre, in any language, without regard to dialogues or recitatives. Mozart referred to *Die Zauberflöte* as his 'teutsche Oper', both informally (in a letter to Constanze of 7–8 October 1791)[2] and in his personal catalogue. Thus I prefer the term 'German opera'.

It has become a commonplace in Mozart scholarship to argue that the composer's early works are somehow less sophisticated than the later ones, adhering to an old biographical principle of 'artistic growth'. It seemed not to matter that it conflicted with another treasured principle, that earlier versions were often deemed superior to later ones (consider the C minor Mass, K. 427, and its later arrangement as the oratorio *Davidde penitente*, K. 469). In fact, the adherence to such a 'principle' obscures an informed appreciation of the breadth of Mozart's accomplishment. One cannot demonstrate according to a convincingly objective standard that Mozart's earlier works (excepting juvenilia) are inferior in quality to his later works. At an early stage Mozart displayed remarkable skill in the details and structure of his music. If he did not impart coherence on as large a scale as he would in the *introduzioni* and finales to *Don Giovanni*, *Così fan tutte*, and *Die Zauberflöte*, neither did his contemporaries. This is because it seems not to have been important to do so until the 1780s, when composers were expected to provide longer musical segments using greater instrumental forces and integrating more varied musical topics and styles.

It was the challenge of writing in a dramatically coherent fashion that Mozart met with such distinction. As a result, his principal compositional virtue in the operatic domain is his consistent achievement of a high musical standard, demanding as much from his listeners as he ultimately rewards them with. Typically a successful late eighteenth-century opera might have had three or four memorable numbers. Mozart could write memorable numbers throughout his operas, however, displaying a masterful use of imagery, coherent dramatic pace, melodic invention, humour and sheer sensuous beauty of sound. Psychological situations are made clearer (that is not to say less complicated) through his musical logic. His scores provide musical stage directions in a way few others did in the period. His music appears to identify directly with each character, good or bad, yet it often seems to suggest ironic distance at the same time.

Nineteenth-century aesthetics – where one finds a pseudo-Darwinian teleology for the development of 'continuous music', the breakdown of aria and recitative distinctions, and the requirement that a libretto has a profound subject – have significantly influenced discussions of late eighteenth-century German opera. We see this in the proliferation of 'hidden sub-text theories' in late twentieth-century commentaries on *Die Zauberflöte*, and in the relatively rare performances of the masterpiece *Der Schauspieldirektor*. But the aesthetics of Mozart's time were associated with pleasure, wit, concinnity and beauty. And in the vernacular theatre, the guiding principle was entertainment and skilled performance.

Mozart's early German opera

Mozart's earliest German opera, *Bastien und Bastienne*, K. 50, is an adaptation by Friedrich Wilhelm Weiskern and Johann Müller of a parody of Jean-Jacques Rousseau's *Le Devin du village* (1752) by Marie-Justine Benoîte Favart, Charles-Simon Favart and Harny de Guerville (*Les Amours de Bastien et Bastienne*).[3] The one-act plot (in seven scenes) is a pastoral story with a feigned magic episode. It was produced for Vienna sometime in autumn 1768, perhaps in the house of Dr Anton Mesmer. Indeed, half of the paper in Mozart's autograph score is Viennese in origin. Johann Andreas Schachtner may have provided the text for additional recitatives to replace dialogue for a later Salzburg performance. The printed libretto (Vienna 1784) survives in Vienna's Gesellschaft der Musikfreunde (henceforth A-Wgm). The autograph score (now located in Kraków, Poland, Biblioteka Jagiellonska, henceforth PL-Kj) comprises an *intrada* and sixteen numbers.

This early work reveals Mozart's precocious mastery of contemporary musical idioms, although the possibility that Leopold contributed to its composition cannot be discounted. There is no tangible gap between the quality of the music by this twelve-year-old boy and that of other mature composers of that time. Take, for example, the wit and skill in the setting of Colas's 'feigned magic' incantation aria, 'Diggi, daggi, schurry, murry', (No. 10). Schachtner's text combines nonsense language and garbled, fragmentary Latin ('quid quo pro'). Mozart's accompaniment in this Andante maestoso in C minor spoofs the serious operatic style of invocation. A steady pulsating bass in quavers supports a simple and slow vocal line with repeated notes and pompously wide leaps. The two oboes play mostly semibreves and minims, enhancing the ominous bass line with sustained wind. The strings accompany with rapid glissandos and repeated notes, reminiscent of a *bruit souterrain*; a few bars with polyphony in the inner voices may actually parody the counterpoint of French 'merveilleux' operas and ballets.

Mozart did not write another German opera until eleven years later, when he returned to Salzburg from his tour of Mannheim and Paris. This project, spanning several months in 1779–80, appears to have been undertaken in the hope of gaining a commission for the Emperor's National Theatre in Vienna. The commission did not materialize and, as a result, the unnamed work remained unfinished (ending just before the dénouement of the plot). Today it is called *Zaide* (K. 344), named by Johann André when he published it in 1838 after purchasing the autograph from Constanze.

Zaide testifies to the contemporary interest in attempting to create a distinctly German operatic genre to rival those French and Italian genres that had achieved supremacy. We learn from the correspondence of Leopold and Wolfgang that this was 'Schachtner's operetta'. Thus the text was by Johann Andreas Schachtner, after *Das Serail, oder Die unvermuthete Zusammenkinft in der Sclaverey zwischen Vater, Tochter und Sohn* (*The Harem, or The Unexpected Reunion of a Father, Daughter and Son in Slavery*) by Franz Joseph Sebastiani. The work had exotic and comic elements, but seems to have been conceived more as a serious than as a comic opera. Linda Tyler has demonstrated that Schachtner stuck close to Sebastiani in Act 1, subsequently deviating from Sebastiani in Act 2.[4]

The untitled autograph score can be found in the Staatsbibliothek zu Berlin (henceforth D-B), but as yet no libretto has been located. The score comprises fifteen complete numbers (set for flutes, oboes, bassoons, horns, trumpets, timpani and strings), although there is no overture or final chorus. Each act begins with a substantial melodrama, longer than any other Mozart composed. One fifty-two-bar sketch survives for aria No. 6. No exact chronology is known, although Alan Tyson has shown that Mozart used the two types of paper found in the autograph extensively in Salzburg in 1779–80.[5]

Linda Tyler has argued that *Zaide* is significant in Mozart's overall development since it reflects his new mastery of operatic conventions. In this respect she comments on 'the streamlining and alteration of traditional aria forms and proportions, characterization through large-scale forms, experiments in phrase structure, more daring representation of text, and the juxtaposition of different operatic conventions'.[6] Irrespective of whether *Zaide* testifies to a true leap in Mozart's compositional development, it certainly contains brilliant examples of his gifts as a musical dramatist and master craftsman. Take, for example, the aria for Zaide in Act 1, 'Ruhe sanft, mein holdes Leben', with its exquisite cantabile (interrupted by a plaintive oboe obbligato). The trio 'O selige Wonne!' in E major that concludes the first act is yet another example of Mozart's mastery of drama, expression and beauty of sound. E major is a key often used for moments of sensuality, as in the 'waves of water' scenes of the chorus No. 15 of *Idomeneo* and the trio 'Soave sia il vento' in *Così fan tutte*. Instead of waves the opening segment of this trio of *Zaide* depicts a vision of moving clouds and a rainbow, using gentle dotted rhythms. The accompanying instrumental motives recall other siciliano-like pieces, such as the 'Laudate Dominum' from the Vespers K. 339 and the 'Et incarnatus est' from the C minor Mass, K. 427. The multi-sectional trio continues with a portentous episode in the minor mode with octave and unison accompaniment, and then a concluding duple-metre segment of determination, hope and calm.

German operas for the Imperial Court

Goethe wrote: 'All our efforts to confine ourselves to the simple went for naught when Mozart appeared. *Die Entführung aus dem Serail* swept away everything else ... and there was no more talk of our carefully worked-out pieces for the stage.'[7] This statement contains perhaps the most salient historical insight ever made on Mozart's most ambitious and original opera to date. Indeed *Die Entführung*, K. 384, was a landmark in the history of German opera, being widely performed and imitated. Popular works such as Emanuel Schikaneder's *Der wohltätige Derwisch* (first performed at the Theater auf der Wieden in early 1791) owe much to Mozart's precedent.

The 'simple and confined things' cultivated by Goethe and his colleagues reflected their concept of a German national idiom, already defined in their proto-Romantic *Volks* poetry that had seized the popular imagination. They desired the same effect in opera, but Mozart's ambition and virtuosity turned the genre in another direction, one that would remain controversial even in the decade following his death. For Mozart cultivated the complex, making demands on his performers and listeners that conflicted with the prevalent aesthetic principles of the day championed by Rousseau. What would make Mozart dear to the early nineteenth century caused consternation to many of his contemporaries.

From the first motives of the 'Turkish' overture, *Die Entführung* presents an array of musical idioms. Some were popular, such as the *Romanze*, the lied, and the exotic Turkish references that delighted the Viennese audience. But Mozart also composed demanding ensembles and the great coloratura aria for Catarina Cavalieri, 'Martern aller Arten'. At the very start the aria's extended introductory ritornello presents a kaleidoscope of 'Instrumenten aller Arten' that seem to suggest the variety of torments mentioned in the text. In fact 'kaleidoscopic' seems the right adjective to describe the governing aesthetic principle of *Die Entführung*, which was composed when vernacular opera was something of a musical variety show punctuated by dialogue, without the long scenes with continuous music that appear later in the decade. But in terms of vivid musical imagery, vital pace and virtuosity in composition, *Die Entführung* is as unmatched by contemporary works as Goethe suggested it was.

Die Entführung had its premiere at the Burgtheater on 16 July 1782. The score for this three-act 'komische Oper' consists of an overture and twenty-two numbers, the text after Christoph Friedrich Bretzner by Gottlieb Stephanie the younger. The autograph of Acts 1 and 3 are held in PL-Kj, Act 3 in D-B, and the libretto (Vienna, 1782) in Vienna's Österreichische Nationalbibliothek (henceforth A-Wn).

In Mozart's letter to his father of 26 September 1781, the composer describes his music for *Die Entführung* and the various expressive devices he employs. The short, rollicking Janissary chorus, for example, was designed to please the Viennese taste, and music in the opera as a whole carefully tailored to the individual singers. Constanze was sung by Cavalieri, Belmonte by Johann Valentin Adamberger, Osmin by Johann Ignaz Ludwig Fischer, Blonde by Therese Teyber, Pedrillo by Johann Ernst Dauer and the Pasha Selim (a speaking role) by Dominik Jautz.

Mozart's next commission for a German opera, *Der Schauspieldirektor*, K. 486, again came from the imperial court, and was also set to a text by Gottlieb Stephanie. The premiere took place in the Orangery at Schönbrunn Palace on 7 February 1786. It was the German companion piece to Antonio Salieri's *Prima la musica e poi le parole*. *Der Schauspieldirektor* then moved to the Kärntnertortheater for performances on 11, 18 and 25 February. The one-act libretto (Vienna, 1786) is preserved in A-Wn. The autograph score, consisting of an overture, ariette, rondò, terzetto, and *Schlussgesang* (a 'vaudeville' for the singing characters), is now located in the New York Public Library. A surviving thirty-eight-bar draft is possibly a fragment of an arietta for this opera; a sketch for a trio also survives. The singers in the cast were from the Emperor's German opera troupe: Adamberger sang Herr Vogelsang, Cavalieri took the role of Madame Silberklang (the first *prima donna*), Aloysia Lange was Madame Herz (second *prima donna*) and Joseph Weidmann sang Buff (bass).

Unlike other German operas by Mozart, this unacknowledged masterpiece has few serviceable recordings and is rarely performed on major stages. Some of the blame for this neglect can be attributed to the rather mediocre text, but most of the problem is in the genre itself, a one-act play with substantial musical components. This kind of piece was popular in the eighteenth century, when there was much greater variability in the form of opera than there is today, but modern audiences are rarely given the opportunity to hear such pieces. Other 'problems' are deemed to be the subject matter of the text, as well as the artificiality and artifice of the music. Such characteristics are not especially admired by those who want to find profundity and seriousness in Mozart.

The plot concerns an impresario's difficulties in assembling a theatrical troupe to perform in (where else?) provincial Salzburg. Although the humour in the spoken text falls flat today, Mozart must have appreciated the situation. In any event, his music is at its highest level of craftsmanship, wit and irony. Donald Tovey believed the overture to be 'actually more polyphonic than that of *The Magic Flute*'.[8] The two *prime donne* compete with virtuoso passages in their arias and the trio. Both coloratura arias are stunning compositions addressed to imaginary lovers. And here again we find Mozart the virtuoso composer creating deeply moving pieces with contrived emotion entirely staged for effect – artifice without the customary illusion. Even the admonitions of Herr Vogelsang, delivered in a reverent legato that sears in its beauty, cannot stop the rivalry of the *prime donne*: 'No artist must speak badly of another for it demeans the art too much.' (This is a principle that Mozart seems rarely to have obeyed!) The brilliant contrapuntal episode that follows fails to convince the two superficial virtuoso singers who continue: 'Ich bin die erste Sängerin!' ('I am the *prima donna!*') Such roles cannot be easily distilled into a representation of Mozart's characters as 'suffering and lamenting' archetypes (Richard Wagner), or at least they cannot be as easily distorted in this respect as the equally false Queen of the Night and each and every character in *Così fan tutte*.

Die Zauberflöte and the Theater auf der Wieden

Mozart apparently did not return to German opera until he became involved with the Theater auf der Wieden, or, as it was called in the period, the 'Wiednertheater'. (It seems not to have been called the Freihaustheater until years after it was demolished.) The three-storey theatre (with approximately 600 seats at that time) was a large, square, brick building located at the rear of the garden within a large complex of residences and businesses called the Stahrembergisches Freihaus. Situated in the district known as the Wieden (really a village for servants and craftsmen), one accessed it most easily through the Carinthian Gate, crossing the empty field that was called the Glacis and a bridge over the river Wien. One then proceeded into the theatre through a long covered wooden walkway; access was also possible through the rear of the Freihaus complex. The theatre had begun producing large-scale German operas in January 1789, adding to its repertory of spoken plays. Emanuel Schikaneder, who became the theatre's director in mid-1789, hired a Kapellmeister, together with an improved roster of musicians and singers. As we learn from Joseph Richter's *Eipeldauer Briefe*, the operas performed at the Wiednertheater became the talk of Vienna, especially the series called *Der dumme Gärtner aus dem Gebürge, oder Die zween Anton*. Schikaneder also produced his series of fairy-tale operas that enjoyed similar success throughout the 1790s.

We do not know exactly when Mozart first began visiting the Wiednertheater or writing music for its productions. Received wisdom claims that this process began after Schikaneder became the director, for he had been a friend of the Mozart family in Salzburg some ten years earlier. Mozart had even written a German aria for one of Schikaneder's productions there. In fact, Mozart may have written the German arias K. 569 and K. 580 for projected operas in the Wiednertheater when Johann Friedel was still the director. At least one aria, if not both, could be connected to Mozart's sister-in-law, Josefa Hofer, the wife of his close friend Franz Hofer. She was the *erste Sängerin* at this theatre well before the arrival of Schikaneder.

The first unequivocal evidence of Mozart composing for the Wiednertheater is found in a partial autograph score of the comic 'cat' duet, 'Nun liebes Weibchen' (K. 625), written for Schikaneder's new heroic-comic opera *Der Stein der Weisen, oder Die Zauberinsel* (premiered on 11 September 1790). The duet was one of the immediate hits of the show and was advertised in the *Wiener Zeitung* shortly after the premiere. While Mozart's manuscript of the duet, preserved in the Bibliothèque Nationale in Paris, is from the original performing score of the opera, the rest of this score is now lost. This loss is significant since it might have confirmed Mozart's role in the composition of the Act 2 finale. In a Viennese manuscript copy of this collaborative opera (from *c.*1795), the Wiednertheater singer, actor and chief copyist Kaspar Weiss specified the contributions of five composers. Most of the music was by the theatre's Kapellmeister, Johann Baptist Henneberg, but the first tenor Benedikt Schack, the first bass Franz Xaver Gerl, Schikaneder and Mozart also contributed music. There are three attributions to Mozart: the cat duet and two segments in the Act 2 finale.

The significance of *Der Stein der Weisen* goes well beyond Mozart's contribution. The text and music of *Der Stein der Weisen* clearly provided the model for *Die Zauberflöte*, K. 620, believed until recently to have been without real precedent in the repertory. Both operas, with texts by Emanuel Schikaneder, were based on fairy tales in Christoph Martin Wieland's *Dschinnistan* (Winterthur, 1786–9), as was Schikaneder's *Der wohltätige Derwisch, oder Die Schellenkappe* (from early 1791). The latter provided a precedent for *Die Zauberflöte* as well, especially in the magic bells and the solemn ceremonial music for the wise dervish (sung by Franz Xaver Gerl, who would create the role of Sarastro six months later). Both *Der Stein der Weisen* and *Die Zauberflöte* have two acts with a long introduction, large episodic finales and similar arias for parallel characters (see table 12.1). The musical numbers for these parallel characters are often placed in similar positions within the operas. For example, both operas have an aria for Schikaneder's comic

Table 12.1. *Structure of* Der Stein der Weisen *and* Die Zauberflöte

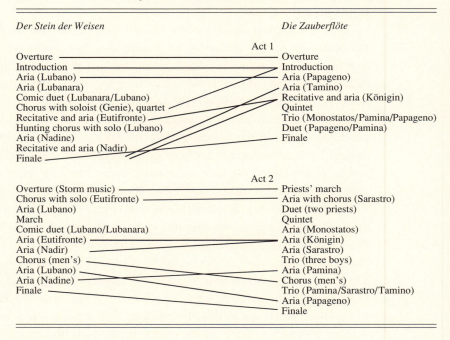

character after the introduction and shortly before the Act 2 finale. Both have male choruses late in Act 2, as well as an aria for the heroine (Nadine or Pamina). The ensembles differ, however, as *Der Stein der Weisen* lacks the elaborate trios and quintets of *Die Zauberflöte*. Nevertheless, both operas present a mixture of solemn, comic, magic and love scenes. Both have musical segments for pantomime and for episodes with machines and magic. The casts of both operas are basically the same, excluding Josefa Hofer, who was on maternity leave when *Der Stein der Weisen* was first produced. (For the two cast lists see table 12.2.) Thus when Mozart came to compose *Die Zauberflöte* he was writing for singers whose voices he knew well, and for a genre with which he was already familiar.

Der Stein der Weisen also presented Mozart with a wealth of musical motives and citations that were subsequently developed in *Die Zauberflöte*. The striking resemblance in the music for Schikaneder's characters (Lubano in *Der Stein der Weisen* and Papageno in *Die Zauberflöte*) may owe something to the input of the impresario himself, who had composed theatre music for many years. Lubano's arias are quite similar to Papageno's, and his exclamations at the end of the first finale seem to have inspired the birdcatcher's 'O wär' ich eine Maus, wie wollt ich mich verstecken' in the first finale of *Die Zauberflöte*, with its similar orchestration, unison and octave

Example 12.1 Attrib. Benedikt Schack, *Der Stein der Weisen*, aria, 'Welch' fremde Stimme', bars 1–3

Sie   klang_____   so   ernst___   und   fei - er - lich!

Table 12.2. *Cast lists* of Der Stein der Weisen *and* Die Zauberflöte

Der Stein der Weisen 11 September 1790 (poster in A-Wgm)	*Die Zauberflöte* 30 September 1791
Astromonte – Hr. [Benedikt] Schack	Sarastro – [Franz Xaver] Gerl
Eutifronte – Hr. [Franz Xaver] Gerl	Tamino – [Benedikt] Schack
Ein Genius – Mlle. [Anna] Schikaneder	Sprecher – [Kosmas Damian] Winter
Sadik – Hr. [Urban] Schikaneder	Erster Preister – [Urban] Schikaneder
Nadir – Hr. [Johann Michael] Kistler	Zweiter Priester – [Johann Michael] Kistler
Nadine – Mlle. [Maria Anna] Gottlieb	Dritter Priester – [Christian H. or Franz?] Moll
Lubano – Hr. [Emanuel] Schikaneder	Königen der Nacht – [Josefa] Hofer
Lubanara – Mad. [Barbara] Gerl	Pamina – [Maria Anna] Gottlieb
Astur – Hr. [Kosmas Damian] Winter	Erste Dame – [Johanna?] Klöpfer
	Zweite Dame – [Antonie?] Hofmann
	Dritter Dame – [Elisabeth] Schack
	Papageno – [Emanuel] Schikaneder
	Ein altes Weib [Papagena] – [Barbara] Gerl
	Monostatos, ein Mohr – [Johann J.] Nouseul
	Erster Sklav – [Karl Ludwig] Giesecke
	Zweiter Sklav – [Wilhelm?] Frasel
	Dritter Sklav – [Johann Nikolaus] Starke
	Priester, Sklaven, Gefolge

sonority and melodic contour. Astromonte's magical arrival, accompanied recitative and multipartite coloratura aria all prefigure the Act 1 scene from *Die Zauberflöte* with the Queen of the Night. Benedikt Schack's beautiful lyric aria 'Welch' fremde Stimme' in *Der Stein der Weisen* seems to have inspired Mozart's setting of 'Dies Bildnis ist bezaubernd schön', written by Mozart for Schack's character Tamino. The key, general style and opening vocal motive (with a soaring high G that immediately descends in scalar motion) are strikingly similar (see example 12.1 for the Schack aria). In addition, a phrase from the Act 1 comic duet (attributed to Gerl) in *Der Stein der Weisen* appears in the Act 1 quintet of *Die Zauberflöte*. Here the common conceit is that of a padlock. In the duet, Lubano places a padlock on the door of his cabin. In the quintet, Papageno has just had a padlock removed from his mouth (see examples 12.2a and 12.2b).

Mozart's association with the theatre's singers continued in the spring of 1791. He composed an aria for Gerl and the contrabassist Friedrich Pischlberger ('Per questa bella mano', K. 612) and a set of eight piano variations on the aria performed by Schikaneder (the original composer of which is unknown) 'Ein Weib ist das herrlichste Ding auf der Welt' (K. 613).

Example 12.2a Attrib. Franz Xaver Gerl, *Der Stein der Weisen*, Act 1 duet, bars 71–6

Example 12.2b Mozart, *Die Zauberflöte*, K. 620, Act 1 quintet, bars 49–52

As hinted above, the basic scholarship on *Die Zauberflöte* (premiered on 30 September 1791) has been more concerned with interpreting the work as an allegory than with its historical context in the theatre. *Der Stein der Weisen* makes us question the multiple interpretations of *Die Zauberflöte* as an allegory of some sort – masonic, whether Rosicrucian, cabalistic or Gnostic – since Schikaneder's fairy-tale operas from both before and after *Die Zauberflöte* have no such demonstrable content. Several other suppositions continue to be asserted as fact: for example, that the original Tamino, Benedikt Schack, performed the flute part (no evidence exists that he even played the instrument); and that the opera's plot was suddenly changed when it was discovered that the Theater in der Leopoldstadt had produced an opera (*Kaspar der Fagottist*) based on the same fairy tale, 'Lulu, oder Die Zauberflöte'. These questionable assertions derive from second- and third-hand accounts, and from commentators unconnected to the theatre or the persons involved in the production.

The autograph of *Die Zauberflöte* is now held in D-B, with some early orchestral parts in A-Wn. The original libretto (Vienna: Ignaz Alberti, 1791; copies in A-Wn and A-Wgm) has been reprinted several times in facsimile. Schikaneder referred to the work as a 'grosse Oper', while Mozart called it a 'teutsche Oper', as we have seen. Above all we must regard *Die Zauberflöte* as an example of the popular musical theatre of the day, an *Operette* designed for a mixed audience, a *Maschinenkomödie*, intended to fill the seats. This status will explain its mixture of styles and its episodic structure, both of which are also apparent in *Der Stein der Weisen*. Accompanied recitative and coloratura aria, popular tunes, comic duets, solemn ceremonial music and instrumental pantomime all contribute to an entertaining evening of musical variety.

While *Der Stein der Weisen* prefigures *Die Zauberflöte* in its comic scenes and characters (it may even exceed the later opera in this regard),[9] it lacks a number of elements that Mozart and Schikaneder included in their later work. First, there is the intricacy and virtuoso compositional accomplishment of the ensembles. *Die Zauberflöte* is unusually demanding in this regard: consider the music for the three ladies in the introduction, the two extensive quintets, the vocal quartet at the beginning of the Act 2 finale, and the trial scene, beginning with the duet for the men in black armour. Together with the solemn and serious tone of the 'feierlich' scenes, and the power and beauty of the reconciliation scenes in the Act 2 finale, these elements made *Die Zauberflöte* very special for its time, and this was recognized by contemporary commentators and reviewers.[10] The uniting of Pamina with Tamino is an emotional high point, extended beyond those of earlier operas such as *Zémire et Azor* and *Der Stein der Weisen* (where the reconciliation is between Astromonte and his son Nadir). From 'Tamino mein, o welche ein Glück' until the end of trial, Mozart creates a series of surging peaks of emotional release unmatched by any similar scene I have been able to find in operas written before *Die Zauberflöte*, probably even exceeding the power of the reconciliation scenes in the three Da Ponte operas; it lingers on the moments of union, moreover, with exquisitely understated elegance. The simplicity of the harmony and the sustained consonant sonority underpin the swells of the vocal lines before and after the two trials of fire and water.

In *Die Zauberflöte* Mozart's music of enchantment is always presented in the style of a march: both episodes with magic flute music use march-like rhythms, as do the three episodes with the magic bells. Mozart is not especially original in choosing the march for his magic scenes; its lockstep power through that most basic rhythm of motion had been a favourite way of illustrating the effect of a magic spell since the seventeenth century. But Mozart's original touch is evident in the fact that his magic bells provide only variations; after hearing the variation the enchanted characters (Monostatos and the slaves in the Act 1 finale, Papageno in the Act 2 finale) magically recognize the theme and sing it out, displaying enchantment through purely musical means.

PART III

Reception

13 Mozart in the nineteenth century

JOHN DAVERIO

... if ever Mozart became wholly comprehensible to me, he would then become fully
incomprehensible to me.   – SØREN KIERKEGAARD, *EITHER/OR* (1843)

I

Implicit in one of the more commonly held beliefs about our understanding of artworks and their creators is an oddly skewed relationship between proximity and distance. According to this view, early critics find themselves in the position of a spectator who, standing just a few inches away from one of Monet's paintings of Rouen cathedral, sees only daubs of paint and vague shapes. Just as the outline of the cathedral emerges only when the viewer takes a few steps back, so the image of the artist and his works is supposed to gain in clarity the farther we withdraw from it in time. This theory of reception has been applied most consistently to figures whose works were first deemed to be particularly challenging and thereafter enjoyed a more or less continuous afterlife. Mozart was such a figure. Recognized by his contemporaries as a prodigious though intractable talent, venerated as a 'classic' by later generations, he continued to pose interpretive challenges even for the most perceptive musicians of the mid- and late nineteenth century. 'We are beginning to understand Mozart', Berlioz wrote in 1862,[1] and, indeed, we are still coming to terms with Mozart today. With increased understanding, however, comes loss – of the sense for precisely those idiosyncrasies that made Mozart's music such a challenge for early audiences. The study of Mozart reception in the nineteenth century is tantamount to a search for lost images, an activity that may ultimately lead us to reconsider our own assumptions about the composer and his works.

As indicated in the selective list of milestones given as table 13.1, there is no dearth of material for this recovery operation. During the course of the nineteenth century, the image of Mozart was refracted through a diverse array of media. While biographers such as Georg Nikolaus von Nissen and Otto Jahn sorted out the details of his life, and critics and theorists including E. T. A. Hoffmann and Gottfried Weber focussed on individual works, practitioners of the relatively young discipline of musicology (Franz Brendel, Friedrich Chrysander, Ludwig Köchel) placed the works within a chronological framework and a historical context. Through the media of

Table 13.1. *Milestones in nineteenth-century Mozart reception*

1793: Friedrich Schlichtegroll, *Nekrolog auf das Jahr 1791*
1798: Friedrich Rochlitz, 'Anekdoten aus W. G. Mozarts Leben', published in *Allgemeine Musikalische Zeitung*
1798: Franz Niemetschek, *Leben des K. K. Kapellmeisters Wolfgang Gottlieb Mozart*
1801: Friedrich Rochlitz, *Don Juan* (adaptation of Da Ponte's *Don Giovanni* libretto as Singspiel text)
1801: *Die Zauberflöte* given as *Les Mystères d'Isis* (adaptation by E. Morel de Chédeville and Ludwig Wenzel Lachner)
1804: performance of the Requiem, K. 626, under Luigi Cherubini, for 'premature' funeral ceremony for Haydn held at Paris Conservatoire
1806: seventeen volumes of the Breitkopf and Härtel 'complete' edition appear by this date (including keyboard sonatas, keyboard and violin sonatas, twelve string quartets, twenty piano concertos, full score of *Don Giovanni*)
1807–9: first published scores of Mozart's orchestral works, including Symphonies Nos. 38–41
1810: E. T. A. Hoffmann counts Mozart among the 'Romantics' in his review of Beethoven's Fifth Symphony (material from review appears in Hoffmann's 1813 essay on Beethoven's instrumental music)
1813: E. T. A. Hoffmann, 'Don Juan' (story)
1828: posthumous publication of Georg Nikolaus von Nissen's *Biographie W. A. Mozarts*
1841: opening of Mozarteum in Salzburg
1841: first Viennese Mozart festival (others follow in 1856, 1879, 1891)
1842: unveiling of Ludwig Schwanthaler's Mozart statue in Salzburg
1843: Alexander Ulïbïshev, *Nouvelle Biographie de Mozart* (German editions 1847, 1859)
1843: Søren Kierkegaard, *Either/Or*
1845: Edward Holmes, *Life of Mozart* (first major biography of Mozart in English)
1855: Eduard Mörike, *Mozart auf der Reise nach Prag* (novella)
1856: first Mozart Salzburg festival
1856: Otto Jahn, *W. A. Mozart*
1862: Ludwig Ritter von Köchel, *Chronologisch-thematisches Verzeichnis sämtlicher Tonwerke Wolfgang Amadé Mozarts*
1863: first edition of Ludwig Nohl's popular biography, *Mozarts Leben*
1860s: Alexander Dargomïzhsky, *The Stone Guest* (opera based on Pushkin's play, musical setting completed by Cesar Cui, orchestrated by Nikolay Rimsky-Korsakov)
1877: appearance of first volumes of the 'definitive' Breitkopf and Härtel collected edition, more or less complete by 1883, all gaps filled by 1905
1887: 500th performance of *Don Giovanni* at Berlin Court Opera on 29 October
1887: Tchaikovsky, Suite No. 4 for Orchestra, 'Mozartiana', Op. 61 (consisting mainly of adaptations of Mozart's keyboard works)
1897: Nikolay Rimsky-Korsakov, *Mozart and Salieri* (opera based on Pushkin's play)

performance and publication, Mozart's compositions were treated as venerable documents of a bygone age (Mendelssohn's 'historical' concerts, held in Leipzig between 1838 and 1847, and the Breitkopf and Härtel collected edition of 1877–1905 were informed by a similar spirit of preservation), or, at the other extreme, as mere blueprints to be realized in accordance with the tastes of a particular audience (for example, the Chédeville–Lachner adaptation of *Die Zauberflöte* as *Les Mystères d'Isis*). Mozart's works provided the stimulus not only for the efforts of later composers (Tchaikovsky's Suite No. 4, 'Mozartiana'), but also for prose fiction (Hoffmann's 'Don Juan' and Mörike's *Mozart auf der Reise nach Prag*) and philosophy (Kierkegaard's *Either/Or*). The greatest musical dramatist of the eighteenth century, Mozart himself became the subject of numerous dramas, among them Pushkin's

Mozart and Salieri, which in turn served as the basis for Rimsky-Korsakov's opera of the same name. Memorialized in the lavish festivals of the mid- and late nineteenth century, depicted as a toga-clad colossus by the sculptor Ludwig Schwanthaler, Mozart was reduced to a domestic ornament in the form of the bric-a-brac on display in the souvenir shops of Salzburg and Vienna.

While all this diversity suggests that the search for a single nineteenth-century image of Mozart would be a futile enterprise, we can at least get our bearings by turning first to biography. In the one hundred years or so after his death, Mozart was the subject of numerous biographical accounts, beginning with Schlichtegroll's *Nekrolog* (obituary) of 1793. More a collection of anecdotes peppered with random observations on the works than a genuine biography, this account focusses on Mozart's earlier years, drawing on material derived in part from Mozart's sister, Nannerl. As argued recently by Maynard Solomon, Schlichtegroll's chronicle bequeathed to the nineteenth century the still prevalent myth of Mozart as the 'eternal child', the 'playful embodiment of love and beauty'.[2] With Niemetschek's volume of 1798, we enter the realm of Mozart biography proper. The work of a writer who worshipped his subject to the point of idolatry, it introduced a hagiographical strand in Mozart reception that was not seriously questioned until well into the twentieth century. Weighing in at over nine hundred pages, Georg Nikolaus von Nissen's posthumously published biography is a rather chaotic affair, though it is still useful as a compendium of documentary material once in the possession of Mozart's widow Constanze, who married Nissen in 1809.[3] The Russian civil servant and musical enthusiast Alexander Ulïbïshev transformed what he called Nissen's 'mortally tedious recitation of minutiae' into a readable narrative in the first volume of his *Nouvelle Biographie de Mozart* (1843), and then proceeded, in its second and third volumes, with detailed analyses of the operas from *Idomeneo* to *La clemenza di Tito*, the Requiem, and instrumental works including the late string quartets, string quintets and symphonies. One of the earliest forays into psychobiography, Ulïbïshev's work built on the typically Romantic premise that an artist's creative output offered a window onto his soul, a notion that led him to view Mozart's compositions in general, and his operas in particular, as revelations of his innermost being.[4] The interdependence of Mozart's life and his art was also a theme in Jahn's monumental biography of 1856, although given the author's training in philology it is hardly surprising that the former receives far more attention that the latter, and that his portrait of Mozart is more cautiously drawn than Ulïbïshev's. Taking as his premise the notion that Mozart's chief virtue was his 'universality' – his transformation of 'every human feeling into a work of art'[5] – Jahn produced a book that was destined to enjoy a distinguished afterlife of its own. The fifth edition, updated and expanded by Hermann Abert, appeared as late as 1919–21.

Among the more intriguing aspects of nineteenth-century Mozart reception is the permeable boundary between factual and fictional portrayals of the composer and his milieu. As Roye Wates observes in a recent article, Mörike's *Mozart auf der Reise nach Prag* is situated at the intersection of biography and world literature. A great favourite with nineteenth-century readers, the novella derived from Ulïbïshev's biography the notion that Mozart was inspired by voices from beyond. At the same time, Mörike's tale had an unmistakable impact on the biographical studies of Jahn – even though he was loath to admit it – and Abert, who embraced Mörike's interpretation of the encounter between the title character and the Commendatore in Act 2 of *Don Giovanni*.[6]

While there is no denying the symbiotic relationship between empirical and poetic elements in nineteenth-century images of Mozart, it is equally important to keep in mind the differences in intent between the media associated with these qualities. Although Hoffmann's 'Don Juan', a typically Romantic blend of fact, fantasy and music criticism, obviously centres on Mozart's *Don Giovanni*, the writer's principal aim is not so much to offer a critique of the opera as to make a statement about the incursion of inexplicable, otherworldly forces on the 'real' world, and to explore the similarities between the dream-state and the process of critical reflection.[7] Similarly, Kierkegaard had much to say about *Don Giovanni* in *Either/Or*, although generally in the context of explaining his theory of the 'musical erotic' – a concept that by the philosopher's own admission he owed 'to Mozart alone'.[8] In both cases, Mozart's opera is a means towards an end, the stimulus for poetic and philosophical reflections on broader themes. In contrast, despite the fact that biographers and historians will often invoke the techniques of imaginative and philosophical prose, they will also tend to focus on Mozart's life and works as ends in themselves.

The realization of Mozart's works in performance raises another significant issue of reception. In speaking of the reception of 'Mozart's' works, we need to remember that the works were at times presented in radically altered versions. For obvious reasons, this is especially true of the operas. Sung in German instead of the original Italian, its recitatives replaced with spoken dialogue, Mozart's opera seria *La clemenza di Tito* would have been known to early nineteenth-century audiences in Vienna and central Germany as *Titus der Grossmütige* or *Titus der Gütige*. *Don Giovanni* underwent a similar transformation from *dramma giocoso* to Singspiel. The most frequently performed of Mozart's operas in the nineteenth century, it was translated into German about twenty times between 1788 and 1900, although the most popular of these versions by far was that of the critic Friedrich Rochlitz. Completed in 1801 and based on Friedrich Ludwig Schröder's translation of 1789, Rochlitz's *Don Juan* divides the original pair of acts into four, such that two of the opera's crucial moments – the entrance of Zerlina and Masetto, and the appearance of the Commendatore's statue in the church-yard scene – occur at the beginnings of the 'new' Acts 2 and 4 respectively. In this way, Rochlitz, like Schröder, underscored the dramatic contrasts implicit in the original, and, by omitting the light-hearted epilogue (a practice adumbrated in Süssmayr's 1798 production of Schröder's version), he in essence converted Mozart's comic drama into a tragic one. As Wates has shown in a perceptive discussion of *Don Giovanni*'s metamorphosis into a Romantic tragedy, Rochlitz's libretto had a decisive influence on Hoffmann's and Mörike's conceptions of the opera, and may even have inspired the design of Liszt's *Don Juan Fantasy* (1841). Indeed, it was in this form – as a Romantic-tragic Singspiel – that *Don Giovanni* would have been known to most of Mozart's nineteenth-century biographers.[9]

Of all of Mozart's major operas, however, probably none was reworked so extensively to satisfy contemporary tastes as *Die Zauberflöte*. Fitted out as a *dramma eroicomico* entitled *Il flauto magico* for a 1794 performance in Prague, it caught the attention of French audiences about a decade later as *Les Mystères d'Isis*. A *dramme lyrique* with exotic touches, this adaptation (also known by the nickname *Les Misères d'ici*) was a far cry from the work premiered at Emanuel Schickaneder's Theater auf der Wieden in 1791. Some of the original music was transposed or otherwise rewritten, and much was cut, although to compensate for the omissions Lachner introduced material from *Figaro*, *Don Giovanni*, *La clemenza di Tito* and even some excerpts from Haydn's 'Drumroll' Symphony, No. 103. Little wonder that a fastidious critic such as Berlioz wrote off this collaborative effort as a 'wretched hotch-potch'.[10] Still, with 134 performances in the twenty-six years after its 1801 premiere, it is not difficult to understand why *Les Mystères* fared so well with the French public. A reflection of the craze for the exotic stimulated by Napoleon's Egyptian campaign, it is but one of the many instances where the nineteenth century remade Mozart in its own image.

II

In his magisterial history of nineteenth-century music, Carl Dahlhaus observes that the reception of Mozart in the century after his death was 'discontinuous' in that a 'romantic stylisation' of the composer in the writings of E. T. A. Hoffmann and other like-minded figures gave way to a 'classical stylisation'.[11] This is a subtle variation on the widespread view that Mozart was first received as a Romantic and subsequently reinterpreted as a Classic. Actually, the situation was considerably more complex. Many of Mozart's early critics understood him as neither a Romantic nor a Classic, but as a difficult composer who made few concessions to the masses. The enthusiastic reception of *Die Zauberflöte* did not significantly alter the prevailing opinion that Mozart's music was intended primarily for *Kenner* (connoisseurs) as opposed to *Liebhaber* (amateurs). As Niemetschek put it in his 1798 biography: 'The true beauty of [Mozart's] music is best appreciated only after several hearings, or serious study.' Indeed, the fact that his music made such demands on the listener constituted 'the real touchstone of [its] classical worth'.[12]

For many critics, even the ones who otherwise had only high praise for his music, Mozart placed such a high premium on originality of expression that he often offended the sensibilities of his audience. Invoking the comparison between Mozart and Raphael that would become one of the leading themes of early nineteenth-century Mozart reception, Rochlitz conceded that while both artists fashioned their ideas into 'beautiful limbs of a single, beautiful body', not all of their works achieved 'the highest, the purest and the most perfect'. As for Mozart, Rochlitz claimed that 'many of his fully textured compositions are congested, his modulations not infrequently bizarre, his transitions rough . . . seldom is he delicate without emitting painful, tension-laden sighs'.[13] A pair of Italian writers cited by Nissen went even further in describing Mozart's vocal melodies as 'forced and sluggish', his harmony as 'harsh and affected', and the overall hue of the operas as 'murky and confused'.[14]

All of these features – originality at any cost, congestion, bizarrerie, harshness, tension, affectation, murkiness – had been subsumed under the notion of the 'characteristic' by the philosopher and critic Friedrich Schlegel in the mid-1790s. Occupying the end of the aesthetic spectrum at the farthest remove from 'beauty', the characteristic, in Schlegel's view, represented the primary tendency in modern art. 'Even in music,' he observed, 'the characterization of individual entities has become increasingly prevalent.'[15] This is not to say that Mozart's early critics copied directly from Schlegel, but rather that their efforts to come to terms with the idiosyncratic features of his music resonated with the leading aesthetic attitudes of their time. And just as Schlegel gave a positive spin to the negative aspects of 'characteristic' art in his developing theories of Romanticism, so too were the more striking elements of Mozart's style co-ordinated with the aesthetic of the 'sublime' (which was often invoked in discussions of the Requiem, the 'Jupiter' Symphony and *La clemenza di Tito*),[16] and soon thereafter with the Romantic ideology.

The primary exponent of the 'Romantic' Mozart was E. T. A. Hoffmann, who in his oft-quoted 1810 review of Beethoven's Fifth Symphony extolled the magical and supernatural qualities of Mozart's instrumental music:

Dread lies all about us, but withholds its torments and becomes more an intimation of infinity. We hear the gentle voices of love and melancholy, the nocturnal spirit-world dissolves into a purple shimmer, and with inexpressible yearning we follow the flying figures kindly beckoning to us from the clouds.[17]

Commenting on *Don Giovanni* in a later essay, Hoffmann derided those early listeners 'who called the great composer a lunatic who could only write confusing rubbish . . . without rhyme or reason'. For Hoffmann, such views betrayed a crude insensitivity to the 'fiery imagination, deeply felt humour, and extravagant abundance of ideas' that made Mozart the 'Shakespeare of music'.[18] Nor was Hoffmann alone in validating the 'characteristic' side of Mozart's art through a comparison with the great English playwright. In his 'Letter Concerning Mozart' of 29 August 1814, Stendhal pointed to the 'sublime fusion of wit and humour' in the works of both figures, noting further that the churchyard scene in Act 2 of *Don Giovanni* represented 'the equivalent, in music, of "terror" as conceived by Shakespeare'.[19] Similarly, in the opinion of Carl Maria von Weber, the supposed peculiarities of Mozart's stageworks were a natural consequence of his 'total grasp of dramatic truth' and his 'delineation of character by declamation'.[20]

Before long, the Romantic-characteristic view of Mozart was displaced by a rather different constellation of aesthetic markers. By the mid-nineteenth century, allusions to the bizarre and eccentric elements of Mozart's style were few and far between. In linking his music with the entire spectrum of qualities that aestheticians associated with the 'beautiful' – perfection, order, symmetry, restraint, harmonious unity, universality, timeless value – critics found in Mozart's works a supreme embodiment of musical classicism.

The assimilation of Mozart's music to an aesthetic of the beautiful was neither abrupt not absolute. On the contrary, late eighteenth- and early nineteenth-century writers (including Rochlitz and Niemetschek) often re-ferred to the consummate beauty and classical worth of his compositions, although generally within a framework that accorded greater emphasis to the 'characteristic' side of his art. Rather than a decisive shift in orientation, it would therefore be more accurate to speak of a gradual transition between complementary aesthetic attitudes. The coexistence of both outlooks in the 1820s and 1830s is evident in the controversy over the slow introduction to the first movement of Mozart's 'Dissonance' Quartet, K. 465. In claiming that Mozart could not possibly have intended the harmonic audacities in the quartet's opening bars, which were almost surely misprints, the critic and theorist François-Joseph Fétis assumed that Mozart was chiefly a vessel for the beautiful in music. In contrast, Gottfried Weber's efforts to analyse the passage as it stood betrays a willingness to accept the 'characteristic' as a vital component of Mozart's stylistic palette.[21]

The image of Mozart as the reigning god of musical classicism was firmly in place in Robert Schumann's writings of the 1830s. In a diary entry of July 1831, Schumann defined the 'classic' as an aesthetic stance in which one force is absorbed into its opposite:

> Classic is the genial in the garb of the folkish, the unfathomable in the guise of the comprehensible . . . the boundless charmingly confined, the weighty made light, the dark in luminous clarity, the corporeal spiritualized, the real ennobled by the ideal.[22]

Three years later, in a review of Hummel's *Studien*, Op. 125, Schumann applied the same aesthetic to Mozart and his followers:

> Cheerfulness, repose, grace, the main features of ancient works of art, are also those of Mozart's school. Just as the Greeks gave their thundering Zeus a merry expression, so too does Mozart withhold his lightning bolts.[23]

Although Schumann thought that Mozart's music was imbued with a classical spirit, he never explicitly assigned the composer to a Classical era, nor did he set Mozart in opposition to Beethoven or to Schumann's 'Romantically' inclined contemporaries. This polarized view first gained currency in the late 1830s with critics and historians who fell under the sway of Hegel's philosophy. Amadeus Wendt, for instance, invoked a typically Hegelian strategy to differentiate Haydn, Mozart and Beethoven, arguing that form overwhelms content in Haydn's music, form and content achieve a state of equilibrium in Mozart's works, and content supersedes form in Beethoven's output.[24] In his *Geschichte der Musik in Italien, Deutschland und Frankreich* (1852), Franz Brendel situated Mozart within a historical framework modelled on Hegel's division of the history of art into 'symbolic', 'Classic', and 'Romantic' phases. Brendel likewise recognized three epochs in music history: a period of 'sublime' style, culminating in the 'combinatorial' art of Bach; a 'beautiful' or 'objective' phase represented by Gluck, Haydn and Mozart; and finally a 'subjective' period inaugurated by Beethoven. As the 'universal genius who bound together all the disparate tendencies [of his time] into one grand organic whole', Mozart emerges in Brendel's panoramic outlook at 'the most beautiful moment in the entire span of [Western musical] history'.[25]

References to Mozart's cultivation of the 'beautiful', his 'classical' status and the 'universality' of his genius constitute the central strands in accounts of his music from the mid- to the late nineteenth century, although writers were hardly unanimous in their understanding of these terms or in the relative weight they placed upon them. For Ulïbïshev, Mozart's classicism consisted principally in his transcendence of the time and place in which his works were conceived. Commenting on the six quartets dedicated to Haydn, which he located at the beginning of Mozart's 'classical' period, Ulïbïshev maintained that 'everything in them is as fresh as if written yesterday, and will remain so for evermore'.[26] Jahn claimed that Mozart derived his 'greatest joy' from the 'production of the beautiful', but equated the composer's genius with his 'universality', that is, his uncanny power of transforming 'inner experience' into 'musical expression'. Moreover, Mozart's universality 'cannot be separated from the harmony of [his] artistic nature, which never allowed . . . his intention and his means to come into conflict'.[27]

While mid- and late nineteenth-century critics acknowledged the 'characteristic' elements of Mozart's style, they tended to subordinate them to the higher unity that resulted from the composer's ability to synthesize antithetical tendencies. One of the chief themes in Gounod's descriptive analysis of *Don Giovanni*, for instance, is the union of beautiful form and emotional truth in the opera: 'By this *truth* Mozart is *human*, by this *beauty* he is *divine*.'[28] In a review of the same work published on 16 January 1874 in the *Russian Gazette*, one of the most passionate Mozart-lovers of the nineteenth century, Pyotr Il'yich Tchaikovsky, lavished special praise on the combination of 'staggering pathos' with 'bewitching beauty of harmony and modulation' in Donna Anna's recitatives.[29] Likewise, Ferruccio Busoni emphasized Mozart's pursuit of the happy medium in several of the aphorisms he wrote on the occasion of the 150th anniversary of the composer's birth:

> He is passionate, but keeps to the forms of chivalry.
> He disposes of light and shadow, but his light does not pain and his
> darkness still shows clear outlines.
> Idealist without losing touch with the earth, realist without ugliness.[30]

Mozart himself would probably have found the last of these aphorisms a fair assessment. In justifying the unusual metrical and tonal design of Osmin's aria 'Solche hergelauf'ne Laffen', in Act 1 of *Die Entführung aus dem Serail*, Mozart observed that 'just as a man in such a towering rage oversteps all the bounds of order, moderation and propriety and completely forgets himself, so must the music too forget itself'. At the same time, however, 'passions, whether violent or not, must never be expressed in such a way as to excite disgust', and 'music, even in the most terrible situations, must never offend the ear, but must please the hearer, or in other words must never cease to be *music*'.[31]

III

A brief sketch such as this cannot do justice to all the nuances in the nineteenth century's changing outlook on Mozart. It also begs the question as to what motivated these interpretive shifts in the first place. No doubt the appearance of Beethoven on the musical scene was a decisive factor in the transformation of Mozart from a representative of Romantic-characteristic tendencies into a purveyor of the 'beautiful' in music. Although E. T. A. Hoffmann claimed that the instrumental works of Haydn, Mozart and Beethoven all 'breathe the same romantic spirit', he qualified this remark by identifying Beethoven as the only 'purely romantic' artist of the trio.[32] In an attempt to revive the early nineteenth-century view of a Romantic Mozart, the critic Alfred Heuss argued in an article of 1906–7 on 'the demonic element' in the composer's works that the reception of Mozart in recent times had been affected by the experience of listening to 'new' music. Modern audiences, he observed, do not respond to fine shadings 'unless they are accompanied by a powerful outward apparatus'.[33] Berlioz had come to the same conclusion over seventy years earlier in a review of a performance of *Don Giovanni* at the Paris Opéra. His advice to the listener who found Mozart's orchestration devoid of 'brilliance and energy' was to 'blame those whose abuse of violence has made you insensitive' – and chief among the culprits he had in mind was almost certainly Meyerbeer.[34] Brendel struck an almost wistful tone in his diagnosis of Mozart's relationship to mid-nineteenth-century audiences. Mozart, he noted, 'has become estranged from current tastes; he no longer speaks to the content of everyday life'.[35] The extent of this estrangement is evident in Eduard Hanslick's review of a Vienna Philharmonic concert that included the Piano Concerto in C major, K. 503. Although in his celebrated treatise on aesthetics, *Vom Musikalisch-Schönen* (1854), Hanslick had extolled Mozart as a paragon of 'absolute' music, in the review he noted dryly that the symmetrical periods and formulaic passagework in the concerto were so naive in conception that the modern listener, 'accustomed to higher temperatures, cannot really warm to them'.[36]

If, however, Hanslick and numerous critics before and after him felt that Mozart's works embodied a kind of beauty that was oddly out of step with contemporary sensibilities, it was perhaps because the nineteenth century craved emblems of precisely this sort. As the bearer of messages from a bygone golden age, Mozart's music offered a welcome relief from the crisis-torn present. Mozart had already assumed this role in the early part of the nineteenth century. As the young Franz Schubert confided to his diary after a performance of one of Mozart's string quintets:

> beautiful impressions like this . . . reveal to us, from within the dark
> recesses of life, a light, bright, beautiful distance in which we may
> confidently place our hope. Oh Mozart, immortal Mozart, how many, oh
> how infinitely many such beneficent impressions of a luminous, higher life
> you have imprinted on our souls.[37]

Mozart's reception by nineteenth-century composers in general and his impact on the history of composition in particular are vast topics in their own right, and well beyond the scope of this survey.[38] One point worth emphasizing, in light of the revelatory qualities commonly ascribed to Mozart's music, is the frequency with which later composers drew on the features of his style in their evocations of an alternative world – whether it was to be an exotic, ideal or idyllic one. When Schumann described Felix Mendelssohn as the 'Mozart of the nineteenth century',[39] he was surely thinking of his colleague's facility, his unerring sense of formal proportion and the elegant finish of his compositions. At times Schumann himself tried to capture what he called the 'heavenly lightness' of Mozart's style,[40] especially during the later phases of his career. The bright woodwind textures and colourful 'Janissary' scoring of the music for the Nile Genies in Schumann's fairy-tale oratorio *Das Paradies und die Peri* (1843) are direct imports from *Die Entführung aus dem Serail*. Likewise, the angelic tone of the music for the four boys positioned around Mignon's bier in the *Requiem für Mignon*, Op. 98b (1849) – a setting of a text from Goethe's *Wilhelm Meister* – stamps the members of Schumann's quartet as close relatives of the Three Boys from Mozart's *Die Zauberflöte*.

In a letter to Nadezhda von Meck dating from the spring of 1878, Tchaikovsky wrote:

> maybe it is precisely because, as a man of my times, I am broken and morally sick that I like to seek peace and consolation in Mozart's music, most of which is an expression of life's joys as experienced by a healthy, wholesome nature, *not corrupted by introspection*.[41]

Hence, when Tchaikovsky wanted to conjure up a realm of Arcadian bliss in the pastoral duet for Daphnis and Chloë in the Act 2 *divertissement* of *The Queen of Spades*, it is hardly surprising that he did so with a pointed allusion to a theme in *volkstümlich* style from the first movement of Mozart's C major Piano Concerto, K. 503. Although Tchaikovsky succinctly stated the aesthetic of his 'Mozartiana' Suite – based largely on selections from Mozart's keyboard works – as 'the past in modern garb', it is also possible to view this four-movement work for chamber orchestra as an oasis of 'peace and consolation' amidst his more turbulent symphonic compositions.[42]

While Schumann and Tchaikovsky, like Schubert and Mendelssohn, embraced the 'beautiful' components of Mozart's art, Brahms seems to have had an affinity for the 'characteristic' side as well. His documented remarks on Mozart include stereotypical references to the perfection of *Figaro* and the beauty of the string quartets,[43] but they also speak to a broader appreciation of Mozart's stylistic range. In conversation late in his life with the critic and composer Richard Heuberger, Brahms mentioned in passing that

Mozart was more daring in his handling of form than Beethoven, and added: 'It's a good thing most people don't know that'.[44] Even though Brahms did not give any specific examples, one of the formal strategies he might have cited to support his claim involves an unusual blend of sonata and rondo principles, variously described as a sonata-rondo form in which one refrain statement (the third) has been omitted, or a binary form with a developmentally expanded second half and a protracted coda. Much favoured by Mozart in the finales of his piano concertos and concertante chamber works, this design was adapted by Brahms to every movement of the sonata cycle, and is represented in nearly twenty instances extending from the Serenade No. 1 in D for Orchestra, Op. 11 (1858), to the Sonata in F minor for Clarinet and Piano, Op. 120 No. 1 (1894).[45] Regardless of the terms we use to designate the form – irregular sonata-rondo or amplified binary – the fact remains that it cannot be adduced as an example of Mozartian perfection, order, symmetry and balance. On the contrary, in employing the design for his own ends, Brahms took as his point of departure one of Mozart's most 'characteristic' approaches to the question of musical form.

In another provocative comment, Brahms once observed that 'Wagner stands much closer to Mozart than most people realize'.[46] Coincidentally, Wagner came to a similar conclusion in dubbing himself 'the last of the Mozartians'.[47] This self-appraisal, dating from the period when he was at work on *Parsifal*, is rather surprising in light of his earlier attitude. In *Opera and Drama* (1851) Wagner criticized Mozart for his lack of discrimination in the selection of operatic texts, and in the essay 'Zukunftsmusik' (1860) he complained of 'the perpetually recurring and noisily garrulous half-closes of the Mozartian Symphony', which called to mind 'the clatter of prince's plates and dishes set to music'.[48] While we will never know in precisely what sense Wagner thought of himself as the last Mozartian, some of his other comments on Mozart at least offer a clue. Pointing to 'the fine humanity' of the Priest's replies to Tamino in Act 2 of *Die Zauberflöte*, he declared Mozart 'the founder of German declamation' in a conversation with Cosima of May 1870, and a decade later traced 'the genesis of the German character' to the same opera.[49] From this perspective, the declamatory monologues for Gurnemanz in Acts 1 and 3 of *Parsifal* represent a Wagnerian realization of tendencies implicit in Mozart's last opera.

Between October 1878 and January 1879, while he was otherwise occupied with the drafting of Act 3 of *Parsifal*, Wagner devoted a considerable amount of time to the study of Mozart's *Figaro*.[50] As different as these two works may be, here too we can identify an area of common ground, though a brief detour will first be necessary. In his essay 'Brahms the Progressive', Arnold Schoenberg described the principle of construction in Mozart's operatic ensembles as follows:

> [Mozart] begins such a piece with a melody consisting of a number of
> phrases of various lengths and characters, each of them pertaining to a
> different phase of the action and mood. They are, in their first
> formulation, loosely joined together, and often simply juxtaposed, thus
> admitting to be broken asunder and used independently as motival
> material for small formal segments.[51]

As a typical example of this procedure, Schoenberg cites the section of
the Act 2 finale of *Figaro* beginning with the Countess's 'Susanna, son morta'.
After presenting the five 'illustrative segments' that form the basis for this
exchange between the Countess, Susanna and the Count, Schoenberg notes
that this 160-bar dramatic unit in B flat major 'contains an astonishingly
great number of segments, all of which are built, almost exclusively, out of
variations of these five little phrases in a constantly changing order'.[52] This
approach to musico-dramatic organization, he goes on to say, 'proves to be
a vision of the future'.[53]

Richard Wagner lay in that future. His leitmotivs bear comparison with
Mozart's 'illustrative segments' not only because they too forge associative
links between musical ideas and different phases of the 'action and mood'
but also because of their potential for presentation in an ever-changing
order. Wagner often exploited the latter property in the scenes of epic nar-
ration that occur with increasing frequency as *The Ring* unfolds, but he
also put it to use at moments of great dramatic power. One such instance
occurs in Act 2 of *Parsifal*, in the monologue beginning with Parsifal's impassioned invocation of the Grail King: 'Amfortas!' An expression of Parsifal's
'cosmic clear-sightedness' after receiving Kundry's kiss, this gripping passage
is based almost entirely on the music of Amfortas's lament from the Act 1
Grail scene – which Parsifal had witnessed, but not comprehended. To underscore Parsifal's self-identification with the ailing Amfortas, Wagner recalls the material of the earlier lament in a chromatically intensified form.
And in arranging this material into an entirely new motivic configuration
he hit upon an effective means of depicting Parsifal's state of psychic shock.
While this hardly suggests that Wagner's methods were directly influenced
by Mozart's, it nonetheless reveals an underlying affinity between their respective approaches to dramatic characterization.

Wagner was not alone in coming to terms with Mozart relatively late in
life. Schumann arrived at a full appreciation of Mozart only in the 1840s, by
which time he had already composed the bulk of the keyboard music and
songs for which he is best remembered. When Berlioz claimed near the end
of his career that 'We are beginning to understand Mozart', he was speaking
just as much for himself as for his contemporaries. This pattern repeats itself
on a broader historical scale as latecomers in the history of Mozart reception
such as Richard Strauss and Schoenberg demonstrated a renewed sensitivity

to the technical and expressive range of Mozart's music. In contrast to the reactionary adherents of the 'Back to Mozart' movement, for whom the composer was a 'rococo' artist par excellence, Schoenberg focussed on the syntactic irregularities in Mozart's dramatic and chamber works. Strauss in turn prized Mozart's comic operas as psychological studies of the highest order, turning to *Figaro* and *Così fan tutte* as models for *Der Rosenkavalier*, and to *Die Zauberflöte* as a model for *Die Frau ohne Schatten*.[54] In other words, Strauss and Schoenberg, each in his own way, were powerfully drawn to the 'characteristic' aspects of Mozart's style, and in this they brought the history of Mozart reception full circle.

14 Mozart and the twentieth century

JAN SMACZNY

At the end of his novel *Lucia in London*, E. F. Benson's heroine, the energetic socialite Emmeline Lucas – Lucia to her friends – suggests to her piano-duet partner, Georgie Pilson, that they have half an hour's practice of 'celestial Mozartino'.[1] In Lucia's cosmology of composers Bach is 'glorious', Scarlatti 'dainty' and Beethoven 'noble',[2] but only Mozart achieves divine, if diminutive, status. Lucia's Mozart is the infant prodigy beloved of the nineteenth century, when, at various stages, England's cultured classes were hot on the trail of successors to the Salzburg genius.[3] Perhaps this is not surprising, since the biographies to which Benson would have had access made much of the infant: for example, Lady Wallace's 1877 translation of Ludwig Nohl's *The Life of Mozart*, which has the child Mozart in Austrian court dress as a frontispiece,[4] or Pauline Townsend's translation of Otto Jahn's monumental *Life of Mozart* published by Novello in 1891, which uses an engraving of Mozart derived from the Verona portrait of 1770.[5]

Nearly twenty years after Benson published *Lucia in London*, van Loon invited Mozart, along with St Francis of Assisi and Hans Andersen, to dinner in his volume of fantasy encounters, *Van Loon's Lives*.[6] His account of Mozart is a flight of fancy based on conventional popular images; Constanze, for example, is described as 'flighty' and 'rather worthless'.[7] There is an emphasis on the purity of the composer's inspiration and the ability of his music to connect the listener with childhood: 'a source of everlasting inspiration and joy for those who have not yet forgotten the laughter and the simple pleasures of their childhood days'.[8]

The *Gemütlichkeit* of Van Loon's treatment of Mozart is as telling as Benson's neutralization of the composer as a rounded figure: touched by the divine spark, a childhood of transcendental achievement can develop into an extended adolescence, but not much beyond. In these classics of popular literature, Mozart simply refuses to grow up. For Adorno, such images locked the composer into an overly comfortable, sanitized image of the age in which he lived: 'A series of falsifications contrives to tailor Mozart to contemporary taste. To begin with he is assigned to the Rococo age whose limits he had just burst asunder.'[9] Adorno might well have been appalled, but almost certainly not surprised, at the phenomenal transformation of the Mozart image in the late twentieth century.

A key corollary to the notion of the divinely touched infant Mozart is the conceit of untutored genius, a trait enunciated by the composer Bohuslav Martinů, who stated fearlessly that Mozart 'never studied, he knew',[10] invoking an image of effortless ability that could only appeal to the 'me'-centred culture of the 1990s. Interestingly, this view occurs fairly consistently throughout the century. A comparative extension of the myth of genius was applied by John Amis to Benjamin Britten and Michael Tippett: of the pair, Britten was Mozart who 'knew where he was going every bar of the piece in advance', whereas Tippett was cast in the role of Beethoven, who 'had the plan but wrestled with material'.[11] Whether or not the comparison holds water (according to Humphrey Carpenter, Tippett was dismissive),[12] it perpetuated an image of transcendental facility, reproducing it for the major musical figures of another age. Even so acute and fastidious a critic as Hans Keller tended to subscribe to the myth when, not entirely willingly, he was seduced into a comparative judgement of Mozart and Britten:

> as one who is soaked in the music of both Mozart and Britten I may be allowed to claim that for the first time Mozart, the universal musician who masters everything with a somnabulistic surefootedness and grace, has found a companion.[13]

This god-like, transcendental Mozart, remote from the perceived heaviness of nineteenth-century Romanticism, was an icon powerfully reinforced for the 1960s generation in the 1961 translation of Hermann Hesse's novel *Steppenwolf* (1927). This tale of an awkward, middle-aged ingénu's sentimental education is billed in its present English-language incarnation in Penguin fiction as: 'The hip bible of 1960s counterculture . . . [capturing] the mood of a disaffected generation and a century increasingly unsure of itself.'[14] The idea of divine youth cut short becomes powerfully totemic in a dialogue between Steppenwolf and the aged Goethe:

> He did not make pretensions in his own life to the enduring and the orderly and to exalted dignity as you did. He did not think himself so important! He sang his divine melodies and died. He died young, poor and misunderstood.[15]

This image of youthful joy as opposed to torpid tradition resonates later in the twentieth century as well, not least in Peter Shaffer's play and Miloš Forman's film *Amadeus*. Mozart's remoteness from Hesse's view of nineteenth-century tendentiousness is celebrated in a hilariously purgatorial scene in which Brahms and Wagner are to be observed traversing a 'desert plain' dragging behind their hoards of 'men in black', the 'players of all those notes and parts of his [Brahms's and Wagner's] scores which according to divine judgement were superfluous. "Too thickly orchestrated, too much material wasted", Mozart said with a nod.'[16]

Hesse's image of Mozart from early in the century may have informed the dialogue that has underpinned the development of his image in the later twentieth century, but the broader picture is not one of stasis. A partial corrective of the seemingly ever-present trope of the infant-adolescent Mozart is found in Sacheverell Sitwell's biography of 1932.[17] Sitwell was among the first to use the portrait of Mozart by his brother-in-law, Joseph Lange, as the frontispiece for a study of the composer. Considering Lange's portrait to be the 'only true' likeness of the composer, Sitwell enthused: 'There is nothing, in all the iconography of great men, to compare with it.'[18] His reasoning introduces what might be described as a more human, psychological and at the same time more Romantic image of Mozart:

> The long shaped head, with space in it for every technical resource . . . the poetical forehead, like the forehead of Keats . . . but there is something of the child still in him. You have only to see the lower part of his face to know of his inexperience in money matters and his weakness in affairs of the world.[19]

Alfred Einstein's far more influential monograph, *Mozart: His Character, His Work*, a standard text for over thirty years, extends, most engagingly, the tendency towards an extensive psychological profile in which the subject, for example, 'could be very rough in dealing with women who had designs upon him'.[20] For Einstein, the adult Mozart is a protean figure who has encompassed all human experience:

> Mozart died in his thirty-sixth year; yet he went through all the stages of human life, simply passing through them faster than ordinary mortals. At thirty he was both childlike and wise; he combined the highest creative power with the highest understanding of his art; he observed the affairs of life and he saw behind them; and he experienced before his end that feeling of imminent completion that consists in the loss of all love for life.[21]

In this summative analysis one again sees Peter Shaffer's *Amadeus* lurking in the wings.

Mozart and musicology in the twentieth century

The apparently settled picture of Mozart in the popular imagination in the early twentieth century does not reflect the situation in musicology. Mozart as an object of study has grown at the same pace as the discipline itself. Gernot Gruber, in his invaluable study *Mozart and Posterity*, outlines the now seemingly curious battles for and against a re-evaluation of Mozart fought in Germany early in the century.[22] The battle lines were drawn around an agenda to demonstrate that Wagnerian progressiveness – led by Paul Zschorlich in his 1906 volume *The Mozart Hypocrisy*[23] – was, for a forward-looking intelligentsia, preferable to the classicism represented by Mozart.[24] The arguments rattled on with Mozart coming to be regarded in Gruber's view as 'an antidote to the heavy, sultry creations of Wagner',[25] a judgement that parallels Hesse's in the 1920s. To an extent musicological attitudes to Mozart's music have developed along similar lines to popular images of the composer. As Boulez perceptively pointed out:

> what I mean is the change in the general attitude to a composer according to which aspect of his music appeals most to the taste of the period. In this way we have heard Bach's music highly 'dramatized' and then reduced to the dry and rather trivial, while Mozart's, once presented as charming, is now tragic.[26]

The foundations of a more objective twentieth-century musicological approach to Mozart were, of course, laid in the nineteenth century, notably in Köchel's *Chronological-Thematic Catalogue of the Complete Works of Wolfgang Amadé Mozart* of 1862,[27] much revised in von Waldersee's new edition of 1905. Later editions and reprints of the Köchel catalogue had a very real impact in refocussing Mozart scholarship at regular intervals during the twentieth century.[28] With the steady tread of discoveries relating to chronology, however, there is a pressing need to produce a more thoroughgoing revision of Köchel.[29] Of crucial significance for a more accurate biography of the composer was Ludwig Schiedermair's edition of *The Letters of W. A. Mozart and His Family* of 1914.[30] In the Anglophone world, Emily Anderson's translation and edition of the letters published in 1938 provided a sound base for Mozart scholarship and Eric Blom's collection of selected letters taken from this edition did much to inform popular images of the composer.[31]

Additional twentieth-century monuments to Mozart scholarship emerged in the post-war era, especially in the run-up to the bicentennial year of 1956. Three numbers of a *Mozart-Jahrbuch* had been published between 1923 and 1929, and three of a *Neues Mozart-Jahrbuch* between 1941 and 1943. A continuous run of the *Jahrbuch*, however, was established in 1950 and later joined by two other serial publications, the *Mitteilungen der Internationalen Stiftung Mozarteum* in 1952 and *Acta Mozartiana*, the proceedings of the German Mozart Society, in 1954. But the greatest resource for both scholars and performers was the founding of a New Mozart Edition[32] in 1955 to replace the nineteenth-century *W. A. Mozarts Werke*. A pendant to the complete correspondence was Deutsch's documentary biography of 1961 (*MDL, MDB*) followed in short order by a new edition of the complete correspondence (*MBA*).

Hermann Abert's early 1920s reworking of Otto Jahn's standard biography of Mozart greatly enriched the contextual appreciation of the composer and to an extent set the agenda for Mozart studies much later in the century.[33] As details of biography fill out and analytical considerations of Mozart's music multiply, one of the most notable features of studies relating to the composer is the need to locate him in his world. A relatively early start was Marcel Brion's *Daily Life in the Vienna of Mozart and Schubert*.[34] Recent years have seen the appearance of volumes that have hugely enlarged our understanding of Mozart's context, working, social and familial.

Another feature of musicological profiling of Mozart in the later twentieth century has been a tendency to look inward; Freud, for example, proved a useful starting point for the examination of Mozart's operas in Brigid Brophy's *Mozart the Dramatist: A New View of Mozart, His Operas and His Age* (London, 1964). Nearly all post-Einstein biographies are inclined to take questions of personal complexity seriously and to shy away from overly simplistic readings of character. Crucial in this development was Wolfgang Hildesheimer's biography, which did much to create the apparently rounded Mozart favoured by the later twentieth century. Growing out of a bicentenary lecture of 1956, Hildesheimer's study strips away cherished myths in assembling a novel psychological portrait of the composer. In taking issue with the conspiracy to neutralize Mozart's existing psychological profile, most tellingly in his critique of Bruno Walter's image of the composer as a 'happy simple-hearted young man', he opened up the potential for richer readings of the composer's character.[35] Of equal importance is Hildesheimer's questioning of how we apply terms to the composer, notably his consideration of Mozart and humour.[36]

Saint-Foix, who with Théodore de Wyzewa and Adolphe Boschot had set up a Société Mozart in Paris in 1901, took analytical study of Mozart to a new level. His exhaustive five-volume assessment of Mozart's music was set against what was then understood of its eighteenth-century contexts. The first two volumes, written with Wyzewa and published in Paris in 1912, consider the music up to 1777;[37] the remaining volumes, covering the rest of Mozart's life and work, were published in Paris in 1936–46.[38] Systematic within its own terms, Saint-Foix's view was in essence evolutionary and in many ways set the agenda for much later analytical work on the composer. Although by no means as comprehensive, Dent's musically and psychologically persuasive study of the operas, *Mozart's Operas: A Critical Study* (London, 1913), proved a standard work through much of the twentieth-century. Analytical commentary on Mozart through the middle years of the century was dominated by approaches to conventionally perceived form. Without doubt, Mozart's pre-eminence in operatic and concerto genres was recognized in books such as Dent's on the former and Arthur Hutchings's on the latter,[39] but context and angle were limited largely to musical considerations. Perhaps the most influential discussion of Mozart's musical language in the last thirty years of the twentieth century was Charles Rosen's in *The Classical Style*, with its fundamental premise that 'a work of music sets its own terms'.[40] Offering not 'a survey of the music of the classical period, but a description of its language',[41] Rosen's perceptive understanding of tonality and, perhaps above all, phrase structure articulated for a generation what appeared to be the fundamental values of Mozart's music.

A purely musical view of Mozart was, however, hardly tenable in the more exploratory climate of the late twentieth century. Where psychology had been applied to Mozart's life, the application of philosophical and other related disciplines would follow for the music. As a focus for deconstruction, Mozart's operas have become a major area of interest in terms of both analysis and psychological profiling. Fruitfully, analysis has also embraced cultural context by drawing in aspects of rhetoric as a means of assessing modes of address in Mozart's music.[42] As a large number of autographs, many of which disappeared during the Second World War, returned to currency in Poland, other aspects of the musicological study of Mozart gained momentum (sketch and paper studies, for example), stretching the credibility of Keller's notion of 'somnambulistic surefootedness'. In particular, Tyson's forensic studies of autograph scores and Wolfgang Plath's pioneering work on sources have done much to illuminate questions of chronology.

In the later twentieth century the study of performance practice developed hand in hand with the rise of performance on early instruments. Ingenious studies of metronome markings for Mozart symphonies from Hummel and Czerny, by Münster and Malloch respectively,[43] offer glimpses of contemporary performance speeds, although, as both writers point out, such speeds are not readily taken up by today's conductors. Broader considerations of performance practice, such as Frederick Neumann's *Ornamentation and Improvisation in Mozart* (Princeton, 1986), have been joined by studies informed by both performance and scholarship, notably in the edited volume *Perspectives on Mozart Performance*,[44] where the violinists Eduard Melkus and Jaap Schröder, for example, offer thoughts on cadenzas and violin performance style respectively. The point of interface between musicology and performance has increasingly fertilized both areas. Neal Zaslaw's now standard study of Mozart's symphonies was begun while the author was working as a musicological adviser to the Academy of Ancient Music during their complete recorded cycle of the symphonies,[45] and the author freely acknowledges an 'inestimable debt' to this orchestra.[46] Such fruitful synergies indicate what might be described as a more holistic approach to Mozart musicology in the later twentieth century.

The Mozart-musicology industry advances: studies of his life, individual works (in particular the operas), context, performance, reception and psychology are unrolled with bewildering frequency, confirming the view of the academic publishing world that Mozart is the most bankable of Classical composers and that anything with his magical moniker will sell to some constituency. But there is a paradox here, since musicology's Mozart mostly flourishes independently of his popular image: as musicology, broadly speaking, demythologizes Mozart, his popular image flourishes more and more in a mythological realm.

Mozart and the performer

The modern manner of presenting Mozart in cleaned-up texts, informed by late eighteenth-century performance practice and with orchestras similar in size and composition to those of Mozart's day, can be attributed to a complex of reasons, but may be traced back to the efforts of performers at the end of the nineteenth and beginning of the twentieth century. Gruber identifies Hermann Levi and Ernst Possart's attempt to present *Don Giovanni* in 'all its original purity and authenticity'[47] in their Munich production of 1896 as a key moment in a process that might be termed 'recovering Mozart'.[48] In fact, there had been a move towards restoration earlier in the nineteenth century in Prague, the city that had commissioned and premiered the opera in 1787. In the newly opened Provisional Theatre, the musical director, Jan Maýr, restored the opera's recitatives (it had been performed as a Singspiel in Prague for decades) and its second-act sextet finale in 1864 and 1865 respectively.[49]

Other important figures in the development of Mozart performance were Strauss and Mahler. Strauss enthusiastically propagated the methods pioneered by Possart and Levi, and Mahler followed suit on his arrival as conductor of the Vienna Hofoper in 1897. Of major significance was Mahler's Mozart cycle (1905–6), whose *Figaro* was taken to the Salzburg Festival of 1906. Gruber's balanced critique of Mahler's practices suggests an interventionist approach where dynamics, transposition and instrumentation were concerned, and a free repetition of parts of the overture or the importation of instrumental items to cover scene changes. Mahler's modernism was vested in a consistent approach to speed, a concentration on ensemble, and an avoidance of both the excessive rubato beloved of earlier decades and ornamentation.[50] Along with this apparently greater respect for the text was the use of lighter orchestral forces and a keyboard continuo.

Strauss took a major lead in promoting Mozart's operas, which extended to making an edition of *Idomeneo* (first performed 16 April 1931). Although much criticized – Dent called it 'a shocking hash'[51] – the edition, from a later perspective overly interventionist, was an honest attempt to habilitate a neglected work. One of Strauss's main contributions to Mozart performance was through his involvement with the Salzburg Festival. There had been sporadic festivals in Salzburg in the late nineteenth and early twentieth centuries,[52] but the birth of the modern festival was in 1920. Michael Steinberg traces the origins of the modern festival to discussions between Hermann Bahr and Max Reinhardt in 1903.[53] Both Strauss and his librettist Hofmannsthal did much to determine the character of the festival in the later stages of planning. Having joined the festival's artistic advisory board in August 1918, Strauss also participated in recruiting financially active 'friends' for the festival on a conducting tour in the United States.[54] Orchestral performances of Mozart began in August conducted by Bernhard Paumgartner of the Mozarteum and performances of Mozart's operas started the following year.[55] These stagings brought some of the finest conductors of the first half of the twentieth century to the festival, including Krauss, Schalk, Walter, Busch and Weingartner.

Fritz Busch was to a large extent responsible for transplanting aspects of the modern Austro-German approach to Mozart to the Glyndebourne festivals, events that were crucial in fixing performance style later in the century. Before the founding of the Glyndebourne festivals in May 1934, performances of Mozart's operas in Britain in the twentieth century were sporadic if occasionally distinctive, notably Beecham's *Die Zauberflöte* at the Aldwych Theatre in 1917, and *Figaro*, *Don Giovanni* and *Die Zauberflöte* at the Old Vic under the regime of Lilian Baylis in successive years from 1920, all of which did much to establish a metropolitan audience for the repertory.[56] Set up by John Christie and his wife, the singer Audrey Mildmay, performances at Glyndebourne began with *Figaro* under Busch, and in subsequent years the festivals were devoted 'almost exclusively to Mozart'.[57] Significantly, on Christie's instructions, all operas were given in their original languages, a practice then rarely followed in Europe. The formative status achieved by Busch's pre-war Glyndebourne performances is reflected in an appreciation by Andrew Porter in a round-up of complete Mozart opera recordings in 1955: 'the sum achieved by the singers and players is something greater than the total of their individual performances'.[58]

The clear implication of Porter's statement is that ensemble performance is the major strength of Busch's interpretations. Listening to Busch's 1936 recording of *Don Giovanni*,[59] the line of descent to the lean, dramatically apt performances of today is clear: tempi are for the most part on the fast side and consistent; the orchestral accompaniment is firm; and the singing, solo and ensemble, is perceptibly theatrical. Cleaner editions and the revival of earlier performing styles made a huge difference to performances of Mozart towards the end of the twentieth century, but in spirit there seems to have been little change from the means and eloquence cultivated so successfully by Busch in early Glyndebourne performances.

If the modern tendency in Mozart opera performance began with a search for authenticity, purging Mozart of the perceived excesses of Romanticism, the quest was impelled powerfully by the greater objectivity sought by a number of influential figures. Bartók's contact with Mozart was largely as a performer and editor.[60] He and his wife included the Concerto for Two Pianos, K. 365, in their repertory, and Bartók played the D major Sonata for Two Keyboards, K. 448, with Dohnányi in 1936.[61] Bartók's approach to Mozart as both performer and teacher prefigures the reformist zeal of the later twentieth century. Szigeti, who played at least two of Mozart's violin sonatas with Bartók, characterized his performance with the composer as 'that kind of unique experience when one starts anew with a clean slate'.[62] As with the music of Bach, in Mozart 'Bartók approved of no emotionalism or sentimentality, but wanted hard *fortes*, and uniform *pianos*'.[63] This fundamentalist view is confirmed by Bartók's pupil, Julia Szekely:

> Through Bartók we could come to know a new Mozart – the real one: hard, almost rapping *fortes*; *pianos* which were not delicate but spoke with a uniform voice; hard-set, closed formal articulations. Never was there any affectation or theatrical mannerism, still less any display of virtuosity.[64]

Stravinsky, too, was certainly important in fixing images of objective approaches to interpretation, indeed non-interpretation, in some ways an extension of his view that 'music, by its very nature, is essentially powerless to express anything at all'.[65] Thus, as Richard Taruskin has pointed out: 'Impersonalism is as old as Stravinsky, who railed against "interpretation", and wanted his performers to be ... obedient "executants" of his will.'[66] The technical underpinning of Stravinsky's attitude was a belief that tempo is the main problem in modern performance. His disquisition on the problem of tempo in 'About Music Today' concludes with the question: 'Isn't this why Mozart concertos are still played as though they were Tchaikovsky concertos?'[67] Stravinsky's potent advocacy of interpreters who do not go beyond the letter of the score had become, by the 1970s, common currency for interpreters of early music, including, needless to say, that of Mozart.[68] Reading without mediation beyond the application of what was known of eighteenth-century performance style was regarded as a way of presenting an untrammelled picture of the composer's music. If the articles that comprise Taruskin's *Text and Act* have gone a long way to exposing the flaws in the arguments for an 'authentic' or even 'historically correct' view of Mozart, the rendition of his music on old instruments and with playing techniques based on a study of contemporary documents now informs the performance of Mozart from opera house to symphony orchestra, from chamber group to solo keyboard player. Collections such as the Academy of Ancient Music's complete Mozart symphonies and John Eliot Gardiner and

Malcolm Bilson's recording of the piano concertos (begun in 1983) have created a new tradition of early-instrument performance. But with this comes
the realization, as Peter Williams states, that

> Performance Practice is so difficult a branch of study as to be an almost
> impossibly elusive ideal. It cannot be merely a practical way of 'combining
> performance and scholarship', for these two are fundamentally different
> activities, each able to inform the other only up to a certain point.[69]

Now, greater liberality in interpretive choice, even in early-instrument performances, seems likely to inform performance.

The composer's Mozart

While the relationship of musicologists and performers to Mozart in the
twentieth century was, on the whole, a developmental dialogue, composers
of most hues, conservative, modern and post-modern, viewed him, largely
consistently, as a source of inspiration and wonderment. There was, of
course, a group of composers among whom Mozart was venerated without
his music being obviously influential. Messiaen, for example, while admiring
Mozart for his rhythm, could sidestep his influence completely.[70] Another
was Sibelius. According to Santeri Levas, Sibelius 'admired Beethoven but
loved Mozart'; it seems that he 'regarded the latter [Mozart] as the greatest
master of orchestration, and several times told me how the G minor Symphony had run through his life like a red thread'.[71] Other composers were
prepared to accept Mozart as a model at formative and later stages: Elgar's
youthful enthusiasm for Mozart prompted him to model a symphony on the
G minor, K. 550, and in the *Strand Magazine* in May 1904 he commented,
unequivocally, that 'Mozart is the musician from whom everyone should
learn form'.[72] This view is echoed, although without the didactic impera-
tive, by Busoni, who heard in the composer 'the joy of life and the beauty
of form'.[73]

Understandably, given the reaction in many quarters to his own music,
Schoenberg made much of Mozart as a progressive artist, misunderstood
in his own day.[74] Schoenberg was also happy to admit that he had learned
fundamental aspects of composition from Mozart, such as 'inequality of
phrase-length; co-ordination of heterogeneous characters to form a thematic unity; deviation from even-number construction in the theme and
its component parts',[75] all of which find a clear echo in Rosen's reading of
Mozart in *The Classical Style*. More specifically, Schoenberg owes a debt to
the finale of Mozart's 'Jupiter' Symphony, K. 551, in the merging of sonata
style and fugue in the last movement of the Suite for Piano, Three Wind and
Three String Instruments, Op. 29.[76]

For two composers in particular, Strauss and Stravinsky, a relationship with Mozart's music was a key aspect of creativity. From his youth, Strauss considered Mozart incomparable, the transcendent Classical figure and a clear model. As Bryan Gilliam notes in his introduction to a series of letters from Strauss to Ludwig Thuille, written when both were in their impressionable teens: 'Strauss's love of Mozart forms an important thread connecting boyhood, adulthood, and old age.'[77] In more than one letter to Thuille, the fourteen-year-old Strauss referred to their idol as 'the divine Mozart'.[78] Strauss then went on to gloss his enthusiasm in immoderate terms: 'All the compositions by this "hero" are so clear and transparent and so rich in melodies and so lovely that with every composition by Mozart I revere him more, and even adore him.'[79] There was little sign of any retreat from this position as Strauss's knowledge and admiration of other composers, in particular Wagner, grew in later life. As an adult, Strauss became a renowned interpreter of the 'Jupiter' Symphony, which he would 'reflect about as the perfect work of art'.[80]

Mozart's style was a constant point of reference for Strauss. In middle-period works, as Leon Botstein explains, 'The Mozartian and the Wagnerian ... in clearly recognizable ways coexisted side by side',[81] a particularly remarkable cohabitation given the views of the musicological ideologists of Germany in the early twentieth century. Mozart does, indeed, have a material influence on late instrumental works in particular, such as the *Symphonie für Bläser* in E flat major, the Concerto for Oboe and Small Orchestra and the Duett-Concertino. In opera, the connections between the two composers are, if anything, more pronounced. Beyond the Mozartian pastiche in Zerbinetta's rondo in *Ariadne auf Naxos* and the importation of opera buffa style in *Arabella*, there is inspiration of a more seminal kind from *Die Zauberflöte* on both Strauss and his librettist Hofmannsthal in *Die Frau ohne Schatten*.[82]

As perspectives shift on the role of composers in the early twentieth century, old definitions break down. As Botstein has pointed out, the convenient view of Strauss as a modernist turned conservative between *Elektra* and *Der Rosenkavalier* requires reconsideration in the light of later works that practise the modes and economies of neo-classicism.[83] Given the potential for rereading Strauss as a neo-classicist, the comparisons with Stravinsky, the arch neo-classicist, no longer seem absurd, and in this rereading Mozart's music occupies almost the role of midwife.

Although prepared to admit that Mozart, with Bach, was among the 'more "perfect" composers',[84] Stravinsky's view of Mozart was by no means unequivocally uncritical. Having played through a number of Mozart Masses bought second-hand in Los Angeles in 1942 or 1943, he suffered indigestion as a result of 'these rococo-operatic sweets-of-sin';[85] the result was a resolution to write his own austerely hieratic setting. Moreover, according to Antheil, in 1922 Stravinsky would have 'cut all the development sections out of Mozart's symphonies. They would be fine then!'[86] Mozart was nevertheless central to his most completely neo-classical work, *The Rake's Progress*, as Stravinsky himself admitted, stating unambiguously that four of Mozart's operas, presumably *Le nozze di Figaro*, *Don Giovanni*, *Così fan tutte* and *Die Zauberflöte*, were 'the source of inspiration for my future opera'.[87] The key work, however, seems to have been *Così* (a further connection with Strauss since this was his favourite Mozart opera), a performance of which both Stravinsky and his librettist W. H. Auden heard in 1947.[88] Both recitative and ensemble music owe much to the 'Italian-Mozartian' style,[89] and although the work as a whole draws on a range of sources beyond Mozart, not least ballad opera, there is clearly enough of his influence to support Stephen Walsh's observation that *The Rake's Progress* is a 'neo-Mozartian' opera.[90]

Mozart's role in the post-modern compositional world is perhaps less overarching, but if his presence has not been reinforced in quite the same way as with neo-classicism, he remains a potent force, whether in realizations of Cage's *HPSCHD* (1967–9) or Michael Nyman's scores for Peter Greenaway's films (notably *The Draughtsman's Contract*, 1982, *A Zed and Two Noughts*, 1985, and *Drowning by Numbers*, 1988). Beyond influence, for composers as much as everyone else, Mozart is not just an exemplar, but perhaps the most potent symbol of excellence in music.

The global Mozart

Visitors to Prague's old town square these days are greeted by a forest of placards on poles advertising a bewildering host of attractions. Alongside advertisements for the Museum of Torture Instruments, an exhibition of 'the world's largest spiders and scorpions' and, perhaps more appropriately, a waxwork display, is a papier-mâché head and torso on a pole in crude imitation of Mozart. This grotesque icon variously draws attention to performances of *Don Giovanni* by marionettes, other of Mozart's operas by real people in eighteenth-century costume, or one of the near-daily renditions of the Requiem. This last work has spawned a veritable industry in the Czech capital, not just for performers but for attendant hawkers who, dressed in costumes modelled on those of Miloš Forman's film of Shaffer's *Amadeus*, thrust bills into the hands of passers-by. Musically, Prague has in its post-revolutionary era constructed itself as a Mozart town. In the early 1990s, the proximity of the Velvet Revolution of the last months of 1989 and the bicentenary of the composer's death produced a kind of Mozartian 'big

bang'. With entrepreneurial enthusiasm the Czechs built on their association with the composer, not just his five visits to Prague and the premiere of
Don Giovanni in the Estates Theatre, but also the fact that parts of the film
Amadeus had been shot in the city. Today, over ten years after the bicentenary,
there is little sign of Prague's Mozart-mania abating. The commercializa-
tion of the Mozart image is seen at its most tawdry, with postcards, mugs,
T-shirts, playing cards and every manner of paraphernalia celebrating the
way Mozart's image bestrides the city for tourists.[91]

This situation could not exist were it not for Mozart's global image as
probably the most visible of all Classical composers. Perhaps the first stir-
ring of what has become a most successful exploitation of the Mozart image
was the arrival of the *Echte Salzburger Mozartkugel*. First manufactured by
Paul Fürst in Salzburg in 1890, the classic manifestation of the now near-
universally available sweet is a marzipan ball enveloped first in hazelnut
nougat cream and finally dark chocolate.[92] Since a reciprocal trade agreement between Germany and Austria in 1981,[93] the *Mozartkugel* has erupted
onto the shelves of delicatessens and duty-free shops the world over, reminding those with a sweet tooth that the Salzburg genius could provide
physical as well as spiritual nourishment. Even the glitzy packaging suggests
that Mozart is in some way the stamp of quality on a favoured product; thus,
both the sweet's and the composer's image is mutually guaranteed. Neither
sweet nor the composer's image, however, have escaped satirical scrutiny as
the artist Wolfgang Ehehalt's *Findings II: Wolfgang Amadeus, Nannerl und
die kleinen Dickmacher* (*Wolfgang Amadeus, Nannerl and the Little Fatten-
ers*) of 1989 shows. This hilarious montage features, among other things,
busts of Mozart, fragments of manuscript and an open Sardine tin filled
with Mozart sweets.[94]

Another vital staging post in the development of the Mozart image
was the popular biography. Where Einstein allowed Benson's 'celestial
Mozartino' to grow into a thoughtful young adult, Marcia Davenport turned
him into a full-blown picaresque hero.[95] If not exactly a 'bodice ripper',
Davenport's biography paints a portrait of the composer almost worthy of
Hollywood, reinforced by the conventional tropes of genius. Of *Don
Giovanni*, she writes:

> Of course, his whole score stood . . . the committing to paper is done
> quickly enough, for everything is, as I said before, already finished, and it
> rarely differs on paper from what it was in my imagination.[96]

There is, of course, the human dimension in Davenport's tale with Mozart
being very much 'one of the lads'. Writing about one of Mozart's stays in
Prague, Davenport goes for colour:

> When the Duscheks did not have a big party on, Wolfgang and Franz, with
> whatever other men were about, would put on their hats and sway off to
> town, to spend the evening in a royal bout of music, wit and noise, in some
> tavern where they were treated like kings.[97]

At moments such as these Davenport's Mozart could almost be the blueprint
for the Shaffer–Forman roistering 'Wolfie'. An important reinforcement to
Mozart's 'laddish' image was the twentieth century's awareness and acceptance of his scatological tendencies. Where the nineteenth and early twentieth century might have preferred to ignore this aspect of a man who was,
after all, the product of an age in which scatology was relatively commonplace in everyday discourse, the later twentieth century would be inclined
to see it as something of an enhancement of his humanity and an aid to uni-
versalizing the composer's image – Mozart as a twenty- or thirty-something
rebel.[98]

In offering the late twentieth century an image of the composer in its
own likeness, Forman's film *Amadeus* was of central significance. Shaffer's
play, premiered in London in 1979, is a sensitive study of the mystery of
genius. Forman's film undoubtedly sensationalized many aspects of the
original for a mass audience. Apart from headlining Mozart's scatological
tendencies allied to the complex wit of genius in a romp with Constanze in
the early scenes, the film externalizes inference and in many ways takes on
the character of a rather glamorous soap opera. Mozart's unquestionable
and unmatchable genius is seen cohabiting with the human and hilarious.
Of Mozart's character as it emerged from play and film, Simon Callow,
who played Mozart in the play and Schikaneder in the film, stated that
Mozart 'was someone whose character was inadequate to his genius'.[99] This
perceptive statement was, in essence, exactly what commended the film's
Mozart to a young, mass audience: genius was unearned and could exist
alongside all of the characteristics of youth, notably rebelliousness against
parents and against authority. Bedecked with eight Oscars, the film *Amadeus*,
of 1984, attracted global attention, and it seems that in celluloid guise Mozart
quite eclipsed (as far as the public were concerned) 'noble Bach' and 'dainty
Scarlatti', not to mention Handel, in their commemorative year, 1985.[100]
The signal inflation of the Mozart image to megastar status meant that he
had become not only the most visible composer but also the most visible
of youthful geniuses. Thus the writer of Channel 4's ground-breaking series
Queer as Folk could put into the mouth of fifteen-year-old Nathan, a capable
artist in revolt from his parents having just 'come out', the following lines:
'I can do what I like, I'm Mozart, I'm fucking Mozart.'[101]

Although Gernot Gruber does not use the word 'global' in *Mozart and
Posterity*, he outlines a situation at the end of the twentieth century that

could clearly be characterized by this term: 'Mozart is known throughout the world and appreciated as never before: to avoid him would give all those concerned with cultural matters a bad conscience.'[102] And not just those 'concerned with cultural matters'. Even before *Amadeus*, the process of what might best be described as the globalization of Mozart was under way. From the Swingles' Grammy award winner of 1965 featuring compositions by Mozart to electric alarm clocks waking people up with a digital version of the opening of the G minor Symphony, his music is part of our environment. As Taruskin put it in a talk at the Lincoln Center during a conference entitled 'Performing Mozart's Music' in 1991, ' "Mozart", as we all know perfectly well, is not just Mozart', adding as gloss on the contemporary situation in the bicentennial year: 'If Mozart were just Mozart, would we have spent a whole year having fits over him?'[103]

The torrential tide of performances, images and information relating to Mozart has turned the composer into an issue. By the end of the twentieth century Mozart was still, in Benson's construction, 'celestial', but the iconic trope was not so much that of the exquisite infant as that of the post-adolescent pop star, an 'A-list' celebrity who, if he were alive, would be on the guest list at any smart society bash. The Mozart of the musicological fraternity may be the most industrialized, contextualized and psychoanalysed of composers, but he has been comprehensively eclipsed by the popular Mozart. Conventional scholarship will certainly continue: Köchel and the *Neue Mozart-Ausgabe* will be revised, the latter perhaps replaced by a new *NMA*; and discoveries will continue to be made about Mozart and his context. Whether any of this will significantly alter the protean, irresistible image of Mozart, the scatological, laddish embodiment of untutored genius remains to be seen. If, as John Daverio suggests in chapter 13 of this volume, the study of Mozart reception in the nineteenth century is tantamount to a search for lost images, then the question for us after a century in which images of the composer were so completely 'in our face' is how to read them. The music of Mozart, so extensively – not to say lovingly – measured, assessed and reassessed by musicologists and performers, collided in the 1980s and 1990s with his popular image. The resulting pile-up is what the twenty-first century will have to sort out.

15 The evolution of Mozartian biography

WILLIAM STAFFORD

The sources for Mozart's biography

The principal source for Mozart's biography is the family correspondence (*MBA*), comprising a large collection of letters from Mozart, his father Leopold, mother, sister Nannerl and wife Constanze. They are marvellously informative but also problematic, in that they are a patchy record of Mozart's life, fullest for those times when, still based in Salzburg, he was travelling and he and his father were writing home. They are much thinner for his final decade in Vienna (1781–91) when the bulk of his great work was written; letters sent to him were not preserved, and letters from him vary in number (only four survive for 1786). The fact that a substantial proportion of the surviving letters from between 1788 and 1790 are to his fellow mason and banker Michael Puchberg requesting loans may have given biographers an exaggerated sense of his financial difficulties and professional distress in those years. The information contained in Mozart's letters was only gradually exploited by biographers. His sister Nannerl consulted some of them in order to answer the queries of his obituarist Friedrich Schlichtegroll. The majority were entrusted by Nannerl to Constanze and her second husband Georg Nikolaus von Nissen, and a heavily (and tendentiously) edited selection was printed in the Nissen biography of 1828. They were deposited in the Salzburg Dommusikverein und Mozarteum in the 1840s and 1850s where scholars could consult them. The majority but not all were made readily available in the editions by Ludwig Schiedermair in 1914 and Emily Anderson in 1938; the definitive seven-volume German edition was issued between 1962 and 1975.

Contemporary documentary evidence constitutes a second source of biographical information – birth, marriage and death certificates, press reports of concerts, official records, masonic lodge records, written comments by those who knew and met Mozart. A fine collection of these was assembled by Otto Erich Deutsch in his documentary biography of 1961 (*MDL/MDB*). He was able to add to it in 1978, and a substantial supplement was published by Cliff Eisen in 1991.[1] We can expect more documentary evidence to emerge as scholars trawl through the archives of former German states, noble households and ecclesiastical institutions.

A third and rather suspect source is the body of alleged eyewitness accounts of the composer communicated after his death, occasionally written by the eyewitness him- or herself, more often recorded by somebody else, sometimes with no better an attribution than 'Salzburg tradition' (or Viennese, or Prague, or Berlin). These 'traditions' continued to outcrop into the biographical record right through the nineteenth century and even into the twentieth.

The first biographies and the standard lives

The first substantial obituary of thirty-one pages and 6000 words, destined to have a disproportionate and arguably malign influence upon the biographical tradition, was published by Friedrich Schlichtegroll in 1793.[2] Schlichtegroll published from Gotha and as far as we know had never met Mozart; he set about collecting his information by writing to men who had known the composer, Joseph Friedrich Retzer in Vienna and Albert von Mölk in Salzburg. Given that less than a page and a half is devoted to the last decade of Mozart's life in Vienna we may surmise that Schlichtegroll got little or nothing from Retzer. Mölk consulted Mozart's sister Nannerl, and the information she carefully provided formed the bulk of the obituary. She in turn consulted an old family friend, Johann Andreas Schachtner, whose stories about Mozart as a child were so delightful that Schlichtegroll could not resist them. But the upshot was that the resulting obituary brought the child and the adolescent into the foreground at the expense of the mature man. On the latter, a judgement was furnished almost certainly by Mölk and perhaps without Nannerl's knowledge or approval:

> Apart from his music he was almost always a child, and thus he
> remained . . . he always needed a father's, a mother's or some other
> guardian's care; he could not manage his financial affairs. He married a girl
> quite unsuited to him, and against the will of his father, and thus the great
> domestic chaos at and after his death.[3]

Much of this was reproduced by Schlichtegroll, thus launching the legend of Mozart the eternal child, who was irresponsible and incompetent outside the realm of music. It has influenced the biographical tradition until the present day, even though it is quite possibly a myth based on Salzburg prejudice and ignorance; Mozart left Salzburg in 1781 under a cloud, at odds with his father and with his employer Archbishop Colloredo.

The next biography was written by Franz Xaver Niemetschek in 1798.[4] He was a citizen of Prague who had met Mozart in 1791; he also knew Mozart's Prague friends and his widow Constanze. Niemetschek's account of the composer's life before 1781 is taken almost entirely from Schlichtegroll, but the majority of the book is concerned with Mozart's final decade in Vienna. It need not surprise us that a disproportionate emphasis is given to Mozart's visits to Prague. Niemetschek's patriotism finds expression in the claim that Mozart was best appreciated in Prague; his opinion that the Viennese by contrast neglected the composer was an influential legacy to the biographical tradition. This too may be a myth. Some of Niemetschek's information almost certainly came directly from Constanze Mozart; later, he concluded that she was not an entirely trustworthy witness. There are demonstrable falsities in what he says about the composition and delivery of the Requiem. Constanze bequeathed contradiction and misinformation to subsequent biographers on that topic. This is understandable to some extent; she was an impoverished widow with two small children who needed to keep the initial down payment for the Requiem, to deliver the score and receive the second instalment, and to make additional money out of the work if she could. She therefore attempted to conceal the extent to which the Requiem was unfinished when Mozart died and collaborated in the construction of romantic stories about its commissioning.

Constanze also provided testimony to Johann Friedrich Rochlitz, who published a series of colourful anecdotes about Mozart between 1798 and 1801 in the Leipzig-based *Allgemeine Musikalische Zeitung*.[5] Most of them were his own, allegedly derived from personal observation and from Mozart's own lips when he visited Leipzig in 1789. Rochlitz is a highly suspect witness: he was employed by Breitkopf and Härtel, who were printing Mozart's scores and wanted some good publicity to boost sales.

Between 1798 and 1828 a series of biographies were almost entirely plagiarized from Schlichtegroll, Niemetschek and Rochlitz, adding fiction and embroidery but virtually no new information of any trustworthiness. The next landmark is Nissen's biography of 1828, the first substantial biography of Mozart and a work of 920 pages.[6] Nissen was a careful, educated man. He had the family correspondence at his disposal, and in addition assiduously collected an archive of printed works. He recorded the eyewitness testimony of his and Mozart's wife Constanze, and of her sister Sophie who had assisted at Mozart's deathbed. But unfortunately Nissen died before the writing up was finished. Constanze was determined to bring the work to completion, as a memorial to both of her husbands, and enlisted Johann Heinrich Feuerstein to help her. The result is a book which, while it contains valuable information not available elsewhere, is in places a mess. For whoever of Nissen, Constanze and Feuerstein was responsible for the final version made a scissors-and-paste job out of the collection of documents, freely plagiarizing earlier biographies. This would not matter unduly if we could conclude that Constanze had reviewed the whole, striking out errors and endorsing the truth of what was left. But evidently she did not: 'Nissen' incorporates blatant contradictions from the sources it plagiarizes, and contains assertions that Constanze knew were false – for example, that most of Mozart's scores had been published by the time he died, and that she made little money out of the rest.

For the next three decades 'Nissen' was the authoritative biography, on which other accounts were based – there is, for example, a well-written life by Edward Holmes.[7] Given the fading of memory and the incidence of mortality, 'Nissen' was the last chance for recording substantial testimony by those who had known Mozart. Although Vincent and Mary Novello came from England in 1829 to interview Constanze, her sisters, Nannerl and others, they got no more than snippets of new information; Constanze's own answers were much shaped by 'Nissen', which she had so recently seen through the press.[8] The biographical tradition as it crystallized in 1828 contained very little in the way of assessments of Mozart the man by educated observers who had known him well; it was already contaminated by fiction and myth and placed undue emphasis on the years of his wondrous childhood. Given the pattern of survival of the letters, the most important source of documentary evidence for Mozart's life, it was likely that this emphasis would persist.

The story of Mozart biography is so far a sorry one: better was to come. In 1856 Otto Jahn published his massive four-volume biography.[9] It was firmly grounded in documentary evidence including the correspondence. Jahn was not a musicologist but he was an academic, a philologist by training, and his work is sober and scholarly. He approaches the evidence and the biographical tradition with a critical eye, leaves open whatever he finds dubious and takes care not to assert what he cannot prove. A case can be argued that Jahn's book is still the standard biographical text. It was twice revised in light of subsequent scholarship – by Hermann Dieters at the end of the nineteenth and beginning of the twentieth centuries and more substantially by Hermann Abert in 1919–21; Abert knew much more about the history of music than Jahn, and greatly enlarged the parts that placed Mozart's achievement within that history. He also added an assessment of Mozart the man and artist, although its status as an advance upon Jahn is debatable.[10]

A professional historian, concerned to track solid and scientific advances in knowledge, will have little more to report about the biographical tradition before he or she arrives at the marvellous growth of scholarly work beginning around 1950. Some work should be mentioned, however, such as that of Ludwig Schiedermair, who wrote a fine biography as well as producing the first edition of the correspondence.[11] The French musicologists Théodore de Wyzewa and Georges de Saint-Foix brought out their five-volume study between 1912 and 1946, in a sense anticipating modern post-structuralism in their intention to explain Mozart's work as the result of a coming together of a series of musical influences and traditions which Mozart progressively absorbed as he toured Europe and finally relocated from Salzburg to Vienna. They identify thirty-four distinct stages in his creative life determined by these experiences.[12]

Themes and narrative patterns

Mozart's death has exerted a powerful shaping influence on the biographical tradition. This is not solely because biographers have felt the need for narrative strategies in order to come to terms with the tragic loss of a composer so young, and with the distressing circumstance of his apparent neglect, poverty and misery at the end of his life. Schubert died even younger and poorer, but his death has not inspired as many stories as Mozart's. In addition, the facts that Mozart died while writing a Requiem Mass, that there were mysteries surrounding its commissioning and completion and that there were rumours of poisoning all contributed to the unleashing of the narrative imagination.

A rumour of poisoning first surfaced in a Berlin weekly less than a month after Mozart's death. In an age when medical science was less advanced than it is now, such a rumour was unremarkable. But the poisoning thesis was entrenched in the biographical tradition in 1798 by Niemetschek, who recounted the story, which he must have heard from Constanze, that a few weeks before he died Mozart told his wife that 'without a doubt, someone has given me poison!' This was by no means the last time she raised the issue, and it is not clear whether she rejected or half believed the rumour. Many subsequent biographers, especially those inclined to sensation or conspiracy theory, lapped this up. The first recorded accusation of Salieri dates from 1823, while the masons were accused in 1861 and the Jews for the first time in 1910; between the two World Wars General Ludendorff and his wife proposed a Jewish–masonic conspiracy.[13] The very idea was absurd in any case: it was almost impossible for a Jew to join the freemasons in Vienna. Followers of Ludendorff still continue to argue that Mozart was offered up in a masonic ritual sacrifice.[14] Finally it has been argued that Mozart was poisoned by Franz Hofdemel because he suspected the composer of seducing his wife.[15] There is absolutely no valid evidence for any of these theories.[16] Mozart's recorded symptoms as he lay dying do not suggest poisoning. We can be perfectly confident that he was not poisoned, because the doctors who attended him – one of whom was a toxicological expert – had a statutory duty to report any suspicious signs and did not do so.

Setting poisoning to one side, there is a large literature on the actual cause of death. Evidently Mozart-loving doctors have been irresistibly impelled to take up the subject; the layperson cannot but be concerned that so many of them are ready to rush to a confident diagnosis on the basis of so little and such unreliable evidence. Today, the main theories in contention are kidney failure or heart failure.[17] If a choice is to be made on the basis of the quality of historical scholarship combined with medical expertise, then we must choose the latter. Carl Bär carefully reads the evidence in context, establishing who the doctors were and how they were qualified, understanding their testimony in light of their medical writings and the medical theories to which they subscribed.[18] Mozart had at least two attacks of rheumatic fever as a child, which probably left him with a damaged heart; a further attack in November 1791, or an infection lodging on a damaged valve, is the most likely cause of death.

Until recent decades, following a storyline elaborated by Niemetschek and Rochlitz, it was generally accepted that Mozart died in abject circumstances, and that the important question was why this was the case. One answer, implied by Schlichtegroll, was that Mozart was in large part responsible for his own downfall, because of his childishness, irresponsibility and sensuality. This proved irresistible to many subsequent biographers, who elaborated on his womanizing, drinking, tactlessness towards potential employers and general extravagance. This story has not only been told by popularizers; authors immersed in the sources, such as Arthur Schurig and Alfred Einstein, have also told it, eventually feeding the travesties of Peter Shaffer's play and Miloš Forman's film *Amadeus*.[19] Schurig elaborated charges suggested by some earlier biographers against Constanze: she was a feckless bohemian who failed to give her husband material, emotional and spiritual support, and she dragged him down to her own disreputable level. The evidence for all of these charges, against both Mozart and Constanze, is poor, debatable or even non-existent. To take an extreme example, it has been contended that Mozart got into debt because he played deep and unsuccessfully at faro;[20] there is absolutely no evidence for this whatsoever. To be sure, there has been a contrary strand in the biographical tradition, beginning with Niemetschek, which has idealized Mozart as a human being; and in recent years Constanze has found her defenders, too.

Another answer to the question of Mozart's downfall is that his star, riding so high until 1785, waned thereafter as the fickle Viennese followed the shifting tides of fashion, or turned to less demanding music. It has been said that his concerts, so numerous and so successful in the early 1780s, dried up as he failed to find subscribers. The story of neglect was launched by Niemetschek writing from Prague and by Rochlitz writing from Leipzig; we have to entertain the possibility that they were motivated by local pride to assert the superior receptivity of their compatriots. Recent work has cast doubt on the idea that Mozart's reputation and popularity declined in Vienna. The absence of documentary records of concerts does not mean that they did not take place; we know of some concerts only from the family correspondence, a source that ran to a mere trickle in later years. Nevertheless, there can be no doubt that Mozart was in financial difficulties at least from 1788. There is now a large literature on Mozart's finances, and modern biographers feel obliged to devote much space to this topic. Before about 1960 the consensus was that Mozart's state was abject when he died; the present consensus is that his fortunes were picking up and looking bright in 1791, a high-earning year even if debts still had to be paid.[21] Moreover, there are explanations for the bad financial years in Mozart's life other than reckless extravagance or Viennese neglect: high inflation and interest rates, a decline in noble incomes and court expenditure and the war with Turkey could all have contributed to a fall in earnings.[22]

An important variant on the story of neglect is the story of Mozart as a social and political rebel. According to this story Mozart acquired a reputation as subversive, in part because of *Le nozze di Figaro* being based on Beaumarchais's anti-aristocratic play and because of his enthusiastic freemasonry; the aristocracy were already withdrawing their patronage before the French Revolution threw them into reaction. And the new Emperor, Leopold II, was more conservative and less well disposed to Mozart than his enlightened reforming predecessor Joseph II. Yet again we trace this story back to Schlichtegroll: one of the questions he asked his correspondents was how Mozart behaved in the presence of the nobility, and Schachtner replied that the child was only interested in playing to music lovers, heedless of rank. Niemetschek, Rochlitz and many subsequent biographers elaborated on this theme; perhaps we should remind ourselves that Mozart biographers tend to be middle-class music lovers and may themselves have anti-aristocratic feelings. Eventually this story fed into systematic neo-Marxist accounts, most notably by Jean and Brigitte Massin and Georg Knepler, of Mozart as a spokesman of the classes in revolt against feudal society.[23]

Grave doubts surround this story of Mozart in revolt. Mozart pens anti-aristocratic sentiments only at two junctures: when his journey to Paris in 1777 in quest of a court appointment was going badly, and in 1781 when he broke with his employer Archbishop Colloredo. There is no recorded reference by Mozart to the French Revolution, and it is logically unsound to claim that his silence demonstrates his fear of falling foul of the police. It is true that among the freemasons there were enlightened progressives highly critical of the social, political and religious order, but it cannot be inferred from this that Mozart was a progressive. More significant is the character of Mozart's own lodge, and the research of Heinz Schuler, for example, has demonstrated that it had a high proportion of aristocrats and churchmen among its members and that it was certainly not anti-Catholic in orientation.[24]

Most fundamentally, the biographical tradition has been shaped by concepts of 'genius'. Mozart's undoubted greatness invites this label, and so accounts of his life and personality are structured by preconceptions of what geniuses should be like, and how they should behave. But the concept of genius has not been static or monothematic between 1756 and the present, and as a result we get a collection of different Mozarts. Mozart's father was the first to project his son as a genius, in accordance with a traditional and religious conception: Mozart's talent was a miracle, a gift from God that he had a duty to fulfil. Later Catholic biographers such as Adolphe Boschot[25] and Wyzewa and Saint-Foix continued this theme in a post-Romantic vein which saw his genius as a divine inspiration coming as it were from outside, speaking through him. Such a conception led to an emphasis upon the spontaneous effortlessness of his compositional activity. It also produced a Mozart who was not only unworldly, as Schlichtegroll and his successors had suggested, but also angelic, a lovable human being as Niemetschek had contended. Such an emphasis upon Mozart's essential goodness, sanity, health and balance squared with the view of him as an essentially classical composer.

Schlichtegroll, by contrast, drew upon a yet older tradition, going back to Aristotle in classical antiquity, according to which the imagination is a lower, subrational faculty of the soul. This suited his story of Mozart as an eternal child, with deep character flaws. Friedrich Schiller's highly influential distinction between naive and sentimental artists fed into this theme, enabling subsequent biographers to construct a naive, childlike, perhaps childish composer who composed without reflection. This view of him is charmingly realized in Mörike's little novel *Mozart auf der Reise nach Prag*.[26] It too proposed a classical composer, for it was natural to assimilate Schiller's naive and sentimental to classicism and Romanticism respectively.

Inevitably these images of Mozart were challenged. For with the rise of Romanticism in the nineteenth century, classicism fell into disfavour in some quarters: it was thought to be shallow, formulaic and non-spiritual. Mozart lovers taking this view wished to reconstruct him as a Romantic. Related to this was an opinion, widespread in Germany, that classicism was French (and inferior) while Romanticism expressed the profundity of the German soul. This leads in turn to a conception of Mozart as a Romantic composer whose music at its greatest expresses dark, demonic inner impulses and forces; a Dionysian rather than Apollonian Mozart, passionate and driven rather than rational and balanced, tragic rather than shallowly optimistic, troubled rather than serene, his music mysterious rather than transparent.

Such a view of him was proposed by E. T. A. Hoffmann in short stories from the early nineteenth century.[27] Nevertheless, for much of the nineteenth century the image of the classical composer prevailed, and so therefore did the tendency to think of Mozart as inferior to, for example, Beethoven and Wagner. Mozart was reclaimed for Romanticism in Alfred Heuss's article,[28] which exerted a crucial influence on the biographical tradition through the writings of Schurig and Abert.

The demonic construction of Mozart placed emphasis on the works in minor keys, and also on *Don Giovanni*, which was understood as an expression of the dark, destructive, death-seeking Dionysian forces in Mozart's soul. It also went with a high evaluation of *Die Zauberflöte* as a work that half lifted the veil to reveal the underlying world of spirit. *Die Zauberflöte* was in German, and this construction of Mozart presented him as a true German who longed to create German opera and who at bottom was out of sympathy with the cosmopolitan Classical style, above all as represented by Italian opera seria. Furthermore, it led to a conception of Mozart the man as an irrational, passionate being whose irresistible inner impulses drove him to self-destruction.

All of these conceptions of genius point to a Mozart utterly out of the common run, whose creativity stems not from his social milieu and his relations with others, but from some divine or demonic inspiration which comes only to the genius. They suit an account of a man who was unworldly, perhaps lacking in common social skills. They downplay the element of skill or craft in his compositions, craft that he would have learned from other composers and musical traditions. Schurig gives us a man utterly lacking in general culture, a Tamino when composing under inspiration, a Papageno in all the common affairs of life. These themes feed into Einstein's celebrated biography, and reach their ultimate expression in Wolfgang Hildesheimer's account, according to which Mozart the genius was so out of the ordinary, so cut off from normal humanity, as to be semi-autistic.[29]

We must suspect a large element of myth-making in all of this, a construction of Mozart and his life in accordance with preconceived ideas. No document survives in which Mozart writes of himself as a genius in this sense; indeed, someone, probably Rochlitz, was tempted to rectify the omission by forging a Mozart letter in 1815 in which Mozart allegedly described his inspired, somnambulist creativity. The real Mozart expressed pride in his craft, in the compositional skills he had learned from other musicians and taken to a high level. Much recent scholarship has emphasized the relationship of his creativity to his social milieu.[30] In place of an unreflective genius who composed in a dream, it has given us, as in Konrad Küster's recent biography, a musician of the highest technical competence for whom composition presented a series of intellectual and aesthetic challenges that could only be surmounted with considerable effort.[31] Such an artist cannot be thought of as a Papageno.

A modern, 'scientific' version of the demonic genius narrative can, to a certain extent, be found in neo-Freudian accounts which relate Mozart's creativity, and the alleged tragedy of his life, to subconscious drives intensified and given a certain direction by his psychological development. Such accounts propose an unbearable conflict between his devotion to the father who gave him so much and an Oedipal revolt against that father in quest of independence and erotic fulfilment. This conflict, it is proposed, gave depth to his creativity but was ultimately destructive. Brigid Brophy developed this thesis and it has been worked out more fully by Solomon.[32] The application of highly debatable Freudian theories by amateur psychologists to a long-dead patient unable to answer for himself on the psychologist's couch cannot command the respect of a sober historian. Solomon's book is an object lesson in how massive learning can be mobilized and shaped to support a dubious thesis. His indictment of Leopold Mozart as a selfish, lying, oppressive and manipulative father has been answered by Ruth Halliwell.[33]

Recent scholarship and future directions

As I have already explained, there has been an explosion of research and scholarly writing about Mozart over the last fifty years, much of it of the highest quality. Fine editions of the scores and the correspondence are now available, as well as fine collections of documents. Detailed and careful study of this evidence, and of the original manuscripts, has corrected and enriched the biographical tradition. For example, the work of Wolfgang Plath on Mozart's handwriting, of Alan Tyson on Mozart's ruled manuscript paper and of John Arthur on the ink used by Mozart has provided valuable information about the dating of his compositions and his methods of working.[34] By drawing upon this and upon the *Neue Mozart-Ausgabe* Küster has demonstrated how much can be learnt about the man and his life from the scores alone.

It is not predominantly new data that is contributing to progress in Mozart biography. To the careful and critical reading of sources available to scholars for a long time we should add as a major cause of advancement the better understanding of these sources by setting them in various contexts. But there are many ways of gaining understanding by reconstructing historical contexts, and some are better than others. Valuable work on the Viennese context of Mozart's last decade has been produced, for example, by Volkmar Braunbehrens and H. C. Robbins Landon. Bär's setting of the medical history into the context of contemporary knowledge and theory has already been noted. We might also mention Dexter Edge's work on Viennese concert life as exemplary,[35] and Julia Moore's setting of the problem of Mozart's finances into the framework of the economic and social history of Vienna.

Robert Gutman's cultural biography is an ambitious attempt to set Mozart into social, political, intellectual and aesthetic contexts.[36] He is right to think that this is what is needed; but his reconstruction of the cultural context sometimes paints with too broad a brush. Europe-wide trends, such as the Enlightenment, or the cult of sensibility, influenced Mozart, but they were mediated to him by specific local circumstances and we need this detailed local knowledge if we are to understand Mozart properly. It is provided, for example, by Schuler's work on Viennese freemasonry and Nicholas Till's on the Austrian Enlightenment,[37] and by Küster's setting of Mozart's work within the generic conventions he shared with contemporary and immediately preceding composers.

Two very different ways of illuminating Mozart's biography by contextualization may be illustrated with reference to the correspondence. Halliwell's study of the Mozart family reads the correspondence as a whole, setting each letter into the framework of the whole corpus; she fills in the background to the letters, explaining references and allusions, identifying the persons and places mentioned. This is empirical work of the highest order. By contrast, David Schroeder's *Mozart in Revolt* is more theoretical and speculative; he reads the letters in light of prevailing epistolary and cultural conventions.[38] Understood historically in this way, aspects of the correspondence – for example, Mozart's obscene letters to his cousin, or the anxious lecturing tone of Leopold's letters to his son – take on new meaning.

If, as I have suggested, Mozart biography must progress by a better understanding of historical contexts, and if, as I and most other historians believe, the complex task of historical reconstruction is never finished in that each age contributes new insights, it follows that there will never be a definitive biography of Mozart. At best we can have biographies like that of Jahn, which sum up the knowledge and insight of their time and which stand as authoritative for a limited period. Is the time now ripe for a new, temporarily standard biography? Before one can be written, fundamental critical work on the early biographical tradition is essential. Such work has been done on Schlichtegroll, Niemetschek and Rochlitz by, for example, Georges Favier, Maynard Solomon, Bruce Cooper Clarke and Ruth Halliwell.[39] What is lacking above all is a fundamental critical study of Nissen and of the sources on which his biography is based; and after that, of the anecdotal evidence that was added later in the nineteenth century. Finally, any new standard life will have to be reflexive, that is to say it will have to recognize in self-conscious fashion the biographical tradition and its legacy of narrative frameworks that have shaped the ways we view the composer. It will have to avoid commitment to any one of these narratives, recognizing that the evidence can often be read in more than one way, leaving open alternative possibilities when a definitive interpretation is not warranted.

Finally, how should the ordinary reader with an interest in Mozart approach the biographical tradition? It would be good to begin with a learned and unfanciful survey, one without a special axe to grind – for example, Stanley Sadie's survey reprinted from the *New Grove*.[40] Next should come the letters, and Anderson's translation (*LMF*), which, although it contains minor inaccuracies and omits letters and passages judged irrelevant to the composer's life, is still commendable. The letters are vivid and fascinating and for large stretches are like a good eighteenth-century epistolary novel. The Deutsch/Eisen documentary biography can also be recommended. After that, the reader might browse according to fancy among the heap of biographies, not neglecting some earlier ones: Holmes, Jahn, Einstein, Hildesheimer, Braunbehrens, Robbins Landon, Solomon, Knepler, Gutman and Küster, for example, will satisfy or provoke. The biographies are of varying reliability; but it is difficult to write a dull one about Mozart.

PART IV

Performance

16 Mozart the performer

KATALIN KOMLÓS

When trying to recreate an image of Mozart as a performer, we must re-member that the word 'performer' conveys a quite different meaning today from what it would have conveyed in the eighteenth century. A knowledge of the craft of music and outstanding musical abilities made a performer exceptional at that time, rather than an ability to play the most technically complex pieces in the fastest possible tempo, after enormous amounts of practice on an instrument. Like so many other modern thoughts about the art of music, the later conception of the 'performer' originated in the first third of the nineteenth century. The Czerny-type of drill and relentless daily practice have brought about a fundamental change in music making.

This is not to say, of course, that Mozart was not a virtuoso performer of the first order. Especially in his last decade, he became the celebrated star of Viennese concert life. He had found the ideal medium for his artistry in the eighteenth-century fortepiano and was, in fact, the first great exponent of that instrument.

Childhood and youth

The versatility of Mozart the *Wunderkind* was so disconcerting that it would have been impossible during his early years as a performer to predict how his future career would develop. Besides composing, he played not only the harpsichord and the clavichord, but also the organ and the violin; he also sang in public. Although the well-known stories connected with the early travels of the Mozart family often remind us of the productions of entertaining troupes, the unique gifts of Wolfgang shine through right from the outset.

Wolfgang's unique gift was an all-round musicianship of the highest level, manifest in every kind of performance. From age six onwards, all of his appearances consisted of sight-reading, improvisation, transposition and so on. He possessed phenomenal aural skills and musical memory. To the credit of contemporary Europe, the unprecedented fame of the young Mozart was due more to his fabulous musicianship than to his dexterous clavier or violin playing. From Paris to London, from Vienna to Italy, he played all types of music at sight (*prima vista*), improvised melody to a given bass, improvised accompaniment to a given melody and extemporized in contrapuntal manner.

What types of music were put in front of Wolfgang in the various centres of Europe during his travels in the 1760s? Unfortunately, Leopold's eloquent reports seem to be more concerned with the income generated than with the programme of these events. Only occasionally do we learn important historical details. We know, for instance, that in October 1762 Wolfgang played music by Wagenseil to the Empress Maria Theresia in Schönbrunn, in the presence of the composer. The name of the revered Hofklaviermeister turns up again in another royal encounter, on this occasion in London in 1764. Leopold describes this encounter in a letter of 28 May 1764:

> The King placed before him not only works by Wagenseil, but those of [Johann Christian] Bach, Abel and Handel, and he played off everything *prima vista*. He played so splendidly on the King's organ that they all value his organ-playing more highly than his clavier-playing. Then he accompanied the Queen in an aria which she sang, and also a flautist who played a solo. Finally he took the bass part of some airs of Handel (which happened to be lying there) and played the most beautiful melody on it and in such a manner that everyone was amazed.[1]

No less remarkable was the musical taste and sensitivity of the seven-year-old Mozart towards the performance of others: he criticized the violin playing of Karl Michael Esser, for example, because he considered it overembellished.[2]

The organ held a special attraction for Wolfgang, an attraction that remained with him for life. (He professed the organ to be his favourite instrument to the *Orgelmacher* Johann Andreas Stein in Augsburg, in October 1777.) His first recorded playing on the instrument took place in the church of Ybbs in 1762; the following year, on his travels again, he learnt to play the pedal in Wasserburg. According to Leopold, he did this standing on the pedal board, for his legs could not reach down from the bench.[3] In subsequent years Mozart acquired a wide knowledge of the various organs in Europe. He played in the Royal Chapel in Versailles and on the King's organ in London, in the cathedral of Antwerp and on the great organ in the church of St Bavo in Haarlem. Much later, in 1778, he played on two different Silbermann organs in Strasbourg; and later still, in 1789, on J. S. Bach's organ in the Thomaskirche in Leipzig. From 1779 to 1781 he held the position of Hoforganist in Salzburg.

Early acquaintance with the organ made Mozart familiar with the particular keyboard action of the instrument on the one hand, and provided practical experience in strict contrapuntal style on the other. (In later years, when Mozart improvised in a fugal manner, he always referred to it as 'orglmässig', or 'im Kirchenstyl'.) His strong inclination towards organ-like thinking led him to have a pedal board attached to his fortepiano in the 1780s.

As the son of one of the leading contemporary authorities on violin playing, it is hardly surprising that Wolfgang was also proficient on the violin from an early age. The first charming story concerns the six-year-old child: Leopold reports in a letter that Wolfgang, in the course of their travels, 'played the customs officer a minuet on his little fiddle'.[4] The following year he performed on both the keyboard and the violin in Nymphenburg and Frankfurt, just as he did elsewhere in his teenage years. Although the keyboard eventually became Mozart's primary artistic medium, he never stopped playing the violin and the viola, the latter being a special favourite.

'You yourself do not know how well you play the violin', wrote Leopold to his son in 1777,[5] in response to Wolfgang's account of an *ad hoc* concert at the Schwarzer Adler inn in Munich, where he played the violin in two string quintets of Michael Haydn as well as in his own keyboard trio K. 254 and Divertimento in B flat major, K. 287. 'I played as though I were the finest fiddler in all Europe', he boasted with his usual sprightliness.[6] One month later he played Vanhal's B flat major Violin Concerto and his own 'Strassburg concerto', K. 216, at the Holy Cross Monastery in Augsburg. 'Everyone praised my beautiful, pure tone', he wrote proudly to his father.[7]

The two great composers Haydn and Mozart often met in Vienna during the 1780s and occasionally played together in string quartets. Michael Kelly remembers that the English composer Stephen Storace gave a quartet party in the summer of 1784, where the participants were Haydn, Dittersdorf, Mozart and Vanhal.[8] Mozart played the viola part, as he usually did in his mature years. In his last known performance of instrumental music, at a private concert in Vienna in April 1791, he played viola in two of his masterworks – the E flat major Trio, K. 563, and the Clarinet Quintet, K. 581.

To return to Mozart the *Wunderkind*, the portrait would not be complete without references to his vocal performances. A natural inclination towards cantabile style and the gift of writing for the human voice were surely in his genes; this was reinforced by the strong musical influences of his Italian travels. It was almost inevitable that Mozart the child would express his musicianship in the most direct manner: through singing. He had the good fortune of receiving singing lessons from the celebrated castrato Giovanni Manzuoli in London. Manzuoli's contract for the 1764–5 opera season coincided with the London sojourn of the Mozart family: he and Wolfgang subsequently became good friends.[9] The philosopher Daines Barrington, who wrote a detailed report on Mozart's extraordinary abilities for the Royal Society in 1765, commented on the boy's singing: 'His voice in the tone of it was thin and infantine, but nothing could exceed the masterly manner in which he sung.'[10]

As far as public appearances are concerned, we know that in July 1766 Wolfgang and Nannerl Mozart gave a concert for two harpsichords in Dijon; in the same programme, Wolfgang sang 'an air of his own composition.'[11] Another family concert with vocal performance took place in the Stift Nonnberg, on a special occasion in 1769. Following a High Mass and a festive dinner, Leopold Mozart and his children crowned the day with music, in the presence of a large clerical assembly. Cajetan Hagenauer (Pater Dominikus) wrote in his diary on 16 October 1769: 'Filius Wolfgangus... sang, and played the violin and the clavier to general amazement.'[12]

Mozart's singing career was confined to his preadolescent years. The last recorded public performances were parts of the prodigious concerts of January 1770 in Verona and Mantua. The long and extraordinarily varied programme of the concert at the Accademia Filarmonica in Mantua has fortunately survived and has often been reproduced in the Mozart litera-ture. Among the surviving items we find the following description: 'Aria composed and sung at the same time by Sig. Amadeo extempore, with the proper Accompaniments performed on the Harpsichord, to words made for the purpose, but not previously seen by him.'[13]

The 19 January 1770 issue of the *Gazzetta di Mantova* described the extraordinary event in glowing terms:

> The incomparable boy Sig. Wolfgango Amadeo Mozart... performed... concertos and sonatas for harpsichord, extemporized, with most judicious variations, and with the repetition of a sonata in another key. He sang a whole aria extempore, on new words never before seen by him, adding the proper accompaniments. He improvised two sonatas on two themes successively given him on the violin by the leader of the orchestra, elegantly linking them both together the second time. He accompanied a whole symphony with all the parts from a single violin part submitted to him on the spot. And what is most to be esteemed, he composed and at the same time extemporaneously performed a fugue on a simple theme given him, which he brought to such a masterly harmonic interweaving of all the parts and so bold a resolution as to leave the hearers astounded; and all these performances were on the harpsichord. Finally he also played marvellously well the violin part in a Trio by a famous composer.[14]

The Mantua concert might be considered a summary of the musical po-tential and artistic achievements of the fourteen-year-old Mozart. After a long period of learning, travelling and performing, he demonstrated not only his prodigious gift, but also the first-class musical education he had re-ceived from his father, and – directly or indirectly – from dozens of eminent musicians across Europe. On the threshold of adulthood, a glorious career lay before him.

Mozart at the keyboard

As it happened, the keyboard – with its polyphonic resources, its suitability for improvisation and its versatility as a solo or an ensemble instrument – was to be the primary medium for Mozart as a performing artist. 'Clavier', a generic term in German-speaking lands, referred to various types of keyboard instruments in the second half of the eighteenth century. The harpsichord, the clavichord and the fortepiano (*Hammerklavier*) were used in varying geographical locations, and for different purposes. The gradual shift from harpsichord to fortepiano as a major solo instrument took place during Mozart's lifetime; the clavichord remained in use as a domestic instrument throughout the century.

Mozart was familiar with all types of keyboard instrument. In the first half of his life he played the harpsichord most of all, in Salzburg and elsewhere. Later in the 1770s, in the course of his travels outside conservative Salzburg, he became acquainted with the new fortepiano. The effect was immediate and profound for his subsequent composition and performance alike. 'Everyone thinks the world of Wolfgang, but indeed he plays quite differently from what he used to in Salzburg – for there are pianofortes here, on which he plays so extraordinarily well that people say they have never heard the like', his mother wrote in December 1777 from Mannheim.[15]

Our first vivid picture of Mozart the fortepianist dates from 1777–8, from the time of the long journey he took with his mother. The two weeks in Augsburg and the months spent in Mannheim were especially rich in brilliant performances, for the inspiring encounter with the excellent fortepianos of Johann Andreas Stein in Augsburg and the high-level musical milieu in Mannheim gave tremendous impetus to Mozart's artistry. His long letters to his father in Salzburg give detailed descriptions of his successes and experiences.

Mozart performed on numerous occasions in Munich, Augsburg and Mannheim – in private circles, in the houses of eminent musicians, at *ad hoc* visits and in public concerts. He played his first six sonatas, K. 279–84, repeatedly, presented his concertos K. 175, 238, 246 and 271, read everything they put before him, *prima vista*, and extemporized everywhere, to the great astonishment of his audiences. The programme of his famous concert in the Augsburg Fugger Hall (22 October 1777) included the Concerto for Three Pianos, K. 242, on three new Stein fortepianos (with the participation of

Stein himself and the organist J. M. Demmler as well as Mozart), the Piano Sonata in D major, K. 284, the Piano Concerto in B flat major, K. 238, and 'another solo, quite in the style of the organ, a fugue in C minor and then all of a sudden a magnificent sonata in C major, out of my head, and a Rondo to finish up with', as Wolfgang wrote to his father.[16]

On private occasions Mozart often played the clavichord. Stein's instruments must have been very common in Augsburg, for Mozart mentions 'a good clavichord by Stein' at various locations in the city. It seems that the small instrument inspired improvisation, mainly in the strict style ('orglmässig' or 'fugirte' playing, in Mozart's words). Wolfgang's account of a long musical evening at the Holy Cross Monastery in Augsburg includes a minutely detailed description of his clavichord improvisation on a given theme: the process, complete with thematic inversions and a closing fugue, might be considered a model of Mozart's 'old-style' extemporizations.[17]

Beyond the information regarding instruments, programmes and venues, the portrait of the young artist comes to life in a number of documents. The twenty-one-year-old Mozart emerges as a born performer, with all the characteristics and attributes of the performer's personality. On the one hand, this implies an urgent eagerness to show off, to prove himself and even to dazzle his audience. On the other hand, the exuberance is complemented, in the highest moments of inspiration, with the feeling of transportation. 'Words fail me to describe my feelings', he confessed about an apparently exceptional performance in the house of the flute player Johann Baptist Wendling in Mannheim.[18]

It was not only for solo performances, however, that Mozart sat down at the keyboard. As an accompanist and continuo player he directed smaller and larger ensembles, according to the custom of the time. By the age of fourteen, he had already directed the premiere of his opera seria *Mitridate, re di Ponto* at the Ducal Theatre in Milan, 'seated at the clavier in the orchestra'. He followed this practice in his mature years in opera productions as well as in oratorio performances, as explained below.

In the early 1780s, Mozart's phenomenal sight-reading and score-reading abilities played a crucial part in the historically important musical gatherings organized by Baron van Swieten in Vienna. An ardent admirer of 'early music', van Swieten produced the works of J. S. Bach, Handel, Graun, C. P. E. Bach and others in his house, every Sunday at twelve noon. The select company went through an enormous repertory, including large-scale compositions. Seated at the fortepiano, Mozart often provided the entire instrumental/orchestral material by himself, while fellow musicians (Salieri, Starzer, Teiber and van Swieten, for example) sang the appropriate vocal parts. Joseph Weigl, a regular attender at these matinees, later wrote in his autobiography:

No one can imagine this pleasure. To hear Mozart play the most difficult scores with his own inimitable skill, and sing the while, and correct the mistakes of the others, could not but excite the greatest admiration.[19]

For years, Mozart never missed these Sunday concerts. The first-hand acquaintance with the masterworks of his predecessors widened his musical horizons, while the encounter with J. S. Bach's music transformed his compositional awareness at a deeper level.

Concert career in Vienna

'Vienna is certainly the land of the clavier!' wrote Mozart enthusiastically to his father from the Imperial city in June 1781.[20] His reputation as an esteemed performer spread quickly: barely half a year after taking up residence in Vienna he was asked by the Emperor Joseph II to compete with the celebrated Muzio Clementi on the fortepiano. The special event took place on Christmas Eve 1781 in the presence of the Emperor and his aristocratic guests, the Grand Duke and Duchess of Russia.

The bold decision of the twenty-five-year-old Mozart to start a freelance career in Vienna was promptly marked with great success. Within two years he had become a sensation as a concert performer, as well as a much sought-after piano teacher. After the first appearances in private *soirées*, he gave an *Akademie* (concert) in the Burgtheater in March 1782, and Prince Galitzin engaged him for a series of concerts in his palace for the winter of 1782–3.

Before going into the details of Mozart's Viennese concert career, we must identify the types of concert in which he performed and the venues in which these concerts took place. In the Vienna of the 1780s, the structure of concert life was still quite backward by comparison with big cosmopolitan centres such as London or Paris. As far as public concerts are concerned, the most prestigious venues were the court theatres; such events were restricted to Lent, however, when performances of plays and operas were suspended. For a series given by a single artist (so-called subscription concerts) one could rent a hall, or a building, or some other similar locality in the city.

The commonest type of Viennese concert was still the private one, taking place in the residences of the higher and lower nobility and the houses of the wealthy middle class. Many aristocratic patrons maintained an orchestra and offered regular concerts. Mozart soon became a favourite in the musical salons of Prince Galitzin, Count Esterházy, Count Zichy, Count Palffy, Prince Kaunitz, Gottfried von Ployer and others.

Mozart's Viennese career – which depended on teaching and concertizing as major sources of income – developed rapidly in the early 1780s. Between

Table 16.1. *Mozart's Viennese concerts during Lent 1784*

| | Public concerts | | |
Date	Mozart's own concerts	Mozart's participation in other concerts	Private concerts
4 March			Prince Galitzin
5 March			Count Esterházy
8 March			Count Esterházy
11 March			Prince Galitzin
12 March			Count Esterházy
15 March			Count Esterházy
17 March	Trattnerhof		
18 March			Prince Galitzin
19 March			Count Esterházy
20 March		Trattnerhof	Count Zichy
22 March			Count Esterházy
24 March	Trattnerhof		
25 March			Prince Galitzin
26 March			Count Esterházy
27 March		Trattnerhof	
29 March			Count Esterházy
31 March	Trattnerhof		
1 April	Burgtheater		
3 April		Trattnerhof	
9 April			Count Palffy
10 April			Prince Kaunitz
11 April		Burgtheater	

1783 and 1785 he gave approximately three to five Akademien per year at the Burgtheater, and several series of subscription concerts at the Trattnerhof and the Mehlgrube. The number of his subscribers for the Trattnerhof series in Lent 1784 was 174, half of them from the nobility; the Mehlgrube series in 1785 attracted over 150 subscribers. Two further series were offered at Advent 1785 and Advent 1786.

The culmination of Mozart's concert activity came in 1784 and 1785. The public concerts outnumbered the private ones in 1785, while the salon appearances were strikingly more frequent in 1784 than in any other year. Within forty days in Lent 1784 Mozart gave a grand total of twenty-three concerts in Vienna: this would be a record for any star performer of today (see table 16.1).[21]

The substantial series of fortepiano concertos Mozart composed for his Viennese concerts begins with K. 414 in A (1782). It is hard to imagine the excitement of those occasions when he premiered these concerto masterpieces from the freshly finished – and at times not even completely finished – manuscript scores. In fact, Mozart often added the final touches to his concertos in his performances of them. In any case, the well-documented success of these concerts was tremendous – in both financial and artistic terms.

It is gratifying to think that Leopold was able to witness Mozart's glorious success in Vienna first-hand, when he was a guest of his son and family in the first half of 1785. 'The concert was magnificent and the orchestra played splendidly', he wrote to his daughter about the first subscription concert at the Mehlgrube, which included the first performance of the Piano Concerto in D minor, K. 466.[22] The presentation of the Piano Concerto in B flat major, K. 456, made an even more profound impression on the usually reserved Leopold, as another excerpt from his letters certainly illustrates: 'I had the great pleasure of hearing so clearly all the interplay of the instruments that for sheer delight tears came into my eyes. When your brother left the platform the Emperor waved his hat and called out "Bravo, Mozart!"'[23] Leopold's ten-week visit must have been a rich reward for fatherly efforts and anxieties stretching back over many years.

In addition to the piano concertos, the eagerly awaited attractions of Mozart's *Akademien* were his improvisations. These always featured in his concerts. For Mozart, extemporization on the fortepiano meant playing variations on well-known tunes of the day. In fact, some of his major variation sets (the two Parisian compositions, K. 264 and 354, and K. 398, 455 and 613 written in Vienna) might be the notated versions of such improvisatory performances. They have a fantasia-like quality, with long cadenzas and other free passages, and their level of virtuosity is very high indeed. These sets and the most technically demanding concertos (probably K. 450 and 451) reflect Mozart's brilliant instrumental mastery.[24]

As well as performing solo, Mozart appeared in concert with other musicians. He played the Concerto for Two Pianos, K. 365, and the Sonata for Two Keyboards, K. 448, with his pupil, Josepha von Auernhammer, at a house concert in November 1781: the latter was composed specifically for this occasion. Mozart and Auernhammer performed K. 365 again the following year at an Augarten concert. Another pupil, Barbara von Ployer, the dedicatee of the concertos K. 453 and 456, was Mozart's partner in a Döbling concert in June 1784 (K. 448). The famous Italian violinist Regina Strinasacchi inspired the Violin Sonata in B flat major, K. 454: she played the sonata with Mozart at her *Akademie* in the Burgtheater in April 1784. In fact, K. 454 and the Quintet for Piano and Winds, K. 452, presented at Mozart's Burgtheater concert in the same month, were the only keyboard chamber works by Mozart to be heard in a public concert.

Mozart's concert activity seems to have declined gradually after 1786. Several explanations have recently been offered for this apparent decline: the general deterioration of Viennese concert life, due to political developments; the decrease in Lent-time concert opportunities in the theatres after the embargo on the performance of plays was lifted; and the lack of documentary evidence detailing Mozart's concerts.[25] While these explanations are correct, the main reason might lie elsewhere. After several years of intense concertizing, composing and teaching, Mozart's energies must have been seriously depleted. Organizing one's own concerts in the late eighteenth century, before managers and agents were on the scene, took enormous effort. The artist had to do everything himself – from the renting of suitable locations and the hiring of orchestral musicians to the publicity and the distribution of tickets. In Mozart's case, this was further complicated by the fact that he had to transport his fortepiano, complete with a heavy fortepiano pedal, to and from every concert venue.

As mentioned above, the considerable income from the Viennese concerts in 1782–6 secured a comfortable living for Mozart and his family. In later years, the lack of this income resulted in severe financial difficulties. (Robbins Landon believes that yet another subscription series was given in 1788, although this cannot be proved.)[26] Travel, illnesses and the immeasurable demands of composition took Mozart in other directions, and when he tried to organize subscription concerts in his own home in 1789 and 1790 – in order to improve his financial situation – it met with little response from the musical public. Outside Vienna he gave isolated, highly successful concerts in Prague (January 1787), Leipzig (May 1789) and Frankfurt (October 1790). Regarding the Frankfurt concert, he wrote wistfully to his wife on 15 October: 'It was a splendid success from the point of view of honour and glory, but a failure as far as money was concerned.'[27]

Another important field of concert activity for Mozart was the performance of oratorios. Supported by a society of noblemen in the late 1780s, Baron van Swieten organized the performance of large-scale works by Handel and other masters, with Mozart playing a key role in the productions. He directed two performances of C. P. E. Bach's oratorio *Die Auferstehung und Himmelfahrt Jesu* in February and March of 1788 at the Esterházy palace; the concert was given for a third time shortly afterwards at the Burgtheater in Vienna. According to Johann Nikolaus Forkel's contemporary review, 'Mozart directed and had the score [*taktirte und hatte die Partitur*], and Umlauf played the harpsichord.'[28] Mozart also directed Handel's *Acis and Galatea* in 1788 and the *Messiah* in March 1789, the latter in Mozart's own orchestration.

According to eighteenth-century practice, Mozart directed the first performances of his operas from the keyboard, which was situated in the orchestra. As Joseph Weigl testifies in his autobiography, Mozart conducted the first three performances of *Figaro* at the Burgtheater, with Weigl taking over for subsequent performances.[29] The same applies to the Viennese premiere of *Don Giovanni*, and perhaps even to *Così fan tutte* as well (although there is no documentary evidence for this). On 30 September 1791, at the

Theater auf der Wieden, Mozart directed the last operatic premiere of his life – that of *Die Zauberflöte*.

Artistic personality

It would appear that Mozart's artistic disposition was characterized by an ideal balance of spontaneity and discipline. He had definite views on the proper way to perform, and was highly critical of the playing of others. Thanks to an abundance of long letters, we know a great deal about Mozart's principles and priorities where performance is concerned. As Siegbert Rampe points out, Mozart has more to say about performance than other eighteenth-century musicians, with the exception of C. P. E. Bach.[30]

The irresistible urge to perform prompted Mozart to take to the organ during Mass on more than one occasion. He relates the unusual course of a Sunday service in the Mannheim court chapel in November 1777 as follows:

> I came in during the Kyrie and played the end of it, and, when the priest had finished intoning the Gloria, I played a cadenza. As my performance was so different from what they are accustomed to here, they all looked round, especially [*Kapellmeister*] Holzbauer . . . Instead of a Benedictus the organist has to play here the whole time. So I took the theme of the Sanctus and developed it as a fugue. Whereupon they all stood gaping. Finally, after the *Ite missa est*, I played a fugue.[31]

A similar event occurred six years later in the Lambach monastery, en route from Salzburg to Linz, where Mozart 'arrived just in time to accompany the Agnus Dei on the organ'.[32]

Highly sensitive (*empfindsamer*) playing, practised primarily by German musicians of the time, allowed – even required – appropriate comportment. Mozart refrained from external habits, whether facial expressions or the swaying of the body. 'I do not make grimaces, and yet play with such expression', he explained to Leopold, reporting the opinion of his admirer J. A. Stein.[33] He ridiculed the 'flopping about' of the young Nannette Stein at the clavier, and found the playing of a certain Miss Hamm 'curiously affected'.[34]

Concerning the essential elements of performance, Mozart considered keeping strict time and playing in moderate tempi indispensable for an intelligible and clear performance. A quiet hand and precision in musical and technical domains were further aspects of performance that he admired.[35]

Mozart upheld the high standards and self-respect of the musical professional to a remarkable degree. 'Give me the best clavier in Europe with an audience who understands nothing, or don't want to understand and who do not feel with me in what I am playing, and I shall cease to feel any pleasure', he wrote in a disillusioned moment in Paris.[36] Fortunately, in the later years of his great success as a performer he experienced the spiritual interchange that can occur between a charismatic performer and a perceptive audience: 'I told you about the applause in the theatre, but I must add that what delighted and surprised me most of all was the amazing silence', he informed Leopold in April 1781.[37]

Two important concepts appear time and again in Mozart's communications about performance: taste and feeling (*Geschmack und Empfindung*). These are the qualities he privileged above all and sought constantly in the performances of others. In his judgement, no kind of technical bravura could compensate for a lack of taste and feeling. As Mozart remarked severely about the famous virtuoso Muzio Clementi: 'He has not a kreuzer's worth of taste or feeling – in short he is simply a *mechanicus*.'[38] Such condemnations – sometimes made humorously, sometimes sharply – did not apply only to keyboard players. Mozart's harsh criticism of a concert given by the flautist Johann Philipp Freyhold in 1784 illustrates this point: 'I found very little to admire in his performance and missed a great deal. His whole tour de force consists in double-tonguing. Otherwise there is nothing whatever to listen to.'[39]

Performers of Mozart's music today should not forget the composer's artistic creed. They should remember the infinite care with which Mozart tried to teach the nuances of an Andante (K. 309) to his pupil Rosa Cannabich, and the 'indescribable pleasure' he felt when she played it 'with the utmost expression'.[40] Performing instructions are marked carefully in Mozart's notation, and a wealth of ideas on music and musical performance survive in his voluminous correspondence. All is available: we can be true Mozart pupils today.

17 Performance practice in the music of Mozart

R O B E R T   D .   L E V I N

Until the second half of the nineteenth century composers tended to work within a *lingua franca*, which did not prevent their music from having a discernible individuality. Their personalities are evident both in matters of style and in peculiarities of notation and terminology. These tend to be overlooked in conservatory training, which dispenses general definitions of terminology with presumed universal validity. The primary sources of performance practice information for Mozart and other eighteenth-century musicians are the treatises, particularly those of Mozart's father on violin playing and that of C. P. E. Bach on keyboard playing.[1]

What follows is an attempt to cover the principal areas of idiomatic performance practice in Mozart. Given the constraints of space, emphasis will be placed upon the relationship between Mozart's notation and its execution. The treatment of individual domains and instruments is drawn both from the treatises and the author's study of Mozart's notational practice.

Society, tempo and character

Mozart's music incarnates a cosmopolitan vernacular depicting a wide range of dramatic and emotional situations, which are intimately bound up with the social conventions of his day. There is scarcely a musical gesture, from the courtly and martial march to the sighing appoggiatura, that is not related to societal relationships and functions, physical gestures, or emotional archetypes. It is Mozart's singular achievement to have enriched this universally understood vocabulary with uncanny acuity of perception in matters of human motivation and character, supported by a sophisticated control of dramatic and structural events from the smallest detail to the largest arc. This in turn is animated by an intense characterization of the individual keys and instruments, an unusually rich harmonic language, a rhythmic style of extraordinary fluidity, and a variety of textures and accompaniment figures that change at split-second speed to mirror the volatile flow of emotions.

There is scarcely a more crucial element to the depiction of a particular dramatic situation than tempo. Mozart uses a consistent hierarchy of tempo indications and modifications. The general speed and character will be clearly implied by the initial theme of a movement, but Mozart's language is intrinsically mercurial. Frequent changes of accompaniment patterns and a rich palette of articulation, harmonic language and expressive gestures are used to delineate impulsive shifts from casual ease to anxiety and high drama; from ardour to charm; from childlike joy to mockery. The tendency of today's instrumental performers to substitute notions of loveliness for Mozart's volatility of character would be unthinkable on the opera stage, as this would be fatal to the intrinsic drama. Musicians who immerse themselves in the stimulating study of Mozart's expressive vocabulary will become aware of his sophisticated rendering of character shifts and will exploit these viscerally in performances of dazzling theatricality in the best sense.

Rubato and tempo flexibility

The eighteenth-century treatises are uniform in emphasizing the importance of a steady tempo. Nonetheless, there are sanctioned ways to underscore the musical rhetoric with discreet tempo inflections. Among the possibilities[2] are emphasis of critical rests to provide dramatic punctuation within a phrase or between two adjoining phrases, tasteful use of agogics (slight stretching of the longer notes of a melody), and *tempo rubato*, described by Mozart in an oft-quoted letter to his father:

> Everyone is amazed that I can always keep strict time. What these people cannot grasp is that in tempo rubato in an Adagio, the left hand should go on playing in strict time. With them the left hand always follows suit.[3]

Repeats

If repeats are considered today as non-binding suggestions, there is strong evidence that Mozart expected performers to respect every repeat he wrote. His deletion of the exposition repeat of the 'Haffner' Symphony, K. 385, shows that there was nothing purely mechanical about such repeats. Those who believe that the occasional prescription 'Menuetto da capo senza replica' should apply universally might reflect that if the suppression of repeats at the da capo had been normative such indications would not appear at all. Mozart's care in these matters is confirmed by the second minuet from the Divertimento for String Trio in E flat major, K. 563. Its first trio concludes with the indication 'Menuetto da capo, le repliche piano': this tells the performers *how* to play the repeat, not that they must take it; and he calls for the omission of the repeats after the second trio.

Beyond these documentary matters is the evidence of the music itself. The dramatic significance of the music that begins the development section in, for example, the first movements of the String Quartet in C major, K. 465 ('Dissonance'), and the Symphony in G minor, K. 550, depends upon the prior repeat having been taken. Such cases are not unusual; one need not have a first and second ending for the necessity of the repeat to be evident.

Observing repeats is as much of a creative challenge as it is part of the style, for a mere replication of the performance in all details will tire the listener.

Dynamics

Like many composers of the period, Mozart assumes that movements begin *f* unless otherwise specified; thus a dynamic appears at the outset only if other than *f*. (This practice is apparent in the sources only, for editors of standard editions insert the *f*.) Mozart generally notates dynamics to the left of the notes to which they apply, using the common eighteenth-century forms *pia:* (*p:*), *for:* (*f:*), *pianiss:* (*pp:*), *fortiss:* (*ff:*), in which the colon denotes abbreviation. The simplified notation (*p*, *f*, *pp*, *ff*) occurs less frequently. Replacement of Mozart's indications by simplified dynamics, uncontroversial though it may seem, engenders difficulties when Mozart's dynamic markings straddle several notes. In placing them where Mozart's *pia:*, *for:* etc. begin rather than where they end, editors may prescribe a dynamic change up to several notes too early.

Nor are the problems limited to placement. Although sharp contrasts of dynamics are integral to Mozart's style, the content and character of his music sometimes suggest the possibility of mediation between dynamics even where no *crescendo* or *decrescendo* indications appear. In such cases the dynamics may serve to denote the moment at which a new level is reached rather than an abrupt shift.[4]

Among Mozart's notational idiosyncrasies are the markings *fp*, *sf* and *dolce*.[5] Mozart tends to treat all three as dynamic markings that remain in force until cancelled by a subsequent *p*. It is noteworthy that this often seems to apply to *fp*, despite the implication of the marking.[6]

Vocal lines and the solo parts of most of Mozart's concertos have few dynamic markings. These are typically limited to echo effects, although concertos written for others to perform sometimes have more dynamics than those in which he was the soloist.

Articulation

The detail of Mozart's slurs and staccati shows the importance of clarity of articulation in his music. In the eighteenth century non-legato was the rule and legato the expressive effect, especially in keyboard writing; the nineteenth century reversed this, mirroring the situation with regard to vibrato. Thus, unarticulated notes are normally played with separation between them, the amount depending upon the expressive content.

There is still controversy over the question of whether Mozart used two signs – the dot and the stroke – for his staccati, as well as over the intended meaning of the two.[7] (It is worth noting that early editions tend to render all staccato signs with one symbol or the other.) His father's violin treatise mentions only the stroke. Although anyone consulting a Mozart autograph will see staccato signs that are clearly strokes and some that seem to be dots, an attempt to sort the vexing middle ground into one or the other is doomed to failure – a contention that is borne out by passages in which two or more instruments, whose parts may have been notated at different times, have the same melody or move in thirds, sixths or octaves with one another.[8] It would seem most likely that, except for dots under slurs (*portato*), Mozart intended only strokes in his autographs for staccati even if through haste these sometimes approximate dots.

The importance of rendering Mozart's staccati as strokes rather than dots in editions relates more to the way musicians are presently trained than to norms of his time. The execution of dots taught today – a short, light articulation – is but one meaning of the stroke. The latter can also denote a more weighty articulation akin to the later accent sign ($>$), which does not appear in Mozart's manuscripts. Strokes appear over long notes ($♩, ♩., 𝅝$) and at the beginnings and endings of slurs, denoting a stressed execution that is incompatible with the meaning of the dot. Most critical for performers is to understand the variety of declamation possible with staccato execution and to display active awareness of the rendering chosen by the editor(s) of a given edition. This will avoid distinctions between dots and strokes that can easily become arbitrary, whilst allowing the performer to determine which type of execution is appropriate within a given context and character.

According to Leopold Mozart and other contemporaneous treatises, slurs are to be understood as *decrescendi*, with the last note normally lighter and shorter.[9] When Alberti basses or related figures are slurred in keyboard music, the bottom note is sustained (finger pedal) throughout the group. Contextual evidence shows that keyboard passages where two or more voices are notated on a single staff are to be performed legato unless otherwise marked. Example 17.1, from the Rondo in F major, K. 494, shows how these principles are interrelated. In bar 19 the slur implies that the first and third crotchets are sustained, whereas the presence of two voices in the following bar implies that the legato execution is continued.

Like most of his contemporaries, Mozart seems to have used shorthand notation for tied and slurred chords, commonly limiting himself to one or

Example 17.1 Mozart, Rondo in F major, K. 494, bars 19–20

two ties/slurs regardless of the number of voices. In the case of tied chords there is little doubt that inner voices are to be sustained when outer ones are so notated, but when there are only outer-voice slurs the performer must decide whether the common tones are to be repeated or tied. Similarly, ties and slurs found in the orchestral bass line of the piano concertos are not always present in the solo keyboard. Such differentiation may have been due to a desire to give the more delicate sound of the period piano greater profile, rather than a product of Mozart's forgetfulness.

Idiosyncrasies of notation and execution

Certain peculiarities of Mozart's notation are worth singling out, as they may have performance implications. Multiple stemming, used for *divisi* orchestral parts, is also used for multiple stops, as well as to indicate the polyphonic basis of much of his piano writing. Mozart's beaming frequently separates individual notes from groups of similar notes to articulate phrase structure and accentuation. As many of these distinctions are eliminated in editions, only study of the manuscripts will reveal this information.

Several of Mozart's habits in notating slurs and ties can lead to confusion:

- He is somewhat more likely to begin a slur to the left of the first note affected by it than to its right, as is the case with his notation of dynamics (see above); this can result in editorial discrepancies.
- He uses combinations of ties and slurs in succession, rather than ties subsumed under lengthy slurs, as rendered in many editions.
- The use of slurs to connect appoggiaturas and grace notes to main notes is highly selective. Although Leopold Mozart prescribes the universal execution of such slurs, even in cases where they are not notated,[10] the evidence of Wolfgang's autographs and performing parts as well as the musical contexts suggest that for him this may not always have been the case, at least from the 1770s onwards. Because individual publishers tacitly add such slurs when absent in the sources or suppress all of them, performers are urged to consult facsimiles, as Mozart's inclusion of such slurs may denote a more cantabile execution than when they are absent.
- Mozart breaks a slur at the point at which the stem direction changes; most often he also breaks slurs at the end of a page. When the parallel passage does not entail

a change of stemming or a new page, Mozart often slurs through, showing that such breaks do not perforce require the articulation associated with the end of a slur. These niceties are not always revealed by printed editions, which sometimes use different stem directions and usually employ a different page layout from the manuscript, thereby giving Mozart's slurring questionable implications.

• Mozart occasionally joins a slur to a previous one. Modern editions tend to replace such multiple slurs with a single, larger one; but there may well be implications of declamation (accentuation) in the more complex notation, as treatises mandate that the first note under a slur is to be executed with more energy.

Another area in which the tacit standardization carried out by editors may distort Mozart's intentions concerns orchestral horn parts. Although Mozart rarely supplies slurs or other articulation to such horn parts, most modern editions tend to add them when found in other wind parts that are doubled (or nearly doubled) by the horns, such as the oboes. Given the care with which Mozart prepared his manuscripts for the copyists providing parts, it is highly unlikely that the paucity of horn articulation stems from an assumption that copyists would simply transfer it from the other winds. When we recall that there was little use of scores – works were almost always circulated and published only in parts – and that orchestral performances without prior rehearsal were common, one may conclude that Mozart actually intended his horn parts to have less slurring and other articulation than the rest of the wind. Indeed, there is every reason to challenge the general aesthetic tendency of modern editions to standardize readings according to parallel passages: it is *variety* of characterization, not consistency, that is an essential trait of the style.

Further details of Mozart's notation will be found in the discussion of ornaments and embellishments below.

Textual issues and conflicts

In many of his compositions Mozart did not write out recurrences of the principal theme or the music that followed it until it diverged from the original passage, instead leaving a brief blank space in the manuscript with the remark 'da Capo [x] Täckt' (x being the number of bars to be repeated). Published versions reprint these passages identically, but the return of the principal theme is a *locus classicus* for embellishment, and Mozart provided embellishments for solo keyboard works published during his lifetime or performed by pupils. An example is the Piano Sonata in C minor, K. 457, in which two separate sets of embellishments for the returns of the second movement's principal theme survive on extra sheets of paper, whereas the manuscript contains only da capos.

Mozart notated his compositions in a multi-tiered process, entering the principal voices first (first violin and bass for orchestral works), from beginning to end, with any colouristic lines in other instruments penned only where they continue the train of thought. In a second stage, the secondary lines are filled in; the purely accompanimental voices are last, and at times there is a final stage in which minor improvements may be made. Differences in quill width and ink tint confirm this process. Its significance for performers is that Mozart sometimes notated the later instruments without examining what he had already written down, creating conflicts or grammatical solecisms that remain uncorrected today. Among such anomalies are:

- two different harmonies unwittingly combined (Piano Concerto in C minor, K. 491/ii, bar 40; Piano Concerto in C major, K. 503/iii, bar 60)
- cross relations (K. 491/i, bar 319, second oboe and solo keyboard)
- parallel fifths (Piano Concerto in C major, K. 415/i, bars 121–2, keyboard right hand and second violin; K. 503/iii, bars 247–8, keyboard right hand and second bassoon)
- one voice appearing twice while another is omitted (Piano Concerto in A major, K. 488/i, bar 38, first and second violins both have A–G♯ whereas one should have C♯–B)[11]
- omissions (K. 491/i, bars 175–7, first bassoon (Mozart almost certainly intended a doubling of the cellos and basses an octave higher) and bars 278–9, violas (likewise))

Finally, there is Mozart's use of shorthand in the piano concertos. Intended arpeggios are delineated by their outer limits in long note values (Piano Concerto in E flat major, K. 482/iii, bars 164–72 and 346–7; K. 491/i, bars 261–2 and 467–70), and broken octaves or thirds are rendered with octaves, single notes or thirds (Piano Concerto in C major, K. 467/iii, bars 302, 304–6, right hand; K. 482/iii, bars 353–6, both hands; K. 491/iii, bars 191 and 198, right hand, bars 245–8 and 262–5, left hand).

Ornaments and embellishments

Mozart's notational conventions often reflect Baroque practice. They include:

- Use of the oblique acciaccatura stroke (𝄀) between the notes of a chord to denote arpeggiation (rendered in standard editions by ♩), which is often signalled in later works by using minims for outer voices with crotchets for the inner ones (𝄀).
- Overdotting, including the possible execution of the sarabande rhythm ♩. ♪ ♫ as ♩.. ♪ ♫ (Piano Concerto in E flat major, K. 271/iii) or of the rhythm ♩. ♪ ♫ ♫ as ♩.. ♪ ♫ ♫ (Concerto for Two Pianos, K. 365/i, bar 32, etc.).
- The execution of ♫ as ♩³♪ in the context of triplets, particularly in moderate to fast tempi (K. 365/iii, bars 223–35, 255–67); cf. Piano Concerto in B flat major, K. 450/i, bar 76, where the dotted rhythms are stemmed together with triplets.
- The afterbeats of trills are not always written out, even though they are conventionally assumed.

- Turns are notated in no fewer than four different ways (see example 17.2). It is to be assumed that each of these implies a slightly different execution, the only point in common being that in all cases the last note of the ornament (c″) coincides with the third quaver of the bar.

Example 17.2 Mozart's notation of turns

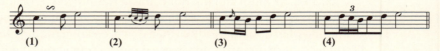

- A single symbol is employed for grace notes and appoggiaturas, with semiquaver ornaments notated as ♪ rather than ♪ and the oblique slash applied to a ♪ for ♪( ), etc. Leopold Mozart observes that the reason for using a smaller note size for the appoggiatura is to show its dissonant, decorative status, in order to prevent poorly educated musicians from adding an additional appoggiatura above it. Both pre-beat (grace-note) and on-beat (appoggiatura) execution are idiomatic to Mozart's music. Since there is considerable latitude of execution for most ornaments of the period, performers are urged to consult both eighteenth- and twentieth-century treatises for detailed explication of the options and their justification.

Essential to idiomatic performance of eighteenth-century music is the addition of decoration to the notated text. This was normally improvised anew at each performance by professional musicians. Amateurs required assistance in such matters; hence, the printed editions of Mozart's piano sonatas contain both more dynamic indications and more decorations than the autographs. Mozart taught the art of embellishment to his pupils, as shown by his embellishments to the aria 'Non sò d'onde viene', K. 294, which were composed for Aloysia Weber,[12] and by an elaborate embellishment of the slow movement of the Piano Concerto in A major, K. 488, by his pupil Barbara Ployer (for whom Mozart wrote the concertos K. 449 and 453).[13] While we may not find everything in the latter to be congruent with Mozart's style, it is extremely unlikely that Ployer would have written demisemiquavers if Mozart himself played only crotchets and quavers.

The places where improvised ornamentation was normally added include:

- Reprises of principal themes of both vocal and instrumental music (mentioned in the preceding section). This is confirmed not only by the published versions of Mozart's keyboard sonatas but also, in the concertos, by written-out embellishments of orchestral iterations of such reprised themes after the soloist has played them. (It would seem scarcely possible that in a concerto the soloist was meant to play simpler versions of main musical material than the orchestra.)
- During the course of slow movements, when the rhythmic surface remains relatively simple. This is documented by Ployer's embellishment of K. 488/ii (see example 17.3).

Example 17.3 Mozart, Piano Concerto in A major, K. 488/ii, bars 22–8

- The piano recitatives in the slow movements of K. 451, 466, 467, 537 and 595, in which prosodic melodic fragments in the keyboard's right hand are accompanied by pulsating repeated quavers in the strings. A surviving authentic embellishment of the passage in K. 451 shows the level and type of embellishment to be supplied (see example 17.4).

Example 17.4 Mozart, Piano Concerto in D major, K. 451/ii, bars 56–63

- Chords may be broken even where not explicitly authorized. As observed in the treatises, this adds a degree of stylish urbanity to a performance when judiciously used and avoids heaviness where an isolated chord appears.

The treatises aver that the goal of embellishment is intensification of expression, not self-aggrandizing display. The ideal is spontaneous declamation of the dramatic and emotional state of each performance, which cannot possibly be represented by a consistently employed solution. Those wary of improvising different rhetoric anew are urged to try a variety of possibilities, noting them one above the other, with an eye to combining the versions into a wide variety of alternatives. (A useful first step is to cut and paste photocopies of Mozart's successive embellishments in the Rondos K. 494 and 511 or the second movement of the Piano Sonata in C Major, K. 309, over the original theme.)

Cadenzas, lead-ins (*Eingänge*) and *Fermaten*

Mozart's concertos and arias contain three types of solo peroration:

- The cadenza is less a prolonged virtuoso display than a decorated cadence, as denoted by its Italian name. It is prompted by the harmonic tension of the orchestra's tonic six-four at the fermata. The soloist bridges the resultant dramatic gap with improvised virtuosity, carrying the tension through the final trill,[14] whose tonic resolution brings on the re-entry of the orchestra.

  Agricola, Arteaga and Mancini aver that vocal cadenzas should be executable in a single breath, but their commentary implies that contemporary practice often violated that convention. While some surviving vocal cadenzas respect this ideal, others, such as Mozart's cadenzas to arias from *Lucio Silla* and *Il re pastore*, push the definition quite far (see example 17.5).[15]

Example 17.5 Mozart, *Lucio Silla*, K. 135, 'Ah se a morir mi chiama' (cadenza)

The metrical freedom displayed by example 17.5 is advocated in the treatises. The brevity of vocal cadenzas precludes the extensive thematic citation found in their instrumental counterparts.[16] They often move to a clear high point, then descend to the trill on the supertonic note and its resolution to the tonic. Harmonically they either outline the tonic triad or adorn it with passagework; the arrival on the dominant is implied rather than arpeggiated.

To judge from the many surviving authentic cadenzas to Mozart's piano concertos, instrumental cadenzas tended to be approximately one-tenth of the total movement length. An important feature is that they never modulate, although a given chord within the principal tonality or its parallel minor can be tonicized momentarily.[17]

Türk's rules for the construction of cadenzas are concise and valuable:

1 ... the cadenza ... should particularly reinforce the impression the composition has made in a most lively way and present the most important parts of the whole composition in the form of a brief summary or in an extremely concise arrangement ...

2 The cadenza, just as every extempore embellishment, must consist not so much of intentionally added difficulties as of such thoughts which are most scrupulously suited to the main character of the composition ...

3 Cadenzas should not be too long, especially in compositions of a melancholy character ...

4 Modulations into other keys, particularly to those which are far removed, either do not take place at all – for example, in short cadenzas – or they must be used with much insight and, as it were, only in passing. In no case should one modulate to a key which the composer himself has not used in the composition. It seems to me that this rule is founded on the principle of unity, which, as is well known, must be followed in all works of the fine arts ...

5 Just as unity is required for a well-ordered whole, so also is variety necessary if the attention of the listener is to be held. Therefore as much of the unexpected and the surprising as can possibly be added should be used in the cadenza . . .

6 No thought should be often repeated in the same key or in another, no matter how beautiful it may be . . .

7 Every dissonance which has been included, even in single-voiced cadenzas, must be properly resolved . . .

8 A cadenza does not have to be erudite, but novelty, wit, an abundance of ideas and the like are so much more its indispensable requirements . . .

9 The same tempo and meter should not be maintained throughout the cadenza; its individual fragments (those parts which are incomplete in themselves) must be skillfully joined to one another. For the whole cadenza should be more like a fantasia which has been fashioned out of an abundance of feeling, rather than a methodically constructed composition . . .

10 From what has been said it follows that a cadenza which perhaps has been learned by memory with great effort or has been written out before should be performed as if it were merely invented on the spur of the moment, consisting of a choice of ideas indiscriminately thrown together which had just occurred to the player.[18]

- The lead-in (*Eingang*) is prompted by a pause on V or V[7] or by an arrival in a related key (that is, a tonality whose tonic triad is diatonic in the main key). Lead-ins usually precede the return of the principal theme or a section in a different tempo. They can employ a motive from the movement or be based upon arpeggios, scales and scale figures or a combination of these. Apart from their slightly shorter length, vocal lead-ins differ little in rhythmic and melodic content from vocal cadenzas. Mozart wrote out lead-ins in the scores of the arias 'Ruhe sanft, mein holdes Leben' (No. 3) from *Zaide*, K. 344, and 'Dalla sua pace' (No. 10a) from *Don Giovanni*, K. 527. Authentic lead-ins also survive for the aria 'Al desio, di chi t'adora', K. 577, and the aria 'L'amerò, sarò costante' from *Il re pastore*, K. 208 (see example 17.6).

Example 17.6 Mozart, *Il re pastore*, K. 208, 'L'amerò, sarò costante', bars 85–6

- *Fermaten* (fermatas) typically appear in arias at the first entry of the vocal soloist and embellish the tonic chord. *Fermaten* are rarely encountered in Mozart's instrumental concertos, though one does appear in the first movement of the Piano Concerto in B flat major, K. 450. Like lead-ins, *Fermaten* are embellished with *fioritura* combinations of arpeggios, scales and scale figures and are to be sung within a single breath. Neumann theorizes that Mozart's use of a broad fermata spanning several notes (or notes and rests) suggests embellishment, although this special symbol does not denote the only places in which lead-ins and *Fermaten* are possible.[19]

Celebrated as the greatest improviser of his age, Mozart would have improvised the cadenzas and lead-ins to his concertos. The fact that authentic cadenzas for the violin and wind concertos do not survive, and that authentic vocal cadenzas to Mozart's arias are exceptional, attests to the fact that their performers did the same. Nonetheless, at least one set (often more) of authentic cadenzas and *Eingänge* survives for all but six of the piano concertos (and for K. 466 and 467 such cadenzas were composed but are now lost). These suggest the length and style of Mozart's improvisations and demonstrate that it is not the number of themes quoted that matters but the question of harmonic instability, which must be preserved through the trill at the cadenza's end.[20]

As with embellishments, performers are advised to compose their own cadenzas as a preliminary step towards attempting true improvisation. Pianists seeking cadenzas to the concertos for which authentic cadenzas and *Eingänge* do not survive often transcribe those by distinguished interpreters. Not all of these respect Mozart's avoidance of modulation; many exceed the compass of Mozart's piano (whose limitations he so adroitly hid); and some have unmistakable hints of later musical styles. Among the finest published cadenzas are those by Marius Flothuis.[21] Stylistically idiomatic cadenzas to most of the non-keyboard concertos have been composed by the author.[22]

Instruments

Instrumentalists, vocalists and conductors should consider the direct relationship between such aspects of the music as texture, articulation and dynamics and the instrument(s) or voice(s) for which the music was conceived, for an expert composer will exploit to the full the characteristics of the instruments and voices at hand. This involves not merely the technical and timbral aspects of the instruments/voices, but the specialized abilities of individual instrumentalists and singers.

Strings

An indispensable source of information regarding Mozartian string technique and general issues of performance practice is Leopold Mozart's *A Treatise on the Fundamental Principles of Violin Playing*, which elucidates issues of bow strokes, articulation, ornamentation and other elements of musical execution. Every string player ought to own this treatise and consult it on a regular basis.

As most of today's performers have been educated in a post-Romantic aesthetic, it may be wise to summarize the most significant changes in string instruments subsequent to the Classical period. These alterations, which affect both the playing style and the sound of the string family, include:

- the realignment of the neck and alteration of the bridge, with a resultant higher tension on the strings
- the adoption of the chin rest for violins and violas and the end pin for cellos
- the change of bow to the Tourte design, resulting in a different balance point on the stick, a different grip and the development of bow strokes not used in earlier times (see below)
- the gradual replacement of gut strings with those of steel

As with all other developments in instrumental design, these physiological changes were precipitated by changes in performance style and the growth of audiences, resulting in larger concert halls. With the advent of virtuosi of all instruments in the early decades of the nineteenth century came a desire for greater brilliance in sound, whose consequences reach to every aspect of music making. A new set of string techniques emerged that were neither idiomatic to nor required by the Classical era, such as *martelé* and off-the-string articulation, whereas others that had been confined to exceptional bravura passages (*spiccato*) became more common, as gradually did the use of vibrato (see below).

Mozart does, however, occasionally prescribe some string techniques that one might associate with later times, such as *sciolto* and *col legno* (*coll'arco al rovescio*) (both, for example, in the Violin Concerto in A major, K. 219).

Vibrato and portamento

For today's players vibrato constitutes the rule; non-vibrato is a special, exceptional effect. Leopold Mozart warns against the use of vibrato on every note, but acknowledges its expressive effect when used judiciously and teaches slow, growing and fast vibrato (*tremolo*), presenting it in the chapter devoted to ornaments. The use of portamento when shifting may not have been normative; but certain of Leopold's fingerings suggest that its use was acceptable at times.[23]

Execution

Stowell's concise treatment of bow grip, fingerings and bow strokes is exemplary,[24] even though it cannot replace Leopold Mozart's indispensable treatise. Stowell notes that 'Leopold Mozart was the first to pinpoint the relationship between bow speed and volume' and continues:

> The *messa di voce* [the seamless crescendo from *piano* to *forte* and back] commonly adorned long notes, often with vibrato, and the so-called 'divisions' (the four types of nuanced bowings – crescendo, diminuendo, *messa di voce* and double *messa di voce* – characterized by Leopold Mozart for the cultivation of tonal purity, variety of expression and mastery of

bowing) were so much accepted practice that sustained strokes without
nuance were exceptions rather than the rule.[25]

Among the central bow strokes of the period enumerated by Stowell are
the various applications of slurred staccato (including the 'Viotti bowing'
of executing a passage of semiquavers with an initial down-bow followed
by pairs of slurred notes against the beat, alternating up- and down-bow)
and slurred tremolo.[26] Regarding the latter, Stowell's assertion that 'the
execution of repeated notes on the same string under one slur ... was played
either staccato (normally indicated by dots or strokes under a slur) or legato
(implied by a slur alone)' surely no longer applies to Wolfgang Mozart. Quite
apart from the fact that the latter notation (common in J. S. Bach) is no
longer found in Mozart, the articulation of dots under a slur is employed by
Mozart for all instruments, not just strings. As example 17.7 from the minuet
of the String Quartet in A major, K. 464, demonstrates, the only possible
intended execution of the dots with slurs in the first violin is *portato*. Clearly,
a staccato stroke on the third crotchet of bar 49 would preclude holding the
note into bar 50, as mandated by the tie. It would seem correct to surmise,
then, that in passages employing dots with slurs the dot refers to the initial
articulation and the slur to the sustaining of the pitch.

Example 17.7 Mozart, String Quartet in A major, K. 464/ii, bars 49–50

Woodwind and brass

In wind writing, like that for strings, vibrato was used sparingly; *portato*
was executed by barely articulating the repeated pitches. During Mozart's
lifetime a number of technological innovations, particularly added keys,
made intonation more reliable; and the lower ranges of the flute and clarinet
were extended. There were undeniable constraints on practicable tonalities:
clarinets were rarely called upon to play in written keys with more than one
sharp or flat.[27] Mozart heeded many of these restrictions, although he did
not avoid the key of E flat major for the oboe, as counselled by contemporary
tutors.[28]

Mozart had an expert understanding of the techniques of every instrument he employed and a precise awareness of the personal technique of
the players for whom he composed solo works. When writing for orchestra
or for ensembles where he had no advance knowledge of the players, he
defaulted to orchestral norms in matters of range, tessitura and technical

demands. It is thus not possible to speak in a general way about Mozart's writing for a particular instrument.

Keyboard

Mozart was acquainted with and wrote for harpsichord, clavichord, organ, clock organ and piano. Whereas his earliest keyboard works, such as the four *pasticcio* concertos K. 37 and 39–41 and his earliest surviving original concertos, are idiomatic to the harpsichord,[29] there seems little doubt that from the sonatas K. 279–84 onwards Mozart's keyboard music was geared to the piano. Given the central importance of the keyboard in Mozart's output, it is relevant for pianists performing his music on standard instruments to understand the differences between the instruments he knew and described with such expertise and today's concert grand. These differences exceed those between eighteenth-century and present forms of other instruments both in number and in degree. As harpsichords, clavichords and organs survive in considerable number, some admirably preserved, others well restored, complemented by an even larger number of historically accurate copies, the following discussion will be devoted to Mozart's pianos, of which a more limited number survive.

The keyboard and general construction of late eighteenth-century pianos are closely related to those of the harpsichord. Unlike harpsichords, however, such pianos are double-strung (that is, two strings per note); triple stringing was later introduced in the treble for added power. The precision and crispness of articulation of the harpsichord, whose action plucks the strings and is extraordinarily sensitive to the speed of attack, is mirrored in Viennese pianos. Their lightness and mechanical simplicity, together with the added velocity due to the reverse positioning of the hammers by comparison with the English-French-American design now standard, result in an action of speed, sensitivity, precision and efficiency based upon a key dip and resistance weight some 50 per cent lighter than that of the present concert grand. Other characteristics are more rapid sound decay, greater focus to the sonority and more pungency. Moreover, the longer and more thinly wound bass strings and parallel stringing produce a lighter sonority, while enabling both hands to play with equal strength without the left hand overpowering the right. In all these respects performers playing on later instruments must make adjustments that will be easier if they have had the experience of playing, however briefly, on a good quality period piano (original or copy).

Mozart never explicitly called for the use of the pedal, although it was available to him (activated by hand levers and knee levers); at least one double-stemmed left-hand passage seems to call for the pedal.[30] The lighter, clearer sound of Mozart's pianos makes possible a more sparing use of the pedal than is customary on today's instruments.

Voice
Apart from physiological changes wrought by altered diets and living conditions, vocal technique, unlike that of instruments, is independent of technology. Considerations of vocal performance practice are thus best approached from the aesthetic perspective of the treatises of the time. Here, as with instruments, systematic use of vibrato does not antedate the nineteenth-century; for both of them vibrato was an important parameter in expression, requiring discretion and taste. Nonetheless, there is a general consensus among voice teachers today that the systematic suppression of vibrato can have harmful consequences. Will Crutchfield rightly observes that 'the degree of vibrato present in an artist's everyday singing is largely a matter of (subconscious) cultivation during training, and . . . during the history of Western artistic singing the steady trend has been towards the cultivation of stronger, wider and slower vibrato'.[31]

In matters of vocal technique, Mancini provides a reliable guide to the tenets of Mozart's era. He places greatest emphasis on the importance of unifying the chest and head registers, cultivating the ability to employ the *messa di voce* throughout the range, a fluent portamento, joining adjacent notes effortlessly, and mastery of the standard vocal embellishments.[32]

In his operas Mozart often relied upon young singers (the first Susanna, Nancy [Ann Selina] Storace, was twenty; the first Donna Anna, Teresa Sopriti, was twenty-four); the more intimate theatres of the time are far removed from today's vocal culture, in which voices develop later and in which power – with its attendant ability to fill houses of more than 2,000 spectators – is crucial.

Orchestral size, make-up and seating arrangements
While there is little explicit documentation concerning the size and make-up of orchestras in Salzburg during the 1770s, references in court documents and in the Mozart family correspondence, together with surviving musical sources, suggest that both public and private orchestras frequently numbered twenty-six to thirty players, including both strings and winds.[33] A letter from Leopold Mozart to his son dated 12 April 1778 describes a private orchestra including eight first violins, six seconds, two violas, five or six cellos, two or three double basses, two oboes and two horns.[34] Surviving salary documents for many Viennese concerts hint at similar numbers of strings, though in a concert of 1781 Mozart had forty violins (today's dimensions) at his disposal, and he was not displeased.[35]

The intended scoring of Mozart's bass line in serenades, divertimenti and concertos – and even in certain chamber works – has been controversial. While most sources give only the generic 'Baßo', meaning bass part in general (and consistent with a scoring of cello or double bass or both), Cliff Eisen has noted that in all concertos in which a bass instrument is explicitly prescribed it is the double bass. Accordingly, in cases such as K. 271, where the part is labelled 'Baßo', Eisen has suggested that a scoring of double basses alone cannot be excluded. Prior to the 1760s, independent concertos did not circulate widely in Salzburg; instead, they derived from the orchestral serenade, which usually included two or more concerto movements, a practice observed by Mozart. Eisen suggests that serenade orchestras frequently did without cellos, thus making it possible that the same was occasionally true of concertos.[36] This view has been contested by James Webster and Wolf-Dieter Seiffert, however, both of whom have presented strong arguments opposing the assumption that the designation 'Baßo' or even 'Contrabasso' perforce excludes the participation of cellos.[37]

In Mozart's time, performances of piano concertos placed the solo instrument either tail forward, lid removed, with the soloist directly facing the audience, or in the opposite direction, with the soloist's back to the audience. The first violins were placed on one side (stage right) and the second violins on the other (stage left). The violas and cellos were behind the first and second violins respectively (although this was sometimes reversed). The string basses were often divided, with some on each side of the stage, so that all other instruments could easily hear the bass line. The wind sat behind the piano. Thus no player was more than ten feet from the piano, and excellent ensemble could be preserved through eye contact between the soloist and leader and through the practice of continuo.

Continuo

Keyboard soloists in Mozart's time accompanied the orchestra during the orchestral ritornellos. In every one of his works involving keyboard and orchestra Mozart directs the soloist to double the string bass line (not the cello line when this diverges from the double basses, or the bassoon when the basses are silent) in orchestral passages, thus delineating a continuo role for the soloist. The earlier concertos provide figuration of the bass during such orchestral sections; often (but not always) these figures were supplied subsequently by his father. Although later concerto autographs omit the figures, the convention is preserved by the indication 'Col Baßo' or its abbreviation 'ColB'.

The validity and relevance of this practice to present-day performance has been attacked for well over a century on several grounds:

- It is said to undermine the essential nature of a concerto, namely, the contest between soloist and orchestra.
- The bass line and figures are now deemed to have been mere cues for the soloist to follow the progress of the work during purely orchestral sections, thus corresponding to the short score simplification of orchestral music that appears in the solo keyboard parts of nineteenth-century concertos.
- The main purpose of continuo playing was to keep the orchestra together – a function that was later taken over by the conductor and thus lacks relevance in present-day performances.

These factors would surely be no less important, however, in passages for wind or for strings when the string basses are silent – places where Mozart does not prescribe continuo. There is, then, no compelling documentary evidence against a continuo role for the soloist.

Where Mozart prescribes continuo, the full range of accompanimental possibilities are invoked: harmonic and/or linear textures, *tasto solo* (the bass line only) and octave doubling of the bass. During many solo passages Mozart accompanies an active right hand by doubling the bass with single notes in the left hand. There is no evidence that he expected the soloist to add continuo-like chords in such passages; indeed, the existence of many notated passages containing left-hand chords may be the strongest argument against supplying them where they are missing.

Although each age executes music from an earlier period according to its own ideas, the nineteenth-century view of Mozart as the embodiment of grace and elegance, coupled with the post-Chopin predilection for singing legato playing, remains the present-day norm, and not just for pianists. It is pianists, in particular, who tend to minimize or ignore completely Mozart's staccato articulations and detailed slurring, holding notes into rests and in general providing as continuous and smooth a surface as possible. (The advent of *Urtext* editions has not prevented performers from continuing to impose a late nineteenth-century aesthetic upon Mozart's music.) Furthermore, the decline of improvisation as a central element in concert life and the ultimate division of musicians into performers and composers has fostered performances, as well as editions, based upon literal readings of the composer's text. This encourages a pietistic approach to a music whose actual substance is theatrical, not decorative. Mozart was above all a dramatist: his performances were crowned by his improvisations and dependent upon the spontaneous realization of a musical surface he often left somewhat bare. This allowed him the necessary freedom to slant the characterization of a given performance in a particular direction.

Everything we know about performance practice in the late eighteenth century suggests that volatile spontaneity was at the core of expression, with the element of risk at the forefront. Modern-day performers are urged to adopt this posture, taking the immense variety of characters mirrored by Mozart's ever-changing accompaniment figures as a guide. His spirit will be most eloquently served when the essential unity between his stage and instrumental works is affirmed.

Notes

The publisher has used its best endeavours to ensure that the URLs for external websites referred to in this book are correct and active at the time of going to press. However, the publisher has no responsibility for the websites and can make no guarantee that a site will remain live or that the content is or will remain appropriate.

Introduction

1 See Friedrich Kerst (ed.), *Mozart: The Man and the Artist Revealed in His Own Words* (New York, 1965; first published London, 1926), p. 1.
2 In one BBC poll (*Your Millennium* series), Mozart finished second behind Paul McCartney. See the article from the BBC website on 3 May 1999: http://www.news.bbc.co.uk/hi/english/entertainment/newsid_334000/334373.stm.
3 H. C. Robbins Landon and Donald Mitchell (eds.), *The Mozart Companion* (London, 1956).
4 Cliff Eisen and Stanley Sadie, '(Johann Chrysostom) Wolfgang Amadeus Mozart', in Stanley Sadie (ed.), *The New Grove Dictionary of Music and Musicians*, 2nd edn (29 vols., London, 2001), vol. 17, p. 276.

1 Mozart and Salzburg

1 Anonymous, *Zeichnungen auf einer Reise von Wien über Triest nach Venedig und von da zurück durch Tyrol und Salzburg. Im Jahre 1798* (Berlin, 1800), p. 335. Translations in this article are based on *LMF* but amended in light of the originals in *MBA*.
2 Salzburg does not figure much in eighteenth-century travel books. One widely circulated guide, Louis Duten's *Itinéraires des Routes les plus fréquentées, ou Journal d'un Voyage aux Villes principales de l'Europe en 1768, 1769, 1770, 1771 & 1777* (London, 1779), does not mention Salzburg, even though the route from Munich to Vienna gives numerous smaller and less important towns as *postes* along the way, including Anzing, Haag, Hampfing, Altenoeting, Markel, Braunau, Altheim, Ried, Unterhag, Lambach, Vels, Ens, Strenberg, Amstotten, Kemmelpach, Moelch, Poelten, Perschling, Sieghartskirchen and Burkersdorf; similarly Hester Thrale says nothing at all about Salzburg, while Thomas Nugent, *The Grand Tour. Containing an Exact Description of most of the Cities, Towns and Remarkable Places of Europe* (London, 1749), mentions the city only briefly, as part of the Bavarian sphere.

3 *Der Morgen und der Abend den Innwohnern der Hochfürstl. Residenz-Stadt Salzburg melodisch und harmonisch angekündigt* (Augsburg, 1759).
4 See Doris Pellegrini-Rainer and Werner Rainer, 'Giuseppe Lolli (1701–1778): ein biographischer Beitrag zur Musikgeschichte Salzburgs', *Mitteilungen der Gesellschaft für Salzburger Landeskunde*, 106 (1966), p. 285.
5 A thoroughly modern politician, Colloredo used his educational reforms both to counter his bad image and to convince Salzburgers of their own good attributes. According to the anonymous *Geographie von Salzburg zum Gebrauche in unsern Schulen* [*Geography of Salzburg, for use in our schools*] (Salzburg, 1796), pp. 8–9: 'Our fatherland is Salzburg: a beautiful German land and noble principality. It is ruled by a good and wise Prince, whom all Salzburgers willingly and happily obey. For he is their lord and master, ordained by God, the lord and master of all men.' And according to the *Abriss der Geographie, zum Gebrauch in und ausser Schulen, nebst der besonderen Geographie des Erzstiftes Salzburg, und einem Unterricht vom Weltgebäude der Globen* (Salzburg, 1782), p. 6: 'The people of Salzburg are known among foreigners as a strong, diligent people. Among mountain dwellers there is still something of that old German uprightness, that is, honesty, candour and open-heartedness, free from pretence.' This is at odds with non-partisan descriptions of the archdiocese; see, for example, Karl Ehrenberts von Moll, 'Des Herrn Karl Ehrenberts von Moll, Ritter und Oesterreichischen Landmanns, Briefe an den Herrn Professor Heinrich Sander in Karlsruhe über eine Reise von Kremsmünster nach Mossheim im Salzburgishen. Im Herbste 1780. (Aus der Handschrift)', in Johann Bernoulli, *Sammlung kurzer Reisebeschreibungen und anderer zur Erweiterung der Länder- und Menschenkenntniss dienender Nachrichten* (Berlin and Leipzig, 1783), vol. 2, p. 457.

6 See Hans Wagner, *Die Aufklärung im Erzstift Salzburg* (Salzburg, 1968).

7 Salzburg, Landesarchiv, Geheime Hofkanzlei XXIX/2b, Fasc. 1, cited in Ernst Hintermaier and Gerhard Walterskirchen, *Aufzüge für Trompeten und Pauken: Musikstücke für mechanische Orgelwerke* (Salzburg, 1977), p. viii.

8 For an account of student musical life in general, not including the school dramas and serenades discussed here, see Walter Salmen, 'Zur Praxis von Nachtmusiken durch Studenten und Kunstpfeifer', in Hubert Unverricht (ed.), *Gesellschaftsgebundene Instrumentale Unterhaltungsmusik des 18. Jahrhunderts: Bericht über die Internationale Fachkonferenz in Eichstätt von 13.10.–15.10.1988* (Tutzing, 1992), pp. 33–45.

9 See Heiner Boberski, *Das Theater der Benediktiner an der alten Universität Salzburg (1617–1778)* (Vienna, 1978), and Sybille Dahms, Maria Cuvay Schneider and Ernst Hintermaier, 'Die Musikpflege an der Salzburger Universität im 17. und 18. Jahrhundert', in *Universität Salzburg 1622–1962–1972: Festschrift* (Salzburg, 1972), pp. 173–92.

10 Dahms *et al.*, 'Die Musikpflege', p. 197.

11 In general, see Andrew Kearns, 'The Orchestral Serenade in Eighteenth-Century Salzburg', *JMR*, 16 (1997), pp. 163–97.

12 See P. Petrus Eder and Gerhard Walterskirchen (eds.), *Das Benediktinerstift St Peter in Salzburg zur Zeit Mozarts: Musik und Musiker – Kunst und Kultur* (Salzburg, 1991).

13 See Franz Esterl, *Chronik des adeligen Benediktiner-Frauen-Stiftes Nonnberg in Salzburg* (Salzburg, 1841); Heinz Dopsch, 'Klöster und Stifte', in Heinz Dopsch (ed.), *Geschichte Salzburgs: Stadt und Land*, vol. 2 (Salzburg, 1983), pp. 1002–53; and Fumiko Niiyama, *Zum mittelalterlichen Musikleben im Benediktinerstift Nonnberg zu Salzburg* (Frankfurt, 1994).

14 Esterl, *Chronik*, p. 155.

15 On civil and military music in Salzburg generally, see Kurt Birsak and Manfred König, *Das grosse Salzburger Blasmusik mit Ehrentafeln der Salzburger Blasmusikkapellen* (Vienna, 1983).

16 *MBA*, vol. 2, pp. 337–8.

17 Ibid.

18 For catalogues of some of these collections, see Nicole Schwindt-Gross, *Die Musikhandschriften der Stiftskirche Altötting, des Collegiatstifts Landshut und der Pfarrkirche Beuerberg, Schnaitsee und St Mang in Füssen* (Munich, 1993); Robert Münster, Ursula Bockholdt, Robert Machold and Lisbet Thew, *Thematischer Katalog der Musikhandschriften der Benediktinerinnenabtei Frauenwörth und der Pfarrkirchen Indersdorf, Wasserburg am Inn und Bad Tölz* (Munich, 1975); and Robert Münster and Robert Machold, *Theatischer Katalog der Musikhandschriften der ehemaligen Klosterkirchen Weyarn, Tegernsee und Benediktbeuern* (Munich, 1971).

19 Italian music circulated freely in Salzburg as well, and Mozart may well have known some of these works. See Cliff Eisen, 'Mozart e l'Italia: Il ruolo di Salisburgo', *Rivista Italiana di Musicologia*, 30 (1995), pp. 51–84.

20 See 'Nachricht von dem gegenwärtigen Zustande der Musik Sr. Hochfürstlichen Gnaden des Erzbischoffs zu Salzburg im Jahr 1757', in Friedrich W. Marpurg (ed.), *Historisch-kritische Beiträge zur Aufnahme der Music* (5 vols., Berlin, 1754–8), vol. 3, pp. 183–98; English translation in Neal Zaslaw, *Mozart's Symphonies: Context, Performance Practice, Reception* (Oxford, 1989), pp. 550–7. Leopold Mozart is presumed to be the author of this notice.

21 *MBA*, vol. 2, p. 490.

22 *MBA*, vol. 3, p. 533. Possibly there was another court performance on 27 August, for Nannerl writes: 'the entertainment [Gesellschaft] and music were at Mirabell today'. Even so, this concert could not have lasted long. By ten o'clock the Mozarts were at home, where they were serenaded by the court violinist Andreas Pinzger.

23 Corbinian Gärtner, *Lebensbeschreibung des Hochwürdigen Fürsten und Herrn Hieronymus Josephus Franciscus de Paula Erzbishofes zu Salzburg, des heiligen apostolischen Stuhles zu Rom gebohrnen Legaten, Primas von Teutschland und Grosskreuzes des kaiserl. österreich. Leopolds-Ordens, aus dem fürstl. Hause Colloredo von Wallsee und Möls* (Salzburg, 1812), p. 6.

24 Joseph Ernst Ritter von Koch-Sternfeld, *Die letzten dreissig Jahre des Hochstifts und Erzbisthums Salzburg*, p. 172. The lack of court entertainments is also mentioned by [Friedrich Schulz] in his *Reise eines Liefländers von Riga nach Warschau, durch Südpreussen, über Breslau, Dresden, Karlsbad, Bayreuth, Nürnberg, Regensburg, München, Salzburg, Linz, Wien und Klagenfurt, nach Botzen in Tyrol* (Berlin, 1795–6), vol. 4, pp. 88–92.

25 Salzburg, Universitätsarchiv, Akten 81 ('Protocollum Praefecturae Scholarum 1759–1769 sub Praefecto P. Mariano Wimmer Seeoneasi'), p. 366.

26 See Michaelbeuern, Stiftsarchiv Fach 65/3 ('Stiftskirche: Abgeschriebene Inventar aus

den Jahre 1824, 1849, 1876, 1920, 1932'),
p. 12.

27 *MDB*, p. 161.

28 It is a curious fact that Mozart's interest in
instrumental music extends even to those
works composed for performance at the
cathedral: while a rich tradition of local and
imported church sonatas can be documented
for the 1730s, 1740s and 1750s, after about
1760 there is no firm source or documentary
evidence for even a single newly composed
church sonata by any other composer.
According to Nikolaus Lange's contemporary
catalogue of Michael Haydn's works, Haydn
composed an undated 'Sonata 2 $^{Vvni.}$ Violone
e Org'. The work does not survive, however,
and it may have been composed before Haydn
moved to Salzburg in 1763 or after Mozart
left for Vienna in 1781.

29 *MDB*, p. 182.

30 *LMF*, pp. 540–1.

31 'Nachricht', p. 186.

32 Michael Haydn's appointment is
reproduced in Gerhard Croll and Kurt
Vossing, *Johann Michael Haydn: sein Leben –
sein Schaffen – seine Zeit* (Vienna, 1987), pp.
66–7 (with facsimile), and Heinz Schuler,
'Salzburger Kapellhauslehrer zur Mozartzeit',
Acta Mozartiana, 35 (1988), p. 31.

33 See Charles H. Sherman and T. Donley
Thomas, *Johann Michael Haydn (1737–1806): A
Chronological Thematic Catalogue of His Works*
(Stuyvesant, NY, 1993), pp. 30–1.

34 In general, see Cliff Eisen, *Orchestral Music
in Salzburg* (Ann Arbor, MI, 1994).

35 Cliff Eisen, *New Mozart Documents: A
Supplement to O. E. Deutsch's Documentary
Biography* (London and Stanford, 1991), p. 23.

36 Ruth Halliwell, *The Mozart Family: Four
Lives in a Social Context* (Oxford, 1998),
pp. 513–14.

37 Letters of 19 July 1763 and 9 July 1778; see
LMF, pp. 25 and 562.

38 Leopold's disengagement is clear from
Wolfgang's letter (in fact written by his
father) to Padre Martini of 4 September 1776.
While it overstates the case – Leopold still
performed numerous duties at the court – it
is nevertheless representative of the ways in
which the family wished both to present itself
and, perhaps more importantly, to think of
itself: 'My father . . . has already served this
court for thirty-six years and as he knows that
the present Archbishop cannot and will not
have anything to do with people who are
getting on in years, he no longer puts his
whole heart into his work, but has taken up
literature, which was always a favourite study
of his.' See *LMF*, p. 266.

39 Letter of 29 December 1755; *MBA*, vol. 1,
p. 28.

40 This may have been the consensus among
some of the Mozarts' Salzburg friends as well.
When Leopold died in May 1787, Dominikus
Hagenauer, Abbot of St Peter's, wrote:
'[Leopold Mozart] was born at Augsburg and
spent most of the days of his life in the service
of the court here but had the misfortune of
being always persecuted . . . and was not as
much favoured by a long way as in other,
larger places in Europe.' *MDB*, p. 293.

2 Mozart in Vienna

1 Letter 4 April 1782, in Robert Spaethling
(ed. and trans.), *Mozart's Letters, Mozart's Life*
(New York, 2000), p. 240; German original in
MBA, vol. 3, p. 102.

2 For an overview of the Hofkapelle in the
eighteenth century, in particular under
Joseph II, see Dorothea Link, 'Mozart's
Appointment to the Viennese Court', in
Dorothea Link (ed.), *Mozart Essays*
(forthcoming). On the theatre under Joseph
II, see Dorothea Link, *The National Court
Theatre in Mozart's Vienna: Sources and
Documents 1783–1792* (Oxford, 1998).

3 Spaethling, *Letters*, p. 243; *MBA*, vol. 3,
p. 106.

4 Spaethling, *Letters*, p. 306; *MBA*, vol. 3,
p. 201.

5 A gulden (abbreviated 'fl.') was worth 60
kreuzer ('x.').

6 Following the death of Joseph II in March
1790, however, Mozart found his chances of
promotion considerably diminished. He and
Salieri had to witness the preferment of
Salieri's apprentice Joseph Weigl to both of
them by Leopold II.

7 Until 1 February 1786, when Joseph
standardized and fixed the value of the ducat
at four and a half gulden, the three types of
ducat in circulation were worth different
amounts at different times.

8 Of the seventy-five Italian operas produced
between Easter 1783 and Easter 1792,
twenty-two were newly commissioned.

9 Lorenzo Da Ponte, *An Extract from the Life of
Lorenzo Da Ponte with the History of Several
Dramas Written by him, and among others, il
Figaro, il Don Giovanni and La scuola degli
amanti, set to music by Mozart* (New York,
1819), p. 12.

10 Da Ponte noted the honour on the title
page of the draft libretto: 'per l'arrivo di Sua
Altezza Reale / Maria Teresa / Arciduchessa
d'Austria: sposa del / Ser. Principe Antonio di
Sassonia'. *MDL*, p. 267; *MDB*, p. 303.

11 *MDL*, p. 267; *MDB*, p. 303.

12 In Vienna a full house yielded between 500 and 600 gulden. Mozart's fee from Guardasoni was probably 450 gulden, as in Vienna. *MDL*, p. 266; *MDB*, p. 303.

13 *MDL*, p. 277; *MDB*, p. 315.

14 Don Ottavio was a poor tenor, Don Giovanni did not have the élan of the Prague original, and Aloysia Lange as Donna Anna simply did not measure up to the better Italian singers.

15 Salieri wrote two numbers before abandoning the opera. It is possible that once Salieri had broken off its composition there was no time to begin afresh, for which reason he resorted to patching together *La cifra* from an earlier opera. For a different interpretation of the events, see John Rice, *Antonio Salieri and Viennese Opera* (Chicago, 1998), pp. 437–41.

16 The lack of close collaboration between Da Ponte and Mozart is perhaps reflected in the ambiguous ending of the opera. Following the conventions of the pastoral play, the libretto convincingly restores the original pairing of the lovers. Mozart's musical setting, however, shows the new pairing to ring more true: Fiordiligi and Ferrando sing in the seria style while the music of Guglielmo belongs to the world of opera buffa, that of Dorabella lying somewhere in between.

17 Dexter Edge, 'Mozart's Reception in Vienna, 1787–1791', in Stanley Sadie (ed.), *Wolfgang Amadè Mozart: Essays on His Life and His Music* (Oxford, 1996), p. 82.

18 Burney cited in Otto Biba, 'Die Wiener Kirchenmusik um 1783', in *Beiträge zur Musikgeschichte des 18. Jahrhunderts, Jahrbuch für Österreichische Kulturgeschichte*, 1/2 (Eisenstadt, 1971), p. 7. This seminal study of the effect of Joseph's church reforms on church music is supplemented by Otto Biba, 'Historical Background: Church and State', in H. C. Robbins Landon (ed.), *The Mozart Compendium: A Guide to Mozart's Life and Music* (London, 1990), pp. 58–61.

19 Biba, 'Church and State', p. 61.

20 As reported in the *Pressburger Zeitung*. See *MDL*, p. 347; *MDB*, p. 395.

21 Letter 26 May 1781, in Spaethling, *Letters*, p. 256; *MBA*, vol. 3, p. 120. On Mozart's pupils, see Heinz Wolfgang Hamann, 'Mozarts Schülerkreis: Versuch einer chronologischen Ordnung', *Mozart-Jahrbuch 1962/63*, pp. 115–39, supplemented by Carl Bär, 'Mozarts Schülerkreis', *Acta Mozartiana*, 11 (1964), pp. 58–64. See also the discussion in Ruth Halliwell, *The Mozart Family: Four Lives in a Social Context* (Oxford, 1998), pp. 390–2.

22 Letter of 7 February 1778 in *LMF*, p. 468; *MBA*, vol. 2, p. 264.

23 'Apparently at least in part in return for some meals'. Halliwell, *Mozart Family*, p. 364.

24 Letter of 12 October 1782 in *LMF*, p. 827; *MBA*, vol. 3, pp. 237–8.

25 *MDL*, p. 252; *MDB*, p. 286.

26 On concert life in Vienna, see Mary Sue Morrow, *Concert Life in Haydn's Vienna: Aspects of a Developing Musical and Social Institution* (Stuyvesant, NY, 1988), and Dexter Edge, 'Review Article: Mary Sue Morrow, *Concert Life in Haydn's Vienna*', *Haydn Yearbook*, 17 (1992), pp. 108–66.

27 Starting in 1786 Joseph allowed plays to be performed during Lent, thereby further reducing the number of nights available for concerts.

28 Letter 12 March 1785, *MBA*, vol. 3, p. 378.

29 Halliwell, *Mozart Family*, p. 393, recalls a plan of Mozart's in 1782 to produce operas at his own expense in order to profit from their success instead of merely receiving a fee for the score. On Schikaneder's operations, see David J. Buch, 'Mozart and the Theater auf der Wieden: New Attributions and Perspectives', *COJ*, 9 (1997), pp. 195–9.

30 Concerning Artaria, see Rupert Ridgewell, 'Mozart's Publishing Plans with Artaria in 1787: New Archival Evidence', *ML*, 83 (2002), pp. 30–74.

31 What follows is a synopsis of the discussion in Halliwell, *Mozart Family*, pp. 395–6.

32 Julia Moore, 'Mozart in the Market-Place', *JRMA*, 114 (1989), p. 25, mentions two other attempts by Mozart to publish his compositions by subscription: two piano sonatas, K. 333 and 284, and the Violin Sonata in B flat major, K. 454, in 1784, and the three string quintets K. 406, 515 and 516 in 1788.

33 Halliwell discusses Constanze's dealings with publishers with riveting clarity in *Mozart Family*, pp. 590–612. For a discussion of Beethoven's difficulties in making a living from his compositions and some of his dealings with publishers, see Julia Moore, 'Beethoven and Inflation', *Beethoven Forum*, 1 (1992), pp. 191–223.

34 This summary is based on Dorothea Link, 'Vienna's Private Theatrical and Musical Life, 1783–92, as Reported by Count Karl Zinzendorf', *JRMA*, 122 (1997), pp. 205–33.

35 The various theories are summarized in Edge, 'Mozart's Reception in Vienna', pp. 66–9.

36 Walter Brauneis, ' ". . . wegen schuldigen 1435 f 32 xr": Neuer Archivfund zur

Finanzmisere Mozarts im November 1791', *Mitteilungen der Internationalen Stiftung Mozarteum*, 39 (1991), pp. 159–63.

3 Mozart's compositional methods: writing for his singers

1 Mozart to his father, letter of 28 February 1778 from Mannheim, *LMF*, p. 497.

2 Mozart to his father, letter of 1 December 1780 from Munich, *LMF*, p. 678.

3 Andew Steptoe, *The Mozart–Da Ponte Operas: The Cultural and Musical Background to 'Le nozze di Figaro', 'Don Giovanni' and 'Così fan tutte'* (Oxford, 1988), pp. 142–5.

4 Mozart to his father, letter of 8 August 1781 from Vienna, *LMF*, p. 756.

5 With the support of a United Kingdom Arts and Humanities Research Board grant, I have been engaged on a study of the autograph manuscript of *Così fan tutte*, Act 1 of which is in Krakow, Act 2 in Berlin.

6 Another example is Dorabella's B flat aria 'È amore' which is preceded by a cadence in E major.

7 Such breaks also occur towards the end of some ensembles, where the likely cause is the need to ensure that the final orchestral postlude matches on-stage dramatic requirements. At the end of the trio 'Una bella serenata', for example, an extra leaf was added to extend its orchestral conclusion.

8 Daniel Heartz, 'When Mozart Revises: The Case of Guglielmo in *Così fan tutte*', in Stanley Sadie (ed.), *Wolfgang Amadè Mozart: Essays on His Life and His Music* (Oxford, 1996), pp. 355–61.

9 For a useful discussion, see John Arthur, 'Some Chronological Problems in Mozart: The Contribution of Ink-Studies', in Sadie (ed.), *Wolfgang Amadè Mozart*, pp. 35–52.

10 Alan Tyson, *Mozart: Studies of the Autograph Scores* (Cambridge, MA, and London, 1987), pp. 177–221.

11 On the tessitura of Guglielmo's aria 'Rivolgete', see Julian Rushton, 'Buffo roles in Mozart's Vienna', in Mary Hunter and James Webster (eds.), *Opera Buffa in Mozart's Vienna* (Cambridge, 1997), p. 423.

12 See Mozart's letter to his father of 26 September 1781, *LMF*, p. 769.

4 Mozart and late eighteenth-century aesthetics

1 These include E. T. A. Hoffmann, Søren Kierkegaard and Eduard Mörike. See William Stafford, *The Mozart Myths: A Critical Reassessment* (Stanford, 1991), p. 164.

2 Arthur Schurig puts forward this view in *Wolfgang Amadeus Mozart: sein Leben und sein Werk* (Leipzig, 1913), pp. 407–10.

3 Alfred Einstein, *Mozart: His Character, His Work*, trans. Arthur Mendel and Nathan Broder (London and New York, 1945), p. 29.

4 Michael Levey, *The Life and Death of Mozart* (London, 1973), p. 31.

5 These include Georg Knepler, *Wolfgang Amadé Mozart*, trans. J. Bradford Robinson (Cambridge, 1994); John Stone, 'Mozart's Opinions and Outlook', in H. C. Robbins Landon (ed.), *The Mozart Compendium: A Guide to Mozart's Life and Music* (London, 1990), pp. 140–57; and especially Stafford, *The Mozart Myths*.

6 See *MBA*. English readers must rely on *LMF*, a translation from 1938 (revised in 1966 and 1985) with often outdated modes of expression.

7 See Gernot Gruber, *Mozart and Posterity*, trans. R. S. Furness (London, 1991), p. 195.

8 Josef Mančal, 'Zum Verhältnis Leopold Mozarts zu Wolfgang "Amadé" Mozart: Prolegomena zur Strukturbestimmung einer personalen Beziehung und der Wirklichkeitorganisation im Zeitalter des Absolutismus und der Aufklärung', *Zeitschrift des Historischen Vereins für Schwaben*, 84 (1991), pp. 191–245; 85 (1992), pp. 233–71; also his 'Neues über Leopold Mozart', *Österreichische Musikzeitschrift*, 42 (1987), pp. 282–91.

9 For a possible explanation of this, see my *Mozart in Revolt: Strategies of Resistance, Mischief and Deception* (New Haven and London, 1999), pp. 44–6.

10 *MBA*, vol. 1, p. 140. All translations from Mozart's letters are mine.

11 Ibid., p. 19, and vol. 2, p. 374.

12 Ibid., vol. 1, p. 309.

13 I discuss this at length in *Mozart in Revolt*, pp. 106–26.

14 *MBA*, vol. 2, p. 389.

15 Wolfgang Hildesheimer, *Mozart*, trans. Marion Faber (London and New York, 1983), p. 193.

16 Hildesheimer calls it a paraphrase in ibid., pp. 192–3.

17 See Joseph Mack, *Die Reform- und Aufklärungsbestrebungen im Erzstift Salzburg unter Erzbischof Hieronymous von Colloredo* (Munich, 1912).

18 *MBA*, vol. 2, pp. 325 and 354.

19 See Eric Blackall, *The Emergence of German as a Literary Language* (Cambridge, 1959), p. 204.

20 Earl of Shaftesbury, *Characteristics of Men, Manners, Opinions, Times*, 4th edn, vol. 3 (London, 1727), p. 228.

21 *MBA*, vol. 3, p. 53.
22 Ibid., p. 60.
23 Robert A. Kann, *A Study in Austrian Intellectual History* (New York, 1960), p. 213.
24 *MBA*, vol. 3, p. 132.
25 Ibid., p. 167.

5 The keyboard music
1 This has, for instance, been articulated with characteristic directness by Charles Rosen: 'with a few magnificent exceptions, [Haydn's and Mozart's] works for piano alone tend to be more inhibited and less rich than the compositions for piano with accompanying instruments'. See *The Classical Style: Haydn, Mozart, Beethoven* (London and New York, 1971), p. 353.
2 Defensive reactions against such connotations are common. For Alfred Brendel, 'a widespread prejudice regards [the sonatas] as teaching matter for children, as secondary pieces for domestic use imbued with the taste of their age'; for Alfred Einstein the sonatas were 'misused as material for teaching beginners'; and Patrick Gale refers to pieces and sonata movements that average concert-goers 'had been allowed to mangle in their youth', continuing that much of this music was 'all too tempting to piano teachers'. See Alfred Brendel, *Alfred Brendel on Music: Collected Essays* (London, 2001), p. 9; Alfred Einstein, *Mozart: His Character, His Work*, trans. Arthur Mendel and Nathan Broder (London and New York, 1945), p. 241; and Patrick Gale, 'Piano: Sonatas and Other Works', in H. C. Robbins Landon (ed.), *The Mozart Compendium: A Guide to Mozart's Life and Music* (London, 1990), pp. 300–1.
3 For a discussion of the traditional imagery, see Nicky Losseff's 'Absent Melody and *The Woman in White*', *ML*, 81 (2000), pp. 532–50. This investigates the use of 'the "divine Mozart" trope' in Wilkie Collins's novel (1859–60), in particular how for the principal character Laura 'the melodies of Mozart . . . embody the qualities of order, peace and contentment' (p. 550).
4 See, for example, Wye J. Allanbrook, 'Two Threads through the Labyrinth: Topic and Process in the First Movements of K. 332 and K. 333', in Wye J. Allanbrook, Janet M. Levy and William P. Mahrt (eds.), *Convention in Eighteenth- and Nineteenth-Century Music: Essays in Honor of Leonard G. Ratner* (Stuyvesant, NY, 1992), pp. 125–71; John Irving, *Mozart's Piano Sonatas: Contexts, Sources, Style* (Cambridge, 1997); and Leonard G. Ratner, 'Topical Content in Mozart's Keyboard Sonatas', *EM*, 19 (1991), pp. 615–19.
5 Malcolm Bilson, 'Execution and Expression in the Sonata in E flat, K282', *EM*, 20 (1992), p. 241.
6 Mark Everist, 'Reception Theories, Canonic Discourses, and Musical Value', in Nicholas Cook and Mark Everist (eds.), *Rethinking Music* (New York, 1999), p. 395.
7 Compare the effect of the cello's pedal point that underpins the piano lead from bar 92 in the first movement. The fact that this pedal was already there in the texture (it had been sounding for four bars) only increases its expressive charge.
8 These more formal textural plots also suggest his leanings towards a 'symphonic' rather than a 'sonata' manner. For the distinction between these two, and discussion of Mozart's strong alignment with the 'symphonic', see Michael Broyles, 'The Two Instrumental Styles of Classicism', *JAMS*, 36 (1983), pp. 210–42.
9 *The Classical Style*, p. 352.
10 The very shape of this figure, involving a turn and a scale fragment, seems like a permutation of what we heard earlier.
11 The sense of an archaic topic is furthered by the arresting brief middle section in which the piano alone repeats a Phrygian cadential progression. This is reminiscent of some curiously archaic passages in Dittersdorf's string quartets, often in trios and thus similarly enclosed structurally. See, for instance, the trios in Quartets No. 3 in G major and No. 4 in C major.
12 This term was coined by Janet M. Levy in her 'Texture as a Sign in Classic and Early Romantic Music', *JAMS*, 35 (1982), p. 489.
13 Alfred Einstein calls this 'a genuinely orchestral effect', yet, aside from the issue of generic borrowings mentioned earlier, it can just as legitimately be heard as a wonderful invention in terms of keyboard sound and gesture. See *Mozart: His Character, His Work*, p. 271.
14 This is also the case in his string quartets, as I have argued in 'The Classical Style: Haydn, Mozart and Their Contemporaries', in Robin Stowell (ed.), *The Cambridge Companion to the String Quartet* (Cambridge, forthcoming).
15 For an account of 'Gothic' tendencies in music of the late eighteenth and early nineteenth centuries, including the role of counterpoint, see Rohan Stewart-MacDonald, 'Towards a New Ontology of Musical Classicism: Sensationalism, Archaism and Formal Grammar in the music of Clementi,

Hummel and Dussek – and Parallels with Haydn, Beethoven and Schubert' (Ph.D. dissertation, University of Cambridge, 2001).

16 See Robert Levin, 'Mozart's Solo Keyboard Music', in Robert L. Marshall (ed.), *Eighteenth-Century Keyboard Music* (New York, 1994), p. 340.

17 In fact, the passage from bar 297 to bar 302 in the primo seems to spoof the precise succession of pitches, so weightily presented, of bars 1–2.

18 James Webster considers the notions of 'entertainment' and 'popularity' in his 'Haydn's Symphonies between *Sturm und Drang* and "Classical Style": Art and Entertainment', in W. Dean Sutcliffe (ed.), *Haydn Studies* (Cambridge, 1998), pp. 218–45.

19 Einstein, *Mozart: His Character, His Work*, p. 264, and William Kinderman, 'Subjectivity and Objectivity in Mozart Performance', *EM*, 19 (1991), p. 593.

20 On this subject see Wye J. Allanbrook, 'Mozart's Tunes and the Comedy of Closure', in James M. Morris (ed.), *On Mozart* (Cambridge, 1994), pp. 169–86.

21 For background information on this issue see Elaine R. Sisman, *Haydn and the Classical Variation* (Cambridge, MA, 1993), especially chapter 1 ('Introduction: Repetition and Decoration'), pp. 1–18.

22 Katalin Komlós, ' "Ich praeludirte und spielte Variazionen": Mozart the Fortepianist', in R. Larry Todd and Peter Williams (eds.), *Perspectives on Mozart Performance* (Cambridge, 1991), p. 39.

23 Komlós states that all pre-1798 sources for K. 398 preserve the music in continuously notated form, and without numbering of the variations. Ibid., p. 38.

24 Sisman demonstrates how Mozart adapted the vocal model to arrive at his theme in *Haydn and the Classical Variation*, pp. 199–202.

25 For background to this set see David J. Buch, 'On the Context of Mozart's Variations to the Aria, "Ein Weib ist das herrlichste Ding auf der Welt", K. 613', *Mozart-Jahrbuch 1999*, pp. 71–80.

26 Arthur Hutchings, 'The Keyboard Music', in H. C. Robbins Landon and Donald Mitchell (eds.), *The Mozart Companion* (London, 1956), p. 62.

27 William S. Newman, *The Sonata in the Classic Era* (Chapel Hill, 1963), p. 483. John Irving has recently offered a more positive account of K. 330–2 as likely teaching pieces, although still betraying some diffidence at the possibility. See *Mozart's Piano Sonatas*, pp. 67–8.

28 Allanbrook, 'Two Threads through the Labyrinth', pp. 155, 147, 145 and 147.

29 Levin, 'Mozart's Solo Keyboard Music', pp. 316, 321, 325 and 338.

30 Bilson, 'Execution and Expression', p. 241. We should bear in mind, however, that great expressive power can also accrue from traditional pianistic approaches.

31 *Alfred Brendel on Music*, pp. 3 and 10.

32 Annette Richards, *The Free Fantasia and the Musical Picturesque* (Cambridge, 2001), p. 134. Richards notes that the word could also have had less stable connotations for Rochlitz.

33 The registral play here is discussed in Cliff Eisen and Christopher Wintle, 'Mozart's C minor Fantasy, K. 475: An Editorial "Problem" and Its Analytical and Critical Consequences', *JRMA*, 124 (1999), pp. 39–41.

34 Eric Blom, *Mozart* (London and New York, 1962), p. 262.

6 The concertos in aesthetic and stylistic context

1 *LMF*, p. 833.

2 Georg Knepler, *Wolfgang Amadé Mozart*, trans. J. Bradford Robinson (Cambridge, 1994), p. 89, and Mark Evan Bonds, *Wordless Rhetoric: Music Form and the Metaphor of the Oration* (Cambridge, MA, 1991), p. 58; V. Kofi Agawu, 'Mozart's Art of Variation: Remarks on the First Movement of K. 503', in Neal Zaslaw (ed.), *Mozart's Piano Concertos: Text, Context, Interpretation* (Ann Arbor, MI, 1996), p. 303; and Ellwood Derr, 'Some Thoughts on the Design of Mozart's Opus 4, the "Subscription Concertos" (K. 414, 413, and 415)', in Zaslaw (ed.), *Mozart's Piano Concertos*, p. 190.

3 On the dual *Kenner/Liebhaber* concept, see Katalin Komlós, *Fortepianos and Their Music: Germany, Austria and England, 1760–1800* (Oxford, 1995), pp. 109–21.

4 See Elaine R. Sisman, *Mozart: The 'Jupiter' Symphony* (Cambridge, 1993), pp. 68–9, and Derr, 'The "Subscription Concertos" ', p. 187.

5 *MDB*, p. 212.

6 Johann Georg Sulzer and Johann Philipp Kirnberger, 'Concert', in Johann Georg Sulzer (ed.), *Allgemeine Theorie der schönen Künste* (4 vols., Leipzig, 1771–4; reprint Hildesheim, 1969), vol. 1, p. 573; Johann Karl Friedrich Triest, 'Remarks on the Development of the Art of Music in Germany in the Eighteenth Century', trans. Susan Gillespie, in Elaine Sisman (ed.), *Haydn and His World* (Princeton, 1997), p. 370; Dittersdorf's remark is given in Chappell White, 'The Early Classical Violin Concerto in Austria', in David

Wyn Jones (ed.), *Music in Eighteenth-Century Austria* (Cambridge, 1996), p. 77.

7 Heinrich Christoph Koch, *Introductory Essay on Composition: the Mechanical Rules of Melody, Sections 3 and 4* (1787–93), trans. Nancy Kovaleff Baker (New Haven and London, 1983), p. 209, reproduced in *Musikalisches Lexikon* (Frankfurt, 1802; reprint Hildesheim, 1964), col. 854. Koch cites C. P. E. Bach's concertos as exemplary in the *Introductory Essay*, presumably encountering Mozart's works between writing the *Introductory Essay* and the *Musikalisches Lexikon*.

8 K. 207 possibly dates back to 1773; see Alan Tyson, *Mozart: Studies of the Autograph Scores* (Cambridge, MA, and London, 1987), pp. 25, 163. Daniel Heartz recently dismissed this idea, however, on circumstantial and stylistic grounds; see Heartz, *Haydn, Mozart, and the Viennese School, 1740–1780* (New York, 1995), pp. 621–2.

9 See Martha Feldman, 'Staging the Virtuoso: Ritornello Procedure in Mozart from Aria to Concerto', in Zaslaw (ed.), *Mozart's Piano Concertos*, pp. 149–86, especially, pp. 151–71.

10 For links between cadential and ending gestures in Mozart's operas and concerto movements, see Wye J. Allanbrook, 'Comic Issues in Mozart's Piano Concertos', in Zaslaw (ed.), *Mozart's Piano Concertos*, pp. 75–105. James Webster challenges the critical orthodoxy on formal connections between Mozart's opera buffa arias from the 1780s and movements from his Viennese piano concertos in 'Are Mozart's Concertos "Dramatic"? Concerto Ritornellos versus Aria Introductions in the 1780s', in Zaslaw (ed.), *Mozart's Piano Concertos*, pp. 107–37.

11 Gotthold Ephraim Lessing, *Hamburg Dramaturgy* (1769), trans. Helen Zimmern (New York, 1962), p. 149.

12 Koch, *Introductory Essay*, p. 209.

13 See Antoine Reicha, *Traité de mélodie* (Paris, 1814), p. 89. Reicha's definition and description is set in historical context in Simon P. Keefe, *Mozart's Piano Concertos: Dramatic Dialogue in the Age of Enlightenment* (Woodbridge and Rochester, NY, 2001), pp. 24–41.

14 The form of the slow movement of K. 467 is a hybrid of concerto and ABA (reflected by my choice of formal terms – ritornello, transition, middle section, reprise etc.); in addition, the tonal and thematic schemes do not initially coincide in the reprise. While the main theme is recapitulated in bar 73 in the flat mediant (A flat), the tonic F is not re-established until bar 88. See Webster, 'Are Mozart's Concertos "Dramatic"?', pp. 113,

127, and Carl Schachter, 'Idiosyncratic Features of Three Mozart Slow Movements: The Piano Concertos K. 449, K. 453, and K. 467', in Zaslaw (ed.), *Mozart's Piano Concertos*, pp. 326–33.

15 For further consideration of dialogue in Mozart's piano concertos, albeit not in K. 467/ii, see Keefe, *Mozart's Piano Concertos*.

16 Cuthbert Girdlestone, *Mozart and His Piano Concertos* (New York, 1964; first published London, 1948), p. 341; Alfred Einstein, *Mozart: His Character, His Work*, trans. Arthur Mendel and Nathan Broder (London and New York, 1945), p. 309; Arthur Hutchings, *A Companion to Mozart's Piano Concertos* (Oxford, 1991; first published London, 1948), p. 140; and Charles Rosen, *The Classical Style: Haydn, Mozart, Beethoven* (London and New York, 1971), p. 238.

17 *LMF*, p. 833.

18 See Daniel Gottlob Türk, *School of Clavier Playing* (1789), trans. Raymond H. Haagh (Lincoln, NE, 1982), p. 111, and Koch, *Musikalisches Lexikon*, col. 272. On the brilliant style as a musical topic see Leonard G. Ratner, *Classic Music: Expression, Form, and Style* (New York, 1980), pp. 19–20.

19 While Joseph Kerman's recent assessment that the soloist in Mozart's piano concerto first movements twice '[traces] a progression away from dialogue toward virtuosity' in the two 'solo spans' is not entirely inaccurate in general terms, it does not adequately reflect the considerable nuances in Mozart's *modus operandi* discussed below. See Kerman, 'Mozart's Piano Concertos and Their Audience' in James M. Morris (ed.), *On Mozart* (Cambridge, 1994), pp. 151–68, at p. 155.

20 In the spirit of preserving the hybrid formal status of Mozart's first-movement concerto form, I designate the principal sections as opening ritornello, solo exposition, middle ritornello, development and recapitulation, following the classification of Daniel N. Leeson and Robert D. Levin in 'On the Authenticity of K. Anh. C14.01 (297b), a Symphonia Concertante for Four Winds and Orchestra', *Mozart-Jahrbuch 1976/77*, pp. 70–96.

21 For more on the types of dialogue at the piano's entry, see Keefe, *Mozart's Piano Concertos*, pp. 76–7.

22 See Keefe, *Mozart's Piano Concertos*, pp. 77–8.

23 K. 491 is exceptional since its elongated solo exposition (bars 100–265) is divided into two by a cadential trill in bars 199–200, creating the impression of 'a double

exposition after the orchestral exposition' in Charles Rosen's words (*The Classical Style*, p. 246). Even in this movement, however, Mozart follows his basic plan in the first half of the section: solo passagework ensues after the secondary theme and lasts until the first cadential trill (see bars 165–200).

24 Semibreves in the string parts in bars 204–7 are not present at the corresponding moment in the solo exposition.

25 For the 'modulatory ritornello' and 'recapitulatory tutti' as they pertain to late eighteenth-century descriptions of first-movement concerto form, see Shelly Davis, 'H. C. Koch, the Classic Concerto and the Sonata-Form Retransition', *JM*, 2 (1983), pp. 45–61. See also Jane Stevens, 'Patterns of Recapitulation in the First Movements of Mozart's Piano Concertos', in Nancy Kovaleff Baker and Barbara Russano Hanning (eds.), *Musical Humanism and Its Legacy: Essays in Honor of Claude Palisca* (Stuyvesant, NY, 1992), pp. 397–418.

26 For more detail on the climactic status of the first movement of K. 491 among Mozart's piano concertos, see Keefe, *Mozart's Piano Concertos*, pp. 75–100.

27 See *LMF*, p. 877; *Allgemeine Musikalische Zeitung*, 3 (October 1800), col. 28.

28 See Keefe, *Mozart's Piano Concertos*, pp. 94–5.

29 See Rosen, *The Classical Style*, p. 259.

30 Tyson suggests that the first and second movements of K. 595 could have been written in the summer of 1788, well in advance of the 5 January 1791 date entered by Mozart in his thematic catalogue, the 'Verzeichnüss aller meiner Werke'. See *Studies of the Autograph Scores*, p. 156.

31 For the 'modulatory ritornello', see Davis, 'Sonata-Form Retransition'. As Davis's study shows, this is an uncommon practice in the first movements of Mozart's concertos; examples include K. 207 and K. 459 as well as K. 622.

32 See *Allgemeine Musikalische Zeitung*, 4 (March 1802), col. 409; trans. William McColl in Colin Lawson, *Mozart: Clarinet Concerto* (Cambridge, 1996), pp. 79–80.

7 The orchestral music

1 Heinrich Christoph Koch, *Musikalisches Lexikon* (Frankfurt, 1802; reprint Hildesheim, 1964), col. 307. For distinctions between these terms in the context of the Salzburg serenading tradition, see Andrew Kearns, 'The Orchestral Serenade in Eighteenth-Century Salzburg', *JMR*, 16 (1997), pp. 165–8.

2 For specific modifications to symphonies and overtures in the course of their reformulation in a new generic context, see Neal Zaslaw, *Mozart's Symphonies: Context, Performance Practice, Reception* (Oxford, 1989).

3 Ibid., p. 49.

4 *MDB*, p. 494. Zaslaw argues (against the prevailing critical trend) that it is unlikely that the symphony concerned is Mozart's earliest, K. 16. See *Mozart's Symphonies*, pp. 17–18.

5 *LMF*, p. 638, letter of 3 December 1778.

6 Ibid., p. 553, letter of 12 June 1778.

7 For the quoted material, see ibid., pp. 565, 558, letters of 9 July and 3 July 1778.

8 See Johann Georg Sulzer (ed.), *Allgemeine Theorie der schönen Künste* (4 vols., Leipzig, 1771–4; reprint Hildesheim, 1969), vol. 4, pp. 478–80; symphony article translated in full in Nancy Kovaleff Baker and Thomas Christensen (eds.), *Aesthetics and the Art of Musical Composition in the German Enlightenment: Selected Writings of Johann Georg Sulzer and Heinrich Christoph Koch* (Cambridge, 1995), pp. 105–108. See also the *Berliner Allgemeine Zeitung* (1805), as given in Thomas Sipe, *Beethoven: 'Eroica Symphony'* (Cambridge, 1998), p. 77; and Friedrich Rochlitz (1830) as quoted in Carl Dahlhaus, *Ludwig van Beethoven: Approaches to His Music*, trans. Mary Whittall (Oxford, 1991), p. 71.

9 For late eighteenth-century theoretical discussion on this point see Mark Evan Bonds, 'The Symphony as Pindaric Ode', in Elaine Sisman (ed.), *Haydn and His World* (Princeton, 1997), pp. 142–6.

10 As given in Zaslaw, *Mozart's Symphonies*, p. 157.

11 See *LMF*, pp. 681, 696, letters of 4 December and 25 December 1780.

12 Franz Xaver Niemetschek, *Life of Mozart* (1798), trans. Helen Mautner (London, 1956), pp. 57–8.

13 See Henry Paolucci (ed. and trans.), *Hegel: On the Arts: Selections from G. W. F. Hegel's 'Aesthetics or the Philosophy of the Fine Arts'* (New York, 1979), p. 133.

14 See *MDB*, pp. 386, 328, and Jérôme-Joseph de Momigny, 'Symphonie', in Jérôme-Joseph de Momigny, Pierre-Louis Ginguené and Nicholas Etienne Framery (eds.), *Encyclopédie méthodique: Musique* (2 vols., Paris, 1791–1818; reprint New York, 1971), vol. 2, pp. 412–13.

15 I understand 'dialogue' to incorporate those technical attributes associated with the concept in the late eighteenth and early nineteenth centuries, as outlined in chapter 6 of this volume, p. 81.

16 It is possible that the clarinets in the second version were not intended to play simultaneously with the oboes. See Dwight Blazin, 'The Two Versions of Mozart's Divertimento K. 113', *ML*, 73 (1992), pp. 32–47.

17 See, for example, Eric Blom, *Mozart* (London and New York, 1962), p. 172; Alfred Einstein, *Mozart: His Character, His Work*, trans. Arthur Mendel and Nathan Broder (London and New York, 1945), p. 223; and Wolfgang Hildesheimer, *Mozart*, trans. Marion Faber (London and New York, 1983), p. 86. In similar fashion, Jens Peter Larsen regards K. 183 – together with K. 201 – as a 'reanimation' of the symphony on Mozart's part, attributing the choice of key to Mozart's acquaintance with Haydn's G minor Symphony No. 39. See Larsen, 'The Symphonies', in H. C. Robbins Landon and Donald Mitchell (eds.), *The Mozart Companion* (London, 1956), pp. 171, 173.

18 *Allgemeine Musikalische Zeitung*, 1 (May 1799), col. 495.

19 Two symphonies dating from the intervening years drew their material from serenades – K. 204 and 250.

20 The inclusion of concerto movements is a standard feature of eighteenth-century orchestral serenades in the Salzburg tradition. See Kearns, 'Orchestral Serenade', pp. 178–83.

21 Daniel Heartz, *Haydn, Mozart, and the Viennese School, 1740–1780* (New York, 1995), p. 635; Konrad Küster, *Mozart: A Musical Biography*, trans. Mary Whittall (Oxford, 1998), p. 98.

22 Stanley Sadie and Cliff Eisen, '(Johann Chrysostom) Wolfgang Amadeus Mozart', in Stanley Sadie (ed.), *The New Grove Dictionary of Music and Musicians*, 2nd edn (29 vols., London, 2001), vol. 17, p. 298.

23 As quoted in Cliff Eisen, 'Mozart's Salzburg Orchestras', *EM*, 20 (1992), p. 98.

24 Robert W. Gutman, *Mozart: A Cultural Biography* (New York, 1999), p. 483. Mozart used the concertante movements from K. 320 for a concert in Vienna on 23 March 1783. See *LMF*, p. 843, letter of 29 March 1783.

25 On typical musical characteristics of the march topic, see Wye Jamison Allanbrook, *Rhythmic Gesture in Mozart: 'Le nozze di Figaro' and 'Don Giovanni'* (Chicago, 1983), pp. 45–8, and V. Kofi Agawu, *Playing with Signs: A Semiotic Interpretation of Classic Music* (Princeton, 1991), p. 38.

26 See Elaine R. Sisman, 'Genre, Gesture, and Meaning in Mozart's "Prague" Symphony', in Cliff Eisen (ed.), *Mozart Studies 2* (Oxford, 1997), pp. 27–84.

27 Rose Rosengard Subotnik's contention that passages such as these reflect a 'critical world view' on Mozart's part whereby sensuous, irrational and illogical elements compromise reason and rationality is countered by Simon P. Keefe in the light of correspondences between these passages and similar material in Mozart's last two piano concertos. See Subotnik, 'Evidence of a Critical World View in Mozart's Last Three Symphonies', in her *Developing Variations: Style and Ideology in Western Music* (Minneapolis, 1991), pp. 98–111, and Keefe, 'A Complementary Pair: Stylistic Experimentation in Mozart's Final Piano Concertos, K. 537 in D and K. 595 in B♭', *JM*, 18 (2001), pp. 678–80. For a consideration of the stylistically progressive nature of one specific gesture – the 'cushion' to the main theme in bar 1 of the first movement – see Glen Carruthers, 'Strangeness and Beauty: The Opening Measure of Mozart's Symphony in G Minor, K. 550', *JM*, 16 (1998), pp. 283–99.

28 For Mozart's comments on the 'Haffner' and 'Linz' symphonies, see *LMF*, pp. 808, 859.

8 Mozart's chamber music

1 Peter Shaffer, *Amadeus* (New York, 1980), p. 18 (Act 1, scene 5).

2 Sébastien de Brossard, *Dictionnaire de musique* (Paris, 1703); Johann Mattheson, *Der vollkommene Capellmeister* (Hamburg, 1739); Jean-Jacques Rousseau, *Dictionnaire de musique* (Paris, 1768); Heinrich Christoph Koch, *Musikalisches Lexikon* (Frankfurt am Main, 1802).

3 See also Charles Burney, *A General History of Music* (London, 1776–89).

4 See James Webster, 'Towards a History of Viennese Chamber Music in the Early Classical Period', *JAMS*, 27 (1974), pp. 212–47.

5 Michael Haydn's notturnos for two violins, two violas and bass of 1773 are isolated examples of strings-only chamber music. It is commonly thought that Haydn's notturnos were the models for Mozart's sole early quintet, K. 174; see Wolf-Dieter Seiffert, 'Mozarts "Salzburger" Streichquintett', in Cliff Eisen and Wolf-Dieter Seiffert (eds.), *Mozarts Streichquintette: Beiträge zum musikalischen Satz, zum Gattungskontext und zu Quellenfragen* (Stuttgart, 1994), pp. 29–67.

6 The Notturno, K. 286, of 1776–7, an elaborated version of the 'standard' divertimento, is composed for four identical

ensembles of strings and horns, which gives rise to a succession of echo effects.

7 In Salzburg Mozart also composed five divertimenti for two oboes, two bassoons and two horns (K. 213, 240, 252, 253, 270, 1775–7) as well as a divertimento for two oboes, two clarinets, two cors anglais, two horns and two bassoons (K. 166, 1773).

8 An isolated first quartet, K. 80, was composed at Lodi, in Italy, on 15 March 1770; originally in three movements, Mozart added a fourth movement in Vienna in 1773 or possibly after his return to Salzburg in 1774.

9 Mozart's earlier sonatas for keyboard and violin include four published in Paris in 1764 (K. 6–9), derived in part from material composed as early as 1762; six composed in London in 1764 (K. 10–15); and six composed at The Hague in 1766 (K. 26–31). The Sonata in C major, K. 296, also composed at Mannheim in 1778, was not published with K. 301–6; together with K. 378, written in Salzburg in 1779 or 1780, it was published with four Viennese sonatas, K. 376, 377, 379 and 380, in 1781.

10 The traditional view is put forward by Ernst Fritz Schmid, 'Mozart and Haydn', in Paul Henry Lang (ed.), *The Creative World of Mozart* (New York, 1963). For a more convincing account of K. 168–73 and the then current Viennese style, see A. Peter Brown, 'Haydn and Mozart's 1773 Stay in Vienna: Weeding a Musicological Garden', *JM*, 10 (1992), pp. 192–230.

11 *MDB*, p. 94.

12 The keyboard concerto K. 175 of December 1773 postdates K. 207. And another four violin concertos – K. 211, 216, 218 and 219 (all 1775) – were written before he turned again to the piano (K. 242, February 1776, for three keyboards, and K. 246, April 1776).

13 *LMF*, pp. 299–300, letter of 6 October 1777.

14 *LMF*, p. 331, letter of 18 October 1777.

15 'I send my sister herewith six duets for keyboard and violin by Schuster, which I have often played here. They are not bad. If I stay on I shall write six myself in the same style.' *LMF*, p. 300, letter of 6 October 1777.

16 *MDB*, p. 214.

17 Ibid., p. 212.

18 At least in part this was to accommodate publishers in Vienna. Where Artaria normally published complete opuses, Hoffmeister, for example, published monthly series including chamber works in a variety of scorings. It is noteworthy that many of Mozart's Viennese chamber works were written for Hoffmeister, including the piano sonatas K. 330, 331 and 533, the rondos K. 485 and 511, the four-hand works K. 426, 501 and 521, the accompanied sonatas K. 481 and 526, the Piano Trio in G major, K. 496, the Piano Quartet in G minor, K. 478, the String Quartet in D major, K. 499, and the Fugue, K. 546. See Cliff Eisen, *New Mozart Documents: A Supplement to O. E. Deutsch's Documentary Biography* (London and Stanford, 1991), pp. 36–7.

19 For the thorny textual question about the relationship between Mozart's autographs and the first edition, see Wolf-Dieter Seiffert, 'Mozart's "Haydn" Quartets: An Evaluation of the Autographs and First Edition, with Particular Attention to mm. 125–42 of the Finale of K. 387', in Cliff Eisen (ed.), *Mozart Studies 2* (Oxford, 1997), pp. 175–200.

20 The introduction to K. 465 was the subject of considerable debate in the nineteenth century; see Julie Anne Vertrees, 'Mozart's String Quartet K. 465: The History of a Controversy', *Current Musicology*, 17 (1974), pp. 96–114. For a recent history, and a new view of the relationship between the introduction and the rest of the quartet, see Simon P. Keefe, 'An Integrated "Dissonance": Mozart's "Haydn" Quartets and the Slow Introduction of K. 465', *Mozart-Jahrbuch 2002*, pp. 87–103 (in press).

21 Mozart may have conceived this possibility as early as 1782 while arranging for string quartet several fugues by Bach and Handel. A similar procedure is found at the conclusion of his versions of the D sharp minor fugue from Book 2 of Bach's *Das wohltemperierte Clavier*. I am indebted to Laurence Dreyfus for this observation.

22 For topics in the six quartets, see in particular Wye J. Allanbrook, ' "To serve the private pleasure": Expression and Form in the String Quartets', in Stanley Sadie (ed.), *Wolfgang Amadè Mozart: Essays on His Life and His Music* (Oxford, 1996), pp. 132–60.

23 See Heinrich Christoph Koch, *Introductory Essay on Composition: The Mechanical Rules of Melody, Sections 3 and 4* (1787–93), trans. Nancy Kovaleff Baker (New Haven and London, 1983), p. 207.

24 For the compositional chronology of the 'Prussian' Quartets, see Alan Tyson, 'New Light on Mozart's "Prussian" Quartets', *MT*, 116 (1975), pp. 126–30, reprinted in Tyson, *Mozart: Studies of the Autograph Scores* (Cambridge, MA, and London, 1987), pp. 36–47.

25 Hans Keller, 'The Chamber Music', in H. C. Robbins Landon and Donald Mitchell (eds.), *The Mozart Companion* (London, 1956), p. 134.

26 Eric Blom, *Mozart* (London, 1935), p. 242.

27 Otto Jahn, *Life of Mozart*, trans. Pauline D. Townsend (3 vols., London, 1891), vol. 3, p. 16.

28 Eisen, *New Mozart Documents*, p. 72.

29 *MDB*, pp. 427–8. In a repeat advertisement of January 1792 Artaria noted that the quartets were received with 'general acclamation'; see *MDB*, p. 436.

30 The slow movement of the accompanied sonata K. 526 is also made up chiefly of accompanimental figures. I am indebted to Wiebke Thormählen for this observation.

9 Mozart as a vocal composer

1 The theologian Hans Küng also finds 'traces of transcendence' in both his instrumental and vocal music. See Küng, *Mozart: Traces of Transcendence*, trans. John Bowden (London, 1992).

2 *MDB*, pp. 95–100, especially p. 98.

3 A facsimile of the autograph was published in Chris A. Banks and J. Rigbie Turner (eds.), *Mozart: Prodigy of Nature* (New York, 1991), p. 20, pl. 7.

4 *MBA*, vol. 2, pp. 304–5.

5 Constanze Weber was the younger sister of two professional singers, Aloysia Lange and Josefa Hofer, both of whom Mozart first met during his trip to Mannheim in 1777–8.

6 *MBA*, vol. 2, p. 264.

7 The Mannheim court was somewhat exceptional in employing two Kapellmeisters: C. P. Grua for 'Kirchen-Musik' and Ignaz Holzbauer for 'Theater-Musik'. See Friedrich W. Marpurg (ed.), *Historisch-kritische Beiträge zur Aufnahme der Musik* (5 vols., Berlin, 1754–8), vol. 2, pp. 567–70. This is confirmed in the local court almanacs or 'Hof-Calender' published annually for the electoral court at Mannheim.

8 *MBA*, vol. 4, p. 107. The petition survives only in a fragment and dates from early May 1790. Mozart uses the occasion to point out that Antonio Salieri, the first Kapellmeister, had never dedicated himself to the church style: 'der sehr geschickte kapellm. Salieri sich nie dem kirchen Styl gewidmet [hat], ich [habe] aber vonn Jugend auf mir diesen Styl ganz eigen gemacht habe.'

9 *MBA*, vol. 2, p. 420.

10 Alfred Einstein, *Mozart: His Character, His Work*, trans. Arthur Mendel and Nathan Broder (London and New York, 1945), pp. 79, 80.

11 These works, mostly fragments of Kyrie and Gloria settings that date from the end of 1787 or later, include K. 91 (186i, a copy of a Kyrie by Carl Georg Reutter), K. 196a (Anh. 16), K. 323 (Anh. 15), K. 323a (Anh. 20) and K. 258a (Anh. 13). See Alan Tyson, *Mozart: Studies of the Autograph Scores* (Cambridge, MA, and London, 1987), especially pp. 26–8, and Tyson 'Proposed New Dates for Many Works and Fragments Written by Mozart from March 1781 to December 1791', in Cliff Eisen (ed.), *Mozart Studies* (Oxford, 1991), pp. 213–26. I do not agree with Tyson, however, regarding the Kyrie in D minor, K. 341, the autograph of which is lost. Tyson suggests that it too may date from the late Viennese period, but there are still strong stylistic grounds to place it in close proximity to *Idomeneo* in 1781. For instance, the Kyrie could have been written as a votive offering for the success of his opera; and the choice of D minor (the main key of *Idomeneo*) would be entirely appropriate for Lent, which began before he was called to Vienna. See also Karl Gustav Fellerer, *Die Kirchenmusik W. A. Mozarts* (Laaber, 1985), p. 15, and Daniel Heartz, *Haydn, Mozart, and the Viennese School, 1740–1780* (New York, 1995), pp. 670–4.

12 For the Italian trips and Mozart's early development, see Ruth Halliwell, *The Mozart Family: Four Lives in a Social Context* (Oxford, 1998), pp. 141–227. Manfred Hermann Schmid, *Mozart und die Salzburger Tradition* (Tutzing, 1976), argues that the significance of these lessons may have been overemphasized in the past.

13 For instance, Johann Friedrich Agricola defines the Italian motet as 'a certain spiritual cantata in Latin for solo voice and instruments, sung in church during mass between the Credo and the Sanctus. Motets consist generally of two arias and two recitatives and end with an Alleluja usually containing many divisions.' See Julianne C. Baird (ed. and trans.), *Introduction to the Art of Singing by Johann Friedrich Agricola* (Cambridge, 1995), p. 181.

14 The works are listed in approximate chronological order, based on the recent handwriting studies of Wolfgang Plath and paper studies of Alan Tyson, in *Studies of the Autograph Scores*, pp. 162–76.

15 Heartz, *Haydn, Mozart, and the Viennese School*, pp. 643–70.

16 *MBA*, vol. 1, pp. 532–3.

17 Konrad Küster, *Mozart: A Musical Biography*, trans. Mary Whittall (Oxford, 1996), p. 37.

18 For a partial reconstruction of the Mozart family library, see Cliff Eisen, 'The Mozarts' Salzburg Music Library', in Eisen (ed.), *Mozart Studies 2* (Oxford, 1997), pp. 85–138, esp. pp. 101–102. See also Leopold Mozart's letters in *MBA*, vol. 2, pp. 200, 337. Ceccarelli became a good friend of the family, and Mozart later wrote a concert aria, K. 374, for him.

19 *MDL*, p. 163. That the Archbishop was not entirely satisfied with Mozart's output is implied in the letter of appointment to his successor, Michael Haydn; see Cliff Eisen, *New Mozart Documents: A Supplement to O. E. Deutsch's Documentary Biography* (London and Stanford, 1991), p. 29.

20 David Charlton (ed.), *E. T. A. Hoffmann's Musical Writings: 'Kreisleriana', 'The Poet and the Composer', 'Music Criticism'*, trans. Martyn Clarke (Cambridge, 1989), p. 370.

21 *MBA*, vol. 3, p. 264.

22 *MBA*, vol. 3, p. 248.

23 See Rosemary Hughes (ed.), *A Mozart Pilgrimage: Being the Travel Diaries of Vincent and Mary Novello in the Year 1829* (London, 1955), p. 96.

24 Tyson, 'Proposed New Dates', p. 219.

25 For an overview of the work, its context, and its reception, see Neal Zaslaw, 'Mozart's Salzburg Sacred Music and His Mass in C Minor, K. 427', in *Mozartiana: The Festschrift for the Seventieth Birthday of Professor Ebisawa Bin* (Tokyo, 2001), pp. 571–88.

26 Here are the relevant entries from Nannerl's diary (in *MBA*, vol. 3, p. 290): 'den 23ten [October] um 8 uhr in der Mess. in capelHaus bey der prob von der mess, meines bruders, bey welcher meine schwägerin die Solo Singt . . . der 25ten [recte 26ten] zu st peter in amt mein bruder sein amt gemacht worder. die ganze hofmusik war dabey'.

27 When Johann André questioned Constanze about the missing sections, she responded on 31 May 1800: 'wegen der Messe zum Davide penitente ist sich in Salzburg, wo sie gemacht or aufgeführt ist, zu erkundigen. den Schluss der Messe hat er gewiss nicht ins Requiem verwandt. Als er die Messe machte, war nicht von dem Requiem, welches viele Jahre jünger ist, die Rede'. See *MBA*, vol. 4, p. 356.

28 Various explanations have been summarized in H. C. Robbins Landon, 'Mozart's Mass in C Minor, K. 427', in Eugene K. Wolf and Edward H. Roesner (eds.), *Studies in Musical Sources and Style: Essays in Honor of Jan LaRue* (Madison, WI, 1990), pp. 419–23.

But Cliff Eisen cautions that the Salzburg manuscript copy (in the Holy Cross Monastery in Augsburg) is 'possibly *not* the one used for the performance, since the paper seems to date from mid-1784 to mid-1785'. See Eisen, 'The Mozarts' Salzburg Copyists: Aspects of Attribution, Chronology, Text, Style, and Performance Practice', in Eisen (ed.), *Mozart Studies* (Oxford, 1991), p. 307. It is possible that the Kyrie, Gloria, Sanctus and Benedictus from K. 427 were sung along with the Credo and Agnus Dei of K. 317 or K. 337.

29 The attribution comes from Abbé Stadler in *A Mozart Pilgrimage*, p. 158.

30 These include the following works, sponsored by van Swieten and Count J. B. Esterházy (with performance dates): Handel's *Judas Maccabaeus* (Lent 1786), *Acis and Galatea* (December 1788), *Messiah* (Lent 1789), *Alexander's Feast* (1790) and C. P. E. Bach's *Die Auferstehung und Himmelfahrt Jesu* (Lent 1788). We can assume that Mozart, rather than Haydn, would have been Baron van Swieten's first choice as the composer for his oratorios *The Creation* and *The Seasons*.

31 See Georg B. Stauffer, *Bach: The Mass in B Minor* (New York, 1997), p. 187 and p. 289, n. 26.

32 The child Raimond Leopold, who was born on 17 June 1783, had been left behind in Vienna with the nursemaid. Neither the exact circumstances of the child's death nor the parents' reaction to the news are known, but a few months later, on 10 December 1783, Mozart wrote to his father: 'We are both very sad about our poor, bonny, fat, darling little boy.' See *LMF*, p. 863.

33 Otto Biba, 'Mozarts Wiener Kirchenmusikkompositionen', in Ingrid Fuchs (ed.), *Internationaler Musikwissenschaftlicher Kongress zum Mozartjahr 1991, Baden–Wien. Bericht* (2 vols., Tutzing, 1993), vol. 1, pp. 43–55.

34 *MBA*, vol. 4, p. 131. His appointment decree is given in *MDL*, p. 346, and *MDB*, p. 395. He would have succeeded Leopold Hofmann at a salary of 2000 florins, but the much older Hofmann lived more than a year longer than Mozart.

35 Franz Xaver Niemetschek, *Life of Mozart* (1798), trans. Helen Mautner as *Life of Mozart* (London, 1956), pp. 85–6.

36 According to Benedikt Schack, on the afternoon before Mozart died a group gathered at his bed to sing through the Requiem. The composer sang the alto part, Schack (the first Tamino) the soprano, Hofer (Mozart's brother-in-law) the tenor, and

Gerle (the first Sarastro) the bass. See *MDL*, pp. 459–60, and *MDB*, pp. 536–7.

37 For an extensive discussion of the literature, fact and fiction, see Christoph Wolff, *Mozart's Requiem: Historical and Analytical Studies, Documents, Score*, trans. Mary Whittall (Berkeley, 1994).

38 Charlton (ed.), *E. T. A. Hoffmann's Musical Writings*, p. 370. 'Compelling and profound though Haydn's settings of the High Mass frequently are, and excellent though his harmonic development is, there is still hardly one of them that is completely without playfulness, without melodies quite inappropriate to the dignity of church style.'

39 Ibid., pp. 374–5.

40 Einstein, *Mozart: His Character, His Work*, p. 374.

41 Gertraut Haberkamp, *Die Erstdrucke der Werke von Wolfgang Amadeus Mozart* (2 vols., Tutzing, 1986), plates 377–80. The *Neue Mozart-Ausgabe* also includes thirty lieder, as well as two complete works and a few fragments in an appendix, but the contents of the two collections do not entirely match.

42 Einstein, *Mozart: His Character, His Work*, pp. 379–80, calls 'Das Veilchen' a 'song that is not a song', also referring to it as 'an "occasional" work in the highest sense' and 'a lyric scena'.

10 The opere buffe

1 Letter of 7 May 1783; *MBA*, vol. 3, p. 268; *LMF*, p. 848.

2 Letter of 5 February 1783; *MBA*, vol. 3, p. 255; *LMF*, p. 839.

3 See *Il teatro comico*, Act 2, scene 1.

4 See, for example, Arnold E. Maurer, *Carlo Goldoni: Seine Komödien und ihre Verbreitung im deutschen Sprachraum des 18. Jahrhunderts* (Bonn, 1982), p. 165.

5 Francesco Bianchi, *Il disertore francese* (Venice, 1784), preface, pp. 8–9. Translations are the author's unless otherwise indicated.

6 See also Johann Georg Sulzer (ed.), *Allgemeine Theorie der schönen Künste* (4 vols., Leipzig, 1791–4; reprint Hildesheim, 1969), vol. 1, p. 488.

7 See, for example, 'Goldoni, Carlo', in Stanley Sadie (ed.), *New Grove Dictionary of Opera* (4 vols., London, 1992), vol. 2, p. 479; and Charles Rosen, *The Classical Style: Haydn, Mozart, Beethoven* (London and New York, 1971), pp. 312–13.

8 Paolo Gallarati, 'Mozart and Eighteenth-Century Comedy', in Mary Hunter and James Webster (eds.), *Opera Buffa*

in *Mozart's Vienna* (Cambridge, 1997), pp. 99, 100.

9 Letter of 30 December 1774; *MBA*, vol. 1, p. 513; *LMF*, p. 256.

10 Daniel Heartz, 'The Creation of the Buffo Finale in Italian Opera', *Proceedings of the Royal Musical Association*, 104 (1977–8), p. 75.

11 See, for example, Stefan Kunze, *Mozarts Opern* (Stuttgart, 1984), pp. 41–2.

12 Johann Adam Hiller, *Wöchentliche Nachrichten und Anmerkungen, die Musik betrefend*, 3/8 (22 August 1768), p. 62.

13 Letter of 29 November 1780; *MBA*, vol. 3, pp. 34–5; *LMF*, p. 674.

14 See, for example, Kunze, *Mozarts Opern*, p. 59.

15 For an analysis of this ensemble, see Wye Jamison Allanbrook, *Rhythmic Gesture in Mozart: 'Le nozze di Figaro' and 'Don Giovanni'* (Chicago, 1983), pp. 233–5, 238–40.

16 See, for example, *Il teatro comico*, Act 2, scene 2.

17 Stefan Kunze, *Don Giovanni vor Mozart: Die Tradition der Don-Giovanni-Opern im italienischen Buffa-Theater des 18. Jahrhunderts* (Munich, 1972), p. 55.

18 Stefano Castelvecchi, 'Sentimental and Anti-Sentimental in *Le nozze di Figaro*', *JAMS*, 53 (2000), pp. 5–11.

11 Mozart and opera seria

1 *Die Zauberflöte* was staged after *La clemenza di Tito*, but was substantially completed before Mozart composed the latter.

2 The performances, on the first day of Carnival, took place on 26 December 1770 and 26 December 1772.

3 Archbishop Schrattenbach died before the intended performance of *Il sogno di Scipione*; the work was eventually performed for the new Prince-Archbishop, Colloredo.

4 Carolyn Gianturco, *Mozart's Early Operas* (London, 1981), includes the German sacred drama *Die Schuldigkeit des ersten Gebots* as the first of Mozart's operas.

5 See Julian Rushton, *W. A. Mozart: 'Idomeneo'* (Cambridge, 1993), pp. 62–8.

6 '. . . ridotta a vera opera': Mozart's thematic catalogue f. 28v. See John A. Rice, *W. A. Mozart: 'La clemenza di Tito'* (Cambridge, 1991).

7 See Christoph-Helmut Mahling, 'Junia's aria in *Lucio Silla*', in Stanley Sadie (ed.), *Wolfgang Amadè Mozart: Essays on His Life and His Music* (Oxford, 1996), pp. 377–94.

8 Barrington's oft-quoted study of Mozart is in *MDB*, pp. 95–100; and in part in

Gianturco, *Mozart's Early Operas*, pp. 13–14.
9 Letter of 24 November 1770; *MBA*, vol. 1,
p. 405.
10 Gasparini's opera was staged at Turin in
1767. Perhaps significantly, Bernasconi had
worked with Gluck, creating the role of
Alceste (Vienna, 1767).
11 'Concert aria' as distinct from an aria
composed for insertion in an opera by
another composer, for which Mozart would
be unlikely to write new recitative.
12 This is K. 316 (300b), 'Io non chiedo',
following the recitative 'Popoli di Tessaglia',
written in 1778.
13 A similar procedure is followed in Gluck's
earlier setting of *Il re pastore*.
14 Campra's *Idoménée* (1712), libretto by
Danchet. See Donald Neville, 'From *tragédie
lyrique* to Moral Drama', in Rushton, *W. A.
Mozart: 'Idomeneo'*, pp. 72–82.
15 This was, however, one of the arias
omitted in the performances, together with
Idomeneo's final aria and, possibly,
Idamante's, resulting in a final act almost
without arias.
16 See Rushton, *W. A. Mozart: 'Idomeneo'*,
and also ' "La vittima è Idamante": Did
Mozart Have a Motive?', *COJ*, 3 (1991),
pp. 1–21.
17 Both this clarinet solo, which descends
below the normal clarinet range and was thus
meant for a 'basset clarinet', and the
basset-horn solo in 'Non più di fiori' were
written for Mozart's friend Anton Stadler. For
the origins of 'Non più di fiori', see Sergio
Durante, 'The Chronology of Mozart's "La
clemenza di Tito" Reconsidered', *ML*, 80
(1999), pp. 560–94.
18 A direct musical connection has been
traced between one of Tito's arias and
Sarastro's 'In diesen heil'gen Hallen'. See
Rice, *W. A. Mozart: 'La clemenza di Tito'*,
p. 77.
19 This solo is accidentally omitted in the
Neue Mozart-Ausgabe (p. 154, bars 117–18).
20 Most of the performances were heavily
altered to suit local tastes and conditions.

12 Mozart's German operas
1 For a discussion of the origins of German
opera, see Thomas Bauman, *North German
Opera in the Age of Goethe* (Cambridge, 1985).
2 *LMF*, p. 967.
3 See Linda L. Tyler, '*Bastien und Bastienne*:
The Libretto, Its Derivation, and Mozart's
Text-Setting', *JM*, 8 (1990), pp. 520–52.
4 Linda L. Tyler, '*Zaide* in the Development
of Mozart's Operatic Language', *ML*, 72
(1991), pp. 214–35.

5 Alan Tyson, *Wasserzeichen-Katalog*, in *NMA*,
Serie 10, Werkgruppe 33, Abteilung 2,
Textband (Kassel, 1992).
6 Tyler, '*Zaide* in the Development of
Mozart's Operatic Language', p. 235.
7 Heinrich Kurz (ed.), *Goethes Werke*
(12 vols., Leipzig, n.d.), vol. 10, 'Bericht
aus Rom', November 1787, p. 380.
8 Donald Francis Tovey, 'Overture, "Der
Schauspieldirektor" (The Theatre-Manager)',
in his *Essays in Musical Analysis* (7 vols.,
London, 1935–1944), vol. 4, pp. 21–2.
9 For instance, the dance duet of Lubano and
Lubanara (Act 1, No. 4), the pantomime with
Lubano and the dwarfs (Act 2, No. 4), the
duets of Eutifronte and Lubano (Act 2, finale)
and the two cat duets in Act 2.
10 Even while criticizing the text, Julius
Friedrich Knüppeln (*Vertraute Briefe zur
Charakteristik von Wien*, 1793) praises Mozart's
music, particularly Sarastro's aria and the
Priests' chorus for their 'feierlich' quality.

13 Mozart in the nineteenth century
1 Quoted in Hugh Macdonald, 'Berlioz and
Mozart', in Peter Bloom (ed.), *The Cambridge
Companion to Berlioz* (Cambridge, 2000),
p. 222.
2 Maynard Solomon, *Mozart: A Life* (New
York, 1995), p. 5. This important though
dubious strand in Mozart reception had its
beginnings in a postscript to a letter in which
Nannerl responded to questions that
Schlichtegroll had originally put to Albert
von Mölk, his Salzburg contact and a friend
of the Mozart family. The postscript, several
paragraphs long, is in Mölk's hand, not
Nannerl's. See Bruce Cooper Clarke, 'Albert
von Mölk: Mozart Myth-Maker? Study of an
Eighteenth-Century Correspondence', in
Mozart-Jahrbuch 1995, pp. 169–79.
3 See Alec Hyatt King, 'Mozart Literature', in
H. C. Robbins Landon (ed.), *The Mozart
Compendium: A Guide to Mozart's Life and
Music* (London, 1990), p. 405.
4 See the comments on Ulïbïshev's outlook in
Ian Bent (ed.), *Music Analysis in the Nineteenth
Century*, vol. 1: *Fugue, Form and Style*
(Cambridge, 1994), pp. 281–2. The German
translation of Ulïbïshev's work went through
two editions: *Mozart's Leben, nebst einer
Übersicht der allgemeinen Geschichte der Musik
und einer Analyse der Hauptwerk Mozart's*,
trans. A. Schraishuon (3 vols., Stuttgart,
1847); the second edition, in four volumes,
was prepared by Ludwig Gantler (Stuttgart,
1859). The first edition in particular was
influential in disseminating Ulïbïshev's ideas
in the German-speaking world.

5 Otto Jahn, *W. A. Mozart* (4 vols., Leipzig, 1856), vol. 4, p. 746.

6 Roye E. Wates, 'Eduard Mörike, Alexander Ulïbïshev, and the "Ghost Scene" in *Don Giovanni*', in *Studies in the History of Music*, vol. 3: *The Creative Process* (New York, 1993), pp. 32–3, 39, 42–3. I would like to thank Professor Wates for her comments on an earlier draft of this chapter. I am especially grateful to her for having drawn my attention to a number of the more egregious errors in that version.

7 E. T. A. Hoffmann, 'Don Juan', in *Fantasy Pieces in Callot's Manner: Pages from the Diary of a Travelling Romantic*, trans. Joseph M. Hayse (Schenectady, NY, 1996), pp. 54–64.

8 Søren Kierkegaard, *Either/Or* (1843), trans. David F. Swenson and Lillian Marvin Swenson (2 vols., Garden City, NY, 1959), vol. 1, p. 58. Since Kierkegaard's treatise was available only in the original Danish until the beginning of the twentieth century, it exercised virtually no impact on the nineteenth-century image of Mozart. Alfred Einstein was one of the first Mozart biographers to cite Kierkegaard's work. See Einstein, *Mozart: His Character, His Work*, trans. Arthur Mendel and Nathan Broder (London and New York, 1945), pp. 432, 434.

9 Roye E. Wates, ' "Die Oper aller Opern": *Don Giovanni* as Text for the Romantics', in Hermann Danuser and Tobias Plebuch (eds.), *Musik als Text: Bericht über den Internationalen Kongress der Gesellschaft für Musikforschung, Freiburg im Breisgau 1993* (2 vols., Kassel, 1998), vol. 2, pp. 209–14.

10 Hector Berlioz, *Memoirs of Hector Berlioz from 1803 to 1865*, trans. Rachel Holmes and Eleanor Newman, annotated and revised by Ernest Newman (New York, 1966), p. 62.

11 Carl Dahlhaus, *Nineteenth-Century Music*, trans. J. Bradford Robinson (Berkeley, 1989), pp. 32–3.

12 Franz Xaver Niemetschek, *Life of Mozart* (1798), trans. Helen Mautner (London, 1956), p. 55.

13 Friedrich Rochlitz, 'Raphael und Mozart', *Allgemeine Musikalische Zeitung*, 2 (1800), cols. 648–9. All translations are the author's unless otherwise indicated.

14 Georg Nikolaus von Nissen, *Anhang zu W. A. Mozarts Biographie*, ed. Constanze, Wittwe von Nissen (Leipzig, 1828), pp. 31, 37.

15 Friedrich Schlegel, *Über das Studium der griechischen Poesie* (1795–6), in *Kritische Friedrich Schlegel Ausgabe*, vol. 1: *Studien des klassischen Altertums*, ed. Ernst Behler (Vienna, 1979), p. 244.

16 On the association of Mozart's music with the aesthetic of the sublime in the writings of Jean Paul, Friedrich Rochlitz and Christian Friedrich Michaelis, see Gernot Gruber, *Mozart and Posterity*, trans. R. S. Furness (London, 1991; first published in German as *Mozart und die Nachwelt*, Salzburg, 1985), pp. 78–9. As Elaine Sisman observes in *Mozart: The 'Jupiter' Symphony* (Cambridge, 1993), pp. 18–20, Kant's 'mathematical' sublime has particular relevance for the reception of Mozart's 'Jupiter' Symphony.

17 E. T. A. Hoffmann, review of Beethoven's Fifth Symphony, in David Charlton (ed.), *E. T. A. Hoffmann's Musical Writings: 'Kreisleriana', 'The Poet and the Composer', 'Music Criticism'*, trans. Martyn Clarke (Cambridge, 1989), p. 238.

18 E. T. A. Hoffmann, 'Further Observations on Spontini's Opera *Olimpia*' (1821), in Charlton (ed.), *E. T. A. Hoffmann's Musical Writings*, p. 440.

19 Stendhal (Henri Beyle), *Lives of Haydn, Mozart and Metastasio*, ed. and trans. Richard N. Coe (London, 1972; a translation of *Vies de Haydn, de Mozart et de Métastase*, 1817, the second edition of *Lettres écrites de Vienne en Autriche*, 1815), pp. 203, 205. For a discussion of several other early nineteenth-century writers who compared Mozart and Shakespeare, see Gruber, *Mozart and Posterity*, pp. 88–90. For Mozart's view of the ghost scene in Shakespeare's *Hamlet*, see Wates, ' "Die Oper aller Opern" ', p. 211.

20 John Warrack (ed.), *Carl Maria von Weber: Writings on Music*, trans. Martin Cooper (Cambridge, 1981), p. 264.

21 For a summary of the controversy, see John Irving, *Mozart: The 'Haydn' Quartets* (Cambridge, 1998), pp. 76–8.

22 Robert Schumann, *Tagebücher*, Band 1: 1827–1838, ed. Georg Eismann (Leipzig, 1971), p. 348.

23 *Neue Zeitschrift für Musik*, 1 (1834), p. 73.

24 See the commentrary on Wendt's *Über den gegenwärtigen Zustand der Musik, besonders in Deutschland und wie er geworden* (Leipzig, 1836) in Arno Forchert, ' "Klassisch" und "romantisch" in der Musikliteratur des frühen 19. Jahrhunderts', *Die Musikforschung*, 31 (1978), p. 412.

25 Franz Brendel, *Geschichte der Musik in Italien, Deutschland und Frankreich* (Leipzig, 1852), pp. 313, 322–3. The discussion of Mozart in Arrey von Dommer's *Handbuch der Musik-Geschichte* (2nd edn, Leipzig, 1878), pp. 563–9, draws liberally on Brendel.

26 Alexander Ulïbïshev, '[Mozart's] String Quartets Dedicated to Haydn', from *Nouvelle*

Biographie de Mozart, in Bent (ed.), *Music Analysis in the Nineteenth Century*, vol. 1, p. 299.

27 Jahn, *W. A. Mozart*, vol. 4, pp. 746–7.

28 Charles Gounod, *Mozart's 'Don Giovanni': A Commentary*, trans. Windeyer Clark (London, 1895), p. 13.

29 Quoted in Alexandra Orlova, *Tchaikovsky: A Self-Portrait*, trans. R. M. Davison (Oxford, 1990), p. 43. After first examining the autograph of the opera, Tchaikovsky wrote in his diary: 'I have seen the score of *Don Giovanni* written IN HIS OWN HAND!!!!!!!!!!' (See Orlova, *Tchaikovsky*, p. 296.)

30 Ferruccio Busoni, 'Mozart: Aphorisms' (originally published in *Lokal Anzeiger*, Berlin, 1906), in *The Essence of Music and Other Papers*, trans. Rosamund Ley (New York, 1965), p. 105.

31 Letter of 26 September 1781 to Leopold Mozart. Translation quoted from Peter Kivy, *Osmin's Rage: Philosophical Reflections on Opera, Drama, and Text* (Princeton, 1988), pp. 59–60.

32 Hoffmann, review of Beethoven's Fifth Symphony, in Charlton (ed.), *E. T. A. Hoffmann's Musical Writings*, pp. 237–8.

33 Quoted in Thomas Seedorf, *Studien zur kompositorischen Mozart-Rezeption im frühen 20. Jahrhundert* (Laaber, 1990), p. 33.

34 Hector Berlioz, 'Don Juan', in Julian Rushton, *W. A. Mozart: 'Don Giovanni'* (Cambridge, 1981), p. 134. It should be noted that Meyerbeer's 1845 revival of the opera in Berlin marked the first time since 1788 that Mozart's recitatives had been heard in public. The concerted numbers were done in Rochlitz's translation, while Da Ponte's text for the original recitatives was also translated into German. See Wates, ' "Die Oper aller Opern" ', pp. 212–14.

35 Brendel, *Geschichte der Musik in Italien, Deutschland und Frankreich*, pp. 329–30.

36 Eduard Hanslick, *Concerte, Componisten und Virtuosen der letzten fünfzehn Jahre, 1870–1885* (2nd edn, Berlin, 1886), p. 62.

37 Diary entry of 13 June 1816. See Otto Erich Deutsch, *Schubert: Die Dokumente seines Lebens*, Franz Schubert: Neue Ausgabe sämtlicher Werke, Serie 8, Supplement, Band 5 (Kassel, 1964), pp. 42–3.

38 Significant contributions in this area include: Karl Gustav Fellerer, 'Mozart in der Musik des 19. Jahrhunderts', *Mozart-Jahrbuch 1980–83*, pp. 1–9; Gruber, *Mozart and Posterity*, pp. 157–77; Jeremy Yudkin, 'Beethoven's "Mozart" Quartet', *JAMS*, 45 (1992), pp. 30–74; R. Larry Todd, 'Mozart According to Mendelssohn: A Contribution

to *Rezeptionsgeschichte*', in R. Larry Todd and Peter Williams (eds.), *Perspectives on Mozart Performance* (Cambridge, 1991), pp. 158–203; Hugh Macdonald, 'Berlioz and Mozart', and Imogen Fellinger, 'Brahms's View of Mozart', in Robert Pascall (eds.), *Brahms: Biographical, Documentary and Analytical Studies* (Cambridge, 1983), pp. 41–57.

39 *Neue Zeitschrift für Musik*, 13 (1840), p. 198.

40 *Neue Zeitschrift für Musik*, 8 (1838), p. 182.

41 Edward Garden and Nigel Gotteri (eds.), *'To my best friend': Correspondence between Tchaikovsky and Nadezhda von Meck 1876–1878*, trans. Galina von Meck (Oxford, 1993), p. 238.

42 See Orlova, *Tchaikovsky*, p. 314. The sources for the movements of 'Mozartiana' are as follows: I, 'Gigue': Gigue for Clavier, K. 574; II, 'Menuet': Minuet for Clavier, K. 355; III, 'Preghiera': Liszt's paraphrase for piano of 'Ave verum corpus', K. 618; IV, 'Thème et variations': Variations for Clavier on 'Les hommes pieusement' from Gluck's *La Rencontre imprévue*, K. 455.

43 See Otto Gottlieb-Billroth (ed.), *Billroth und Brahms im Briefwechsel* (Berlin and Vienna, 1935), p. 315; and Brahms's letter of June 1869 to Simrock, in Max Kalbeck (ed.), *Johannes Brahms Briefwechsel*, vol. 9: *Johannes Brahms Briefe an P. J. und Fritz Simrock* (Berlin, 1917), p. 75.

44 Richard Heuberger, *Erinnerungen an Johannes Brahms* (1885–97) (Tutzing, 1971), p. 22.

45 See my 'From "Concertante" Rondo to "Lyric Sonata": A Commentary on Brahms's Reception of Mozart', in David Brodbeck (ed.), *Brahms Studies*, vol. 1 (Lincoln, NE, and London, 1994), pp. 111–38.

46 Heuberger, *Erinnerungen*, p. 68.

47 Martin Gregor-Dellin and Dietrich Mack (eds.), *Cosima Wagner's Diaries*, trans. Geoffrey Skelton, vol. 2: 1878–1883 (New York and London, 1980), p. 199, entry of 12 November 1878.

48 *Richard Wagner's Prose Works*, trans. William Ashton Ellis (London, 1893), vol. 2, p. 36, and vol. 3, p. 334.

49 Gregor-Dellin and Mack (eds.), *Cosima Wagner's Diaries*, vol. 1: 1869–1877 (New York and London, 1976), p. 225, entry of 30 May 1870; and vol. 2, p. 557, entry of 11 November 1880.

50 See Gregor-Dellin and Mack (eds.), *Cosima Wagner's Diaries*, vol. 2, pp. 167–8, 254–5, 261–2.

51 Arnold Schoenberg, 'Brahms the Progressive', in *Style and Idea: Selected Writings*

of Arnold Schoenberg, ed. Leonard Stein, trans.
Leo Black (Berkeley, 1984), p. 411.
52 Ibid., p. 412.
53 Ibid., p. 413.
54 Richard Strauss, *Recollections and
Reflections*, ed. Willi Schuh, trans. L. J.
Lawrence (Westport, CT, 1974), pp. 73, 75–6.
For the 'Back to Mozart' movement, see Leon
Botstein, 'Nineteenth-Century Mozart: The
Fin-de-Siècle Mozart Revival', in James M.
Morris (ed.), *On Mozart* (Cambridge, 1994),
pp. 204–5, 208, 215–18, 225; and Seedorf,
*Studien zur kompositorischen Mozart-Rezeption
im frühen 20. Jahrhundert*, pp. 34–6.

14 Mozart and the twentieth century
1 E. F. Benson, *Lucia in London* (first
published London, 1927). There are
numerous editions of this volume, as there
are of all of Benson's popular 'Lucia' novels.
Reference is made here to the Penguin
compendium of the first three, *Lucia Rising*
(Harmondsworth, 1991), p. 721.
2 Ibid., p. 4.
3 See Christina Bashford, 'Varieties of
Childhood: John Ella and the Construction of
a Victorian Mozart', in Dorothea Link (ed.),
Mozart Essays (Woodbridge and Rochester,
NY, forthcoming).
4 Ludwig Nohl, *The Life of Mozart*, trans.
Grace Wallace (London, 1877). In the
translator's preface (p. vi) Wallace anticipates
Benson's Lucia to some extent in describing
Mozart in the following terms: 'He who of all
musicians was the most "heaven-born", and
naturally the most joyous'.
5 Otto Jahn, *The Life of Mozart*, trans. Pauline
D. Townsend (3 vols., London, 1891),
frontispiece.
6 Hendrik Willem van Loon, *Van Loon's Lives*
(London, 1943), pp. 320–52.
7 Ibid., p. 335.
8 Ibid., p. 337.
9 Theodor W. Adorno, *Quasi una Fantasia:
Essays on Modern Music*, trans. Rodney
Livingstone (New York, 1994), p. 45.
10 See Martinů's 'O Dvořákovi' ('About
Dvořák'), a letter addressing the union of
Czechoslovak composers and writers, in
Hudební rozhledy, 7 (1954), p. 267.
11 Quoted in Humphrey Carpenter,
Benjamin Britten: A Biography (London,
1992), p. 196.
12 Ibid.
13 Quoted in ibid., p. 316.
14 Hermann Hesse, *Steppenwolf*, trans. Basil
Creighton, rev. Walter Sorell (London, 1965),
back cover.

15 Ibid., p. 114.
16 Ibid., p. 239.
17 Sacheverell Sitwell, *Mozart* (Edinburgh,
1932).
18 Ibid., pp. 36, 37.
19 Ibid., p. 37.
20 Alfred Einstein, *Mozart: His Character, His
Work*, trans. Arthur Mendel and Nathan
Broder (London and New York, 1945), p. 79.
21 Ibid., p. 80.
22 Gernot Gruber, *Mozart and Posterity*, trans.
R. S. Furness (London, 1991; first published
in German as *Mozart und die Nachwelt*,
Salzburg, 1985).
23 Paul Zschorlich, *Mozart-Heuchelei: Ein
Beitrag zur Kunstgeschichte des 20. Jahrhunderts*
(Leipzig, 1906).
24 Gruber, *Mozart and Posterity*, p. 190.
25 Ibid., p. 191.
26 From Pierre Boulez, *Orientations: Collected
Writings*, ed. Jean-Jacques Nattiez, trans.
Martin Cooper (London, 1986), p. 474.
27 Ludwig Ritter von Köchel,
*Chronologisch-thematisches Verzeichnis
sämtlicher Tonwerke Wolfgang Amadé Mozarts*
(Leipzig, 1862).
28 Köchel's catalogue was revised by Alfred
Einstein in 1937 and reprinted in 1958 and
1963, and published with a supplement in
1947. A further revision by F. Giegling,
A. Weinmann and G. Sievers was published
in 1964 and reprinted in 1965. Additional
corrections and supplements were provided
by P. W. van Reijen in the *Mozart-Jahrbuch
1971/72*, pp. 342–401.
29 Neal Zaslaw (ed.), *Der Neue Köchel*, in
preparation.
30 Ludwig Schiedermair (ed.), *Briefe W. A.
Mozarts und seiner Familie* (Munich and
Leipzig, 1914); this collection includes an
iconography.
31 Emily Anderson (ed. and trans.), *The
Letters of Mozart and His Family* (London,
1938). The edition was revised in 1966 and
further revised in 1985 (*LMF*). Eric Blom
(ed.), *Mozart's Letters* (Harmondsworth,
1956).
32 Ernst Fritz Schmid, Wolfgang Plath and
Wolfgang Rehm (eds.), *W. A. Mozart: Neue
Ausgabe sämtlicher Werke* (Kassel, 1955–).
33 Hermann Abert, *W. A. Mozart: Neu
bearbeitete und erweiterte Ausgabe von Otto
Jahns 'Mozart'* (Leipzig, 1919–21).
34 Marcel Brion, *Daily Life in the Vienna of
Mozart and Schubert*, trans. Jean Stewart
(New York, 1962).
35 Wolfgang Hildesheimer, *Mozart*, trans.
Marion Faber (London and New York, 1983),
p. 7.

36 Ibid., pp. 116ff.

37 Théodore de Wyzewa and Georges de Saint-Foix, *W.-A. Mozart: Sa Vie musicale et son oeuvre*, vols. 1 and 2 (Paris, 1912).

38 Georges de Saint-Foix, *W.-A. Mozart: Sa Vie musicale et son oeuvre*, vols. 3–5 (Paris, 1936–46).

39 Arthur Hutchings, *A Companion to Mozart's Piano Concertos* (London, 1948).

40 Charles Rosen, *The Classical Style* (London and New York, 1971), p. 9.

41 Ibid.

42 See, for example, Elaine R. Sisman, *Mozart: The 'Jupiter' Symphony* (Cambridge, 1993).

43 See Robert Münster, 'Autentische Tempi zu den sechs letzten Sinfonien W. A. Mozarts?', *Mozart-Jahrbuch 1962/63*, pp. 179–94; William Malloch, 'Carl Czerny's Metronome Marks for Haydn and Mozart Symphonies', *EM*, 16 (1988), pp. 72–82.

44 R. Larry Todd and Peter Williams (eds.), *Perspectives on Mozart Performance* (Cambridge, 1991).

45 Neal Zaslaw, *Mozart's Symphonies: Context, Performance Practice, Reception* (Oxford, 1989). The recordings were issued on Decca L'Oiseau-Lyre, 1979–83: D167D3–D170D3, D171D4–D172D4, D173D3.

46 Zaslaw, *Mozart's Symphonies*, p. xii.

47 Possart quoted in Gruber, *Mozart and Posterity*, p. 184.

48 Gruber, *Mozart and Posterity*, pp. 183–4.

49 See Jan Smaczny, *The Daily Repertoire of the Prague Provisional Theatre* (Prague, 1994), p. 117, n. 30, p. 118, n. 26.

50 See Gruber, *Mozart and Posterity*, pp. 185–7.

51 See Edward J. Dent, 'The Modern Cult of Mozart', in *Opera Annual: 1955–6*, ed. Harold Rosenthal (London, 1955), p. 15.

52 See Michael P. Steinberg, *Austria as Theater and Ideology: The Meaning of the Salzburg Festival* (Ithaca and London, 1990), p. 42.

53 Ibid., pp. 42ff.

54 Ibid., pp. 47, 67.

55 Ibid., pp. 216–17, 65.

56 Dent, 'The Modern Cult of Mozart', pp. 15–16.

57 Ibid., p. 17.

58 Andrew Porter, 'Mozart Complete Opera Recordings: A Discography', in *Opera Annual: 1955–6*, ed. Rosenthal, p. 71.

59 Glyndebourne Festival Chorus and Orchestra, conducted by Fritz Busch, Naxos, Great Opera Recordings, 8.110135–37.

60 Bartók edited twenty of the sonatas and the fantasies in C minor, K. 396, and D minor, K. 397.

61 See Malcolm Gillies, 'Bartók and His Music in the 1990s', in Gillies (ed.), *The Bartók Companion* (London, 1993), p. 66.

62 Malcolm Gillies (ed.), *Bartók Remembered* (London, 1990), p. 102.

63 Gillies, 'Bartók and His Music in the 1990s', p. 83.

64 Gillies (ed.), *Bartók Remembered*, p. 136.

65 Igor Stravinsky, *An Autobiography* (New York, 1962), p. 54.

66 See Richard Taruskin, *Text and Act: Essays on Music and Performance* (Oxford and New York, 1995), p. 167.

67 Igor Stravinsky and Robert Craft, *Conversations with Igor Stravinsky* (London, 1958–9), p. 120.

68 See Taruskin, *Text and Act*, pp. 360–7.

69 Todd and Williams (eds.), *Mozart Performance*, p. xii.

70 See Paul Griffiths, *Olivier Messiaen and the Music of Time* (London, 1985), p. 15.

71 Santeri Levas, *Sibelius: A Personal Portrait*, trans. Percy M. Young (London, 1972), p. 60.

72 Quoted in Jerold Northrop Moore, *Edward Elgar: A Creative Life* (Oxford, 1984), p. 80.

73 Quoted in Michael H. Kater, *Composers of the Nazi Era: Eight Portraits* (New York, 2000), p. 269, sourced in turn to Albrecht Riethmüller, *Die Walhalla und ihre Musiker* (Laaber, 1993), p. 27.

74 See Leonard Stein (ed.), *Style and Idea: Selected Writings of Arnold Schoenberg* (New York, 1975), p. 508.

75 Ibid., p. 173.

76 See Humphrey Searle, *Arnold Schoenberg: His Life, World and Work*, trans. Hans Stuckenschmidt (London, 1977), p. 306.

77 Bryan Gilliam (ed.), *Richard Strauss and His World* (Princeton, 1992), p. 194.

78 Ibid., pp. 202, 204.

79 Ibid., p. 204.

80 Kater, *Composers of the Nazi Era*, p. 211.

81 Leon Botstein, 'The Enigmas of Richard Strauss: A Revisionist View', in Gilliam (ed.), *Strauss and His World*, p. 19.

82 See Norman del Mar, *Richard Strauss: A Critical Commentary on His Life and Works* (3 vols., London, 1978), vol. 2, pp. 157–8, 161, 202, 204.

83 See Botstein, 'Enigmas of Richard Strauss', pp. 12–13.

84 Igor Stravinsky and Robert Craft, *Memories and Commentaries* (London, 1959–60), p. 23.

85 Igor Stravinsky and Robert Craft, *Expositions and Developments* (London, 1962), p. 77.

86 See Eric Walter White, *Stravinsky: The Composer and His Works* (London, 1966), pp. 270–1.
87 Quoted in Stephen Walsh, *The Music of Stravinsky* (Oxford, 1988), p. 205, from a letter of 9 November 1947.
88 See White, *Stravinsky*, p. 418.
89 According to White in *Stravinsky*, p. 418.
90 Walsh, *The Music of Stravinsky*, p. 209.
91 Literally so in the case of one T-shirt, designed by J. Vortruba and copyrighted by Fun Explosive, in which, it seems, Mozart's legs stand above a representation of Prague's Baroque architecture.
92 See *Echte Salzburger Mozartkugel: A History*, at: http://www.mozartkugel.at/englisch/links/sortiment/kugel/geschichte.html.
93 Gruber, *Mozart and Posterity*, p. 244.
94 See the exhibition catalogue, *Mozart in Art: 1900–1990* (Stuttgart, 1990), p. 109.
95 Marcia Davenport, *Mozart* (New York, 1979; first published 1932).
96 Ibid., p. 296.
97 Ibid., p. 298–9.
98 For an engagingly contextual consideration of scatology and Mozart's 'Bäsle letters', see David Schroeder, *Mozart in Revolt: Strategies of Resistance, Mischief and Deception* (New Haven and London, 1999), pp. 127–40.
99 Simon Callow, 'Being Mozart', in *Mozart 200*, part 2 (booklet to accompany the bicentenary celebrations of 1991 at the Barbican Centre).
100 See Gruber, *Mozart and Posterity*, p. 242.
101 Russell T. Davis, *Queer as Folk* (Channel 4, 1999), episode 4.
102 Gruber, *Mozart and Posterity*, p. 183.
103 See Taruskin, *Text and Act*, p. 173. For other constructions of Mozart in the late twentieth century, see *Text and Act*, pp. 263–72.

15 The evolution of Mozartian biography

1 Cliff Eisen, *New Mozart Documents: A Supplement to O. E. Deutsch's Documentary Biography* (London and Stanford, 1991).
2 Friedrich Schlichtegroll, 'Johannes Chrysostomos Wolfgang Gottlieb Mozart', in *Nekrolog auf das Jahr 1791* (Gotha, 1793), pp. 82–112.
3 *MDB*, p. 462.
4 Franz Xaver Niemetschek, *Leben des K. K. Kapellmeisters Wolfgang Gottlieb Mozart, nach Originalquellen beschrieben* (Prague, 1798), trans. Helen Mautner as *Life of Mozart* (London, 1956).
5 Maynard Solomon, 'The Rochlitz Anecdotes', in Cliff Eisen (ed.), *Mozart Studies* (Oxford, 1991), pp. 1–59.
6 Georg Nikolaus von Nissen, *Biographie W. A. Mozarts* (Leipzig, 1828).
7 Edward Holmes, *Life of Mozart* (London, 1845).
8 Rosemary Hughes (ed.), *A Mozart Pilgrimage: Being the Travel Diaries of Vincent and Mary Novello in the Year 1829* (London, 1955).
9 Otto Jahn, *W. A. Mozart* (4 vols., Leipzig, 1856).
10 Hermann Abert, *W. A. Mozart: Neu bearbeitete und erweiterte Ausgabe von Otto Jahns 'Mozart'* (Leipzig, 1919–21).
11 Ludwig Schiedermair, *Mozart: Sein Leben und seine Werke* (Munich, 1922).
12 Théodore de Wyzewa and Georges de Saint-Foix, *W.-A. Mozart: Sa Vie musicale et son oeuvre* (5 vols., Paris, 1912–46).
13 Mathilde Ludendorff, *Mozarts Leben und gewaltsamer Tod* (Munich, 1936).
14 G. Duda, *'Den Göttern gegeben': Ein 'Bauopfertod'* (Pähl, 1994).
15 Francis Carr, *Mozart and Constanze* (London, 1983).
16 Otto Erich Deutsch, 'Die Legende von Mozarts Vergiftung', *Mozart-Jahrbuch 1964*, pp. 7–18; William Stafford, *Mozart's Death: A Corrective Survey of the Legends* (London, 1991).
17 Aloys Greither, 'Noch einmal: Woran ist Mozart gestorben?', *Mitteilungen der Internationalen Stiftung Mozarteum*, 19/3–4 (1971), pp. 25–7; Peter J. Davies, 'Mozart's Illnesses and Death', *MT*, 125 (1984), pp. 437–41, 554–61.
18 Carl Bär, *Mozart: Krankheit – Tod – Begräbnis* (Salzburg, 1967).
19 Arthur Schurig, *Wolfgang Amadeus Mozart: Sein Leben und sein Werk* (Leipzig, 1913); Alfred Einstein, *Mozart: His Character, His Work*, trans. Arthur Mendel and Nathan Broder (London and New York, 1945).
20 Uwe Kraemer, 'Wer hat Mozart verhungern lassen?', *Musica*, 30 (1976), pp. 75–84.
21 H. C. Robbins Landon, *1791: Mozart's Last Year* (London, 1988).
22 Volkmar Braunbehrens, *Mozart in Vienna, 1781–1791*, trans. Timothy Bell (New York, 1989); Julia Moore, 'Mozart in the Market-Place', *JRMA*, 114 (1989), pp. 18–42.
23 Jean Massin and Brigitte Massin, *Wolfgang Amadeus Mozart* (Paris, 1959); Georg Knepler, *Wolfgang Amadé Mozart*, trans. J. Bradford Robinson (Cambridge, 1994).

24 Heinz Schuler, *Mozart und die Freimaurerei* (Wilhelmshaven, 1992).

25 Adolphe Boschot, *Mozart* (Paris, 1935).

26 Eduard Mörike, *Mozart auf der Reise nach Prag* (Stuttgart, 1856), trans. Leopold von Loewenstein-Wertheim as *Mozart's Journey to Prague* (London, 1957).

27 E. T. A. Hoffmann, 'Don Juan', 'Kreisleriana', in *Fantasiestücke in Callots Manier* (Bamberg, 1814).

28 Alfred Heuss, 'Das dämonische Element in Mozarts Werken', *Zeitschrift der Internationalen Musikgesellschaft*, 5 (1906–7), pp. 175–86.

29 Wolfgang Hildesheimer, *Mozart*, trans. Marion Faber (London and New York, 1983).

30 Neal Zaslaw, 'Mozart as Working Stiff', in James M. Morris (ed.), *On Mozart* (Cambridge, 1994), pp. 102–12.

31 Konrad Küster, *Mozart: A Musical Biography*, trans. Mary Whittall (Oxford, 1996).

32 Brigid Brophy, *Mozart the Dramatist: A New View of Mozart, His Operas and His Age* (London, 1964); Maynard Solomon, *Mozart: A Life* (New York, 1995).

33 Ruth Halliwell, *The Mozart Family: Four Lives in a Social Context* (Oxford, 1998).

34 Wolfgang Plath, 'Beiträge zur Mozart-Autographie II: Schriftchronologie 1770–1780', *Mozart-Jahrbuch 1976/77*, pp. 131–73; Alan Tyson, *Mozart: Studies of the Autograph Scores* (Cambridge, MA, and London, 1987); John Arthur, 'Some Chronological Problems in Mozart: The Contribution of Ink-Studies', in Stanley Sadie (ed.), *Wolfgang Amadè Mozart: Essays on His Life and His Music* (Oxford, 1996), pp. 35–52.

35 For example, Dexter Edge, 'Mozart's Reception in Vienna, 1787–1791', in Sadie (ed.), *Wolfgang Amadè Mozart*, pp. 66–117.

36 Robert W. Gutman, *Mozart: A Cultural Biography* (New York, 1999).

37 Nicholas Till, *Mozart and the Enlightenment: Truth, Virtue and Beauty in Mozart's Operas* (London, 1992).

38 David Schroeder, *Mozart in Revolt: Strategies of Resistance, Mischief and Deception* (New Haven and London, 1999).

39 Georges Favier, *Vie de W. A. Mozart par Franz Xaver Niemetschek précédée du nécrologe de Schlichtegroll* (St-Etienne, 1976); Solomon, 'The Rochlitz Anecdotes'; Bruce Cooper Clarke, 'Albert von Mölk: Mozart Myth-Maker? Study of an Eighteenth-Century Correspondence', *Mozart-Jahrbuch 1995*, pp. 155–91; Halliwell, *Mozart Family*.

40 Stanley Sadie, *The New Grove Mozart* (London, 1982).

16 Mozart the performer

1 *LMF*, p. 47.

2 Remembered by Leopold Mozart in a letter of 7 December 1780; ibid., p. 683.

3 Letter of 11 June 1763; ibid., p. 20.

4 Letter of 16 October 1762; ibid., p. 5.

5 Letter of 18 October 1777; ibid., p. 331.

6 Letter of 6 October 1777; ibid., p. 300.

7 Letter of 23 October 1777; ibid., p. 338.

8 *MDL*, p. 456; *MDB*, pp. 531–2.

9 For details, see Ian Woodfield, 'New Light on the Mozarts' London Visit: A Private Concert with Manzuoli', *ML*, 76 (1995), pp. 187–207.

10 *MDL*, p. 88; *MDB*, p. 96.

11 *MDL*, p. 56; *MDB*, p. 57.

12 *MDL*, p. 86; *MDB*, p. 94 (translation slightly adapted). See also Christoph-Hellmut Mahling, ' "... new and altogether special and astonishingly difficult": Some Comments on Junia's Aria in *Lucio Silla*', in Stanley Sadie (ed.), *Wolfgang Amadè Mozart: Essays on His Life and His Music* (Oxford, 1996), pp. 377–9.

13 *MDL*, p. 96; *MDB*, p. 106.

14 *MDB*, p. 107.

15 Letter of 28 December 1777; *LMF*, p. 436.

16 Letter of 23 October 1777; ibid., p. 340.

17 Letter of 23 October 1777; ibid., p. 339.

18 Letter of 8 November 1777; ibid., p. 363.

19 *MDB*, p. 519.

20 Letter of 2 June 1781; *LMF*, p. 739.

21 All data in this table is taken from Mary Sue Morrow, *Concert Life in Haydn's Vienna: Aspects of a Developing Musical and Social Institution* (Stuyvesant, NY, 1988), pp. 237–384.

22 Letter of 16 February 1785; *LMF*, p. 886.

23 Ibid.

24 See details in Katalin Komlós, ' "Ich praeludirte und spielte Variazionen": Mozart the Fortepianist', in R. Larry Todd and Peter Williams (eds.), *Perspectives on Mozart Performance* (Cambridge, 1991), pp. 31–42.

25 Mary Sue Morrow, 'Mozart and Viennese Concert Life', *MT*, 126 (1985), pp. 453–4; Morrow, *Concert Life in Haydn's Vienna*, pp. 234–5; Dexter Edge, 'Mozart's Reception in Vienna, 1787–1791', in Sadie (ed.), *Wolfgang Amadè Mozart*, pp. 66–117.

26 H. C. Robbins Landon, *1791: Mozart's Last Year* (London, 1988), pp. 31–3.

27 *LMF*, p. 946.

28 Quoted in Morrow, *Concert Life in Haydn's Vienna*, p. 11.

29 *MDB*, p. 519.

30 Siegbert Rampe, *Mozarts Claviermusik: Klangwelt und Aufführungspraxis* (Kassel, 1995), p. 88.

31 Letter of 13 November 1777; *LMF*, p. 370.

32 Letter of 31 October 1783; ibid., p. 859.

33 Letter of 23 October 1777; ibid., p. 340.

34 Letters of 23 October and 16 October 1777; ibid., pp. 339 and 322.

35 See further in Komlós, 'Mozart the Fortepianist', pp. 52–3.

36 Letter of 1 May 1778; *LMF*, p. 532.

37 Letter of 8 April 1781; ibid., p. 722.

38 Letter of 16 January 1782; ibid., p. 793.

39 Letter of 20 February 1784; ibid., p. 867.

40 Letter of 6 December 1777; ibid., p. 408.

17 Performance practice in the music of Mozart

I would like to express my thanks to Cliff Eisen for his permission to include materials here that were drawn up for our Breitkopf and Härtel edition, *Mozart: Konzert für Klavier und Orchester ('Jeunehomme'), Es-dur, KV 271* (Wiesbaden, 2001).

1 Leopold Mozart, *Versuch einer gründlichen Violinschule* (Augsburg, 1756); trans. Editha Knocker as *A Treatise on the Fundamental Principles of Violin Playing* (Oxford, 1948). Carl Philipp Emanuel Bach, *Versuch über die wahre Art das Clavier zu spielen* (Berlin, 1753); trans. William J. Mitchell as *Essay on the True Art of Playing Keyboard Instruments* (New York, 1949). Johann Joachim Quantz, *Versuch einer Anweisung die Flöte traversière zu spielen* (Berlin, 1752); trans. Edward R. Reilly as *On Playing the Flute* (New York, 1975). Daniel Gottlob Türk, *Klavierschule* (Leipzig, 1789); trans. Raymond H. Haggh as *School of Clavier Playing* (Lincoln, NE, 1982). Among the important twentieth-century treatises are Paul and Eva Badura-Skoda, *Mozart-Interpretation* (Vienna, 1957); trans. Leo Black as *Interpreting Mozart on the Keyboard* (New York, 1962). Frederick Neumann, *Ornamentation and Improvisation in Mozart* (Princeton, 1986). Sandra P. Rosenblum, *Performance Practices in Classic Piano Music: Their Principles and Applications* (Indianapolis, 1988).

2 For more details, see Rosenblum, *Classic Piano Music*, chapter 10, pp. 362–80.

3 Letter of 23–5 October 1777; *LMF*, p. 340.

4 See, for instance, bars 62–8 of the first movement of the Piano Sonata in G major, K. 283. I would like to thank Malcolm Bilson for pointing out this example.

5 For *dolce* as a dynamic as well as a character prescription, see Robert D. Levin, 'The Devil's in the Details: Neglected Aspects of Mozart's Piano Concertos', in Neal Zaslaw

(ed.), *Mozart's Piano Concertos: Text, Context, Interpretation* (Ann Arbor, MI, 1996), p. 32–5.

6 See, for example, the Piano Concerto in E flat major, K. 271/i, bars 83–4, 86, 212–13, 215.

7 For a recent presentation of both sides of this argument, including extensive accounts of the literature, see Frederick Neumann, 'Dots and Strokes in Mozart', *EM*, 21 (1993), pp. 429–35, and Clive Brown, 'Dots and Strokes in Late Eighteenth- and Nineteenth-Century Music', *EM*, 21 (1993), pp. 593–610.

8 See, for example, the Rondo in D major for Piano and Orchestra, K. 382.

9 Leopold Mozart, *Fundamental Principles of Violin Playing*, p. 136.

10 Ibid., p. 166. It is worth noting, however, that the examples in this treatise frequently dispense with slurs from grace notes to main notes.

11 The standard correction is to raise the first violin a third, as this is the voice leading used by the solo keyboard later in the movement; but as the second violin was not notated until the second phase it could be argued that Mozart's original intention was for the seconds to play a sixth below the firsts.

12 The complete embellished version appears in the *Neue Mozart-Ausgabe*, II/7 (arias), vol. 2, pp. 151–66. Neumann gives the complete embellished and original vocal lines without the accompaniment in *Ornamentation and Improvisation*, pp. 235–8. The embellished version consists of two sheets. The first, comprising the A section of the aria, apparently dates from the time of composition (1778); the second, containing the reprise of the A section, probably dates from 1783. The structure of the aria was modified at the time of the revival. Mozart also embellished the aria 'Ah se a morir mi chiama il fato mio crudele' (No. 14) from *Lucio Silla*, K. 135 (*Neue Mozart-Ausgabe*, II/5, vol. 7, part 2, pp. 471–84; the two versions of the solo vocal part are given in Neumann, *Ornamentation and Improvisation*, pp. 231–33), and arias by Johann Christian Bach and Antonio Sacchini. A number of his vocal cadenzas are collected in the sixth edition of the Köchel catalogue under the number K. 293e, to appear in the *Neue Mozart-Ausgabe*, X/28, Abt. 3–5, part 2: *Sonstige Bearbeitungen und Kopien*. (My thanks to Dr Faye Ferguson of the *Neue Mozart-Ausgabe* for this information.)

13 See Robert D. Levin, 'K. 488: Mozart's Third Concerto for Barbara Ployer?' in

Mozartiana: Festschrift for the Seventieth Birthday of Professor Ebisawa Bin (2001), pp. 555–70. Ployer's embellishment is reproduced in the critical report for this concerto in the *Neue Mozart-Ausgabe* (V/15, vol. 7), prepared by Hermann Beck. It appears in a diplomatic version with an additional staff that rationalizes the rhythms (excerpted in example 17.3 in the present chapter), as well as in facsimile.

14 In piano concertos a dominant-seventh chord is played under the trill by the left hand. In string concertos the soloist can create the chord through multiple stops. For wind instruments, brass instruments and the voice, the chord is implied.

15 See also the cadenzas cited in note 20 below.

16 Giambattista Mancini, however, advocates motivic citation. See Mancini, *Pensieri, e riflessioni pratiche sopra il canto figurato* (Vienna, 1774), p. 124.

17 See the later of the two cadenzas to K. 271/i, bars 20–9.

18 Türk, *School of Clavier Playing*, pp. 298–301. Türk's, examples and discussion of poor cadenzas on pp. 304–7 are illuminating and amusing.

19 Neumann, *Ornamentation and Improvisation*, pp. 218–27.

20 Indeed, the first-movement cadenza to the Piano Concerto in A major, K. 488, uses none of the many memorable themes of that movement; for the origin of the quotation at the beginning of the cadenza, see note 13 above. For general precepts of vocal cadenza construction, see Johann Adam Hiller, *Anweisung zum musikalisch-zierlichen Gesange* (Leipzig, 1780), pp. 108–28; Mancini, *Pensieri, e riflessioni pratiche sopra il canto figurato*, pp. 122–9. For discussion in twentieth-century treatises, see Badura-Skoda, *Interpreting Mozart on the Keyboard*, pp. 214–34; Robert D. Levin, 'Instrumental Ornamentation, Improvisation and Cadenzas', in Howard Mayer Brown and Stanley Sadie (eds.), *Performance Practice: Music after 1600* (London, 1989), pp. 267–91, especially pp. 279–87, for instrumental cadenzas; Will Crutchfield, 'The Classical Era: Voices', in Brown and Sadie (eds.), *Performance Practice*, pp. 292–319, for vocal cadenzas.

21 See the Broekmans and van Poppel editions of K. 466 and 491 (Amsterdam, 1959), and K. 467, 503, 482 and 537 (Amsterdam, 1964). In addition, Flothuis

composed cadenzas for the Concerto for Flute and Harp, K. 299, and for the violin concertos K. 211, 216, 218 and 219.

22 Robert D. Levin, *Mozart: Kadenzen zu Mozarts Violinkonzerten* (Vienna, 1992). This contains two versions with combinatorial possibilities for all cadenzas and lead-ins in the concertos K. 207, 211, 216, 218 and 219. Similar cadenzas and lead-ins have been published by G. Henle for the flute concertos K. 313 (673) and 314 (674), for the Andante in C major, K. 315 (675), and for the Oboe Concerto, K. 314 (695), the horn concertos K. 447 (703) and 495 (in press), and the Concerto for Flute and Harp, K. 299 (in press). Cadenzas and lead-ins to numerous arias remain unpublished.

23 See Leopold Mozart, *Fundamental Principles of Violin Playing*, pp. 246, 179; quoted in Robin Stowell, 'The Classical Era: Strings', in Brown and Sadie (eds.), *Performance Practice*, p. 245.

24 Stowell, 'Strings', pp. 239–51.

25 Stowell, 'Strings', p. 247.

26 Ibid., p. 248.

27 See Daniel N. Leeson and Robert D. Levin, 'Mozart's Deliberate Use of Incorrect Key Signatures for Clarinets', *Mozart-Jahrbuch 1998*, pp. 139–52.

28 David Charlton, 'The Classical Era: Woodwind and Brass', in Brown and Sadie (eds.), *Performing Practice*, pp. 252–66.

29 The concertos K. 175, 238 and 246 are effective on the harpsichord, and K. 175 could conceivably have been intended for organ. (Its top note is d''' and the treatment of the lower bass range is congruent with the epistle sonatas for organ.) The Concerto for Three Keyboards, K. 242 (1776), contains dynamics, including numerous occurrences of *fp* as well as *crescendo*, thereby implying performance with pianos.

30 See the Sonata in D major, K. 311/ii, bars 86–90. More generally, see David Rowland, *A History of Pianoforte Pedalling* (Cambridge, 1993).

31 Crutchfield, 'Voices', in Brown and Sadie (eds.), *Performing Practice*, pp. 295–6.

32 Ibid., p. 295.

33 Cliff Eisen, 'Mozart's Salzburg Orchestras', *EM*, 21 (1992), pp. 89–104.

34 *LMF*, pp. 526–7; *MBA*, vol. 2, p. 338.

35 *LMF*, p. 724; *MBA*, vol. 3, p. 106.

36 Cliff Eisen, 'The Orchestral Bass Part in Mozart's Salzburg Piano Concertos: The Evidence of the Authentic Copies', in

Zaslaw (ed.), *Mozart's Piano Concertos*, pp. 411–26.

37 James Webster, 'The Bass Part in Haydn's Early String Quartets and in Austrian Chamber Music, 1750–1780' (Ph.D. dissertation, Princeton University, 1973); Webster, 'Violoncello and Double Bass in the Chamber Music of Haydn and His Viennese Contemporaries, 1750–1780', *JAMS*, 29 (1976), pp. 413–39; Webster, 'The Scoring of Mozart's Chamber Music for Strings', in Allan W. Atlas (ed.), *Music in the Classic Period: Essays in Honor of Barry S. Brook* (Stuyvesant, NY, 1985), pp. 259–96; Wolf-Dieter Seiffert, *Mozarts frühe Streichquartette* (Munich, 1992).

Selected further reading

The secondary literature on Mozart is vast. The following citations – taken for the most part from readily available sources – represent a diverse range of starting points for those wishing to pursue specific interests. Subsections in 'Secondary literature on specialized topics' correspond to the topics of chapters in this volume. Although each source is listed once only, in the subsection in which it is likely to prove most relevant, many writings will clearly be of interest to readers in several areas. Readers are therefore encouraged to survey the bibliography in its entirety, rather than limiting their line of enquiry to literature listed under a single topic.

Reference works

Anderson, Emily (ed. and trans.). *The Letters of Mozart and His Family*, 3rd edn, London, Macmillan, 1985. (*LMF*)

Bauer, Wilhelm, Otto Erich Deutsch and Joseph Eibl (eds.). *Mozart: Briefe und Aufzeichnungen, Gesamtausgabe*, 7 vols., Kassel, Bärenreiter, 1962–75. (*MBA*)

Caplin, William E. *Classical Form: A Theory of Formal Functions for the Instrumental Music of Haydn, Mozart and Beethoven*, New York, Oxford University Press, 1998.

Clive, Peter. *Mozart and His Circle: A Biographical Dictionary*, New Haven and London, Yale University Press, 1993.

Deutsch, Otto Erich. *Mozart: Die Dokumente seines Lebens*, Kassel, Bärenreiter, 1961 (*MDL*); trans. Eric Blom, Peter Branscombe and Jeremy Noble as *Mozart: A Documentary Biography*, Stanford and London, Stanford University Press, 1965 (paperback edn London, Simon and Schuster, 1990). (*MDB*)

Eisen, Cliff. *New Mozart Documents: A Supplement to O. E. Deutsch's Documentary Biography*, London and Stanford, Stanford University Press, 1991.

Halliwell, Ruth. *The Mozart Family: Four Lives in a Social Context*, Oxford, Clarendon Press, 1998.

Heartz, Daniel. *Haydn, Mozart, and the Viennese School, 1740–1780*, New York, Norton, 1995.

Köchel, Ludwig Ritter von. *Chronologisch-thematisches Verzeichnis sämtlicher Tonwerke Wolfgang Amadé Mozarts*, eds. F. Giegling, A. Weinmann and G. Sievers, 6th edn, Leipzig, Breitkopf and Härtel, 1964.

Küster, Konrad. *Mozart: A Musical Biography*, trans. Mary Whittall, Oxford, Clarendon Press, 1996.

Landon, H. C. Robbins (ed.). *The Mozart Compendium: A Guide to Mozart's Life and Music*, London, Thames and Hudson, 1990.

Marshall, Robert L. (ed.). *Mozart Speaks: Views on Music, Musicians and the World*, New York, Schirmer, 1991.

Ratner, Leonard G. *Classic Music: Expression, Form, and Style*, New York, Schirmer, 1980.

Rosen, Charles. *The Classical Style: Haydn, Mozart, Beethoven*, London and New York, Norton, 1971 (expanded edn New York, Norton, 1997).

Spaethling, Robert (ed. and trans.). *Mozart's Letters, Mozart's Life*, New York, Norton, 2000.

Tyson, Alan, and Albi Rosenthal (eds.). *Mozart's Thematic Catalogue*, Ithaca and London, Cornell University Press, 1990.

Zaslaw, Neal, and William Cowdery (eds.). *The Compleat Mozart*, New York, Norton, 1990.

Secondary literature on specialized topics
Mozart in context
Mozart and Salzburg

Birsak, Kurt, and Manfred König. *Das grosse Salzburger Blasmusik mit Ehrentafeln der Salzburger Blasmusikkapellen*, Vienna, Brandstatter, 1983.

Dahms, Sibylle. 'Das musikalische Repertoire des Salzburger Fürsterzbischöflichen Hoftheaters (1775–1803)', *Österreichische Musikzeitschrift*, 31 (1976), pp. 340–55.

Dopsch, Heinz (ed.). *Geschichte Salzburgs: Stadt und Land*, vol. 2, Salzburg, Universitätsverlag Pustet, 1983.

Eisen, Cliff. 'The Mozarts' Salzburg Copyists: Aspects of Attribution, Chronology, Text, Style, and Performance Practice', in Cliff Eisen (ed.), *Mozart Studies*, Oxford, Clarendon Press, 1991, pp. 253–307.

'Mozart's Salzburg Orchestras', *EM*, 20 (1992), pp. 89–103.

'The Mozarts' Salzburg Music Library', in Cliff Eisen (ed.), *Mozart Studies 2*, Oxford, Clarendon Press, 1997, pp. 85–138.

Hintermaier, Ernst. 'Die Salzburger Hofkapelle von 1700 bis 1806: Organisation und Personal', Ph.D. dissertation, University of Salzburg, 1972.

Schmid, Manfred Hermann. *Mozart und die Salzburger Tradition*, Tutzing, Hans Schneider, 1976.

Mozart in Vienna

Biba, Otto. 'Die Wiener Kirchenmusik um 1783', in *Beiträge zur Musikgeschichte des 18. Jahrhunderts, Jahrbuch für Österreichische Kulturgeschichte*, 1/2 (Eisenstadt, 1971), pp. 7–67.

'Historical Background: Church and State', in H. C. Robbins Landon (ed.), *The Mozart Compendium: A Guide to Mozart's Life and Music*, London, Thames and Hudson, 1990, pp. 58–61.

Brauneis, Walter. ' "... wegen schuldigen 1435 f 32 xr": Neuer Archivfund zur Finanzmisere Mozarts im November 1791', *Mitteilungen der Internationalen Stiftung Mozarteum*, 39 (1991), pp. 159–63.

Edge, Dexter. 'Mozart's Fee for *Così fan tutte*', *JRMA*, 116 (1991), pp. 212–35.

'Review Article: Mary Sue Morrow, *Concert Life in Haydn's Vienna*', *Haydn Yearbook*, 17 (1992), pp. 108–66.

'Mozart's Reception in Vienna, 1787–1791', in Stanley Sadie (ed.), *Wolfgang Amadè Mozart: Essays on His Life and His Music*, Oxford, Clarendon Press, 1996, pp. 66–117.

Hamann, Heinz Wolfgang. 'Mozarts Schülerkreis: Versuch einer chronologischen Ordnung', *Mozart-Jahrbuch 1962/63*, pp. 115–39.

Link, Dorothea. 'Vienna's Private Theatrical and Musical Life, 1783–92, as Reported by Count Karl Zinzendorf', *JRMA*, 122 (1997), pp. 205–33.
The National Court Theatre in Mozart's Vienna: Sources and Documents 1783–1792, Oxford, Clarendon Press, 1998.

Moore, Julia. 'Mozart in the Marketplace', *JRMA*, 114 (1989), pp. 19–42.
'Beethoven and Inflation', *Beethoven Forum*, 1 (1992), pp. 191–223.

Morrow, Mary Sue. *Concert Life in Haydn's Vienna: Aspects of a Developing Musical and Social Institution*, Stuyvesant, NY, Pendragon Press, 1988.

Rice, John. *Antonio Salieri and Viennese Opera*, University of Chicago Press, 1998.

Ridgewell, Rupert. 'Mozart's Publishing Plans with Artaria in 1787: New Archival Evidence', *ML*, 83 (2002), pp. 30–74.

Mozart's compositional methods

Arthur, John. 'Some Chronological Problems in Mozart: The Contribution of Ink-Studies', in Stanley Sadie (ed.), *Wolfgang Amadè Mozart: Essays on His Life and His Music*, Oxford, Clarendon Press, 1996, pp. 35–52.

Brandenburg, Sieghard (ed.). *Haydn, Mozart, and Beethoven: Studies in the Music of the Classical Period*, Oxford, Clarendon Press, 1998.

Hertzmann, Erich. 'Mozart's Creative Process', in Paul Henry Lang (ed.), *The Creative World of Mozart*, New York, Norton, 1963, pp. 17–30.

Konrad, Ulrich. *Mozarts Schaffensweise: Studien zu den Werkautographen, Skizzen und Entwürfen*, Göttingen, Vandenhoeck und Ruprecht, 1992.
'Mozart's Sketches', *EM*, 20 (1992), pp. 119–30.

Plath, Wolfgang. 'Beiträge zur Mozart-Autographie I: Die Handschrift Leopold Mozarts', *Mozart-Jahrbuch 1960/61*, pp. 82–117.
'Beiträge zur Mozart-Autographie II: Schriftchronologie 1770–1780', *Mozart-Jahrbuch 1976/77*, pp. 131–73.

Somfai, László. 'Sketches during the Process of Composition: Studies of K. 504 and K. 414', in Stanley Sadie (ed.), *Wolfgang Amadè Mozart: Essays on His Life and His Music*, Oxford, Clarendon Press, 1996, pp. 53–65.

Tyson, Alan. *Mozart: Studies of the Autograph Scores*, Cambridge, MA, and London, Harvard University Press, 1987.

Wolff, Christoph (ed.). *The String Quartets of Haydn, Mozart and Beethoven: Studies of the Autograph Manuscripts*, Cambridge, MA, Harvard University Department of Music, 1980.

Aesthetics

Blackall, Eric. *The Emergence of German as a Literary Language*, Cambridge University Press, 1959.

Bonds, Mark Evan. *Wordless Rhetoric: Musical Form and the Metaphor of the Oration*, Cambridge, MA, Harvard University Press, 1991.

Kann, Robert A. *A Study in Austrian Intellectual History*, New York, Frederick A. Praeger, 1960.

Levey, Michael. *The Life and Death of Mozart*, London, Sphere Books, 1973.

Mack, Joseph. *Die Reform- und Aufklärungsbestrebungen im Erzstift Salzburg unter Erzbischof Hieronymous von Colloredo*, Munich, O. Böck, 1912.

Mančal, Josef. 'Neues über Leopold Mozart', *Österreichische Musikzeitschrift*, 42 (1987), pp. 282–91.

  'Zum Verhältnis Leopold Mozarts zu Wolfgang "Amadé" Mozart: Prolegomena zur Strukturbestimmung einer personalen Beziehung und der Wirklichkeitorganisation im Zeitalter der Absolutismus und der Aufklärung', *Zeitschrift des Historischen Vereins für Schwaben*, 84 (1991), pp. 191–245; 85 (1992), pp. 233–71.

Schroeder, David. *Mozart in Revolt: Strategies of Resistance, Mischief and Deception*, New Haven and London, Yale University Press, 1999.

Schurig, Arthur. *Wolfgang Amadeus Mozart*, Leipzig, Insel-Verlag, 1913.

Stafford, William. *The Mozart Myths: A Critical Reassessment*, Stanford University Press, 1991.

The works

Keyboard music

Allanbrook, Wye J. 'Two Threads through the Labyrinth: Topic and Process in the First Movements of K. 332 and K. 333', in Wye J. Allanbrook, Janet M. Levy and William P. Mahrt (eds.), *Convention in Eighteenth- and Nineteenth-Century Music: Essays in Honor of Leonard G. Ratner*, Stuyvesant, NY, Pendragon, 1992, pp. 125–71.

Bilson, Malcolm. 'Execution and Expression in the Sonata in E flat, K282', *EM*, 20 (1992), pp. 237–43.

Eisen, Cliff, and Christopher Wintle. 'Mozart's C minor Fantasy, K. 475: An Editorial "Problem" and Its Analytical and Critical Consequences', *JRMA*, 124 (1999), pp. 26–52.

Irving, John. *Mozart's Piano Sonatas: Contexts, Sources, Style*, Cambridge University Press, 1997.

Komlós, Katalin. *Fortepianos and Their Music: Germany, Austria and England, 1760–1800*, Oxford, Clarendon Press, 1995.

Levin, Robert. 'Mozart's Solo Keyboard Music', in Robert L. Marshall (ed.), *Eighteenth-Century Keyboard Music*, New York, Schirmer, 1994, pp. 308–49.

Mercado, Mario R. *The Evolution of Mozart's Pianistic Style*, Carbondale, Southern Illinois University Press, 1992.

Ratner, Leonard G. 'Topical Content in Mozart's Keyboard Sonatas', *EM*, 19 (1991), pp. 615–19.

Smallman, Basil. *The Piano Trio*, Oxford, Clarendon Press, 1990.

Somfai, Lászlo. 'Mozart's First Thoughts: The Two Versions of the Sonata in D major, K284', *EM*, 19 (1991), pp. 601–14.

Concertos

Berger, Karol. 'Toward a History of Hearing: The Classic Concerto, a Sample
 Case', in Wye J. Allanbrook, Janet M. Levy and William P. Mahrt (eds.),
 *Convention in Eighteenth- and Nineteenth-Century Music: Essays in Honor of
 Leonard Ratner*, Stuyvesant, NY, Pendragon, 1992, pp. 405–29.
Blume, Friedrich. 'The Concertos: (1) Their Sources', in H. C. Robbins Landon
 and Donald Mitchell (eds.), *The Mozart Companion*, London, Rockliff, 1956,
 pp. 200–33.
Ferguson, Linda Faye. 'The Classical Concerto: Some Thoughts on Authentic
 Performance', *EM*, 12 (1984), pp. 437–45.
Girdlestone, Cuthbert. *Mozart and His Piano Concertos*, New York, Dover, 1964
 (first published London, Cassell, 1948).
Grayson, David. *Mozart: Piano Concertos No. 20 in D Minor, K. 466, and No. 21 in C
 Major, K. 467*, Cambridge University Press, 1998.
Hutchings, Arthur. *A Companion to Mozart's Piano Concertos*, Oxford University
 Press, 1991 (first published London, Oxford University Press, 1948).
Keefe, Simon P. 'A Complementary Pair: Stylistic Experimentation in Mozart's
 Final Piano Concertos, K. 537 in D and K. 595 in B♭', *JM*, 18 (2001),
 pp. 658–84.
 ' "An Entirely Special Manner": Mozart's Piano Concerto No. 14 in E flat
 K. 449 and the Stylistic Implications of Confrontation', *ML*, 82 (2001),
 pp. 559–81.
 Mozart's Piano Concertos: Dramatic Dialogue in the Age of Enlightenment,
 Woodbridge and Rochester, NY, The Boydell Press, 2001.
Keller, Hans. 'K. 503: The Unity of Contrasting Themes and Movements', *Music
 Review*, 17 (1956), pp. 48–58, 120–9.
Kerman, Joseph. 'Mozart's Piano Concertos and Their Audience', in James M.
 Morris (ed.), *On Mozart*, Cambridge University Press, 1994, pp. 151–68.
Landon, H. C. Robbins. 'The Concertos: (2) Their Musical Origin and
 Development', in H. C. Robbins Landon and Donald Mitchell (eds.),
 The Mozart Companion, London, Rockliff, 1956, pp. 234–82.
Lawson, Colin. *Mozart: Clarinet Concerto*, Cambridge University Press, 1996.
McClary, Susan. 'A Musical Dialectic from the Enlightenment: Mozart's *Piano
 Concerto in G Major, K. 453*, Movement 2', *Cultural Critique*, 5 (1986),
 pp. 129–69.
Zaslaw, Neal (ed.). *Mozart's Piano Concertos: Text, Context, Interpretation*, Ann
 Arbor, University of Michigan Press, 1996.

Orchestral music

Blazin, Dwight. 'The Two Versions of Mozart's Divertimento K. 113', *ML*, 73
 (1992), pp. 32–47.
Eisen, Cliff. 'The Symphonies of Leopold Mozart: Their Chronology, Style and
 Importance for the Study of Mozart's Early Symphonies', in *Mozart-Jahrbuch
 1987/88*, pp. 181–93.
 'New Light on Mozart's "Linz" Symphony, K. 425', *JRMA*, 113 (1988),
 pp. 81–96.

'The Salzburg Symphonies: A Biographical Interpretation', in Stanley Sadie (ed.), *Wolfgang Amadè Mozart: Essays on His Life and His Music*, Oxford, Clarendon Press, 1996, pp. 178–212.

Kearns, Andrew. 'The Orchestral Serenade in Eighteenth-Century Salzburg', *JMR*, 16 (1997), pp. 163–97.

Sisman, Elaine R. *Mozart: The 'Jupiter' Symphony*, Cambridge University Press, 1993.

'Genre, Gesture, and Meaning in Mozart's "Prague" Symphony', in Cliff Eisen (ed.), *Mozart Studies 2*, Oxford, Clarendon Press, 1997, pp. 27–84.

Subotnik, Rose Rosengard. 'Evidence of a Critical World View in Mozart's Last Three Symphonies', in her *Developing Variations: Style and Ideology in Western Music*, Minneapolis, University of Minnesota Press, 1991, pp. 98–111.

Zaslaw, Neal. *Mozart's Symphonies: Context, Performance Practice, Reception*, Oxford, Clarendon Press, 1989.

'Mozart's Orchestral Flutes and Oboes', in Cliff Eisen (ed.), *Mozart Studies*, Oxford, Clarendon Press, 1991, pp. 201–11.

Chamber music

Agawu, V. Kofi. *Playing with Signs: A Semiotic Interpretation of Classic Music*, Princeton University Press, 1991.

Allanbrook, Wye J. ' "To serve the private pleasure": Expression and Form in the String Quartets', in Stanley Sadie (ed.), *Wolfgang Amadè Mozart: Essays on His Life and His Music*, Oxford, Clarendon Press, 1996, pp. 132–60.

Brown, A. Peter. 'Haydn and Mozart's 1773 Stay in Vienna: Weeding a Musicological Garden', *JM*, 10 (1992), pp. 192–230.

Eisen, Cliff, and Wolf-Dieter Seiffert (eds.). *Mozarts Streichquintette: Beiträge zum musikalischen Satz, zum Gattungskontext und zu Quellenfragen*, Stuttgart, Steiner, 1994.

Hellyer, Roger. 'Mozart's Harmoniemusik', *Music Review*, 34 (1973), pp. 146–56.

Irving, John. *Mozart: The 'Haydn' Quartets*, Cambridge University Press, 1998.

Keefe, Simon P. 'An Integrated "Dissonance": Mozart's "Haydn" Quartets and the Slow Introduction of K. 465', *Mozart-Jahrbuch 2002*, pp. 87–103.

Maguerre, Kurt. 'Mozarts Klaviertrios', *Mozart-Jahrbuch 1960/61*, pp. 182–94.

Seiffert, Wolf-Dieter. 'Mozart's "Haydn" Quartets: An Evaluation of the Autographs and First Edition, with Particular Attention to mm. 125–42 of the Finale of K. 387', in Cliff Eisen (ed.), *Mozart Studies 2*, Oxford, Clarendon Press, 1997, pp. 175–200.

Vertrees, Julie Anne. 'Mozart's String Quartet K. 465: The History of a Controversy', *Current Musicology*, 17 (1974), pp. 96–114.

Webster, James. 'Towards a History of Viennese Chamber Music in the Early Classical Period', *JAMS*, 27 (1974), pp. 212–47.

Vocal music

Baird, Julianne C. (ed. and trans.). *Introduction to the Art of Singing by Johann Friedrich Agricola* (1757), Cambridge University Press, 1995.

Biba, Otto. 'Mozarts Wiener Kirchenmusikkompositionen', in Ingrid Fuchs (ed.), *Internationaler Musikwissenschaftlicher Kongress zum Mozartjahr 1991, Baden – Wien. Bericht*, 2 vols., Tutzing, Hans Schneider, 1993, vol. 1, pp. 143–55.

Fellerer, Karl Gustav. *Die Kirchenmusik W. A. Mozarts*, Laaber-Verlag, 1985.

Haberkamp, Gertraut. *Die Erstdrucke der Werke von Wolfgang Amadeus Mozart*, 2 vols., Tutzing, Hans Schneider, 1986.

Küng, Hans. *Mozart: Traces of Transcendence*, trans. John Bowden, London, SCM Press, 1992.

Landon, H. C. Robbins. 'Mozart's Mass in C Minor, K. 427', in Eugene K. Wolf and Edward H. Roesner (eds.), *Studies in Musical Sources and Style: Essays in Honor of Jan LaRue*, Madison, WI, A-R Editions, 1990, pp. 419–23.

Marpurg, Friedrich W. (ed.). *Historisch-kritische Beiträge zur Aufnahme der Musik*, 5 vols., Berlin, 1754–8 (reprint Hildesheim, Georg Olms, 1970).

Stauffer, Georg B. *Bach: The Mass in B Minor*, New York, Schirmer, 1997.

Tyson, Alan. 'Proposed New Dates for Many Works and Fragments Written by Mozart from March 1781 to December 1791', in Cliff Eisen (ed.), *Mozart Studies*, Oxford University Press, 1991, pp. 213–26.

Wolff, Christoph. *Mozart's Requiem: Historical and Analytical Studies, Documents, Score*, trans. Mary Whittall, Berkeley, University of California Press, 1994.

Opera (general)

Dent, Edward J. *Mozart's Operas: A Critical Study*, London, Chatto and Windus, 1913 (2nd edn Oxford University Press, 1947).

Gianturco, Carolyn. *Mozart's Early Operas*, London, Batsford, 1981.

Heartz, Daniel. *Mozart's Operas*, ed. (with contributing essays) Thomas Bauman, Berkeley, University of California Press, 1990.

Kunze, Stefan. *Mozarts Opern*, Stuttgart, Reclam, 1984.

Till, Nicholas. *Mozart and the Enlightenment: Truth, Virtue and Beauty in Mozart's Operas*, London, Faber, 1992.

Webster, James. 'The Analysis of Mozart's Arias', in Cliff Eisen (ed.), *Mozart Studies*, Oxford, Clarendon Press, 1991, pp. 101–99.

Opera buffa

Allanbrook, Wye Jamison. *Rhythmic Gesture in Mozart: 'Le nozze di Figaro' and 'Don Giovanni'*, University of Chicago Press, 1983.

Brown, Bruce Alan. *W. A. Mozart: 'Così fan tutte'*, Cambridge University Press, 1995.

Carter, Tim. *W. A. Mozart: 'Le nozze di Figaro'*, Cambridge University Press, 1987.

Castelvecchi, Stefano. 'Sentimental and Anti-Sentimental in *Le nozze di Figaro*', *JAMS*, 53 (2000), pp. 1–24.

Heartz, Daniel. 'The Creation of the Buffo Finale in Italian Opera', *Proceedings of the Royal Musical Association*, 104 (1977–8), pp. 67–78.

Hunter, Mary. *The Culture of Opera Buffa in Mozart's Vienna*, Princeton University Press, 1999.

Hunter, Mary, and James Webster (eds.). *Opera Buffa in Mozart's Vienna*, Cambridge University Press, 1997.

Kunze, Stefan. *Don Giovanni vor Mozart: Die Tradition der Don-Giovanni-Opern im italienischen Buffa-Theater des 18. Jahrhunderts*, Munich, Wilhelm Fink Verlag, 1972.

Rushton, Julian. *W. A. Mozart: 'Don Giovanni'*, Cambridge University Press, 1981.

Steptoe, Andrew. *The Mozart–Da Ponte Operas: The Cultural and Musical Background to 'Le nozze di Figaro', 'Don Giovanni' and 'Così fan tutte'*, Oxford, Clarendon Press, 1988.

Opera seria

L'Avant-scène Opéra, 54 (1983), *Mitridate*; 89 (1986), *Idomeneo*; 99 (1987), *La clemenza di Tito*; 131 (1990), *Il re pastore* and *Il sogno di Scipione*.

Cairns, David. 'Idomeneo', in his *Responses: Musical Essays and Reviews*, London, Martin Secker and Warburg, 1973, pp. 55–77.

Durante, Sergio. 'Mozart and the Idea of *vera opera*: A Study of *La clemenza di Tito*', Ph.D. dissertation, Harvard University (1993).

'The Chronology of Mozart's *La clemenza di Tito* Reconsidered', *ML*, 80 (1999), pp. 560–94.

Heartz, Daniel. 'The Great Quartet in Mozart's *Idomeneo*', *Music Forum*, 5 (1980), pp. 233–56.

Hocquard, Jean-Victor. *Idoménée*, Paris, Aubier Montaigne, 1982.

Hortschanksy, K. 'Mozarts *Ascanio in Alba* und der Typus der Serenata', *Analecta Musicologica*, 18 (1978), pp. 148–59.

McClymonds, Marita P. 'Mozart's *La clemenza di Tito* and Opera Seria in Florence as a Reflection of Leopold II's Musical Taste', *Mozart-Jahrbuch 1984/85*, pp. 61–70.

Münster, Robert (ed.). *Wolfgang Amadeus Mozart: Idomeneo 1781–1981*, Munich, Piper, 1981.

Neville, Donald. '*Idomeneo* and *La clemenza di Tito*: Opera Seria and *vera opera*', *Studies in Music from the University of Western Ontario*, 2 (1977), pp. 138–66; 3 (1978), pp. 97–126; 5 (1980), pp. 99–121; 6 (1981), pp. 112–46; 7 (1983), pp. 107–36.

'Cartesian Principles in Mozart's *La clemenza di Tito*', *Studies in the History of Music*, 2 (1988), pp. 97–123.

Rice, John A. *W. A. Mozart: 'La clemenza di Tito'*, Cambridge University Press, 1991.

Rushton, Julian. ' "La vittima è Idamante": Did Mozart Have a Motive?', *COJ*, 3 (1991), pp. 1–21.

W. A. Mozart: 'Idomeneo', Cambridge University Press, 1993.

Warburton, Ernest. 'Lucio Silla, by Mozart and J. C. Bach', *MT*, 126 (1985), pp. 726–30.

German opera

Bauman, Thomas. *North German Opera in the Age of Goethe*, Cambridge University Press, 1985.

Branscombe, Peter. *W. A. Mozart: 'Die Zauberflöte'*, Cambridge University Press, 1991.

Buch, David J. 'Fairy-Tale Literature and *Die Zauberflöte*', *Acta Musicologica*, 64 (1992), pp. 30–49.

'Mozart and the Theater auf der Wieden: New Attributions and Perspectives', *COJ*, 9 (1997), pp. 195–232.

'On Mozart's Partial Autograph of the Duet "Nun, liebes Weibchen"', K.625/592a', *JRMA*, 124 (1999), pp. 53–85.

'On the Context of Mozart's Variations on the Aria, "Ein Weib ist das herrlichste Ding auf der Welt", K.613', *Mozart-Jahrbuch 1999*, pp. 71–80.

'*Der Stein der Weisen*, Mozart, and Collaborative Singspiels at Emanuel Schikaneder's Theater auf der Wieden', *Mozart-Jahrbuch 2000*, pp. 89–124.

'Eighteenth-Century Performing Materials from the Archive of the Theater an der Wien and Mozart's *Die Zauberflöte*', *MQ*, 84 (2000), pp. 287–322.

Deutsch, Otto Erich. *Das Freihaustheater auf der Wieden, 1787–1801*, 2nd edn, Vienna and Leipzig, Deutscher Verlag für Jugend und Volk, 1937.

Rommel, Otto. *Die Maschinenkomödie*, Darmstadt, 1974 (first published Leipzig, 1935).

Die Alt-Wiener Volkskomödie, Vienna, Anton Schroll, 1952.

Tyler, Linda L. '*Bastien und Bastienne*: The Libretto, Its Derivation, and Mozart's Text-Setting', *JM*, 8 (1990), pp. 520–52.

'*Zaide* in the Development of Mozart's Operatic Language', *ML*, 72 (1991), pp. 214–35.

Reception

Nineteenth-century reception

Brendel, Franz. *Geschichte der Musik in Italien, Deutschland und Frankreich*, Leipzig, Breitkopf and Härtel, 1852.

Charlton, David (ed.). *E. T. A. Hoffmann's Musical Writings: 'Kreisleriana', 'The Poet and the Composer'; 'Music Criticism'*, trans. Martyn Clarke, Cambridge University Press, 1989.

Daverio, John. 'From "Concertante" Rondo to "Lyric Sonata": A Commentary on Brahms's Reception of Mozart', in David Brodbeck (ed.), *Brahms Studies*, vol. 1, Lincoln, NE, and London, University of Nebraska Press, 1994, pp. 111–38.

Fellinger, Imogen. 'Brahms's View of Mozart', in Robert Pascall (ed.), *Brahms: Biographical, Documentary and Analytical Studies*, Cambridge University Press, 1983, pp. 41–57.

Gounod, Charles. *Mozart's 'Don Giovanni': A Commentary*, trans. Windeyer Clark, London, Robert Cocks, 1895.

Kierkegaard, Søren. *Either/Or* (1843), trans. David F. Swenson and Lillian Marvin Swenson, 2 vols., Garden City, NY, Anchor Books, 1959.

Stendhal (Henri Beyle). *Lives of Haydn, Mozart and Metastasio* (1815), ed. and trans. Richard N. Coe, London, Calder and Boyars, 1972.

Todd, R. Larry. 'Mozart According to Mendelssohn: A Contribution to *Rezeptionsgeschichte*', in R. Larry Todd and Peter Williams (eds.), *Perspectives on Mozart Performance*, Cambridge University Press, 1991, pp. 158–203.

Wates, Roye E. 'Eduard Mörike, Alexander Ulïbïshev, and the "Ghost Scene" in *Don Giovanni*', in *Studies in the History of Music*, vol. 3: *The Creative Process*, New York, Broude Brothers, 1993, pp. 31–48.

' "Die Oper aller Opern": *Don Giovanni* as Text for the Romantics', in Hermann Danuser and Tobias Plebuch (eds.), *Musik als Text: Bericht über den Internationalen Kongress der Gesellschaft für Musikforschung, Freiburg im Breisgau 1993*, 2 vols., Kassel, Bärenreiter, 1998, vol. 2, pp. 209–14.

Twentieth-century reception

Busoni, Ferruccio. 'Mozart: Aphorisms' (1906), in *The Essence of Music and Other Papers*, trans. Rosamund Ley, New York, Dover, 1965.

Csobadi, Peter, Gernot Gruber, Jürgen Kuhnel, Ulrich Muller and Oswald Panagl (eds.). *Das Phänomen Mozart im 20. Jahrhundert: Wirkung, Verarbeitung und Vermarktung in Literatur, bildender Kunst und den Medien*, Salzburg, Muller-Speiser, 1991.

Gruber, Gernot. *Mozart and Posterity*, trans. R. S. Furness, London, Quartet Books, 1991.

Mozart in Art, 1900–1990, Stuttgart, Hugo Mattheas Verlag, 1990.

Seedorf, Thomas. *Studien zur kompositorischen Mozart-Rezeption im frühen 20. Jahrhundert*, Laaber-Verlag, 1990.

Steinberg, Michael P. *Austria as Theater and Ideology: The Meaning of the Salzburg Festival*, Ithaca and London, Cornell University Press, 1990.

Taruskin, Richard. *Text and Act: Essays on Music and Performance*, Oxford and New York, Oxford University Press, 1995.

Biographies and biographical literature

Abert, Hermann. *W. A. Mozart: Neu bearbeitete und erweiterte Ausgabe von Otto Jahns 'Mozart'*, Leipzig, Breitkopf and Härtel, 1919–21.

Braunbehrens, Volkmar. *Mozart in Vienna, 1781–1791*, trans. Timothy Bell, New York, Grove Weidenfeld, 1989.

Clarke, Bruce Cooper. 'Albert von Mölk: Mozart Myth-Maker? Study of an Eighteenth-Century Correspondence', *Mozart-Jahrbuch 1995*, pp. 155–91.

Davies, Peter J. 'Mozart's Illnesses and Death', *MT*, 125 (1984), pp. 437–41, 554–61.

Deutsch, Otto Erich. 'Die Legende von Mozarts Vergiftung', *Mozart-Jahrbuch 1964*, pp. 7–18.

Einstein, Alfred. *Mozart: His Character, His Work*, trans. Arthur Mendel and Nathan Broder, London and New York, Oxford University Press, 1945.

Favier, Georges. *Vie de W. A. Mozart par Franz Xaver Niemetschek précédée du nécrologe de Schlichtegroll*, St-Etienne, Centre Interdisciplinaire d'Etudes et de Recherches sur l'Expression Contemporaine, 1976.

Gutman, Robert W. *Mozart: A Cultural Biography*, New York, Harcourt, 1999.

Hildesheimer, Wolfgang. *Mozart*, trans. Marion Faber, London and New York, Dent, 1983.

Holmes, Edward. *Life of Mozart*, London, Folio Society, 1991 (first published London, Chapman and Hall, 1845).

Hughes, Rosemary (ed.). *A Mozart Pilgrimage: Being the Travel Diaries of Vincent and Mary Novello in the Year 1829*, London, Novello and Company, 1955.

Jahn, Otto. *W. A. Mozart* (1856), trans. Pauline D. Townsend, New York, Cooper Square Publishers, 1970.

Knepler, Georg. *Wolfgang Amadé Mozart*, trans. J. Bradford Robinson, Cambridge University Press, 1994.

Landon, H. C. Robbins. *1791: Mozart's Last Year*, London, Thames and Hudson, 1988.

Massin, Jean and Brigitte. *Wolfgang Amadeus Mozart*, Paris, Club Français du Livre, 1959.

Mörike, Eduard. *Mozart's Journey to Prague* (1856), trans. Leopold von Loewenstein-Wertheim, London, John Calder, 1957.

Niemetschek, Franz Xaver. *Life of Mozart* (1798), trans. Helen Mautner, London, Leonard Hyman, 1956.

Nissen, Georg Nikolaus von. *Biographie W. A. Mozarts*, Leipzig, Breitkopf and Härtel, 1828.

Sadie, Stanley. *The New Grove Mozart*, London, Macmillan, 1982.

Schiedermair, Ludwig. *Mozart: Sein Leben und seine Werke*, Munich, C. H. Beck'sche Verlagsbuchhandlung, 1922.

Schlichtegroll, Friedrich. 'Johannes Chrysostomos Wolfgang Gottlieb Mozart', in *Nekrolog auf das Jahr 1791*, Gotha, Justus Perthes, 1793, pp. 82–112.

Schuler, Heinz. *Mozart und die Freimaurerei*, Wilhelmshaven, Florian Nötzel Verlag, 1992.

Schurig, Arthur. *Wolfgang Amadeus Mozart: Sein Leben und sein Werk*, Leipzig, Insel-Verlag, 1913.

Solomon, Maynard. 'The Rochlitz Anecdotes', in Cliff Eisen (ed.), *Mozart Studies*, Oxford University Press, 1991, pp. 1–59.

   Mozart: A Life, New York, Harper Collins, 1995.

Stafford, William. *Mozart's Death: A Corrective Survey of the Legends*, London, Macmillan, 1991.

Wyzewa, Théodore de, and Georges de Saint-Foix. *W.-A. Mozart: Sa Vie musicale et son oeuvre*, 5 vols., Paris, Desclée de Brouwer, 1912–46.

Zaslaw, Neal. 'Mozart as Working Stiff', in James M. Morris (ed.), *On Mozart*, Cambridge University Press, 1994, pp. 102–12.

Performance

Mozart the performer

Komlós, Katalin. ' "Ich praeludirte und spielte Variazionen": Mozart the Fortepianist', in R. Larry Todd and Peter Williams (eds.), *Perspectives on Mozart Performance*, Cambridge University Press, 1991, pp. 27–54.

Mahling, Christoph-Hellmut. ' "... new and altogether special and astonishingly difficult": Some Comments on Junia's Aria in *Lucio Silla*', in Stanley Sadie (ed.), *Wolfgang Amadè Mozart: Essays on His Life and His Music*, Oxford, Clarendon Press, 1996, pp. 377–94.

Morrow, Mary Sue. 'Mozart and Viennese Concert Life', *MT*, 126 (1985),
    pp. 453–4.
Rampe, Siegbert. *Mozarts Claviermusik: Klangwelt und Aufführungspraxis*, Kassel,
    Bärenreiter, 1995.
Woodfield, Ian. 'New Light on the Mozarts' London Visit: A Private Concert with
    Manzuoli', *ML*, 76 (1995), pp. 187–207.

Mozart and performance practice
Bach, Carl Philipp Emanuel. *Versuch über die wahre Art das Clavier zu spielen*,
    Berlin, C. F. Henning, 1753; trans. William J. Mitchell as *Essay on the True Art
    of Playing Keyboard Instruments*, New York, Norton, 1949.
Badura-Skoda, Paul and Eva. *Mozart-Interpretation*, Vienna, Eduard Wancura
    Verlag, 1957; trans. Leo Black as *Interpreting Mozart on the Keyboard*, New York,
    St. Martin's Press, 1962.
Beicken, Suzanne J. (ed. and trans.). *Treatise on Vocal Performance and
    Ornamentation by Johann Adam Hiller* (1780), Cambridge University Press,
    2001.
Brown, Clive. *Classical and Romantic Performing Practice, 1750–1900*, Oxford
    University Press, 1999.
Brown, Howard Mayer, and Stanley Sadie (eds.). *Performance Practice: Music after
    1600*, London, Macmillan, 1989.
Hudson, Richard. *Stolen Time: The History of Tempo Rubato*, Oxford, Clarendon
    Press, 1994.
Marty, Jean-Pierre. *The Tempo Indications of Mozart*, New Haven, Yale University
    Press, 1988.
Mozart, Leopold. *Versuch einer gründlichen Violinschule*, Augsburg, 1756; trans.
    Editha Knocker as *A Treatise on the Fundamental Principles of Violin Playing*,
    Oxford University Press, 1948.
Neumann, Frederick. *Ornamentation and Improvisation in Mozart*, Princeton
    University Press, 1986.
Quantz, Johann Joachim. *Versuch einer Anweisung die Flöte traversière zu spielen*,
    Berlin, J. F. Voss, 1752; trans. Edward R. Reilly as *On Playing the Flute*,
    New York, Schirmer, 1975.
Rosenblum, Sandra P. *Performance Practices in Classic Piano Music: Their Principles
    and Applications*, Indianapolis, Indiana University Press, 1988.
Türk, Daniel Gottlob. *Klavierschule*, Leipzig, Schwickert 1789; trans. Raymond H.
    Haggh as *School of Clavier Playing*, Lincoln, University of Nebraska Press, 1982.
Whitmore, Philip. *Unpremeditated Art: The Cadenza in the Classical Keyboard
    Concerto*, Oxford, Clarendon Press, 1991.

General index

Index of Mozart's works

Chamber works
Chamber works for wind and strings
K. 285, in D (flute quartet) 108
K. 285a, in G (flute quartet) 108
K. 370, in F (oboe quartet) 108
K. 407, in E♭ (horn quintet) 116
K. 581, in A (clarinet quintet) xvii, 34, 114, 217

Chamber works for keyboard and strings
K. 254, in B♭ (piano trio) 65, 217
K. 452, in E♭ (quintet for piano and winds) xvi, 62–3, 72, 112, 114, 116, 223
K. 478, in g (piano quartet) xvi, 63–4, 69, 112, 256
K. 493, in E♭ (piano quartet) xvi, 64, 112
K. 496, in G (piano trio) 65–6, 256
K. 498, in E♭ ('Kegelstatt' trio for piano, viola and clarinet) xvi, 112
K. 502, in B♭ (piano trio) xvi, 32, 66, 112
K. 542, in E (piano trio) xvii, 32, 66
K. 548, in C (piano trio) xvii, 32, 66
K. 564, in G (piano trio) xvii, 32, 113–14

Divertimenti and serenades
K. 136–8, in D, B♭, F (divertimenti for string quartet) xiv
K. 166, in E♭ (divertimento for wind ensemble) 256
K. 213, in F (divertimento for wind ensemble) 256
K. 240, in B♭ (divertimento for wind ensemble) 256
K. 247, in F (divertimento for horns and solo strings) xiv, 107
K. 251, in D (divertimento for oboe, horns and solo strings) xiv
K. 252, in E♭ (divertimento for wind ensemble) 256
K. 253, in F (divertimento for wind ensemble) 256
K. 270, in B♭ (divertimento for wind ensemble) 256
K. 286, in D (notturno for horns and solo strings) 255
K. 287, in B♭ (divertimento for horns and solo strings) 107, 108, 217
K. 334, in D (divertimento for horns and solo strings) 16, 17, 107
K. 361, in B♭ (serenade for wind ensemble, 'Gran partita') xvi, 105, 106, 118

K. 375, in E♭ (serenade for wind ensemble) xv
K. 525, in G ('Eine kleine Nachtmusik' for solo strings) xvi

Sonatas for violin and keyboard
K. 6–9 256
   K. 6–7, in C and D xii
   K. 8–9, in B♭ and G xii
K. 10–15, in B♭, G, A, F, C, B♭ xii, 256
K. 26–31, in E♭, G, C, D, F, B♭ xiii, 256
K. 296, in C xiv, 110, 256
K. 301–6 108, 110, 256
   K. 301, in G xiv, 109
   K. 302, in E♭ xiv
   K. 303, in C xiv, 109
   K. 304, in e xiv, 109
   K. 305, in A xiv, 109
   K. 306, in D xiv
K. 376–80 110
   K. 376, in F xv, 256
   K. 377, in F xv, 256
   K. 378, in B♭ 17, 256
   K. 379, in G 256
   K. 380, in E♭ xv, 256
K. 454, in B♭ xvi, 110, 223, 249
K. 481, in E♭ xvi, 110, 256
K. 526, in A xvi, 110, 256, 257
K. 547, in F xvii

String quartets
K. 80, in G xiii, 256
K. 155–60 108
   K. 155–8, in D, G, C, F xiv, 108
   K. 159, in B♭ xiv, 108
   K. 160, in E♭ xiv
K. 168–73 xiv, 108, 256
   K. 168, in F 108
   K. 173, in d 108
'Haydn' Quartets 31, 112, 113, 115, 178
   K. 387, in G xv, 113
   K. 421, in d xv, 112
   K. 428, in E♭ xv, 112
   K. 458, in B♭ xvi, 113
   K. 464, in A xvi, 112, 240
   K. 465, in C xvi, 113, 177, 229, 256
K. 499, in D ('Hoffmeister') xvi, 112, 256
K. 546, in c (Adagio and Fugue) 113, 256
'Prussian' Quartets 113, 114–15
   K. 575, in D xvii, 32, 117
   K. 589, in B♭ xvii, 32
   K. 590, in F xvii, 32, 117

Cambridge Companions to Music

Composers

The Cambridge Companion to Bach
Edited by John Butt

The Cambridge Companion to Bartók
Edited by Amanda Bayley

The Cambridge Companion to Beethoven
Edited by Glenn Stanley

The Cambridge Companion to Berg
Edited by Anthony Pople

The Cambridge Companion to Berlioz
Edited by Peter Bloom

The Cambridge Companion to Brahms
Edited by Michael Musgrave

The Cambridge Companion to Benjamin Britten
Edited by Mervyn Cooke

The Cambridge Companion to John Cage
Edited by David Nicholls

The Cambridge Companion to Chopin
Edited by Jim Samson

The Cambridge Companion to Debussy
Edited by Simon Trezise

The Cambridge Companion to Handel
Edited by Donald Burrows

The Cambridge Companion to Mozart
Edited by Simon P. Keefe

The Cambridge Companion to Ravel
Edited by Deborah Mawer

The Cambridge Companion to Schubert
Edited by Christopher Gibbs

The Cambridge Companion to Stravinsky
Edited by Jonathan Cross

Instruments

The Cambridge Companion to Brass Instruments
Edited by Trevor Herbert and John Wallace

The Cambridge Companion to the Cello
Edited by Robin Stowell

The Cambridge Companion to the Clarinet
Edited by Colin Lawson

The Cambridge Companion to the Guitar
Edited by Victor Coelho

The Cambridge Companion to the Organ
Edited by Nicholas Thistlethwaite and Geoffrey Webber

The Cambridge Companion to the Piano
Edited by David Rowland

The Cambridge Companion to the Recorder
Edited by John Mansfield Thomson

The Cambridge Companion to the Saxophone
Edited by Richard Ingham

The Cambridge Companion to Singing
Edited by John Potter

The Cambridge Companion to the Violin
Edited by Robin Stowell

Topics
The Cambridge Companion to Blues and Gospel Music
Edited by Allan Moore

The Cambridge Companion to Grand Opera
Edited by David Charlton

The Cambridge Companion to Jazz
Edited by Mervyn Cooke and David Horn

The Cambridge Companion to the Orchestra
Edited by Colin Lawson

The Cambridge Companion to Pop and Rock
Edited by Simon Frith, Will Straw and John Street